Kinship Organization
in Late Imperial China
1000–1940

China Proper during the Ch'ing Dynasty

Kinship Organization in Late Imperial China 1000–1940

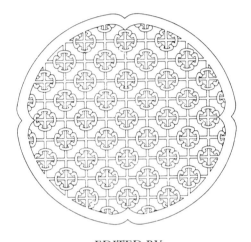

EDITED BY

Patricia Buckley Ebrey
and James L. Watson

UNIVERSITY OF CALIFORNIA PRESS

Berkeley · Los Angeles · London

UNIVERSITY OF CALIFORNIA PRESS
Berkeley and Los Angeles, California

University of California Press, Ltd.
London, England

Typeset by Asco Trade Typesetting Ltd., Hong Kong
Printed in the United States of America

1 2 3 4 5 6 7 8 9

Library of Congress Cataloging in Publication Data
Main entry under title:
Kinship organization in late imperial China, 1000–1940.
(Studies on China; 5)
Bibliography: p.
Includes index.
1. Kinship—China—History—Addresses, essays, lectures.
2. China—Social life and customs—Addresses, essays,
lectures.   I. Ebrey, Patricia Buckley.   II. Watson,
James L.   III. Series.
GN635.C5K56   1986   306.8'3   85–1139
ISBN 0–520–05416–4

CONTENTS

TABLES

ILLUSTRATIONS

PREFACE

One of the most important questions currently facing scholars of China is how Chinese society held together. It is now well known that China was marked by great diversity. In the realm of social customs, not only were there broad regional or class differences, but also, at a local level, the people in one village might adopt a different set of practices from those of neighboring communities. Yet the majority of these varied practices seem to have fit within a frame that was distinctly Chinese. Thus scholars must also ask how people of dissimilar occupations and economic interests, living in widely separated parts of the country, came to recognize and act on a common set of cultural beliefs. Explaining the variations in Chinese society requires minute knowledge of local conditions. Explaining the uniformities requires historical understanding of the processes involved in the spread of ideas and practices and the ways by which some came to be considered standard. Given the available sources on Chinese society, neither of these tasks is simple.

The study of kinship and kinship organization provides one of the best ways to approach the coexisting uniformities and variations of Chinese society. A major component of what made people consider themselves Chinese—and identify others as outsiders and non-Chinese—was adherence to fundamental aspects of a "Chinese" family and kinship system. Moreover, the kinship system itself played a part in integrating Chinese society by bringing together distant relatives whose economic and social status could vary considerably. Yet, as scholars have shown in case after case, what was considered an undesirable or unattainable variant in one place might be accepted as common practice elsewhere. In some communities, for instance, the problem of family succession was never solved by resorting to uxorilocal marriage, whereas in other communities this course was considered the reasonable one to take. In some areas where large numbers of men related patrilineally lived near each other, these agnates would organize themselves for collective activities, own property in common, and face the rest of the community as a group. In other places, local sets of agnates would remain a collection of separate families with no more than a dim sense of their common origins. Kinship, thus, provides perhaps the most straightforward example of how a shared cultural system can lie behind and provide coherence to great diversity in practice.

The collaboration of historians and social scientists is required if we are to learn enough about kinship in Chinese society to explain both the uniformities and the variations. This volume presents a special form of such collaboration. The substantive papers are all written by historians, but these historians have raided the stock of anthropological terms, models, and theories, tried to use technical terms in a consistent and well-defined way, implicitly addressed anthropologists on the issues that seem to fascinate them, and responded to the suggestions and criticisms of the anthropologists who have read their papers. At the same time, however, they remain historians and do not ignore the types of issues (such as historical context and change over time) with which historians have always dealt. The editors believe that this type of collaboration has distinct advantages over the more usual approach to transcending disciplinary boundaries by placing articles by historians and social scientists side by side in the same volume. If we have been successful, social scientists should find issues of interest in the chapters, and historians should find them full of the substance of history and not too long-winded in belaboring the obvious.

This volume has its origins in a multidisciplinary conference held in January 1983 at Asilomar, California, on "Family and Kinship in Chinese History." The conference was sponsored by the National Endowment for the Humanities and the Joint Committee on Chinese Studies of the American Council of Learned Societies and the Social Science Research Council, with funds from the Mellon Foundation. At the conference, papers were presented on a wide variety of topics, including theoretical models, sources and methods, and studies of household composition, inheritance, adoption, and child-rearing. For this volume, however, the topic has been narrowed to kinship organization. Most of the other papers have been or will soon be published elsewhere.

The contributors to this volume owe a great debt to the other participants at the conference who criticized their papers and provided the intellectual intensity that led to a sharpening of our conceptual focus. These participants include Richard Barrett, Katherine Carlitz, Charlotte Furth, Mary Rankin, Steven Sangren, Ann Waltner, and Rubie Watson. We were also extremely fortunate to have three discussants who brought to our project a wide range of knowledge, wit, and historical acumen; they were Eugene Hammel,

Ts'ui-jung Liu, and G. William Skinner. The two rapporteurs, Michael Marme and Janice Stockard, were conscientious in keeping records of the proceedings and also participated in many of the discussions.

Bringing together twenty scholars working on family and kinship forced all of us to look closely at our evidence and the inferences we were drawing from it. The conference papers included in this volume were all substantially rewritten to take into account the new insights or new questions that came up during the conference discussions. Moreover, chapters 1, 2, 5, and 9 were written after the conference specifically for this volume; they are most directly a consequence of the conference, as they pursue themes that emerged during the course of our discussions. The author of chapter 5 was not at the conference, but he wrote his chapter partly in response to the papers that were presented there.

Most of the technical terminology that we employ in this book is defined in chapter 1. For the sake of readers, we have attempted to attain some degree of uniformity in our use of terms. With regard to one usage we have, however, remained divided; this is whether to say "the Wangs" or "the Wang" when referring to the members of a Wang lineage or descent group. Generally, we agree that "the Wang" implies a greater sense of group cohesion than "the Wangs," but some authors, for stylistic reasons, prefer not to use "the Wang" even when referring to a cohesive unit. We hope that this inconsistency in our usage will not be too troublesome to the reader.

P. B. E.

J. L. W.

CONTRIBUTORS

Richard L. Davis is Assistant Professor of History at Duke University and earlier taught at Middlebury College. His dissertation, completed at Princeton in 1980, has been published as a book titled *Court and Family in Sung China* (1986). His other publications include an article in *T'oung Pao* and three chapters on the political history of the late Southern Sung for the *Cambridge History of China*.

Jerry Dennerline is Associate Professor of History at Amherst College. He also taught at Pomona College and Yale University. Author of *The Chia-ting Loyalists* (1981), he has also contributed chapters to *Conflict and Control in Late Imperial China* (1975), *From Ming to Ch'ing* (1979), and the *Cambridge History of China*. He is currently working on a manuscript on rural gentry life in Soochow and Wu-hsi at the turn of the century.

Patricia Buckley Ebrey is Professor of Asian Studies and History at the University of Illinois at Urbana-Champaign. Her major research interests have been in the social history of the Han through Sung periods. She is the author of *The Aristocratic Families of Early Imperial China* (1978) and *Family and Property in Sung China* (1984) and editor of *Chinese Civilization and Society: A Sourcebook* (1981). Currently she is engaged in research on marriage and family rituals in Sung China.

Keith Hazelton is Research Associate at Princeton University. In 1984 he completed his dissertation there, titled "Lineages and Local Elites in Hui-chou, 1500 to 1800." He has published *A Synchronic Chinese-Western Daily Calendar, 1341–1661 A.D.* (1984) and plans to continue his research on descent groups in Hui-chou during the Ming and Ch'ing periods.

Robert P. Hymes is Assistant Professor in the department of East Asian Languages and Cultures at Columbia University. His dissertation, completed in 1979 at the University of Pennsylvania, has been revised as a book titled *Elite, State, and Locality in Sung China*, to be published in 1986. He is at present beginning work on the social history of Taoism between the Sung and Ming.

Susan Naquin is Associate Professor of History at the University of Pennsylvania. Her research has focused on sectarian movements during the Ch'ing dynasty. She is author of *Millenarian Rebellion in China* (1976) and *Shantung Rebellion* (1982). Currently she is writing on Chinese society in the eighteenth century.

Evelyn S. Rawski is Professor of History at the University of Pittsburgh. Her research interests are in social and economic history from the late imperial period to the twentieth century. She is the author of *Agricultural Change and the Peasant Economy of South China* (1972) and *Education and Popular Literacy in Ch'ing China* (1979) and is a co-editor of *Popular Culture in Late Imperial China* (1985).

James L. Watson is Professor of Anthropology at the University of Pittsburgh. From 1973 to 1983 he taught at the School of Oriental and African Studies, University of London, and served as Head of the Contemporary China Institute (1978–81). He is author of *Emigration and the Chinese Lineage* (1975) and editor of *Asian and African Systems of Slavery* (1980) and *Class and Social Stratification in Post-Revolution China* (1984).

ONE

Introduction

Patricia Buckley Ebrey and James L. Watson

In the Chinese tradition, kinship has always been a matter of both philosophical and political importance. Since ancient times the Chinese have written about the theoretical basis and ideal expressions of agnatic, matrilateral, and affinal kinship, developing models for patrilineal descent groups (the *tsung* system) and grades of the "closeness" of relatives of all types (the mourning grades). Throughout the imperial period, not only were family and kinship of major importance to ordinary people, as they have been everywhere, but they were central to the practical, political, and ethical concerns of the elite. Kinship organization provided a means of preserving property and privilege and of developing bodies of followers and allies. Different forms of organization were better suited to some needs than others, and over the centuries the forms that appeared in different parts of the country varied considerably.

The study of kinship and kinship groups in Chinese history draws on two traditions: social history and social anthropology. The anthropological study of kinship in Chinese society has paralleled intellectual developments in the larger discipline of social anthropology. Early research on Chinese kinship took the form of community studies (Kulp 1925; Fei 1939; Yang 1945) or focused on principles of descent, kinship terminology, and incest taboos (Hsu 1940; Hu 1948; Feng 1948). After the theory of unilineal descent groups was elaborated by British social anthropologists such as Evans-Pritchard (1940) and Meyer Fortes (1945, 1953), this approach was applied to China by Maurice Freedman, particularly in his classic study *Lineage Organization in Southeastern China* (1958; see also his 1966 sequel).

The work of Freedman and those who followed him in studying lineages has had great impact on the study of Chinese society. One reason for this is that the theoretical framework Freedman brought to the subject is entirely

1

different from the traditional Chinese way of looking at the matter. Earlier issues in the study of kinship, such as principles of descent and methods of classifying kin, were easily translated into Chinese ideas and the Chinese had already written in detail on these subjects. But traditional Chinese scholars had not analyzed kinship in terms of control and allocation of resources or the formation of segmented groups. Rephrasing the questions allowed scholars to see phenomena that they had not noticed before.

The anthropologists who followed Freedman have refined a model of the Chinese lineage as it has existed during the last century, especially in the areas where scholars could engage in field research, that is, in the New Territories of Hong Kong and in Taiwan (Ahern 1973, 1976; Baker 1968, 1979; Cohen 1969; Pasternak 1969, 1972; Potter 1968, 1970; J. Watson 1975a, 1975b, 1982a; R. Watson 1982, 1985). These scholars have provided a large body of ethnographic description, a set of well-developed terms and concepts (see below), and also some well-focused issues: How were lineages formed? Why did strong lineages appear in some environments and not in others? How did control of estates shape the internal dynamics of lineages? What role did ancestral rites play in lineage organization? Why were some lineages more segmented than others? How could lineages dominate communities? (For an overview, see J. Watson 1982a.)

Social historians have also investigated Chinese kinship organization, usually because understanding kinship was crucial to the exploration of historical issues concerning social mobility, the power and resources of the elite, or the dynamics of local society (see, especially, Beattie 1979; Dardess 1974; Dennerline 1981a, 1981b; Ebrey 1978, 1984; Ho 1964; Johnson 1977a, 1977b; Hsiao 1960; Kuhn 1970; Liu 1959; Twitchett 1959; Wakeman 1966). How these features of Chinese society varied and changed over time are basic questions in social history; they are also the issues most directly addressed by the authors of this volume.

Historians usually analyze social mobility in terms of changes in social status from one generation to the next; this, by definition, concerns families and lines. Some authors start with an assumption that the "business" of lines is the preservation or enhancement of social and economic position. Kinship groups can stand in several relations to this process. For an elite family, membership in a descent group composed largely of much poorer families could prove to be a burden, given that the wealthier family might be asked to pay for a disproportionate share of group activities and that poor kinsmen might make regular requests for assistance. But the general assumption has been that the descent group would benefit the richer and more educated members at the expense of the less affluent. Lineages in particular provided the wealthy with a set of allies in local politics; lineages also endowed schools and subsidized the expenses of examination candidates, services of most benefit to the wealthier members. At any rate, fear that one's descendants might fall into poverty and lose their social status as educated men seems often to have motivated endowments of lineage schools. When the richer families in a lineage also controlled its assets—and the assets were substantial—they might be able to exploit the estate for their own purposes and reinforce their dominant position in the process (cf. R. Watson 1985).

Elite groups often seem to have derived much of their economic and political power from a rural local base, but the nature of this local base—and how members of elite groups interacted with local commoners—has remained largely a matter of surmise. Most scholars take for granted that kinship relations and economic relations, including systems of production and marketing, were fundamental at this level (see, e.g., Skinner 1964). But how kinship and economic relations reinforced or countered each other is still poorly understood. Studying particular descent groups in their local context has proved one way to gain an insight into the complexities of local social life and provide some basic empirical evidence concerning the organization of specific communities.

These basic historical issues cannot be investigated in any depth without coming to grips with the variability of Chinese society. It is now well known that economic conditions, social customs, and religious practices all varied in significant ways from place to place. From the work presented in this volume and earlier studies, it seems fair to conclude that agnatic kinship organization was at least as variable as other social practices (see Harrell 1981; Wolf and Huang 1980; Sangren 1984). This variability was not only at the macro-level, reflecting differences between regions and change over time, but also at a micro-level: One set of agnates in a county could be highly organized while another one nearby of similar size and genealogical depth might not be. One major approach to the explanation of variability of this sort is Skinner's model of core and periphery areas within macro-regions, each with its own economic cycle (Skinner 1976, 1977). Examining the variations in kinship practices in a region provides a way to investigate these issues and brings us closer to understanding the dynamics of Chinese civilization.

Historians, of course, are seldom interested solely in social organization at a fixed moment of time. Usually they phrase questions of social mobility, elite resources, and kinship organization in terms of how they changed. An historian, in looking at a descent group, is very likely to want to know when it began and the stages through which it developed. When anthropologists look at a group's past it is usually to find explanations for present adaptations; for historians earlier stages are generally of as much interest as later ones.

Despite these differences in emphasis and problematique, the historians who have contributed to this volume have learned much from the anthropologists, especially in the use of concepts and terms. They have also drawn on models for local and regional social organization and lineage development. But there are special problems in studying kinship without access to living informants; these make some modifications in approach and even in termi-nology necessary.

To avoid the misleading use of terms, historians need analytical categories broad and flexible enough to allow them to deal with historical phenomena that may differ significantly from those observed in modern times. Judging historical evidence by models based on field research can lead to interesting insights when the models fit well, but this approach is much less profitable when the models fit poorly (Ebrey 1983). In addition, historians who deal regularly with incomplete information need terms that will not imply that they know more than they do. For example, if they know only that a group of people were linked by agnation (ties based on patrilineal descent), it is best not to use the term "lineage," which implies a particular form of organization (see below). Historians thus need a vocabulary that will allow them to indicate not merely differences in structural features, but also differ-ences in the adequacy of their knowledge about sets of people.

One of the simplest ways to overcome the problem of mislabeling is to start at an elementary level and ask basic questions every time signs of kinship activity are encountered: What categories of kinsmen were involved (e.g., patrilineal, affinal, matrilateral)? Did these kinsmen form a *group*, or were they acting together or aiding each other because of personal links, independent of any enduring group? (To be called a "group" would require, at the minimum, some definition of who belonged and who did not and evidence of collective endeavors or responsibilities.) Were these links based on non-kinship principles (e.g., common residence or shared occupation) or kinship ones. If a *group* did exist, what common goals were involved? Who belonged to it, and how were questions of membership resolved? What collective activities were undertaken? Did members engage in corporate behavior of a ritual, economic, and political nature? Did the group own property or other assets in common?

It is important to be able to discuss these and other issues of general com-parative significance without distorting or forcing the Chinese evidence. Accordingly, in this volume we use a very general set of terms for kinship units, adapted from an earlier survey of ethnographic and historical re-search by J. L. Watson (1982a). Following are some general definitions of the terms we propose to use.

Family: The term "family" will be reserved for domestic groups, the basic unit of production, consumption, and political authority, whose members normally reside together and share a common budget for everyday expenses. In this sense it is largely synonymous with *chia* in its core meaning (see below).

Line/patriline: This concept, crucial to ancestor worship, refers to the genealogical link from father to son to grandson, and continuing indefinitely. A man's line extends backward as a single strand through all of his patrilineal ancestors and will be continued, perhaps by many strands, through his patrilineal descendants. Property and social status are normally transmitted along the line.

Agnates: The term "agnates" will be used for the general *category* of people related patrilineally, when no enduring group organization or group activity is evident or clearly implied.

Descent group: The term "descent group" will be used to refer to *groups* of agnates, defined by *descent* from a common ancestor, who are not all members of a single *chia* or a single line. Thus "descent group" is a *group* (by contrast to a loose collection of agnates), whose members are aware of their kinship connections, but corporate behavior may be limited to activities such as ancestral rites or compilation of genealogies. As employed in this book, the term "descent group" will imply little about the internal organization of the unit in question. Generally, when it is clear from the historical sources that a set of agnates formed a group or had a well-developed sense of group consciousness, they will be called a descent group even if positive evidence of principles of recruitment and ritual activities are absent.

Lineage: "Lineage" will be reserved for descent groups that have strong corporate bases in shared assets, usually, but not exclusively, land. "A lineage is a *corporation* in the sense that members derive benefits from jointly-owned property and shared resources; they also join in corporate activities on a regular basis. Furthermore, members of a lineage are highly conscious of themselves as a *group* in relation to others whom they define as outsiders. A lineage is not, therefore, a loosely-defined collection of individuals" (J. Watson 1982a:594). A diagnostic feature of lineages (as opposed to other descent groups) is that a lineage has ownership of collective assets vested in the group or segments of the group (and not with individuals). The main reason for distinguishing lineages from other descent groups is that, when a group provides material benefits for members, this fact will affect not only how individuals look on membership but also the internal dynamics of the group and the power the group can exert in society. There are, of course, highly developed, complex lineages as well as simple lineages with small estates (see Freedman 1958); but the gradation in the size of estates does not affect their classification here as lineages. The real question is whether or not the estate provides an economic base for corporate activities. In this volume, only when there is specific evidence of a corporate estate will the group be called a lineage.

Localized lineage or descent group: A localized lineage or descent group is one whose members live in a well-defined area—usually a village or set of neighboring communities. Generally, one can assume a greater intensity of interaction among the members of a localized group than among those of a dispersed one.

Higher-order lineage: A higher-order lineage is the "umbrella organization" that ties together several patrilineally related localized lineages. Usually it has a hall or other property located in a market town or a county seat; activities in the hall bring together members of the constituent lineages on regular ritual occasions.

Branch: "Branch" will be used here in two senses. When a man has many lines of descendants, all those descended from him can be called a branch of the larger descent group or set of agnates. The decision to label them a branch is the observer's. But some descent groups and lineages formally divided themselves into segments along descent lines (usually called *fang*, *chih*, or *p'ai*), and these we also call "branches." Such branches normally had names.

Surname group or *surname category*: These terms will be reserved for any group or category of people who are united solely on the basis of shared surname and very distant presumed kinship.

Clan: Clan is used as the term for organizations composed of lineages or descent groups. The agnatic links between these constituent units are extremely remote and most likely fictionalized. In this sense they are linked by "stipulated" rather than "demonstrated" descent. Clans, as such, do not figure in this volume.

Although the historians writing in this volume are using terminology derived from anthropological research, they are pursuing historical issues and are often more interested in explaining change than in analyzing structures. In most cases, they have chosen their "units of analysis" on principles different from those employed by anthropologists. Anthropologists, pursuing issues of kinship organization and development, have generally chosen as their unit of analysis well-developed lineages or multi-lineage communities. Historians, pursuing the types of issues outlined above, have had to deal with kinship in other, less distinct forms. If they wish to focus on change they need to cover a long historical span. Similarly, if the focus is on a community or the elite of a community, historians have had to devise ways to account for not only powerful and wealthy lineages, but also lineages with modest estates, or descent groups whose only focus was ritual, and even the sorts of kinship connections that existed when there was no discernable group organization at all.

Descent groups whose only joint activities were ritual did not die out to be replaced by powerful lineages. Even if statistically the predominant form of kinship organization in late imperial China was of this sort, these descent groups have so far received much less study than powerful lineages. Did descent groups with no property aside from tombs, shrines, and tiny endowments for ancestral rites ever become significant forces in local politics? If so, was their power based on corporate unity, or did it derive simply from the power of their wealthiest or highest-ranking members? Did the compilation of genealogies or the construction of ancestral halls significantly enhance the internal cohesion of this sort of descent group? Several of the studies in this volume deal with groups of agnates whose primary focus seems to have been ritual activities and not corporate land, contributing in a preliminary way to our understanding of the workings of Chinese descent groups.

Investigating these historical issues is made more difficult for historians by a poor match between the conceptual framework employed by modern social scientists and that employed by the writers of historical documents, forcing historians to go back and forth between two separate conceptual systems. Chinese writers of the Sung through Ch'ing dynasties used a wide variety of terms to discuss matters that fall under the domain we define as "kinship," and most of these terms were of considerable antiquity. At one end of the scale, there was in Chinese a highly elaborate set of terms for labeling kinsmen. Chinese terminology bears many similarities to systems employed elsewhere, marking age, generation, sex, and the sex of the intermediate links (e.g., distinguishing among cousins related through father's brother, father's sister, mother's brother, and mother's sister). Traditional Chinese vocabulary also had highly precise ways to talk about sets of relatives presumed to form the core of each person's kinship activities, that is, the mourning grades. These schemes show clear understanding of progressively more distant collateral lines. They also distinguish between lineal relatives, whose obligations are asymmetrical, and collateral relatives, who have reciprocal obligations (see, e.g., Feng 1948; McCoy 1970; Weller 1981).

Despite the availability of highly precise terms for kinship relationships, most discussions of kinship matters in Chinese texts use vaguely defined terms to refer to "family," "relatives," "kinsmen," and "group of kinsmen." In general, these terms (like most terms in classical Chinese) had both "core" meanings and also extended meanings that tended to proliferate over time. In this volume we have made every effort not to confuse modern anthropological concepts and Chinese terms. We do not equate *tsu* and "lineage." We use anthropological concepts as best we can to describe and analyze the types of organization for which we find evidence in historical sources. But one of the major ways evidence of this sort is discovered is through careful reading of Chinese references to kinship matters. Without understanding the vocabulary Chinese writers used—and the distinctions they employed—we literally cannot read what they wrote.

Below is a brief discussion of some of the core meanings and common

extended uses of terms frequently employed by Chinese writers to refer to
relatives and groups of relatives.

Chia: The core meaning is the property-holding group that normally re-
sides together. In this sense it can usually be translated as "family." In its
extended meanings it can refer to patrilineal groupings of very large size and
depth, especially if they have some common assets.

Ku-jou: "Bone and flesh." A common term used to mean close consan-
guineal relatives (that is, including those related through mothers and daughters, not merely through men). The idea of shared substance (*t'i*, body, and
ch'i, vital force) is implied by the use of this term. In later use, some sources
distinguished the bones as deriving from the father and the flesh from the
mother (cf. J. Watson 1982b), but as a compound this distinction does not
seem to have been strongly felt.

Ch'in: Since this is a very common word for "close" or "personal," it has
several meanings with regard to kinship, depending on context. Two of the
most common meanings are "parents" and "close relatives," including, in
particular, affinal and matrilateral relatives. *Ssu-ma ch'in* are relatives of the
ssu-ma (fifth) grade of mourning. Frequently *ch'in* is used in distinction to
tsu or *tsung* to refer specifically to affinal and matrilateral relatives of all sorts
(including, for instance, the families of one's children's spouses).

Tsu: The core meaning seems to be "agnates" as a set of people. Several
oft-cited classical phrases refer to "collecting (*shou, ho, chü*) the agnates"
(*tsu*). In particular contexts these can be very close relatives, but a common
use is for those beyond the realm of specific kinship terms, as in *tsu-jen* or
tsu-ti (agnate and younger agnate of the generation to be a brother, more
distant than second cousin). *Mu-tsu* means the agnates of one's mother. *Tsu-
ch'in* means agnates and affines/matrilateral relatives. *Tsu* could refer to a set
or group of people distinguished by age, size, prestige, power, and so on in
phrases like *ta-tsu, wang-tsu, shih-tsu*. A group referred to as a *tsu*, set of
agnates, could also be a *chia*, functioning as a single economic unit.

Tsung: The core meaning of *tsung* seems to be patrilineal descent line.
Whereas *tsu* normally refers to physically identifiable people, *tsung* evokes
the abstract principle of agnatic kinship, especially the lineal relationships.
Ancestral rites and related notions of obligation and piety were usually discussed with reference to *tsung*. *Tsung* carried positive overtones from its
association with *tsung-fa*, the schematic system of branching descent groups
described in the classics (see Ebrey 1984). The "line" from father to son to
grandson, with its obligations of "continuing the sacrifices," could be referred to as *pen-tsung*. *Tsung* also had a very common extended meaning of the
people related through patrilineal descent in its broadest possible sense;
t'ung-tsung, those who share a descent line, could be loosely applied to any-

one with the same surname. *Tsung-tsu* was a common term for patrilineal descent group from early times. When one wished to describe a large set of related descent groups, the groups would be called *tsu* and the overarching set of them *tsung* (as in *tsung* genealogies that link *tsu*).

Hsing and *shih*: In ancient times family names appear to have been linked much more than they were in later times to descent groups known as *hsing* (the larger unit) and *shih* (the subunit). Already by the time of Ssu-ma Ch'ien in the Former Han (202 B.C.–A.D. 9) the ancient distinctions between the two were poorly understood, and *hsing* became the common term for surname, with *shih* relegated to restricted usages (especially as part of terms of reference, as in Chang *shih*, the person surnamed Chang). In later periods, both *hsing* and *shih* retained some of their sense of agnatically conceived groups but seem to have continued to carry an overtone of "name" in most usages, meaning perhaps "name-group" (i.e., Lu *shih* could mean the group with the name Lu). It was common, for instance, in Ming and Ch'ing times for a genealogy to be titled *X-shih tsu-p'u*, "a listing of the agnates of the X name-group" or "a listing of the lineage of the X name-group."

From this brief examination, it should be clear that those who wrote in Chinese in imperial times did not make the types of distinctions that have seemed significant to modern analysts. They distinguished agnates from nonagnatic relatives; but they did not distinguish sets of agnates conceived as a category of people who shared only the attribute of common descent from sets of agnates who acted as a group. Nor did they have different terms for localized and dispersed groups, or groups with corporate property and those without. Moreover, they did not always distinguish clearly among what we call family, line, and descent group.

Several explanations can be offered to account for the imprecision of Chinese terminology in these regards. One is the conservatism of kinship practices. Many basic kinship principles and practices continued with only minor changes from the Han (202 B.C.–A.D.220) through the Ch'ing (1644–1911) dynasties. Throughout this period, men did not marry agnates but saw them as the preferred source of adoptive heirs. Close agnates were seen as the most appropriate recipients of charity and guidance for any well-educated or well-to-do person. Sets of agnates settled in one place would meet for family and ancestral rituals, especially weddings and funerals. Nevertheless, throughout this period local groups of agnates were seen as potentially disorderly unless they had educated men to act as their leaders. All of these continuities in attitude and practice led to a great similarity in the language used to discuss kinship matters over the centuries, even after significant innovations were introduced in group organization. Writers, it would seem, preferred to evoke the principles and practices sanctified by tradition rather than to draw attention to changes.

The blurring of the realms of the family, line, and descent group probably has a different explanation. In terms of practice, areas of overlap between these three realms were great. Inheritance could be seen as a matter for the family or the line. Large undivided families could be called in Chinese both *chia* and *tsu*. Ancestral rites could be done strictly on a family or line basis, or they could be conducted as a rite for a larger descent group. Decisions generally left to family heads (such as marriage and adoption) could infringe on group identity (if pure patrilineality was a part of this identity) or group interest (where substantial land and income from it were at stake). For all of these reasons, it may have been difficult for many people to think of family, line, and descent group as separate realms.

Since Chinese writers did not always distinguish among different types of groups formed by agnation, one might conclude that the differences among these groups were unimportant in their social life. This is certainly a possibility worth pursuing—and undoubtedly it was true of many writers. But where other evidence of the importance of these features is present, it should be kept in mind that distinctions among different sorts of groups may have been made orally that were not put in writing. In formal writing, it may often have been expedient to associate a group "on the ground" with an elevated, fully legitimated concept, such as *tsu* or *tsung*, without qualifying it in any way; in other words, authors may purposely have obscured some of the crucial features of the group (J. Watson 1982a:592–93). But it is also possible that the authors of many texts were not aware of the importance of some of the principles governing the formation of descent groups, even ones to which they belonged. For instance, they may not have distinguished between groups of agnates who assembled twice a year for ancestral rites paid for by voluntary contributions and a similar group that had a plot of land, the income from which was used to defer these expenses. Their failure to see the consequences of owning property in common does not alter the situation.

For these reasons, in this volume we have tried to be careful both in our use of modern anthropological concepts and in the inferences we draw from Chinese terms. We try to use anthropological concepts as precisely as possible, not only in order to be able to communicate with comparative social scientists generally, but also because these concepts bring to our attention important structural features of Chinese society. Yet, in doing so, we must recognize that the Chinese conceptual framework was based on a different set of distinctions and attempts to make direct translations from one set of ideas to the other are sure to result in misunderstandings.

In this introduction we have set out the common framework upon which the chapters in this volume are based. Although each chapter explores a different case or question, the authors share a common set of interests.

In chapter 2, Patricia Ebrey traces the evolution of the repertoire of forms of agnatic kinship organization, especially the appearance of group ancestral rites at graves and halls, the formation of corporate estates, and the elaboration of a modern-style genealogy. She looks beyond what educated men wanted to institute to find evidence of what might have been happening in local society, on the hypothesis that the crucial changes may well have developed there, even if the elite bias of sources tends to obscure this process.

In chapter 3, Richard Davis begins with a question of social mobility: How effective was the high officials' privilege of nominating relatives to office in enabling their descendants to retain high political status? He approaches this question by examining the fate of the descendants of a few closely related political leaders of the Southern Sung. These questions bring him to explore the type of kinship organization that existed among these Shih as they proliferated and to question whether politics and kinship organization were mutually beneficial. Did high officials gain anything by forming descent groups? Could active descent groups be disrupted by the political success of a few of their members?

Robert Hymes, in chapter 4, poses a related question concerning elite strategies: How does emphasis placed on descent affect strategies for marriage alliances, and vice versa? To answer this question he examines the resources of the elite, especially the relationship between elite status and a local base. He argues that a shift in the basis of this relationship, brought on by changes in opportunities for political careers, had a major effect on the concern that highly educated men took in organizing their kinsmen. Through a study of the elite in one prefecture of Kiangsi, he shows that a "lineage orientation," a desire to form or strengthen agnatic kinship organization, was becoming more common among highly educated men as they shifted their focus from national to local level concerns.

In chapter 5, Keith Hazelton examines a lineage in Hui-chou, Anhwei, one of the areas in which lineage organization developed earliest. Basing his study on a genealogy written in 1528 and a prefecture-wide survey of descent groups compiled in 1551, he is able to describe in detail the type of group the Wu of Hsiu-ning city comprised in the early sixteenth century. He knows how numerous they were, how much property they had for ritual activities, what ritual activities they performed, who they married, and where they were buried. He pays particular attention to the question of leadership in lineage activities and the compilation of genealogies; he concludes that, even in a lineage where members' wealth came mostly from commerce, it was the lines of politically successful men who took the lead in compiling genealogies, endowing land, and formulating rites. He argues that this pattern was probably typical of "Lower Yangtze" lineages.

Jerry Dennerline, in chapter 6, examines the development of two higher-order lineages in the Lower Yangtze region. He relates his study to the local economy, to the interests of family heads in ensuring the continuation of the family line, to the needs of women for support in widowhood, and to the moral and ideological commitments of the elite. By examining these questions over an extended period of time, Dennerline shows convincingly that kinship organization in this area changed significantly over the centuries. Given the richness of his data, he is able to explore many of the issues anthropologists have considered regarding the structure and operation of lineages. He argues that in Wu-hsi in the eighteenth and nineteenth centuries lineages were as much involved in regulating relations with affines as separating agnates from outsiders. In his view, charitable activities, often directed at widows, were central to the development of corporate lineages.

In chapter 7, Susan Naquin takes up the issue of variability at two levels. First, she implicitly compares the type of kinship organization found in Hopei with that reported for Southeast China, and second, she compares the history and organization of two descent groups in one prefecture. These descent groups were contemporaneous, but their members pursued different social strategies, one producing many lower-degree holders and the other sectarian leaders. Nevertheless, patterns of growth and leadership show considerable similarities. Naquin's study makes it clear that we must reexamine the assumption that landownership is the corporate base for all lineage development.

In chapter 8, Evelyn Rawski looks especially at local society and the ways a set of kinsmen could dominate a community. Her chapter deals more than any other with the issue of landownership and the overlapping or sometimes competing interests of families and lines with the demands of a more encompassing kinship group. She argues that a set of agnates could be perceived as a corporate group by outsiders, that they could demonstrate kinship solidarity in their naming patterns, and dominate their community—all without having any corporate land or organized group activities. Rawski concludes with the apt observation that the highly developed lineages of Southeastern China may be aberrant in national terms. Lineages of the type she describes are more likely to be found in the North and may be more "significant" in statistical terms than the Southeastern lineages described by fieldworking anthropologists.

In chapter 9, James Watson, the only contributor who is not an historian, offers an anthropological perspective on the issues discussed in the previous chapters. In his view, the evidence in this volume suggests that Chinese "descent groups" functioned quite effectively without corporately owned land (taken by anthropologists to be the single most important aspect of lineage organization). Only a few of the descent groups examined here were landowning corporations and yet the others survived, as coherent units of social organization, in some cases for centuries. Watson discusses the implications of these findings and highlights other issues that may surprise anthropologists and historians who work on Chinese society: the leading role of women in the formation of agnatic groups, the importance of uxorilocal residence among the Chinese elite, and the significance of mortuary rites as a determining factor in the emergence of formal descent groups.

REFERENCES

Ahern, Emily M. 1973. *The Cult of the Dead in a Chinese Village*. Stanford: Stanford University Press.

———. 1976. "Segmentation in Chinese Lineages: A View from Written Genealogies." *American Ethnologist* 3:1–16.

Baker, Hugh D. R. 1968. *A Chinese Lineage Village: Sheung Shui*. Stanford: Stanford University Press.

———. 1979. *Chinese Family and Kinship*. New York: Columbia University Press.

Beattie, Hilary J. 1979. *Land and Lineage in China: A Study of T'ung-ch'eng County, Anhwei, in the Ming and Ch'ing Dynasties*. Cambridge: Cambridge University Press.

Cohen, Myron. 1969. "Agnatic Kinship in South Taiwan." *Ethnology* 15:237–92.

Dardess, John W. 1974. "The Cheng Communal Family: Social Organization and Neo-Confucianism in Yuan and Early Ming China." *Harvard Journal of Asiatic Studies* 34:7–52.

Dennerline, Jerry. 1981a. *The Chia-ting Loyalists: Confucian Leadership and Social Change in Seventeenth-Century China*. New Haven: Yale University Press.

———. 1981b. "The New Hua Charitable Estate and Local Level Leadership in Wuxi County at the End of the Qing." In *Select Papers from the Center for Far Eastern Studies* (University of Chicago), 4 (1979–80):19–70.

Ebrey, Patricia Buckley. 1978. *The Aristocratic Families of Early Imperial China: A Case Study of the Po-ling Ts'ui Family*. Cambridge: Cambridge University Press.

———. 1983. "Types of Lineages in Ch'ing China: A Re-examination of the Chang Lineage of T'ung-ch'eng." *Ch'ing-shih wen-t'i* 4.9:1–20.

———. 1984. "Conceptions of the Family in the Sung Dynasty." *Journal of Asian Studies* 43:219–45.

Evans-Pritchard, E. E. 1940. *The Nuer*. Oxford: Oxford University Press, Clarendon Press.

Fei, Hsiao-t'ung. 1939. *Peasant Life in China: A Field Study of Country Life in the Yangtze Valley*. London: Routledge.

Feng, Han-yi. 1948. *The Chinese Kinship System*. Cambridge, Mass.: Harvard-Yenching Institute Publications.

Fortes, Meyer. 1945. *The Dynamics of Clanship among the Tallensi*. Oxford University Press.

———. 1953. "The Structure of Unilineal Descent Groups." *American Anthropologist* 55:17–41.

Freedman, Maurice. 1958. *Lineage Organization in Southeastern China*. London: Athlone Press.

———. 1966. *Chinese Lineage and Society: Fukien and Kwangtung*. London: Athlone Press.

Harrell, Stevan. 1981. "Social Organization in Hai-shan." In *The Anthropology of*

Taiwanese Society, ed. Emily M. Ahern and Hill Gates. Stanford: Stanford University Press.

Ho, Ping-ti. 1964. *The Ladder of Success in Imperial China*. New York: Columbia University Press.

Hsiao, Kung-chuan. 1960. *Rural China: Imperial Control in the Nineteenth Century*. Seattle: University of Washington Press.

Hsu, Francis L. K. 1940. "The Problem of Incest Tabu in a North China Village." *American Anthropologist* 42:122–35.

Hu, Hsien Chin. 1948. *The Common Descent Group in China and Its Functions*. New York: Viking Fund Publications in Anthropology, no. 10.

Johnson, David G. 1977a. "The Last Years of a Great Clan: The Li Family of Chao Chün in late T'ang and Early Sung." *Harvard Journal of Asiatic Studies* 37:5–102.

———. 1977b. *The Medieval Chinese Oligarchy*. Boulder: Westview Press.

Kuhn, Philip A. 1970. *Rebellion and Its Enemies in Late Imperial China*. Cambridge, Mass.: Harvard University Press.

Kulp, Daniel M. 1925. *Country Life in South China*. New York: Columbia University Press.

Liu, Hui-chen Wang. 1959. "An Analysis of Chinese Clan Rules: Confucian Theories in Action." In *Confucianism in Action*, ed. David S. Nivison and Arthur F. Wright. Stanford: Stanford University Press.

McCoy, John. 1970. "Chinese Kin Terms of Reference and Address." In *Family and Kinship in Chinese Society*, ed. Maurice Freedman. Stanford: Stanford University Press.

Pasternak, Burton. 1969. "The Role of the Frontier in Chinese Lineage Development." *Journal of Asian Studies* 28:551–61.

———. 1982a. "Chinese Kinship Reconsidered: Anthropological Perspectives on Historical Research." *China Quarterly* 92:589–622.

Potter, Jack M. 1968. *Capitalism and the Chinese Peasant*. Berkeley: University of California Press.

———. 1970. "Land and Lineage in Traditional China." In *Family and Kinship in Chinese Society*, ed. Maurice Freedman. Stanford: Stanford University Press.

Sangren, P. Steven. 1984. "Traditional Chinese Corporations: Beyond Kinship." *Journal of Asian Studies* 43:391–415.

Skinner, G. William. 1964. "Marketing and Social Structure in Rural China." *Journal of Asian Studies* 24:3–43.

———. 1976. "Mobility Strategies in Late Imperial China: A Regional Analysis." In *Regional Analysis*, vol 1., *Economic Systems*, ed. Carol Smith. New York: Academic Press.

———. 1977. "Cities and the Hierarchy of Local Systems." In *The City in Late Imperial China*, ed. G. William Skinner. Stanford: Stanford University Press.

Twitchett, Denis. 1959. "The Fan Clan's Charitable Estate, 1050–1760," in *Confucianism in Action*, ed. David S. Nivison and Arthur F. Wright. Stanford: Stanford University Press.

Wakeman, Frederic, Jr. 1966. *Strangers at the Gate: Social Disorder in South China*. Berkeley: University of California Press.

Watson, James L. 1975a. "Agnates and Outsiders: Adoption in a Chinese Lineage." *Man* 10:293–306.

———. 1975b. *Emigration and the Chinese Lineage*. Berkeley: University of California Press.

———. 1982a. "Chinese Kinship Reconsidered: Anthropological Perspectives on Historical Research." *China Quarterly* 92:589–622.

———. 1982b. "Of Flesh and Bones: The Management of Death Pollution in Cantonese Society." In *Death and the Regeneration of Life*, ed. Maurice Bloch and Jonathan Parry. Cambridge: Cambridge University Press.

Watson, Rubie S. 1981. "Class Differences and Affinal Relations in South China." *Man* 16:593–615.

———. 1982. "The Creation of a Chinese Lineage: The Teng of Ha Tsuen, 1669–1751." *Modern Asian Studies* 16:69–100.

———. 1985. *Inequality among Brothers: Class and Kinship in South China*. Cambridge: Cambridge University Press.

Weller, Robert P. 1981. "Affines, Ambiguity, and Meaning in Hokkien Kin Terms." *Ethnology* 20:15–29.

Wolf, Arthur P., and Chieh-shan Huang. 1980. *Marriage and Adoption in China, 1845–1945*. Stanford: Stanford University Press.

Yang, Martin C. 1945. *A Chinese Village: Taitou, Shantung Province*. New York: Columbia University Press.

TWO

The Early Stages in the Development of
Descent Group Organization

Patricia Buckley Ebrey

Twenty-five years ago, Denis Twitchett wrote that "one of the most urgent tasks confronting the social historian writing on China is to provide a dynamic picture of the developments in clan organization over the past two millennia" (Twitchett 1959:97). However urgent this task may have seemed, since Twitchett's own study of the Fan estate and its management, very little research has been done on the historical issues of change and development. Scholars have added a dozen or more case studies of lineages, but most of these have concentrated on analyzing how lineages operated in a static, ideal form, rather than examining how forms of organization developed or spread (for exceptions, see Pasternak 1969 and R. Watson 1982). Moreover, scholars have often assumed that there was only one type of lineage and that features important in modern lineages, especially corporately owned landed property and genealogies, played the same roles everywhere and in all stages of lineage development (for objections to this view, see Ebrey 1983, Sangren 1984). Even the broad surveys of lineages done a generation ago by the Japanese legal and sociological historians Niida, Shimizu, and Makino, which drew together great quantities of information, did not altogether escape these failings (Niida 1942:103–235; Shimizu 1949; Makino 1939, 1949). This essay, therefore, will try to correct the balance by looking at the development of kinship organization in a historical context, concentrating on the period 1000–1400.

As I organized material for the overview that follows, I kept in mind three underlying questions. The first is the question of what, precisely, changed. Many of the activities of descent groups and lineages (ancestral rites, charity along kin lines, compilation of genealogies) were practiced long before there were descent groups of the type that appeared in the Sung and

16

later. What were the crucial innovations that can be linked to the appearance of this type of descent group, and when did they appear?

The second question is why these innovations appeared. Given the great continuity in kinship attitudes and practices, what social, economic, religious, or intellectual developments can account for the appearance or transformation of forms of agnatic organization? Was one change the crucial one, leading to the others, or were several independent changes in practices and attitudes involved?

The third question is the relationship between elite leadership and descent group formation. Historical sources largely present educated men as the catalysts of descent group or lineage organization. Acting on the basis of their own interests, values, or needs, educated men could certainly have tried to establish kinship groups. But for these groups to thrive and endure, they must also have served the needs of kinsmen who did not belong to the educated class. Sometimes it was undoubtedly the latter who formed the organization that educated men later tried to develop further. In order to detect evidence of kinship organization among uneducated commoners, I have paid special attention to cases where educated men seem to have been responding to the needs of local agnates, rather than imposing on them their own ideas.

In the survey presented here, conclusive answers are not provided for any of these questions; rather, I attempt to bring attention to the most relevant evidence and suggest plausible explanations. I have organized this overview in terms of changes in the basic repertoire of agnatic kinship practices. I adopted this framework because the notion of a cultural repertoire provides the most satisfactory way to grasp both the variability and the uniformity in people's ways of dealing with kin. This repertoire of ideas and practices related to kinship evolved over time, and its content increased significantly during the four centuries reviewed here; yet there were always a great many alternate forms, all socially acceptable and suited to different needs. Individuals and groups could actively draw from this repertoire to select appropriate courses of action, but also, often at a less conscious level, they would try to remold or reinterpret ongoing activities to fit into recognized forms.

By concentrating on the cultural repertoire, I am largely setting aside consideration of local economic conditions. There is little doubt that the development of forms of kinship organization was tied to patterns of migration, settlement, and land tenure practices. These varied considerably over the Sung, both geographically and temporally (Hartwell 1982 and McDermott 1984). A complete history of the processes by which certain forms of kinship organization came to be practiced where they did must therefore await fuller understanding of regional developments.

The Basic Repertoire of Extra-household
Agnatic Kinship

The primary focus of agnatic kinship from the Han period (202 B.C.–A.D. 220) on was always the family and family line, the men in the household and their patrilineal ancestors and descendants (see Ebrey 1984a). Here, however, I will only examine agnatic kinship activities outside this sphere, looking particularly at the relations among agnates whose common ancestor was further back than their grandfather. The classical prescription for these relations can be summarized in a sentence: Second and third cousins were mourning relatives and therefore had a variety of specific and diffuse obligations toward each other; fourth cousins, however, were not, and in the classics it was said that kinship ended at that point.

In practice, however, by the Han, certain forms of behavior were extended to agnates much more distant than fourth cousins. Above all, people had a concept of agnate (*tsu-jen*) that was applied to those believed to share a common ancestor, even a distant one, but in practice mainly when the person lived in the same locality. One way agnates were treated differently from other people was by use of kinship terms. Agnates would refer to each other as *tsu* uncle, *tsu* cousin, *tsu* nephew, and call each other "uncle," "nephew," and so on. More significant, the category of agnate was used in regulating marriage and adoption. One did not marry agnates, that is, people of the same surname known to share a patrilineal ancestor (Dull 1978:29–30). Agnates were, however, the preferred source of adopted male heirs, though this preference does not seem to have been especially strong (Ch'ü 1972:18–20).

By the Han, if not much earlier, agnates often lived near each other in local communities (Ebrey 1986; for later periods see Johnson 1977b:114–15). Local agnates were seen as the inner layer in an educated man's social world, closely associated with the local community, as in expressions like "He was cordial to his agnates and neighbors." Educated men were expected to offer help and guidance to their agnatic kinsmen. This could mean financial aid, especially to widows, orphans, and those having trouble paying for weddings and funerals. In the *History of the Later Han* men were often praised for using their income to aid their kinsmen or kinsmen and neighbors (e.g. HHS 26:920, 31:1093, 62:2049). Leadership was also supposed to be involved. In times of crisis, educated men were expected to lead their agnates and other local residents to defend themselves or move to safety. Since educated men were supposed to serve as leaders for the entire community, it would be a mistake to infer kinship organization from this sort of leadership. Although historical sources look with favor on groups of local agnates led by educated men, they reveal distrust of groups without educated leaders, for such groups might fall under the sway of a local strongman or bully

(Ebrey 1986).[1] These patterns remained common through the Six Dynasties (A.D. 220–589) (Ebrey 1978:55–58, Johnson 1977a:18; T'ang 1959).

Before the Sung, local agnates living in separate households did not often hold property together, not even it would seem the gravesites of their ancestors. Grave lands could be passed down to one son rather than remain the property of all (e.g. WS 57:5b), and nowhere have I found the implication that these graves were a group responsibility or a group resource, rights to be buried there controlled by decision of the group as a whole or its representative. Graves were of great significance, but to individuals much more than to groups. Filial sons spent great sums on building tombs and on moving coffins back to old graveyards; in the Han they often spent the period of mourning for their parents by the side of their tombs (S. T. Yang 1933:82–299). In the Han, sacrifices were offered at graves (SMYL 74 or Ebrey 1974:187), and halls (*tz'u*) might be built there (Ebrey 1980:336–37). But the greatest emphasis was on the graves of recent ancestors, so that there is little indication that graves were a focus for distantly related agnates.

In the Han through T'ang (618–906) period, men saw their agnates at weddings, funerals, and in some cases the seasonal sacrifices (e.g., SMYL 68, 74; PS 33:33; PCS 46:6a). How wide a group of agnates assembled seems to have depended on how many lived nearby. Some aristocratic families seem to have maintained common graveyards, but others spread their graves over several locations, even when they lived in the same city or county (Ebrey 1978:91–93; Johnson 1977a; Twitchett 1973:52–53).

So far I have been discussing agnates who lived near each other, especially commoners. During the Six Dynasties and the T'ang, some men retained recognition that they shared a common ancestry with people living scattered across the country. This practice, however, was probably restricted to the upper class, since its purpose was to establish and define social status within an aristocratic social system (Johnson 1977b; Ebrey 1978). To characterize this system very briefly, after a "family" (probably more accurately termed a line or set of lines, since ancestors were included) gained national fame, descendants or collaterals who settled elsewhere would still use the place name of the famous "family" as a qualifier to their surname, that is, as a choronym (Johnson 1977b:29–30). Thus the Ch'ing-ho Ts'uis were distinct from the

1. What to call these groups still remains a problem. Elsewhere (Ebrey 1986) I have called them "clans," using Fried's (instead of J. Watson's 1982:610–12) definition of "clan." Fried sees clans as inclusive groups organized for collective security, which therefore easily absorb marginal members ("stipulated descent"), in contrast to the exclusive practices of lineages (1970:20–33). Very little is known about the internal organization or membership of the groups the historians saw as troublesome sets of local agnates. However, they cannot be called "descent groups" as the term is defined in the introduction to this book, since there is no evidence that they joined for ancestral rituals or insisted on demonstrated descent linkages. All that is clear is that they could often dominate a community.

Po-ling Ts'uis, and each set of Ts'uis had many members living far from
their ancestral area. Some of these aristocratic lines seem to have functioned
as kinship groups, but the majority probably did not (Ebrey 1978:55–61,
126 nn. 25 and 26, 146 n. 20).

Since the various governments of the Northern and Southern Dynasties
(317–589) ranked these "great families" by status and used these ranks in
allocating access to political privileges, genealogies were needed to prove
membership in a ranked line. In the local context a man was a Ho-tung
Chang because he was a Chang living in Ho-tung, and no one had challenged the presumption of his common origin with the other Changs. But if
he wanted to claim to be a Ho-tung Chang while living in Ho-nei, he needed
a genealogy documenting descent from known members of the line. Especially during the Southern Dynasties, the government took the lead in compiling these genealogies, collecting ones for all the leading lines and publishing them together. But private genealogists also flourished along with the
aristocratic system, lasting well through the T'ang. No T'ang or pre-T'ang
genealogies survive, but from scattered references to their contents, modern
scholars have inferred that they were concerned primarily with clarifying
lines of descent and offices held by male members. Because lines that did not
produce officials were irrelevant for these purposes, they probably were not
recorded in any detail (Johnson 1977b:33–55, 98–107).

There is no particular reason to think that these aristocratic practices had
any influence on kinship organization at the local commoner level. There is
no evidence that commoners kept genealogies or concerned themselves with
kinsmen who lived in distant areas.

Ch'ing-ming and Worship at Graves

Almost without exception, the forms of behavior toward agnatic kin that
have been described above continued into the Sung and later. Men referred
to distant agnates as tsu-jen; did not marry them; saw them as appropriate
recipients of charity and guidance; and would meet with them at weddings,
funerals, and other rites. Local groups of agnates without educated men as
leaders could be seen as disorderly.[2] Even the practice of labeling "great
families" with choronyms unrelated to contemporary residence continued
(Hartwell 1982:406–13). What changed in the T'ang and Sung were additions to the repertoire, much more than subtractions. The additions, however, were significant and subtly altered the relationships of the old constants.

Ancestral worship at graves during the Ch'ing-ming festival was one of

---

2. All of these assumptions and practices can be found referred to in the *Precepts for Social
Life* of Yuan Ts'ai (ca. 1140–ca. 1195) (Ebrey 1984b). For an example of a large local group of
agnates in the early Sung, see Matsui 1968.

the most important of the additions to the basic repertoire of kinship activities. The Ch'ing-ming festival was held in the spring, 105 days after the winter solstice. In recent times it has been the most significant occasion for ancestral offerings at graves in both North and South China (Uchida 1950:258; Hu 1948:34–35; Hazelton, this volume), but this was not always the case. Since the end of the Han, the "Cold Food" (*han-shih*) festival, involving extinguishing fires for three days, had been held at the solar period named "Ch'ing-ming." However, scholars of folklore have not found references to it as an occasion for visiting graves before the T'ang period (Shang 1941:440–43). Perhaps the earliest reference to this practice is in a Buddhist text dating from the 660s, which refers in passing to a man in the Sui period (581–617) who took food and wine to make a sacrifice (*chi*) at the graves on the day of Cold Food (TTC 53:720).

By the mid-T'ang the association between Cold Food or Ch'ing-ming and rites at graves was well-established. An edict of 732 noted that although the ritual classics had not mentioned visiting graves at the Cold Food festival, it had become customary in recent times. The edict gave approval to the custom: "For gentlemen and commoners who do not get together to make offerings in family altars (*chia miao*), how else can they exhibit their filial sentiments? They should be allowed to visit the graves and together perform the rituals of bowing and sweeping at the tombs" (TT 52:300B). The edict went on to state that the sacrifice (*chi*) should be made outside the southern gate of the burial ground (*ying*), and that at its conclusion the leftover food should be taken and eaten elsewhere. These rules were to be made a permanent part of the ritual code and are included in the ritual compendium, the *K'ai-yuan li* (KYL 78/6a–7a).

From this edict it is clear that by mid-T'ang, visiting graves at Ch'ing-ming was already recognized as *the* occasion for agnates (other than high officials who were allowed family altars)[3] to get together to express reverence for ancestors. Its popularity in this period is confirmed in a letter Liu Tsung-yuan (773–819) wrote from exile lamenting his forced absence from his ancestors' graves. Whenever the Cold Food festival arrived, he was reminded of "how the country roads are filled with men and women, how slaves, servants, and beggars are all able to visit their parents' graves, and how not one of the ghosts of horse doctors or field laborers is left without care" (CTW 573:3a–6b). Late T'ang etiquette books even include models of complimentary letters to write on the occasion of visiting graves at Ch'ing-ming (e.g. THPT 40:72–75).

3. According to T'ang government regulations, officials of rank five or higher were allowed three altars (*miao*), one each for their deceased father, grandfather, and great-grandfather. The very highest officials could have four altars, and if they had noble titles they could also make offerings to the first ancestor to receive the title. Lower officials and commoners, not allowed altars, were to make offerings in their living quarters (TT 48: 277A).

During the Sung dynasty, there is abundant evidence of the importance of Cold Food/Ch'ing-ming as an occasion for sacrifices (*chi*). The *Sui-shih tsa-chi* of Lü Hsi-che (ca. 1050–1120) quoted the statement that "Northerners all use this day to sweep and make offerings (*sao-chi*) at their ancestors' tombs" (SSKC 15:155), implying that Southerners did not. During the Southern Sung, customs from Kaifeng and elsewhere in the North spread to the capital, Hangchow, and elsewhere in the South. Chou Mi (1232–1308) wrote an account of the annual observances of the Ch'ien-tao and Ch'un-hsi periods (1165–89) that described grave visits to offer sacrifices as a major activity of residents of Hangchow, participated in not only by men but also by women leading children (CCSSC 14b–15a). A gazetteer for Fu-chou (Fukien) written in 1182 described a flourishing celebration led by the well-to-do within a set of agnates:

> The people of this prefecture always bow before the graves at the Cold Food spring sacrifice. The rich houses (*fu shih*) and great surnames (*ta hsing*) have land set aside to support the graveyards. When the sacrifice is over they assemble their agnates (*ho tsu*). The largest groups have several hundred people, the smallest a few dozen. Afterward they have a feast, arranging themselves in order and showing their respect. This is their way to "honor ancestors and encourage warm feelings among agnates" (*tsun tsu mu tsu*). (SSC 40:5a)

During the Sung it also became common to visit graves at other festivals, especially the Buddhist All Souls' Feast (fifteenth of the seventh month) and the Buddhist Stove Lighting festival on the first of the tenth month (TCMHL 8:218, 9:225; MLL 4:24, 6:45; SSKC 37:404–5; Gernet 1962:191–95). The Fu-chou gazetteer records a different set of dates, the second or third of the first month and the winter solstice (SSC 40:2a, 9a).

While visiting tombs to make announcements to ancestors was mentioned in the classics, sacrificing (*chi*) to them there was not. According to long-established beliefs, individuals had two souls, a *p'o* that stayed with the body in the grave, and a *hun* that left the body and could be settled in an ancestral tablet. In the classics sacrifices were made to the spirit in the tablet but not the *p'o* in the grave. In the Sung, Confucian ritualists gave the custom of sacrifices to ancestors at their graves qualified acceptance. Ch'eng I (1033–1107) argued that the spirits (*shen*) of the dead did not reside in their graves but in spirit tablets (*shen-chu*), thus meaning that offerings at tombs accomplished nothing. He thought that rulers had taken to making offerings at imperial tombs out of acquiescence to popular customs. He did, however, admit that sacrifices at graves did no great harm to righteous principles (IS 1:6, 18:240). Some other Confucian ritualists accepted the concept of grave rites but wanted to separate their practice from the popular festivals by picking different days by divination, the classical rule for determining the dates for domestic rites (HLTCS 21:29a–30b). Chu Hsi (1130–1200) gave lukewarm acceptance to grave rites but drew the line at using the fifteenth of the seventh month because of its Buddhist associations (CWKCC 30:29a–30a; HLTCS 19:9b, 21:20a).

What is the significance of grave rites to the development of descent group organization? First, it should be stressed that sacrifices at graves developed at the level of local custom. I see no evidence at all that ideological motives led Confucian scholars to promote worship at graves. Rather, those concerned with classical ritual forms tried to find ways to accommodate practices that had become popular. This level of custom appears to have had associations with Buddhism, although the Ch'ing-ming festival itself was never considered a Buddhist celebration.[4] Yet Buddhist monks had for centuries held ceremonies to pray for the dead, and these seem to have been, at the popular level at least, partially assimilated to the more purely Chinese practice of ancestor worship. As Kenneth Ch'en points out, Buddhists actively promoted the idea that their ways of caring for the dead were the most filial (Ch'en 1973:50–55). Buddhist notions of death, souls, and the uses of prayers or offerings to the dead were of course different from classical ones, and these new ideas could have helped encourage worship of distant ancestors. Indeed, the sutra that is the source for making offerings on behalf of ancestors on the All Souls' Feast stated that they should be made for ancestors up to seven generations back, three more than the Confucian classics allowed (Ch'en 1973:24–25). The practice of attaching a Buddhist shrine, with monks, to look after a family's graves is a further indication of ties to Buddhism. This practice, often referred to as "merit cloisters," had been common since the mid-T'ang (Ch'en 1973:139–40). It is perhaps also significant that Fukien—where there were large group rites already in the twelfth century—was a major stronghold of Buddhism in the Sung (Chikusa 1956).

For the development of group consciousness among sets of local agnates, two innovations are particularly important: the inclusion of *early ancestors* in rites and the practice of everyone visiting graves on *the same day*. Since at least the Han, men often visited graves to make offerings or announcements, but they could choose any day significant to them, and they would not expect to meet distant kin there. From T'ang times on, on Ch'ing-ming and the summer or fall festivals, people would meet with their local agnates at graveyards in a context that stressed their lines of descent. Whether distant ancestors were regularly included in these rites in the T'ang is uncertain from surviving sources. By the Sung, however, there is clear evidence that old

---

4. Ch'ing-ming or Cold Food is mentioned only a half-dozen times in the Buddhist Canon (at least according to the meticulous forty-odd volume index, *Taishō shinshū daizōkyō sakuhin*). Moreover, the only actual discussion of the festival in the Canon concerns whether Buddhist monks should participate in this non-Buddhist custom (*su*). The answer offered was that it would be acceptable to visit the graves of parents but not to join in any partying with relatives (TTC 54:p. 309).

graves were sites of worship (see below). In such cases the entire group of
local agnates would be assembled for the rites for the first ancestor to be
buried in that locality, which undoubtedly ties in with the new interest in
"first ancestors" that appears in the Sung. Rather than all of these people
making separate offerings, they might well have come to hold a group ceremony, a step which would certainly increase their group consciousness.[5] In
the Fu-chou case a group feast had become part of the Ch'ing-ming celebra-
tions. Occasionally, as in the Fu-chou case, men may have sought to ensure
regular funding for these rites by setting aside land (such estates will be
discussed in more detail below).

This process may have had a kind of "snowball" effect. As grave rites
became more popular (for religious and social reasons), it would have become more crucial to bury agnates near each other: Some concentration of
graves would ensure that as the number of generations increased, old tombs
would not be neglected, for many graves could then be visited on a single
day. As more generations of graves came to be visited, a larger descent group
would have a ritual focus. This focus would provide a principle for deciding
who was a member of the descent group (whether or not he was a descendant of the "first ancestor"), excluding later migrants who claimed a common ancestor of an even earlier date. And as the association between grave
rites and descent groups came to be recognized, people who wished to
promote group cohesiveness among their local agnates could have begun by
initiating or restoring joint rites to their earliest ancestors. (Some examples
of such initiatives will be given below.)

The importance of grave rites and the association of graves and descent
groups is made explicit in the writings of a few Sung men. Here I will cite
evidence from the writings of four men, presenting them in chronological
order. The first author is Han Ch'i (1008–75), a noted scholar who served as
prime minister under three emperors (Jen-tsung, Ying-tsung, and Shen-
tsung). Han Ch'i wrote a manual for sacrifices (*Chi-i*), no longer extant,
which was quoted in a later source as supporting the practice of grave
worship on the Cold Food and first of the tenth month festivals (WKCL
160a). Another source quoted him as saying, "Being conscientious with the
family records and never forgetting the ancestral tombs are the major elements of filial piety" (CSCC 2:29). Han Ch'i also wrote an account of an
impressive ceremony he performed on Cold Food at the graves of his parents and grandparents. He followed this ceremony by lecturing to his sons

---

5. From surviving sources it is not clear whether people held one ceremony for all the
ancestors buried in a graveyard, or separate ones for each ancestor. The general rule was that
people should make offerings only to their own ancestors. This practice would favor dividing
up after a rite for the first ancestor, but some references (such as the 732 edict above and Huang
Kan's discussions below) seem to imply one ceremony for all the ancestors by all the descendants.

and nephews, urging them to be good and to continue to bury all of their relatives near these two graves where the *hun* and *p'o* souls of his father and grandfather could give them peace, and warning them definitely not to let the advice of a burial specialist (a geomancer, presumably) lead them to bury elsewhere in the hopes of gaining good fortune.[6] Should anyone act so barbarously, the descent group (*tsung-tsu*) should punish him (AYC 2:10a–b).

In 1045 Han Ch'i acted on his own advice and constructed two complex tombs, each with several chambers, each chamber to house a husband and wife or wives plus any children who died young or heirless (AYC 46:9a–17a). In 1051, 1062, and 1071, additional tombs were built for younger relatives, one of these to be used entirely for descendants who died without heirs (AYC 46:6a, 21a–26b). (Here Han Ch'i admitted consulting a burial specialist to select the spot within the graveyard for this tomb, AYC 47:26b). Perhaps the best evidence of Han Ch'i's preoccupation with graves, however, is the extraordinary efforts he took to locate the graves of his great-grandfather and great-great-grandfather, left behind in Hopei when their descendants moved south to Honan. His persistent inquiries went on for over thirty years, as he queried men surnamed Han who came from his ancestors' native place and delegated friends and relatives to pursue leads for him. As he noted, his search was a continuation of his father's attempt to reconstruct the family genealogy by collecting tomb inscriptions (AYC 46:2b–3a, 22:3b).

Han Ch'i's local descent group in Honan had very little genealogical depth, going back only to his grandfather. Although he refers to it as *tsung-tsu*, the group cannot have been very large. His concern to keep all of the graves together, however, would have provided a clearer focus for later generations (and saved them the sense of dereliction of duty Han Ch'i felt at never having visited his ancestors' tombs). There are also examples of men who belonged to sizable local descent groups who were concerned to preserve group burial. Ch'en Liang (1143–94), a noted political thinker from Chin-hua (Chekiang), wrote that his father was much concerned with the tombs of his ancestors. The grave of Liang's great-great-great-grandfather was still in existence, even though those of his great-great-grandfather and great-grandfather were not, apparently in part because they were not eldest sons and perhaps as such were not given graves intended to be focal points of worship (CLC 27:396).[7] Ch'en Liang's father in 1167

---

6. Grave geomancy has not been fully studied for the Sung, but it did exist. A Sung text on "Combatting Delusions" discussed it, particularly criticizing the way it led to delay in burials (CCPP 2). Hung Mai's *I-chien chih* also includes some references to geomancers (*feng-shui chia*) (e.g. ICC *san-jen* 1:1475). Maurice Freedman discussed the tensions between geomantic burial practices and lineage solidarity in modern times in 1966:118–43.

7. Ch'en's father is quoted as saying, "My great-great-grandfather's tomb is still extant, but my great-grandfather was a youngest son, so I do not dare *tsu* it [treat it as an ancestor?].

wanted to start a new pattern of having all the descendants buried together, not unlike Han Ch'i's project, but he specified that they should be put in generational (*chao-mu*) order, making the graveyard resemble a genealogical chart (*p'u-hsi*) (CLC 27:396). (In strict *chao-mu* order, the odd-numbered generations would be on one side and the even-numbered ones on the other, both sides arranged in order of age, along the pattern specified in the classics for an ancestral shrine. Sometimes, however, the term *chao-mu* order is loosely used to mean in order by generation, and that may be what was meant here.)

At the time Ch'en Liang's father urged this plan, the Ch'en comprised a recognizable descent group. Ch'en Liang wrote that in this period the Ch'en were flourishing and a hundred or more people would assemble for the seasonal rites (CLC 22:347). He also described a great-uncle who because he remained healthy into old age came to be the leader of his descent group (*chang ch'i tsu*). Ch'en Liang described this man's activities by remarking that since he had died, within his descent group "who will care for the young? Who will discipline the wayward? Who will commiserate with the sick? Who will manage affairs for the dead?" (CLC 22:347). Thus Ch'en Liang would seem to imply that the descent group benefited when someone took on a leadership role, but that this role was not institutionalized, depending instead on a suitable volunteer.

Another aspect of the connection between graves and descent groups is found in the writings of Huang Kan (1152–1221), a resident of Fu-chou (Fukien). Huang Kan was a disciple (and son-in-law) of Chu Hsi, and therefore undoubtedly knew of the ideas of the Neo-Confucian philosophers on "restoring the *tsung*," to be discussed below. However, in his passages on tombs and the descent group organized around them he does not seem to have been acting on ideological principles so much as responding to the needs of an existing group. He had no qualms about worship at graves. In one of his judicial decisions he declared, "People's graves are the place where descendants make sacrifices for a hundred years" (MCC 33:14a). He may have felt strongly about this because he and his kinsmen fought encroachment on an old graveyard for over twenty years.

In his last effort to bring this case to court, Huang Kan wrote a detailed charge, giving the history of the graveyard. It was over three hundred years old and was located in a Buddhist shrine built by his ancestors. Since its founding, his kinsmen had been getting together every spring and fall to make sacrifices. Unfortunately, Huang Kan's father had lent a female cousin

---

Neither my great-grandfather's nor my grandfather's tombs survive, so I am unable to *tsu*" them (CLC 27:396). The implication seems to be that only the primary heirs should *tsu* a grave. This would fit in with the *tsung* ideology of differentiated descent lines, but I have found no other reference to its applicability to tombs.

and her husband named Chao use of the study in this shrine as a place to live, and their sons later came to occupy the whole shrine. As a result the Huangs had to use the monk's quarters when coming or going to make offerings. In the years that followed disputes kept recurring, leading to brawls, vandalism, and lawsuits. Even the so-called "forbidden area" of the tombs was violated.[8] In his final plea Huang Kan argued against a settlement by division of the property: "In the spring and fall when we bow and sweep the graves, outside of an area to lay out a mat there is hardly room for a person, causing me great sorrow. If the area is divided, how will I be able to face my ancestors in the world below?" (MCC:32b–34b).

Undoubtedly influenced by his family's long struggle over the old graveyard, in 1221, on the day of the Ch'ing-ming festival, Huang Kan decided to endow a fund to pay for sacrifices at the graves. He wrote:

> Whenever I think of the importance of the grave mounds I become distressed and grieve that I am already seventy and could die any day without having made a plan to enable my descendants to continue the sacrifices.... When graves are close by, one can expect sons and grandsons to assist each other in maintaining them. Still, the four areas of my ancestors' tombs at the Common Blessings Shrine have been in existence for three hundred years. Although my agnates each spring and fall contribute money to pay for the sacrifices, there are poor ones among them who find this a serious strain. As the generations go by it is easy for people's affections to become remiss. Outside of the sacrifices, few of them visit the graves. (MCC 34:13b–14a)

Consequently Huang Kan donated land of more than four *mou*, with an annual income of sixteen piculs, to pay for the sacrifices. (Some details on its management will be discussed later under estates.) Endowments of the sort described in the Fu-chou gazetteer may have provided models for Huang Kan, since he lived in Fu-chou, though little is known of the size or management of earlier endowments for graves or grave rites.

Finally, let us look at a text, probably dating from the thirteenth century, written by one Chao Chi-ming and preserved in a Yuan encyclopedia for popular reference (CCPYSL, *I* 4:72a–77b). It is called "A Diagram of Descent Group Burial." The author outlines a plan whereby the first ancestor is placed in the center of the graveyard, facing south. South of him, on the east would be the *chao* ranks, sons in one row, great-grandsons in the next row further south, and so on. On the west would be the *mu* ranks, first a row of grandsons, then a row of great-great-grandsons, and so on. Descendants were to be buried strictly in order of age, irrespective of who their fathers were; thus the arrangement would match the tablets in an ancestral hall, not a genealogy. This pattern, by de-emphasizing separate lines of descent, would stress the unity of the group and its common origin. (This point will

8. On the "forbidden area" of graves, eighteen paces long, see CMC:371–76.

be elaborated below with regard to name and number systems). To the north of the founding ancestor would be buried all those born into the family who did not live to marry, arranged by generation, boys on the east and girls on the west. They were members of the group, but not ancestors.

The commentary to this graveyard diagram explicitly justified this practice of rank-ordered burials in terms of convenience for getting together to offer sacrifices. The author also explained that while family rites extend back only to the great-great-grandfather, at the graves they go back to the first ancestor, making graves particularly important. Although it is difficult to evaluate how many people followed this plan (for some Yuan cases, see SHSWC 30:542–43, 34:606), it continued to be cited in reference books, de Groot finding it in manuals in use in Fukien in the late nineteenth century (de Groot 1892–1910, III:832–34); even in the twentieth century it was practiced in some places (Gamble 1963:261–62).

There are several inferences that can be drawn from the writings of these four men. The first is that graves and descent groups were associated in the authors' minds. The second is that there was an interest in burying people together—overcoming the conflicting imperatives of geomancy if need be—in order to be able to visit more graves at ritual occasions and obtain greater benefits from the spirits of deceased ancestors. Third, there was an interest in arranging burials in patterns that would reflect the descent and seniority principles important in ancestral rites, thereby stressing the unity of the group rather than its separation into lines. Fourth, association with an old graveyard, as in Huang Kan's case, could lead to a group identity as those responsible for it had to protect it from outsiders, in his case affines. Fifth, collecting money to pay for group rites may have been one of the earliest forms of descent group organization. In Huang Kan's case it was first done through annual solicitations (resembling Buddhist clubs in this regard), but later property was set aside to provide a regular income for it. When annual solicitations are made, the group is essentially a voluntary one; once it owns property in common, its nature changes. People no longer have to decide each year whether they wish to contribute and participate; they have a right to participate based on descent from the named ancestor. So long as the property is competently managed (not an easy assumption to make) the rites continue and the group maintains its existence.

It should of course be stressed that not all sets of agnates in the Sung had common graveyards or common rites at graves. But then neither did all sets of agnates in later times develop into descent groups. The question is whether there is an association between common grave sites/rites and the development of descent group organization. The Shihs described by Richard Davis in chapter 3 did not have common burial areas, and as he shows their group identity lasted only about two centuries. By contrast the Wus studied by Keith Hazelton in chapter 5 favored a particular burial ground from at least the eleventh century and began compiling genealogies and formulating rules for ritual observances in the mid-thirteenth century.

All considered, I think it can be argued that a key element in the emergence of descent groups in the Sung and later was a change in religious ideas and ritual practices related to graves and ancestors, a change that fostered the development of group consciousness among local agnates. This is not to deny that the process would often have been a dynamic one; once the social effects of worshiping at graves came to be understood, people who wished to promote solidarity among their kin probably would urge that rites at the grave of their earliest ancestor be instituted. Yet I would stress the significance of the grave rites in and of themselves.

By putting emphasis on the rituals, I am going counter to the general model of Chinese kinship development that draws largely on the tradition of British social anthropology (for criticisms of this approach, see Sangren 1984 and R. Watson 1985). Broadly speaking, this school sees economic and political needs leading to the formation of groups, which then adopt rituals to help strengthen the group's solidarity. There are two main reasons why I give primacy to the change in ritual practices in explaining the broader historical change. One is chronology: The changed approach to graves—probably stimulated by the tremendous influence of Buddhism—was well under way in the T'ang, considerably before stronger group identity among local agnates becomes evident in the historical sources. The second reason concerns the widespread popularity of sacrifices at graves. The worship of ancestors at their graves, so long as they were located not far from one's home, seems to have become a common practice from Sung times on, by no means limited to members of recognizable descent groups. And a sense of group identity, characterized by a consciousness of a focal, apical ancestor, became fairly common, at least in places where migration and settlement patterns led to large numbers of agnates living near each other (e.g. M. Yang 1945:134–42). Much less common was the leap from group consciousness (which is enough to call the set of people a group in a weak sense) to the solidification of the descent group into a lineage that possessed corporate property and acted as a unit in local politics (cf. J. Watson 1982:606–7). Lineages, once they appeared, naturally elaborated their ritual activities to serve group purposes (as in building halls for subbranches). But the needs of members of lineages—a tiny fraction of all sets of local agnates—cannot account for the rituals practiced by the rest; nor would they diminish the consequences such rituals would have had for people's sense of a "we" group.

Communal Families

Even if group ritual practices helped foster a greater awareness of descent principles and greater sense of group consciousness among local agnates, these attitudes need not have resulted in a particular type of group organization. During the T'ang and Sung dynasties, most historical references to organized groups of agnates were to ones of the form called "communal families" and not to descent groups or lineages.

A "communal family" was a domestic unit that had not divided—either property or members—for five, six, or even ten generations. In Chinese terminology this was spoken of as though the unit in question was both a *chia*, a family with common assets, and a *tsu*, an organization including distant agnates. In other words, their concept of agnates (*tsu*) did not preclude the possibility that they lived together with a common budget: To the contrary, this was seen as the moral and ritual ideal, extremely difficult to attain in practice but much to be admired. These communal families had some resemblance to the kinship system described in the classics (the *tsung* system) but do not seem to have been the product of conscious efforts to revive ancient forms; indeed they were as likely to be found among commoners as among the educated. The state celebrated their existence, honoring them with banners and tax and labor service exemptions, but the motivation underlying these state actions does not seem to have been to try to get a higher percentage of commoners to organize themselves as communal families, but rather to promote traditional moral values of family solidarity by honoring extreme examples of their fulfillment. One reason why communal families inspired such awe among Sung and Yuan literati is probably that most upper class families found it difficult to stay together even a few decades after losing a father as a family head (cf. Ebrey 1984b:92–96).

Communal families can be seen as precursors of lineages in the sense that they were large localized groups that shared in a common estate and were organized on a basis of patrilineal descent. And some may have been protolineages; for lack of an adequate range of concepts, observers may sometimes have labeled as *chia* any patrilineal kinship unit organized around a property base, since to them *tsu* implied a much looser grouping without shared property. (This understanding of *tsu* would change in time as corporate estates became more common.)

The late T'ang and Five Dynasties periods appear to have been a time when families in many parts of the country chose to stay together with a common estate; in all probability they took this course as a way to provide self-protection in a time of endemic disorder. The economic base of these families is almost always unknown, so whether they fared best in specific economic contexts is a matter for speculation.[9] Chapter 456 of the *Sung History*, on the filially righteous, describes briefly numerous communal

9. See Satake 1973 for an attempt to explore the economic organization of some of these families. See also Cohen 1976 for a discussion of the economic conditions that could lead to delaying division of a family for a few decades.

families singled out for their exceptional size. For instance, the Hsu family of Chiang-chou (Kiangsi) "maintained a common household of eight generations' depth, with 781 people, young and old." In 982 a special banner honoring them was awarded by the court (SS 456:13390). The family of Fang Kang in Ch'ih-chou (Anhwei) had "shared a stove" for eight generations and comprised seven hundred people in six hundred rooms. The history says that they met every morning and ate together. In 1005 they were honored with a banner, and about fifteen years later they had their taxes partially remitted (SS 456:13396). Six more cases of families with over seven hundred people are listed, plus another twenty that had remained undivided for eight to ten generations (SS 456:13390–400). In the *Draft Continuation of the Comprehensive Mirror (Hsu tzu-chih t'ung-chien ch'ang-pien)* and the *Sung Collected Documents (Sung hui-yao)*, there are many more citations of communal families, including some which had one or two thousand members (Niida 1937:550–53). As Niida points out, these families were found all over the country, with no particular area standing out. There do seem to be some temporal differences, however, as many more were recorded for the first century of the Sung than for the next two. (Could it be that this form of organization declined as political stability set in? Or could it be that similar kinship units were later classed as *tsu*? Or is this change no more than an historiographical illusion?)

In most of these cases the members of the families seem to have been commoners.[10] A family in Ho-chung prefecture (Shansi) that was noted for its filial piety in the T'ang remained undivided into the Sung. When they reached ten generations, Emperor Jen-tsung (r. 1023–63) excused them from labor service. By the end of the eleventh century they had reached thirteen generations. The historian commented:

> The Yao family have been farmers for generations and include no one who studies. The family is not especially rich; it owns several dozen *ch'ing* of land for over a hundred assembled agnates (*chü-tsu*). The junior members do all the farming and sericulture in person, diligently working to provide food and clothing. For over three hundred years no one has separated from the family. Through the wars of the late T'ang and Five Dynasties the descendants preserved their graves, and "bone and flesh" did not separate (SS 456:13403)

10. Large communal families were not entirely restricted to commoners. The *Sung History* cites the case of a family in Hung prefecture (Kiangsi) with several hundred members. It built a school, collecting ten thousand books and inviting teachers from afar. In 985 it was honored with the banner (SS 456:13390). Another case was of a family in Chiang prefecture (Kiangsi) that was descended from T'ang officials. At the beginning of the Sung it had seven hundred people, who are said to have met for every meal. The family was excused from labor service by the government and given grants of grain to feed its members, now reaching one thousand. It also ran a school and several of the family managers were made officials (SS 456:13391–92; see also Satake 1973).

All of the cases discussed so far were recorded because of the unusual size and genealogical depth. Among men of literary or political note, one also comes across communal families, but more often ones of four or five generations' depth and perhaps a hundred members. Ssu-ma Kuang (1019–86) and Lu Chiu-shao (b. ca. 1138) both wrote brief instructions on the management of these sorts of families (SMSSI 4:41–45; SYHA 57:118–19). From the point of view of the development of descent group organization, their writings are illuminating in three ways. First, in these families the only distinctions drawn among members were the traditional kinship ones of age, generation, and sex, and efforts were taken to keep differences in individual wealth from leading to differing standards of living. Second, in each case, rules for management, budgeting, and even everyday courtesies were very much stressed, reflecting undoubtedly the complexities of these organizations. Chao Ting (1085–1147), a noted scholar and political figure, wrote a similar set of rules for his descendants in the hope that they would never divide their property and thus would in time become a communal family (CHPL:1–4). Thus, despite Fan Chung-yen's invention of the charitable estate in 1049, through the eleventh and twelfth century it was common for educated men to see the ideal descent group (i.e., group of *tsu-jen* or *tsung-jen*) as one organized as a *chia*. Indeed, communal families continued to appear—and be praised—through the Yuan, Ming, and Ch'ing (see Xu 1980:33–50; see also the example described by Dennerline in chapter 5). The Cheng family of Chin-hua, perhaps the most famous communal family, was founded in the eleventh century and attracted much notice in the late Yuan and early Ming; even long after the family's demise it continued to be admired and copied (Dardess 1974; Langlois 1981).

The breakup of communal families in some cases led to the formation of descent groups. That is, agnates who were no longer able to keep all of their property together still tried to preserve some group organization and maybe some common assets. For instance, the Wangs of Wu-yuan in Hui-chou compiled a genealogy in the mid-eleventh century at the seventh generation, and another in 1211 at the tenth, and a third in 1236 at the twelfth generation.[11] Each stressed that the Wangs had earlier been a communal family and

---

11. Morita 1979 restricts his discussion of Sung genealogies to the nineteen prefaces found in collected works of Sung literati, arguing that ones preserved in later genealogies are often forged. While ones attributed to famous scholars (and not found in their collected works) may often be later forgeries, that does not mean that all prefaces labeled "Sung" are unreliable. Frequently the circumstantial evidence in the genealogies to support the date and authorship of a preface is convincing. In the case of the two prefaces quoted here, the authors are members of the family and their existence is confirmed by the highly detailed *Hsin-an ming-tsu-chih* (HAMTC 2:89b–90a), which also records the Wangs' earlier status as a communal family. Moreover, the nature of the Sung data in the genealogy makes it likely that a table was compiled at the date listed. The first preface is also quoted in later prefaces, even in ones in other descent groups' genealogies.

that something of this spirit could be revived through genealogical compilation. According to these authors, the family's founder died in 960; he had eleven sons whose names all included the character "Jen," twenty-four grandsons (names, "Wen"), and fifty-one great-grandsons (names, "Te"). "From 960 to 1024, some sixty-five years, they lived as a communal family with four generations' depth, comprising 326 people" (WSTP 1211 preface).

> All internal and external affairs, major or minor, were governed by rules, just like a government office, and no one dared violate them. When seniors were sitting in the hall, anyone walking by would scurry deferentially. Everyone was diligent, and would not dare make excuses. Not until the twelfth month of each year would people be given clothes, cloth, and floss. Eating was signaled by drumbeat, and if someone failed to show up, no one would eat. Whenever scolded, they would act fearful and submit. They had several hundred *mou* of average fields that they set aside for the expenses of entertaining and paying taxes. There was never the slightest deception in the handling of the family's accounts in money and grain. Whenever an emergency arose, then without exception they would unite to provide aid. (WSTP old preface)

The author of this preface went on to lament the great decline in family behavior that had occurred after the break-up of the communal family. The author of the second preface (1211) noted that the descent group of Wangs currently had officials and wealthy men, but also illiterates and people without an inch of land; it had monks and others who had abandoned the family graveyards to move elsewhere, plus boatmen, peddlers, craftsmen, and government menials. (The last category the author thought was too lowly to record in the genealogy.) Such a diverse group could not form a communal family. But they do seem to have formed a descent group; the repeated updating of their genealogy is evidence of a strong sense of group identity among their educated members and perhaps even of ongoing organization. (The Hui-chou descent group described in Hazelton's chapter already had some organization in the late Sung.)

As the author of this preface implied, communal families probably survived best when there were no great differences of wealth or social status among their men, for their underlying principle was distribution of income to all members equally according to need, just as though they were members of a small family. Officials' salaries would have to go into a common pool, and the sons of officials would get no benefits the sons of others did not get. Because this went counter to so much of Chinese thinking on the status of literati and officials, it probably seldom worked. Even the famous Cheng family succumbed to the pressure to divide within a few generations after producing officials (Dardess 1974:33–44).

More detail on the transformation of a communal family is given in an account written by Wang Yung. In 1246 he visited the village in Kuei-chi (Chekiang) that was the home of a communal family named Ch'iu. This

family had been described in the *Sung History* and elsewhere as having
already stayed together for nineteen generations when they were awarded
the banner in 1011, the longest period of joint residence listed for any family
in the *Sung History* (SS 456:13400). According to the *Kuei-chi chih*, a local
gazetteer written in 1201, the family head (*tsu-chang*) did such things as
organize the hundred-odd children under thirteen to pick melons (KCC
13:24b–25a). When Wang Yung visited the Ch'iu in 1246 he found that they
were no longer strictly speaking a "communal family," having in recent
times separated their family finances. Yet, as he noted, they still retained
some central organization, which we might characterize as lineage-like.
According to Wang:

> Every generation the Ch'iu choose one man to be head (*chang*). Whenever
> anything needs to be settled, he acts as judge. There is a bamboo rod that is also
> passed from one generation to the next. The *tsu-chang* uses it if he wishes to
> punish an offender. At the seasonal sacrifices everyone assembles. Up until
> today they are still exempted from labor service. How many generations
> beyond nineteen they have now reached, I do not know.
>   I pondered this. The Ch'ius are working farmers, without a scholar-official
> among them, which is how they have been able to stay together for so long
> without scattering. If there had been a high-ranking or prominent person
> among them, then he would have been beyond the control of the *tsu-chang*....
> Although the Ch'ius lack prominent members, their descendants have pre-
> served their patrimony for generations and are a great descent group (*ta-tsu*).
> How much better this is than sudden upward and downward changes. (YIIML
> 5:47–48).

Wang Yung seems to have hit upon a crucial point. Officials were regularly transferred and had to go where the government sent them. For a
communal family, producing a great many officials would bring not only
differences in status but also geographic dispersal. The looser, secondary
ties of descent groups might offer advantages in these cases, proving more
resilient to the exodus of members and changes in their status.

As a local kinship unit, organized to protect group interest, communal
families probably were gradually superseded by lineages. After the idea of
corporate estates separate from family property gained widespread recognition (see below), it seems likely that many groups of kinsmen who wished to
strengthen their local political and economic power would have set up a
lineage estate rather than remain an undivided family. Leaders of a lineage
did not have as complete control over its members as the head of a communal family did, but lineages escaped many of the tensions of an undivided
family while still providing a means for defense of group interest. The process by which lineages superseded communal families as units in local society, however, does not belong to the early stages of descent group development. During the Sung and Yuan periods, local sets of agnates sharing an
estate seem more often to have been communal families than lineages.

The Efforts of Intellectuals to "Revive the *Tsung*" and Promote Genealogy Compilation

At this point I will switch from the signs of organized activity among local kinsmen that can be detected in Sung sources to the steps taken by intellectuals in an effort to reform kinship practices among members of their own social class (*shih-ta-fu*). Their writings provided the ideological justification for promoting descent group organization for the next several centuries.

In the mid-eleventh century, during the same period when Han Ch'i was searching for his ancestors' graves and constructing a new graveyard, his acquaintances in the capital, Ou-yang Hsiu (1007–72), Fan Chung-yen (989–1052), and Su Hsun (1009–66), and the scholars Chang Tsai (1022–78) and Ch'eng I (1033–1107) all came to promote reforms in agnatic kinship practices. Fan's establishment of his famous "charitable estate" was formalized in 1049, and in 1051 he compiled a genealogy of the kinsmen to share in this estate. In 1055 both Su Hsun and Ou-yang Hsiu independently compiled genealogies of their kin. The comments by Chang Tsai and Ch'eng I on "reviving the *tsung*" are undated, but in all probability they took shape after 1055. These men, each in different ways, wished to reform society. They sensed that something was missing in the family life of most educated, upper class men, oriented toward the family line and descendants. The family spirit they sought seemed to be more often attained by commoners, long settled in a community, who either maintained communal families or at least got together periodically to make offerings together.

The background of Fan Chung-yen's action has already been fully described by Denis Twitchett (1959), and only a few points need to be highlighted here. First and foremost, there does not seem to have been an active, preexisting descent group of Soochow Fan before Fan Chung-yen took the initiative to set up an estate. Second, the group he created did not have much genealogical depth, going back only four generations.[12]

---

12. The rules Fan Chung-yen established refer constantly to the "various *fang*," here apparently meaning households (*fang* means "room" and refers to collateral divisions within a kinship unit, from nuclear families in a household to branches of a lineage) (FWCKWC 8:97). The meaning of *fang* in these rules can be seen from the 1051 genealogy. According to the preface Fan Chung-yen wrote to the genealogy, since the time his great-great-grandfather Fan Sui had migrated south with the fall of the T'ang, knowledge of their ancestry had become confused. Sui had six sons, but they had scattered to the four directions. The old genealogy had been lost, so Fan had to get his relatives to look among their old family papers to find enough information to reconstruct a genealogy, which he then called a "continued genealogy" (*Hsu chia p'u*). When the work was done, Fan Chung-yen was able to trace his own ancestry back for four generations, plus detail the currently existing divisions among the younger generation (Makino 1949:121, FWCKWC 6:86). Later recensions of the genealogy report that since the Sung there had been sixteen *fang* and list the heads of each. These heads were all descendants of Fan Sui, four generations back, and thus during Fan Chung-yen's lifetime all but the youngest

Only a few years after Fan Chung-yen founded his estate and compiled a
genealogy through research, Su Hsun compiled a genealogy for the descendants of his great-great-grandfather and had it carved on stone and the stele
erected at the ancestral graveyard. Su Hsun explicitly related his efforts to
the classical descent line system, the *tsung* system. He described how the
ancient *tsung* system worked, with its division into the "great *tsung*" of the
primary line that continues indefinitely and the nesting "lesser *tsung*" that
break off from it every generation and are composed, respectively, of the
descendants of great-great-grandfather, great-grandfather, grandfather, and
father, each led in ritual by a "son of the *tsung*" (*tsung-tzu*), the representative of the senior line descended from that ancestor (CYC 13:130–31). Su
Hsun noted that only the lesser *tsung* was applicable to ordinary educated
men in his day. He argued for the social benefits of instituting the *tsung*
system, for it would lead to improvements both to kin behavior and to the
moral climate of local communities. When the *tsung* system operated, he
said, close agnates mourned each other and informed each other at the event
of deaths, burials, or marriages (CYC 13:125). This was at odds with what
he saw around him where relatives became strangers from the time they
began to live apart (CYC 13:126). He noted that although he did not have
many agnatic kinsmen (less than a hundred within the circle of mourning
obligations), they did not celebrate seasonal sacrifices and festivals together,
and "those at all distant do not visit each other" (CYC 13:132). Carving the
genealogy of the descendants of his great-great-grandfather on stone and
placing it *by the grave of that ancestor* he thought would allow all the descendants to see how closely they were related and remedy this deplorable
situation. Clearly Su Hsun did not belong to the kind of descent groups
Ch'en Liang or Huang Kan did, but he had hopes of fostering one.

The genealogy Su Hsun wrote was a compromise between lesser *tsung*
principles and filial piety to his direct ancestors, most of whom were
younger sons. Thus, he singled out the primary line of descent from each
of his own ancestors (that is, his cousins who were responsible for the rites
to his grandfather, great-grandfather, and great-great-grandfather). But he
gave vital data (age at death, death dates, and wife's surname) only for his
own ancestors. In other words, the genealogy was written from Hsun's particular point of view, a tack he explicitly defended (CYC 13:126), but which
never became a standard feature of genealogies. The postface to it reads
much as a "family account," giving stories of his direct ancestors (CYC

were within Fan Chung-yen's mourning circle and the "small *tsung*" of his great-great-
grandfather. Some were of Fan Chung-yen's generation (brother, first cousin, second cousin),
and some of up to three generations younger (great-grandson of a third cousin) (Makino
1949:123–24). (These *fang* headed by men two or three generations below Fan Chung-yen were
probably not in existence in 1049 or 1051 but created later in the Sung.)

13:132–34). Other kinsmen could use the genealogy as a skeleton, which they could then fill in for their own relatives.

Ou-yang Hsiu's genealogy bears many similarities to Su Hsun's. It also covered only the descendants of his great-great-grandfather, and it also was carved on stone and erected at the graves of his ancestors. Its format was different from Su Hsun's, providing data on individuals in a commentary after the table proper. Data were very uneven, mostly on offices, with some references to age at death and wife's name. Many men were annotated only as "fact missing," but in a few cases Ou-yang Hsiu included the man's number within his row (to be discussed below) (OYHCC 21:510–23).

In Ou-yang Hsiu's case, it could be that kinsmen wished to strengthen ties with him rather than the other way around. As Kobayashi (1980) points out, Ou-yang Hsiu did not spend much time in his native place, and compiling this genealogy on the five-generation basis may have been an attempt to restrict the scope of the descent group toward which he had obligations as a wealthy and prominent man. It is of course understandable why Su and Ou-yang both had the genealogies erected at the graves: This was the place, and probably the only place, that agnates routinely gathered.

Within much the same intellectual climate, the philosophers Chang Tsai and Ch'eng I called for a more thoroughgoing revival of the *tsung* system of antiquity. Chang Tsai wrote an essay on the *tsung fa* (system of classical descent groups) in his *Explications of the Classics (Ching-hsueh li-k'u)*. It opens with an often-quoted statement also found in Ch'eng I's sayings (IS 6:85):

> In order to control the hearts of the people of the world, to bring together agnates (*tsung-tsu*), and to improve social customs so that people never forget their origins, it is necessary to clarify the genealogical order of descent groups (*tsu*) and institute the system of differentiated descent lines (*tsung-tzu-fa*). (CTC 4:258)

Chang Tsai then continued:

> When the system of differentiated descent lines is not practiced, people do not know the organization of the lines or the places that they came from. Very few people in ancient times were ignorant of their places of origin. After the system of differentiated descent lines decayed, later generations still honored genealogical writing, so that some of the spirit persisted. Now that genealogical writing has also decayed, people do not know where they come from; there are no hundred year families (*chia*); there is no organization to "bone and flesh kin"; even the closest relatives (*chih-ch'in*) feel no more than slight obligation to each other. Moreover, without the establishment of the system of differentiated descent lines, the court can have no hereditary officials. For instance, a minister can rise up in a day from a poor and humble position. If he does not set up a *tsung* system, once he dies his agnates (*tsu*) will scatter and his house

(*chia*) will not continue.... Nowadays those who accumulate wealth or honor can only plan for thirty or forty years. They may build a residence and occupy it but when they die their sons will divide and separate and soon be bankrupt, so that the house (*chia*) does not survive. If, in this way, they cannot preserve their houses, how can they preserve the state? (CTC 4:258–59).

Ch'eng I's comments on relations with agnates and the descent group system were not as organized as Chang Tsai's, but if anything they were more influential, being regularly quoted in later genealogies. Particularly noteworthy are his arguments for assembling agnates and compiling genealogies:

Family rules (*chia-fa*) should provide that whenever an agnate (*tsu-jen*) comes from a distant place, there should be a meeting of the entire descent group (*tsu*). Even when nothing is happening there should be a meeting once a month. One can copy the practice of the Wei family of the past, which had descent group meetings (*tsung hui*) under flowering trees. Also at births, deaths, marriages, and the like, agnates (*tsu-jen*) must join in the rituals, so that the idea of "flesh and bone" links are constantly reinforced. The reason that "flesh and bone" relatives every day become more distant is that they do not see each other and are not involved with each other. (IS 1:7)

When the system of differentiated descent lines is in decay, people do not know where they come from, to the point where they wander off in all directions and then do not recognize each other although they are still within the mourning grades. Now let's have one or two families (*chia*) of great men try to put this system into practice. The procedures should be ones that can be strictly adhered to. As in the T'ang system of ancestral altars and halls of fasting, there should be no division of the ancestral property; rather, one man should be given charge of managing it all. (IS 15:150)

Instituting the system of differentiated descent lines is a Principle of Heaven. It can be compared to a tree: There must be a trunk growing up from the roots, but there also are side branches. Or like a river: There must be a main source, however far away, but there are also streams that divert water away. These are natural tendencies. (IS 18:242)

Ch'eng I also discussed at some length the forms to be followed for ancestor worship. For ancestors up to great-great-grandfather, he said offerings of fresh food should be made at household altars on the first of each month, with full sacrifices (*chi*) in the second, fifth, eighth, and eleventh months. Besides this there were to be only three other sacrifices. At the winter solstice one could sacrifice to the First Ancestor (*shih tsu*), defined as the first to have descendants in the line, and thus someone of remote antiquity. On the day of "establishing spring," one could sacrifice to ancestors between the founder and one's great-great-grandfather. Finally, in the last month of fall, there should be sacrifices to ancestors in general (IS 18:240). The rites to distant ancestors, while perhaps a concession to popular custom, were not to be done at graves or descent group shrines, but at family altars, and the participants would be the same ones who normally joined in family rites. Despite these qualifications, Chu Hsi, who usually deferred to Ch'eng I's judgment, declared that rites to early ancestors were presumptuous on the part of all but rulers and nobles (CWKCC 63:19a–20a; HLTCS 21:25a). Chu Hsi's opinion, however, was largely ignored; in fact, Ch'eng I's approval of *household* offerings to ancient ancestors came to be regularly cited to justify the quite different practice of *descent group* rites to apical ancestors ("first migrant ancestors," *shih ch'ien tsu*).

In the generations after Ch'eng I and Chang Tsai, many scholars committed to their philosophy tried to act on their advice. Although I have found no cases of scholars successfully instituting the system of differentiated descent lines, many did try to bring agnates together for group rituals (e.g. LTLWC 4:67, 10:241–50). Others also followed their advice in compiling genealogies (which, of course, had also been recommended by Ou-yang Hsiu and Su Hsun). Often all we know are the steps taken and the goals sought: Whether they led to the creation of an enduring descent group cannot be answered. In a few cases, however, scholars have left records of their efforts to celebrate or reform preexisting descent groups. A few of these cases will be discussed in a later section of this essay.

Philosophers' motivation for advocating the strengthening of ties to kinsmen was undoubtedly complex, tied to their goals of bringing order to society at all levels, formulating means of governing the uneducated that were humane and effective, finding ways to maintain some independence from the government for educated men so that they would be free to criticize it, and so on. Leaving these questions of motivation aside, one question should be raised at this point: Were Chang Tsai and Ch'eng I advocating that upper class men (*shih-ta-fu*) take steps to develop descent groups organized around rituals and genealogies because of any changes in local kinship organization? Although impossible to prove, I think that they may have written as they did in part because they knew of descent groups that had features (such as group rituals and communal property) that seemed morally preferable to the family or family line orientation typical of the upper class. These descent groups would have included the communal families discussed above but also local descent groups that met for ritual occasions, such as the ones Ch'en Liang and Huang Kan described. That such families also seemed models of social order, led by the educated, stable over generations, would only have added to their attractiveness.[13]

13. Recently some questions have been raised about the significance of the new ideas of the eleventh century—especially the idea of the charitable estate, the sanctioning of rites to early ancestors, and the renewed interest in writing genealogies. First, J. L. Watson, commenting in part on the notion that the invention of the charitable estate by highly educated men could lead

Endowed Estates and Lineage Formation

In anthropological theories on Chinese kinship organization, attention
has been concentrated on lineages, that is, descent groups with substantial
corporate properties (e.g. Freedman 1966, Baker 1979, J. Watson 1982).
Moreover, the estate has been seen as the central feature of these lineages, for
they are looked on above all as property-owning organizations. A review of
the early stages of descent group organization provides some perspective on
this interpretation by showing that from the beginning there was considerable variety in the size of estates, the length of time they survived, the purposes to which they were dedicated, and the ways they were managed. Years
ago Hui-chen Wang Liu noted that of 116 nineteenth- and twentieth-
century lineages whose genealogies she analyzed, seventy-six had graveyards
and fifty-seven had lands set aside to pay the expenses of rituals, but only
twelve had charitable estates (Liu 1959:108). This predominance of small
estates dedicated to ritual expenses seems to go back to the Sung. Moreover,
even a small estate did not necessarily provide a permanent base for kinship
organization. Shimizu Morimitsu, in his broad survey of lineage estates,
found very few estates that lasted more than a couple of centuries (1949:64).

---

to its adoption by commoners, wrote that "it is difficult for many anthropologists, given their
frog in the well view of Chinese society, to accept that lineages and related social forms...
emerged as a consequence of an ideological transformation among the national elite"
(1982:618). He also proposed that, from his perspective, the ideological shift from the T'ang to
the Sung seemed to be a shift from alliance to descent as a major organizing principle of society
(p. 617). Denis Twitchett responded to this formulation by saying that there really was no new
ideology, only a new attitude toward existing ideology that had always stressed descent, and he
cautioned against concentrating too much on terms that had only imprecise meanings (1982).
David Johnson (1983) came to Watson's defense and argued that words were not used as impre-
cisely as Twitchett had said, and that written words influence behavior as much as concrete
interests and political pressures do (p. 364). Meanwhile Robert Hymes, in his paper in this
volume, argues against opposing alliance and descent, showing that there was no turning away
from concern with marriage alliance on the part of the Sung elite, even if their interest in
organizing along lines of descent grew stronger. Here I have argued that the ideas of Neo-
Confucian writers reflected changes in society as much as they helped promote them. That is,
grave rituals and associated ideas about ancestors led to an increased group consciousness
among local agnates and this "family spirit" attracted intellectuals. Their writings never made
anyone start a lineage, but they helped gloss what was going on with a classical vocabulary,
something important to the well-educated. I agree that there was no shift from alliance (never
provided with much theoretical underpinning) to descent, nor even much of a tension between
these principles. But I do see, as I argue elsewhere (Ebrey 1984a), a conceptual tension between
the strain of thought centered on the *chia*, the family as a property-owning group, and the *tsung*
principles of "pure kinship," elaborated by Ch'eng-Chu philosophers. In the latter, genealogical linkage greatly outweighed ties based on common interests in property. Generally speaking,
glorification of *tsung* principles would have favored the development of descent groups by
allowing the well-educated to see their efforts to develop such groups as righteous.

This tendency for estates to succumb to pressures toward division was also evident from the beginning.

The ideal model of the lineage estate was of course that established by Fan Chung-yen (989–1052). His charitable estate (*i-t'ien* or *i-chuang*) was started with a gift of 3,000 *mou* of land, the benefits from which would go to those of his agnatic relatives who lived in Soochow. As discussed earlier, at the time these relatives were not especially distant, falling within the canonical four generations of the "lesser *tsung*." Benefits were distributed for special expenses (births, marriages, deaths) and on a per capita basis. Financial matters were handled by a manager chosen from among the younger members (Twitchett 1960:107). The truly poor had a further advantage of getting free lodging in a "charitable hostel." Chung-yen's son made an additional contribution of 1,000 *mou* for *chi-t'ien*, "sacrificial lands," to be handled by the monks of an attached Buddhist shrine (Twitchett 1959:103). He also had the rules modified to subsidize examination candidates and provide the salary for a teacher who would instruct the boys of member families, thus starting a lineage school (Twitchett 1959:110–11).

As Denis Twitchett has noted, Fan Chung-yen's decision to set up a permanent estate may have been inspired by Buddhist institutions. Monasteries, with their great landed estates, survived for centuries unaffected by the deaths of individual abbots (1959:102–4). Moreover, monasteries sometimes had fields singled out to provide for charitable activities, the so-called "fields of compassion" (Ch'en 1973:297–300). Since Fan's estate was large enough to subsidize basic living expenses of all the members, it also bore similarities to communal families in which all members had their expenses provided from a common fund. And like communal families, this estate required rules of operation and managers. However, unlike communal families, there were independent households that could hold separate assets, beyond their shares in the estate, and no uniform standard of living was imposed.

Fan Chung-yen's action was much admired, and it continued to be praised for centuries. To some extent, at least, this admiration may have been based on the belief that the charitable estate solved the problem of the upper class man and his obligations to his kin (on this point, see Hymes's essay, chapter 4). Communal families would find it hard to maintain everyone at upper class status for generations. But a separation of descent group property from household property would make it possible for upper class families to continue with their higher standard of living, while larger descent groups including many commoners could also continue, without recurrent subsidy from the more wealthy, as ritual and charitable expenses were ensured through the endowment. Just as the well-to-do in a community might get together to endow an estate to pay for all local labor service obligations, saving themselves from repeated annoyance, others might endow a fund to provide for poor orphans and widows among their kin so that they would

not have to deal with them individually. Endowing a lineage school, however, probably had a different appeal. It would be especially attractive to
the educated members of the lineage who then would not need to worry as
much about their descendants losing social status for lack of access to
schooling.

The government gave positive encouragement to descent group estates (as
it did also to communal families). In 1092 the land law was specifically
amended to allow officials and commoners to set aside "land or houses to
pay for the expenses of sacrifices to their ancestors." Local government
officials were to certify this, changing the tax registration of the property
and preventing descendants from ever dividing it. If a surplus resulted, the
descent group was permitted to use this for aid to agnates (SHY *shih-huo*
61:5904). Nevertheless, the number of wealthy men who imitated Fan
Chung-yen seems to have been very small. Shimizu, in a careful study of this
subject, found only a dozen references in Sung sources to men setting up
charitable estates to aid their agnates (Shimizu 1949:37–45; cf. Kyō
1976:303–5). Most of these were only for the poor in a lineage, and when the
size of the estate is given, it is usually much smaller than the Fan's, a few
hundred *mou*. As Lu Yu (1125–1210) noted in 1207, very few people in the
world had been able to copy Fan's example. "Their failure is not due to not
considering it righteous, but to lack of means" (LFWCC 21:124). (Even the
estate Lu praised, started with a gift of 700 *mou*, did not last very long. Hu
Chu [fl. 1300–50] recorded that it had long been out of existence [CPCLK
19:178].) Nor were all of the estates established strictly for agnates; some
were for agnates and maternal or other "external" relatives (e.g. CWKCC
95B:41b, KKC 89:1221). One woman in the Northern Sung is recorded to
have used her dowry to set up charitable fields to benefit equally relatives
through marriage and agnates (presumably this meant the agnates of her
husband and son and also the families tied to them by marriage, such as her
own natal family and the families her daughters married into) (SHSWC
42:738).

The relatively small number of references to lineage estates must be compared to the dozens of references to communal families and the hundreds of
references to men acting charitably toward their kinsmen (including affines)
by supplying them when they were in need from their own income. There
are probably even more references to unsuccessful attempts to found estates
than to estates that survived for over a century (e.g. HTHSTCC 79:10b–
12a; CWKCC 88:16a). If anything, Fan's example may have had greater
influence in areas outside kinship. Endowments for charitable purposes became extremely common in the Sung, but if surviving references are any
indication of their prevalence at the time, most were for community-based
activities. These included charitable schools, charitable granaries, and estates
to defray labor service costs (on the latter see McKnight 1971:157–70).

Sometimes these community services were seen as particularly aiding the donor's agnates, presumably because the community was largely composed of his agnates (e.g. MSC 10:22a, 28a).

In all probability, estates that provided no more than ritual expenses provided the material base for lineage formation more often than charitable estates did (see also Hazelton's chapter in this volume).[14] Most Sung references to sacrificial fields refer to very small descent groups. Among Sung legal cases there are several references to estates set up to pay for sacrifices, the control of the estate to be rotated among a set of brothers. In one case the estate was based on the dowry of a wife who had died along with her husband and only son. Rather than establish an adoptive heir for the husband, his parents, who had three living sons, had the three rotate management of her dowry land and take charge of the sacrifices (CMC:348–55). (On the relationship of dowry and women's interests to estate formation, see also the chapter by Jerry Dennerline in this volume.)

The advantages of rotation as a means of managing small estates can be seen in a case decided by Liu K'o-chuang (1187–1269) (HTHSTCC 192: 10a–11a). A father who was worried about the differing ability of his four sons had divided his property unequally, with the older two getting less and the younger two more. He had also set up a charitable estate to provide for rites at the tombs, complete with rules for its management and allocation. At issue now was the management of the estate attached to the tombs. Each brother wanted the management, claiming "I am the eldest," "I am an official," "I am the most able." There was also an argument that the land should either be divided equally or donated to a temple. But Liu K'o-chuang rejected donation because then the "spirit would starve" and provided instead for the sons to rotate management, keeping records that would be open to all of them. He quoted a legal ruling to the effect that if a father feared his sons would be unable to preserve their land, it could be made into an inalienable estate, to be handled in rotation to pay for sacrifices.[15]

Sometimes management of sacrificial lands could call for extensive rules. Huang Kan reports that in 1216 Ch'en Fu-tao showed him a three-chapter "Compact for the Sacrificial Fields" for which Huang Kan then wrote a

---

14. The *Family Rituals (Chia li)* circulated under Chu Hsi's name endorsed setting up "sacrificial lands," with separate plots for each ancestor, recommending that 5 percent of a man's land be put aside for this purpose at the time of family division. After the four generations of domestic worship were completed, this land could become "grave fields" (CL 1:3a). Although this type of sacrificial field system would not lead to an enduring descent group, the association of Chu Hsi's name with sacrificial fields seems to have encouraged their formation. See Tai 1936 for a full discussion of sacrificial fields and Ueyama 1982 on Chu Hsi's authorship of the *Chia li.*

15. Communal families also sometimes started with a dying wish not to see sons divide property (e.g. NCCIK 16:310–11).

colophon (MCC 22:10b–11a). To deserve such lengthy rules, this estate was probably larger than the one Huang Kan established himself in 1221. Of the management of the latter, Huang Kan wrote that its annual income of sixteen piculs was too slight to allow each household to manage it in turn. Instead, six piculs should be set aside for the sacrifices, and the leaders of the descent group should use the rest for taxes and a contingency fund. Any remaining surplus was to be reinvested to increase the holdings. "After ten years, if the increase is substantial, by rotation, it can be used to supply agnates in need" (MCC 34:14b).

Thus, although the Fan example of selecting elders and managers to run the estate may well have been copied by lineages with large estates, the practice of rotation was already well-established in the Sung and may well have been the most common form where joint properties were slight. (For its use in later periods, see Makino 1949:135–50, Uchida 1953, Hu 1948:82–83, Tai 1936:116–22).

It has been necessary to discuss estates and their management in some detail because of their importance in the literature on lineages. It should be apparent, however, that I have not found evidence of many lineages with great estates during the early stages of descent group development. Nor do estates always seem to have been the central feature of the lineages that owned them. Even a lineage/descent group strongly identified with an estate might survive its loss. Sung Lien (1310–81) reported that the Lin of P'u-t'ien in Fukien by the late Sung had accumulated 2,000 *mou* of "sacrificial fields," allowing them to conduct more impressive ancestral ceremonies than other descent groups in the area. Yet after this land was lost with the Yuan takeover, the sense of group identity was not extinguished; two generations later the leaders of these Lins erected an ancestral hall as a new focus for descent group activities (SHSWC 24:455–56).

Later Directions in Genealogy Writing and Elite Strategies for Promoting Descent Group Formation

Although genealogists up to the twentieth century regularly cited the pioneering examples of Ou-yang Hsiu and Su Hsun, within a century after they wrote their genealogies, their model was largely abandoned; the limitation at five generations was ignored and new sorts of information came to be regularly included in genealogies. These new directions appear to be closely related to developments in descent group organization and to a "localist strategy" on the part of officials and other members of the national elite. On the one hand, active descent groups often asked literati (sometimes their own members) to help them compile genealogies, but the kinds of genealogies they wanted were ones that would match their needs, stressing their first (apical) ancestor, any transfers of residence or burial grounds, the name and number patterns they used to distinguish themselves, and the location of all ancestors' graves. But the process could also occur in the opposite order, with politically ambitious men trying to strengthen their local network of allies by compiling a genealogy; this act, they believed, would give group identity to their nearby agnates (see Hymes's chapter in this volume). As more and more genealogies were written, they came to be increasingly important in establishing pedigree and social status; they became public documents, shown to relatives through marriage who might well write prefaces or postfaces for them. Similarly they could be used to foster alliances between distantly related local descent groups. Thus genealogies came to serve both the internal and external needs of descent groups and compiling them became a major practical and symbolic act of descent groups, handled almost exclusively by the more highly educated of their members. Indeed, as "public" genealogies became a central concern of descent groups with elite members, such descent groups may have progressively diverged from ones composed entirely of commoners of little education (on elite-centered descent groups see Ebrey 1983 and Hazelton, this volume).

The information included in a genealogy often provides a good indication of the needs or goals of the group that produced it. The significance of listing the location of graves in genealogies should be obvious from the argument so far; one had to know where graves were to make offerings at them. Concern with "first migrant ancestors" and shifts of residence seems to reflect a concern with specific groupings of people "on the ground," the ones who joined in rites. As mentioned earlier, it was at the grave of the "first migrant ancestor" that an entire local descent group would assemble and it clearly had a special importance in defining the boundaries of the group. Already in the mid-twelfth century (1166) Tseng Feng referred to "first migrant ancestors" (*shih-ch'ien chih tsu*) eight generations back to define two branches (*p'ai*) of Tseng in Lin-ch'uan (YTC 17:1b). Thereafter this became very common. From the late Sung on, great attention also came to be given to every transfer of residence (e.g. WSHSWC 9:331–32; SHSWC 6:131; see also Hymes and Hazelton, this volume), a trait of written genealogies that persisted until recent times (Ahern 1976). This departure from Ou-yang Hsiu's and Su Hsun's model was explicitly justified by Cheng Yü (1298–1358), who said that mourning rules and their limitation at four generations had nothing to do with genealogies, which are concerned with tracing origins (SSWC 1: 7a–b).

Naming patterns of various sorts had been followed by high status families since the Northern and Southern Dynasties (Grafflin 1983). In the fifth and sixth centuries brothers (and less frequently first cousins) were often given patterned names, the pattern either in a common radical of a one-character name, or in a common character in a two-character name. This system continued to be very common through the T'ang and was sometimes even extended to second or third cousins, though such cases were rare (see the genealogical tables in HTS 70–75). The Wangs of Wu-yuan, discussed above as a communal family, had generational names from the late T'ang. On naming patterns used by descent groups in the Sung and later, see the chapters in this volume by Davis, Naquin, and Rawski.

In genealogies, very often name and number patterns are discussed together. In the preface Ou-yang Shou-tao (1209–67+) wrote for a genealogy, he said that the descent group in question could trace back sixteen generations, giving ancestors' names (*ming*), informal names (*tzu*), numbers (*ti*), rows (*hang*), death dates, and tomb locations (SCWC 21:9a). (Rows refer to generations and numbers to a person's seniority by date of birth within a generation.) Tai Piao-yuan (fl. 1260–90) described a name and number pattern that was consciously put into practice as part of an effort to establish a descent group. He reported that after a man named Sun Yao did extensive research to compile the genealogy of his large descent group (which had included many officials in the previous century), he got together "the worthy and able" and together they assembled their agnates. At this meeting, one generation was selected to be the first row (*hang*) and a naming pattern was designed, using twenty characters in the order of production of the Five Phases; this pattern would be continued indefinitely, returning to the beginning after twenty generations. "Thus for a hundred generations the seniority in the *chao-mu* ranks will not become disordered" (YYC 10:145–46).[16] In other words, the express purpose of this naming system was to make it easy to recognize differences in generations among the members of a large descent group. Some recorded name and number systems follow slightly different principles; for instance one described by Wu Hai (fl. 1350–70) used the ten celestial stems as generational markers in the numbering system (WKCC 1:2–3).

Number patterns are less well understood than name patterns. Rather than emphasizing membership in a generation, numbers indicate exact seniority within a generation. Seniority was of course important in Chinese family ethics (the elder brother–younger brother relationship) and this may account in part for the practice. Numbering of people within a family or a small ritual group (e.g., among descendants of a great-grandfather) seems to have been a common practice among the upper class in the T'ang; T'ang poems and elegies were often dedicated to Wang 11 or Chang 22. In the Sung commoners were often referred to by a name and a number. In legal cases and anecdotes, people of the lowest status were often called Wang 3 or Li 5.

16. Exactly which generation was being designated the first row is unclear. Since one could not rename deceased ancestors, it presumably was the youngest generation then alive or being born. At any rate, since a genealogy had been carefully researched, this was not an attempt to fudge a genealogy by declaring all the adults then alive to be of the same generation.

Most often one finds low numbers, which could mean only brothers were included within the sequence.

From the earliest stages of descent group development, there seems to have been an association between numbers and descent groups. Ou-yang Hsiu had recorded some numbers in his genealogy, and in 1098 the Fan estate had required that numbers be recorded for infants (FWCKWC 8:107 or Twitchett 1960:14). Why did people number sons within a large descent group instead of a family or small ritual group? One possible reason is that the significance of numbers was in ancestor worship (where people and tablets were to be lined up in this order), and the unit involved in ancestor worship in their cases was large. Moreover, as mentioned above in the context of patterned graves, emphasis on seniority within a generation would counter the tendency to divide into separate lines of descent. Genealogies, by their very arrangement, reveal descent lines (referred to as branching, *chih-fen p'ai-pieh*); that is, they place each man under his own father. If each person's birth order number was also added, something of this emphasis on lines could be countered. Whatever the reason, in the Sung it seems to have become common to refer to ancestors by their number[17] and genealogists, by recording these numbers, seem to have adapted the genre of genealogical writing to the requirements of active descent groups.

Sung and Yuan genealogies with the features described above seem to have been written by and large for preexisting descent groups, groups with well-defined needs for recording information. But not all genealogies were of this sort or written for this purpose. Among the upper class at least, genealogies could be used to assert status and establish ties between families. Morita (1979) shows how genealogy writing became a more public activity in the late Sung and Yuan, as men turned to famous writers to write prefaces and postfaces. Wen T'ien-hsiang (1236–83), for instance, wrote four prefaces/postfaces, Wu Ch'eng (1247–1331) wrote thirty-seven, and Sung Lien (1310–81) wrote twenty. In addition, to make genealogies more widely

---

17. An additional reason for recording numbers in genealogies may have been the taboo on using a deceased father's *ming*. Officials received posthumous titles by which their descendants could refer to them, but for commoners, finding the appropriate term was not so easy. The practice of calling even commoners after they were dead "so-and-so *kung*" ("lord") had started by the early Sung. (Ch'en Liang says his descent group started to follow the custom [*shih-su*] of calling ancestors "*kung*" in about A.D. 1000, CLC 27:395.) In some genealogies, the early ancestors' *ming* have been lost and they are known only as "Lord 24" or "Lord Mu 12." The preface to a genealogy written in 1297 gives some insight into how this worked. Hu Yen-wu recorded that when he was a very young child a local teacher asked him if he knew his ancestors' row numbers. When he replied that he did not know them all, the teacher taught him six numbers: 4, 6, 2, 10, 7, and 8. Later at five *sui* when he entered school, he learned that his first ancestor was "Lord 4" (perhaps the fourth son in a family) and that *six* generations later there were four branches (*p'ai*). (Presumably the man who was his own ancestor was called "two," and so on.) (HSTP:1297 preface.)

available men began to make multiple copies by printing them. In chapter 4, Robert Hymes describes this trend in Fu-chou, where he relates it to changes in the elite's place in local society.

The importance of genealogies in establishing status was perhaps most acutely developed in Hui-chou, where men even published genealogical gazetteers, the first one in 1316 (Zurndorfer 1981 and Hazelton, this volume). This may well have had something to do with marriage ties. Shu Ti (1304–77) from Hui-chou wrote prefaces for the genealogies of the families of his maternal grandfather, his father's sister, and his wife's brother (CSCC 2:7a–8a, 22b–29a). But the relationship between marriage and genealogy compilation was not limited to Hui-chou. Lou Yueh (1137–1213) describes a man in his native Ming-chou who was thoughtful to all of his relatives, even, for instance, paying his respects to the tombs of his mother's family as well as his own. He also compiled a table of the descent lines and branches of all the families related to his by marriage over the generations (KKC 88:1203). This then was a genealogy not of a single descent line but of several intermarried ones.[18]

Besides helping in establishing ties to affines, genealogies could also be used to link patrilineally related descent groups and thus to form "higher-order" descent groups. This practice had appeared by the late Sung. When Ou-yang Shou-tao broke the precedent set by his ancestor Ou-yang Hsiu of compiling a genealogy for only five generations, he justified this by saying he wanted a genealogy that would connect all of the descent groups of Ou-yang in Lu-ling. By the Yuan dynasty, writing genealogies explicitly to document the connections between separate descent groups became quite common. Describing a descent group in his home community, Sung Lien praised a man who "compiled a genealogy of relatives of the same surname in order to connect their descent groups" (SHSWC 69:1099–1100). In another case, a Tseng wanted to compile a genealogy to record the connections among thirty-five branches (*fang*) under one of the nine segments (*chih*) of the Tsengs of Ch'a-lin in Kiangsi. This was difficult because he had to get access to other descent groups' genealogies; many had lost theirs in the wars, and others who had preserved them considered them secret treasures they would not show anyone (SHSWC 40:700).

There could be several reasons why men might want to establish links among descent groups. As Robert Hymes argues in his chapter, it could be

---

18. Another example of the relation between genealogies and marriage is described by Huang Chin (1277–1357). After he finished making an announcement of posthumous rank at the grave of his grandmother in front of an assembly that included agnates, affinal relatives, and local residents, a relative of his grandmother (a grandson of her first cousin) brought out a copy of their genealogy and asked Huang Chin to fill in the dates and burial place of his grandmother (HWHKC 7B:300–301). In other words, they were using the genealogy as a means of maintaining contact with a family into which one of their women had married three generations earlier.

useful to define a set of potential allies, even if no joint endeavor was under consideration at the moment. Moreover, prestige was probably also involved. A descent line that had branches throughout the region would seem more glorious than one limited to a single place. Men would like to know that they belonged to such a ramified descent group.

Genealogies could be written not only to create, document, or link descent groups, but also to purify them. This is seen especially in the works of Wu Hai (fl. 1350–70), a native of Min county in Fukien, who seems to have had an intense distaste for any violation of patrilineal principles. In several prefaces to genealogies he decried the prevalence of nonagnatic adoption, in one place asserting that it confused the family lines of 50 to 60 percent of descent groups (WKCC 1:20–21). In one genealogy he recorded a rule that anyone who had someone of another surname made heir would be excised from the genealogy and not recorded. He noted that this policy raised questions in some people's minds:

> Some say, "Although he is of a different surname, he has been a successor to our line for a long time; it would be difficult to exclude him. Couldn't he be recorded in an appendix?" I say, "No. Anyone of another surname who abandoned his ancestors and attached himself to our ancestors, discarding his own surname and hiding under ours, should be labeled unfilial and inhumane!" (WKCC 1:24)

In another case, the descent group's "first ancestor" had been an adoptee, and compiling the genealogy was an effort to rectify the error, returning to the original surname. Some of these nonagnatic adoptions were with "external" relatives. As Wu Hai complained in one preface, "Today people do not follow the ritual rules; they take a son-in-law or a daughter's son to be their heir without limit. They are destroying themselves because they cannot go beyond their wives' viewpoint" (WKCC 1:12).[19] For Wu Hai, compiling genealogies was a way to overcome this tendency.

Understanding the purposes for compiling genealogies can help us evaluate them as historical sources for the organization or leadership of descent groups. Even from this brief review, it should be evident that not all genealogies correspond in their tables to descent groups. Many Sung and Yuan

---

19. One such case concerned the Ni of Kuei-ch'i and the Fu of Chin-ch'i, neighboring areas in Kiangsi. These two lines had intermarried for generations, so when one line among the Ni had no heir, a Fu was adopted. Five generations passed, and one of the descendants asked Wu Hai what he should do. Wu Hai said that there was only one choice, to return to the Fu name. The man replied that a hundred years had passed; reverting would arouse suspicion, and his other agnates did not want to follow him. Wu Hai said he should revert by himself if necessary, compiling a genealogy so that if any of them later wanted to do the right thing, the evidence would be available to them. The man then replied: "The Ni line trusted us to be their heirs. If I revert, will it be all right to cut off their line?" Wu Hai's solution was to set up a Ni as the heir and marry a Fu girl to him (WKCC 1:13–14).

genealogies are explicitly stated to have been products of research in sources such as epitaphs, intended to facilitate formation of descent groups rather than to represent the membership list of an existing one. The genealogies written to link descent groups may well be like the huge compilations done during the last century, which as Freedman noted need not be charters for groups about to embark on joint action; they could simply be history, inspired by "filial piety, hunger for prestige, and scholarly appetite for writing history" (1966:28). Such genealogies should be easily recognized by the statements in the prefaces or the patchy quality of the vital data they contain. A genealogy that includes fairly good vital data for all branches can probably safely be taken as evidence of the existence of a descent group, for a group that got together only once a year for ancestor worship would have records of ancestors and maybe of living members. Yet even a highly detailed genealogy need not indicate that the descent group was a lineage with extensive property unless explicit reference to such property is given. As Johanna Meskill pointed out, lineages barely needed to exist for genealogies to be produced; all that was needed were a few wealthy individuals (1970:141).

With regard to leadership, genealogies usually portray members of the elite—officials especially—as the active agents in the development of the group. In some cases, this may be the result of recasting what had actually happened into the language of Neo-Confucianism discussed above. In other cases it is probably because the best educated, especially officials, were the active members of the group and those most concerned with presenting the group to outsiders (see Hazelton's chapter here and Ebrey 1983). And in yet other cases the prominence of educated men in descriptions of descent group activities could be because the only actual descent group activity was the intellectual one of defining themselves as a group through compiling a genealogy (see Hymes's chapter below).[20]

20. Near the end of his chapter in this volume, Robert Hymes argues that what was new in the Southern Sung was not the existence of groups or quasigroups of agnatic kinsmen, but "the role of the elite—at even its highest bureaucratic levels—in their promotion, celebration, and, in some cases, creation" and the "new impulse of the elite to define themselves as members of the same groups as (in principle) all their local agnates." Thus he places particular emphasis on the compiling of genealogies in the late Sung and Yuan. Taking a longer historical perspective, I evaluate the relative weight of changes in elite strategies and changes in the groups themselves differently. Because historical sources are much thinner before the Sung, especially before the Southern Sung, we know very little about the local activities of those in the elite who did not rise to high posts in the capital. Presumably many educated men in the T'ang and earlier had always followed a localist strategy as the only one available to them; however, they did not develop descent groups or lineages of the sort that appear after Sung. There were also long periods (such as the Later Han) when the highest-ranking men sought to be identified with their local community and local agnates; yet lineages were not created. Moreover, many "modern-style" descent groups seem to have emerged without being celebrated or promoted by members of the national elite (although we learn about them in our sources only after this occurred). To

Ancestral Halls

The last major addition to the repertoire of agnatic kinship practices made in the Sung and Yuan periods was the establishment of ancestral halls as foci for descent groups or "high-order" descent groups.

In Sung sources probably 99 percent of the references to halls (*tz'u*) have nothing to do with descent group organization. Men who had made contributions to a community or to the state were often honored after their deaths by having halls established for them where ritual offerings could be made. Often it was the local county or prefectural government that sponsored the construction of the hall and later looked after upkeep and sacrificial offerings. Not infrequently halls were dedicated to two or three great men. Besides this sort of hall, families of high officials might have *miao* (ancestral altars) in their residences (see n. 3 of this chapter), and Chu Hsi was said to have recommended that families set up halls (*tz'u-t'ang*) to the east of their main room (CL 1:1a–10b). Both of these types of ancestral shrines were for domestic rites, going back only the canonical four generations. During the Yuan period, however, one begins to find references to ancestral halls of the more recent type, permanently focused on an apical ancestor, detached from anyone's residence.[21]

Wu Hai, whose objections to contamination of the patrilineal line were cited above, described an ancestral hall (*tz'u-t'ang*) of the Lins of Lo-t'ien (Hupei). In this hall were tablets for all the ancestors, going back twenty-one generations, including members of the lineage who had died without descendants. These were all in *chao-mu* order. On the first and fifteenth of each month one of the kinsmen would pay his respects, and on a day chosen by divination in the spring and fall, sacrifices would be performed. In his reformist zeal, Wu Hai wanted this stopped. He said only nobles were allowed

---

me what is new in the Sung is not the desire of some men of education, property, and ambition to gain all the local allies they could, but the focus for organization of localized groups of agnates in rites to the first ancestors buried there, the "invention" of the inalienable estate, and the moral value assigned to organizing on patrilineal lines by Sung thinkers. Educated men could try to take over, manipulate, or develop for their own purposes the organizations that developed. But when there was no incipient organization, the efforts of elites to create them— even the compilation of genealogies—may well have resulted in a group of significance to those elite members who tried to promote it, but of little importance to anyone else "defined" as belonging to it. Descent groups were much more likely to have "public" genealogies when they had officials among their members (see Hazelton's chapter), but it is not obvious that this sort of genealogy was a necessary feature of all types of descent groups (many Kwangtung ones lacked them), though it seems to be typical of what Hazelton calls here a "Lower Yangtze" type.

21. What might have been a late Sung transitional form is found in HTHSTCC 91:13b–15b. A shrine dedicated to four heroes of one family was later restored by one of the descendants, who arranged to have all his mourning relatives make offerings there.

to have halls of this sort; commoners were to make offerings in their homes. So he had the Lins bury the tablets (the classical way to dispose of tablets retired from family altars), recording their distant ancestors on a chart instead. On the winter solstice and New Year's Day, this chart could be displayed and all the lineage members could gather to bow before it, all ranked in order, after which they could have a meeting to encourage moral behavior. Consequently Wu Hai had the name of the building changed from hall to "Building for Descent Group Meetings," using a term from Ch'eng I (WKCC 2:41–42).

Other scholars were not so inhospitable to ancestral halls (see Dardess 1974:48–49). Sung Lien (1310–81), a highly respected scholar and teacher, wrote essays on seven he had come across, explicitly justifying their innovative aspects. In one essay he wrote:

> The ancients did not have halls at graves, and commoners could only offer sacrifices to their fathers. This was the ritual. In the Han there were halls at graves, and sacrifices went back to great-great-grandfathers. One cannot say that this was contrary to ritual. The Lins of Kai-chu in P'ing-yang [Chekiang] have set up a hall at the grave of their first migrant ancestor and make sacrifices there. How can one say this is contrary to ritual? (SHSWC 73:1165)

Sung Lien noted that after twelve generations, the descendants of this first ancestor lived scattered in different villages and their ties to each other had become weak. Thus one of their members, an official, wanted to set up a hall at the first ancestor's grave so they would not forget their common origin. His son finished the project, and the whole lineage assembled for the seasonal sacrifices, which were followed by a group feast. In addition, a school was attached to the hall for the education of lineage members. Sung Lien ended with strong praise for this institution, saying that a descent group with great depth will have such diverse members (rich and poor, weak and strong) that group rituals will be the only way to overcome their distance (SHSWC 73:1166).

In another case, in Sung Lien's home area of Chin-hua, a hall was erected in 1365–66 to unite through ritual three descent groups (*san ta-tsu*) of Chang who were related ten generations back. The first migrant ancestor and his three sons, the apical ancestors of the three descent groups, were the foci of the hall. Because the elapsed time was so great, the organizers thought that they would not try to offer the seasonal sacrifices at this hall but rather use it to get the entire higher-order descent group together there each New Year festival. On that occasion all recently born sons who had already been named would have their names recorded in the genealogy. Some sacrificial fields were established to pay for these rites, which the three descent groups would handle in rotation (SHSWC 10:183–84).

In another case discussed by Sung Lien, a hall was explicitly described as a functional replacement for "sacrificial fields" that had been lost with the Yuan takeover. The hall united the three branches (*fang*) of the Lin of P'u-t'ien (Fukien) and had five "spirit boards" (*shen-pan*), each four feet high, listing all of the ancestors. On each summer solstice the descent group held a joint sacrifice. The essay explicitly noted that "small *tsung*" sacrifices to each person's four most recent ancestors would continue to be done separately in homes. The hall, however, would be used for greetings at New Year's and for cappings, weddings, and announcements to ancestors (SHSWC 24:455–56).

Two features are striking about the reports by Wu Hai and Sung Lien concerning the descent groups they came across. The first is their high level of organizational complexity. They had great genealogical depth; they conducted ancestor worship as a group ceremony; they did this on a regular schedule; they had records of their ancestors' names written on tablets or boards and arranged in significant ways. The second striking feature is their variability. Some made offerings in the spring and fall, others at New Year's, others at the summer solstice. Whether this reflects regional differences requires further research, but it is possible that many variations co-existed. Indeed, in Sung Lien's home county of Chin-hua quite different forms and stages of kinship organization existed side by side, for it was the home not only of the "higher-order" Chang descent group but also of the Cheng communal family and several of its imitators.

Finally I should perhaps note that Sung Lien's student, the eminent scholar Fang Hsiao-ju (1357–1402), wrote a series of essays on descent groups in which he advocated as ideal many of the practices that had appeared over the previous four centuries. In several different essays he stressed joint sacrifices at the tomb of the first migrant ancestor and at halls, followed by banquets, the compilation and regular updating of comprehensive genealogies, and the establishment of estates to provide for rituals, charity, and education (SCCC 1:41b–45a; 8:22a; 13:1a–2a). In his writings, the repertoire of descent group activities appears in essentially complete form.

Conclusion

In this cursory overview of the development of descent group organization in the Sung and Yuan dynasties, I have tried to describe the new practices that appeared, expanding the repertoire of known and accepted ways to interact with local agnatic kinsmen. In 1350 descent groups had a variety of features (halls, sacrificial fields, regularly updated genealogies, and so on) that were not to be found in 1000. Almost all Sung and Yuan references to these features are from areas south of the Huai River, the region in which lineages were most highly developed in Ch'ing times. It is true that a few features common in nineteenth- and twentieth-century lineages and descent groups had not yet appeared. Not until mid-Ming were detailed rules of behavior, with sanctions against violation, printed in lineage genealogies (Tso 1964:105)[22] or halls erected for all those of one surname in a prefecture or province (Makino 1939:197–201). Nevertheless, a surprisingly large number of features characteristic of later descent groups and lineages did appear during the eleventh through fourteenth centuries.

My emphasis on innovations should not obscure the larger conservatism of kinship practices. As I mentioned earlier, the repertoire of agnatic kinship practices that existed in the T'ang dynasty largely continued into the Sung; it also continued into the Ming and Ch'ing. Even after the widespread acceptance of worship at graves, concern with first migrant ancestors, and innovations in genealogy writing, estates, and shrines, there were always men who would have concurred with Su Hsun that they seldom saw even their agnates within their mourning circle. Some anthropologists have talked of "lineage atrophy" as a process of social change in areas where well-developed lineages are part of the cultural repertoire (Pasternak 1968; Anderson 1970). Although some lineages have certainly atrophied, the general trend was just the opposite. As Makino pointed out many years ago, there was a slow but gradual trend toward more organization in the activities of agnates, not less (Makino 1949:566–68). Nevertheless, most sets of agnates remained at various less-organized levels. Japanese scholars like Uchida found groups of agnates in North China whose only joint activities might be celebration of the Ch'ing-ming sacrifices, responsibility rotated among households or segments (Uchida 1953). In this regard, the finding by Evelyn Rawski reported in chapter 8 that a set of wealthy agnates identified as a group by outsiders did not function like a lineage need not be surprising; it was undoubtedly true of many other comparable sets of agnates elsewhere. In fact, the only cases reported in this volume that seem to have had all the standard features of lineages as defined in the introduction to this volume are the ones in Hui-chou and Wu-hsi, and Jerry Dennerline argues that corporate property came relatively late in the development of the Wu-hsi lineages (chapter 5).

By way of conclusion I would like to suggest ways in which a knowledge of the early stages of descent group development adds to our understanding of agnatic kinship in China. In doing so I do not wish to confuse historical and sociological explanation. As I stated in my opening paragraph, features important in the early stages of descent group development need not be the crucial features of fully developed ones, or vice versa. In other words, the fact that in a highly developed lineage a genealogy serves a recognizable function in maintaining the lineage surely cannot be taken as evidence that genealogies were invented or developed to serve those purposes. Nor, if I am correct in stressing the role of innovations in ancestor worship as fostering a

---

22. They had, however, earlier appeared in rules for communal families. See Langlois 1981.

broad shift in conceptions of how to deal with agnates, can I then go on to argue that ancestral rites were the catalyst for the formation of particular groups, or even a central feature of all fully developed descent groups.

This caveat aside, I am enough of an historian to think that the historical explanations for a phenomenon provide some insight into its dynamics. Thus I wish to reiterate the central place of ancestral rites in descent group formation. The importance of graves to descent groups has been emphasized throughout this essay. Genealogies and ancestral halls appear to be key features of more developed descent groups, and both had major ritual purposes. Genealogies are in large part lists of ritually relevant information, especially about ancestors. Location of graves, birth and death dates, and seniority within a generation were all ritually significant items of information. This is not to deny that ritual groups could come to play other roles, to act as units in local politics, own property, or dominate communities. But whether or not this happened would have depended on circumstances. I am arguing that there was no internal logic moving all ritual, ancestor-focused descent groups in this direction.

In the early stages of descent group development I have found little sign that membership in a descent group was so basic to social life that it restricted other social activities. It is well known that Chinese literati and officials participated in complex social networks, based on varied ties to friends, teachers, relatives of all sorts, and superiors and subordinates in office. In the Sung and Yuan periods at least full and enthusiastic membership in a ritually focused descent group does not seem to have infringed on these other relations. Kinship solidarity would not necessarily take precedence over other solidarities, and communities where several large descent groups resided would not always divide along kin lines.[23]

In stressing the importance of ancestral rites in descent group formation I am also by implication downgrading the part played by corporate estates. Lineages organized around large estates appear to be the functional successors of communal families; like communal families they exerted considerable

23. The patrilineality of Sung and Yuan descent groups does not seem to have been so pronounced that it interfered with relations with affines or with individuals' needs to arrange for heirs from outside the descent group. Of all the authors of Sung and Yuan genealogy prefaces and other descent group documents that I have read, Wu Hai was the only one strongly to condemn nonagnatic adoption and uxorilocal marriage. His contemporary Sung Lien, a much more highly regarded teacher, had great praise for families that found ways to "continue the sacrifices" through their daughters (SHSWC 46:809–10). Moreover, many genealogy prefaces, in recording the movements of ancestors, remark that the moves were made to join a wife's parents (usually without change of surname) without implying in any way that this compromised the group (e.g. YYC 5:75; SHSWC 10:183–84; see also Dennerline, this volume). Indeed, genealogies often seem to have been important among upper class groups precisely to help them arrange good marriages. After all, they document ancestry, proving family standing, something much involved in establishing marriage ties.

control over individuals, regulated their access to material benefits, and acted as a social and political unit in the larger society. Thus lineages should not be looked on as the most fully developed descent groups, but as a certain special type of descent group. The more usual type of descent group could flourish without an income-producing estate; to enhance and strengthen its central purpose, its leaders would find ways to finance ancestral halls, genealogies, and schools; estates could be a means to this end, but they were not an essential one.

REFERENCES

Chinese Primary Sources

AYC   *An-yang chi* 安陽集, by Han Ch'i 韓琦. 1740 ed. of Lo-an chiang.

CCPP   *Chü-chia pi-pei* 居家必備 (anon.). Ming ed.

CCPYSL   *Chü-chia pi-yung shih-lei* 居家必用事類 (anon.). Kyoto: Chūmon 1979 facsimile of Japanese 1673 ed.

CCSSC   *Ch'ien-ch'un sui-shih chi* 乾淳歳時記 by Chou Mi 周密. Taipei: Sui-shih hsi-su tz'u-liao hui-pien ed., I-wen yin-shu kuan.

CHPL   *Chia-hsun pi-lu* 家訓筆錄, by Chao Ting 趙鼎. Ts'ung-shu chi-ch'eng ed.

CL   *Chu Tzu chia li* 朱子家禮, attr. Chu Hsi 朱熹. 5 ch., Pao-kao-t'ang ed., Ch'ing dynasty.

CLC   *Ch'en Liang chi* 陳亮集, by Ch'en Liang 陳亮. Taipei: Ho-lo t'u-shu ch'u-pan she punctuated ed.

CMC   *Ming-kung shu-p'an ch'ing-ming chi* 名公書判清明集 (anon.). Tokyo: Koten kenkyūkai 1964 facsimile ed. of Seikadō Bunko copy.

CPCLK   *Ch'un-po chai lei-kao* 純白齋類稿, by Hu Chu 胡助. Ts'ung-shu chi-ch'eng ed.

CSCC   *Chen-su chai-chi* 貞素齋集, by Shu Ti 舒頔. Ssu-k'u chen-pen ed.

CTC   *Chang Tsai chi* 張載集, by Chang Tsai 張載. Peking: Chung-hua shu-chü.

CTW   *Ch'üan T'ang wen* 全唐文, by Tung Kao 董誥 et al. Taipei: Ching-wei reprint of 1814 ed.

CWKCC   *Chu Wen-kung ch'üan chi* 朱文公全集, by Chu Hsi 朱熹. Ssu-pu ts'ung-k'an ed.

CYC   *Chia-yu chi* 嘉祐集, by Su Hsun 蘇洵. Wan-yu wen-k'u ed.

FWCKWC   *Fan Wen-cheng kung wen-chi* 范文正公文集, by Fan Chung-yen 范仲淹. Ts'ung-shu chi-ch'eng ed.

HAMTC   *Hsin-an ming-tsu chih* 新安名族志. Peiping National Library Rare Books Microfilm, roll 916.

HHS   *Hou Han shu* 後漢書, by Fan Yeh 范曄. Peking: Chung-hua shu-chü.

HLTCS   *Hsing-li ta-ch'üan-shu* 性理大全書. Ssu-k'u chen-pen ed.

HSHS   *Ho-shan hsien-sheng ta-ch'üan chi* 鶴山先生大全集, by Wei Liao-weng 魏了翁. Ssu-pu ts'ung-k'an ed.

HSTP   *Kuei-ch'i Hu-shih tsu-p'u* 貴溪胡氏族譜, by Hu Tzu-li 胡自立. 1468.

HTHSTCC   *Hou-ts'un hsien-sheng ta-ch'üan chi* 後村先生大全集, by Liu K'o-chuang 劉克莊. Ssu-pu ts'ung-k'an ed.

HTS *Hsin T'ang shu* 新唐書, by Ou-yang Hsiu 歐陽修 and Sung Ch'i 宋祁. Peking: Chung-hua shu-chü.

HWHKC *Huang Wen-hsien kung chi* 黃文獻公集, by Huang Chin 黃溍. Ts'ung-shu chi-ch'eng ed.

ICC *I-chien chih* 夷堅志, by Hung Mai 洪邁. Peking: Chung-hua shu-chü, 1981.

IS *Ho-nan Ch'eng-shih i-shu* 河南程氏遺書, by Ch'eng I 程頤. In *Erh Ch'eng chi*. Peking: Chung-hua shu-chü.

KCC *Kuei-chi chih (Chia-t'ai)* 會稽志,嘉泰, by Shih Su 施宿. Ssu-k'u chen-pen ed.

KKC *K'ung-k'uei chi* 玫媿集, by Lou Yueh 樓鑰. Ts'ung-shu chi-ch'eng ed.

KYL *K'ai-yuan li* 開元禮, ed. Hsiao Sung 蕭嵩 et al. Ssu-k'u chen-pen ed.

LFWCC *Lu Fang-weng ch'üan chi* 陸放翁全集, by Lu Yu 陸游. Hong Kong: Kuang-chih shu-chü punctuated ed.

LTLWC *Lü Tung-lai wen-chi* 呂東萊文集, by Lü Tsu-ch'ien 呂祖謙. Ts'ung-shu chi-ch'eng ed.

MCC *Mien-chai chi* 勉齋集, by Huang Kan 黃榦. Ssu-k'u chen-pen ed.

MLL *Meng liang lu* 夢粱錄, by Wu Tzu-mu 吳自牧. Ts'ung-shu chi-ch'eng ed.

MSC *Ming-shui chi* 洺水集, by Ch'eng Pi 程泌. Ssu-k'u chen-pen ed.

NCCIK *Nan-chien chia-i kao* 南澗甲乙稿, by Han Yuan-chi 韓元吉. Ts'ung-shu chi-ch'eng ed.

OYHCC *Ou-yang Hsiu ch'üan-chi* 歐陽修全集, by Ou-yang Hsiu 歐陽修. Taipei: Chung-kuo wen-hsueh ming-chu chi ed., Shih-chieh shu-chü.

PCS *Pei Ch'i shu* 北齊書, by Li Te-lin 李德林 and Li Po-yao 李百藥. Peking: Chung-hua shu-chü.

PS *Pei shih* 北史, by Li Yen-shou 李延壽. Peking: Chung-hua shu-chü.

SCCC *Sun-chih chai-chi* 遜志齋集, by Fang Hsiao-ju 方孝孺. Ssu-pu ts'ung-k'an ed.

SCWC *Sun-chai wen-chi* 巽齋文集, by Ou-yang Shou-tao 歐陽守道. Ssu-k'u chen-pen ed.

SHSWC *Sung hsueh-shih wen-chi* 宋學士文集, by Sung Lien 宋濂. Wan-yu wen-k'u ed.

SHY *Sung hui yao chi-pen* 宋會要輯本, ed. Hsu Sung 徐松 et al. Taiwan: Shih-chieh shu-chü reprint, 1964.

SMCC *Ssu-ma Wen-cheng kung ch'uan-chia chi* 司馬文正公傳家集, by Ssu-ma Kuang 司馬光. Wan-yu wen-k'u ed.

SMSSI *Ssu-ma shih shu-i* 司馬氏書儀, by Ssu-ma Kuang 司馬光. Ts'ung-shu chi-ch'eng ed.

SMYL *Ssu-min yueh-ling* 四民月令, by Ts'ui Shih 崔寔. In *Ssu-min yueh-ling chiao-chu*, by Shih Sheng-han. Peking: Chung-hua shu-chü, 1965.

SS *Sung shih* 宋史, ed. T'o T'o 脫脫 et al. Peking: Chung-hua shu-chü ed.

SSC *San-shan chih* 三山志, by Liang K'o-chia 梁克家. Ssu-k'u chen-pen ed.

SSKC *Sui-shih kuang-chi* 歲時廣記, by Ch'en Yuan-ching 陳元靚. Ts'ung-shu chi-ch'eng ed.

SSWC *Shih-shan wen-chi* 師山文集, by Cheng Yü 鄭玉. Ssu-k'u chen-pen ed.

SYHA *Sung Yuan hsueh-an* 宋元學案, by Huang Tsung-hsi 黃宗羲. Shanghai: Commercial Press.

TCMHL *Tung-ching meng-hua lu* 東京夢華錄, by Meng Yuan-lao 孟元老. Taipei: Shih-chieh shu-chü.

THPT   *Tun-huang pao tsang* 敦煌寶藏, ed. Huang Yung-wu 黃永戊. Taipei: Hsing-wen feng, 1981.

TT   *T'ung-tien* 通典, by Tu Yu 杜佑. Taipei: Hsin-hsing shu-chü reprint of Shih-t'ung ed.

TTC   *Ta tsang ching* 大藏經. Taipei: Hsin-wen-feng reprint of Taisho ed., 1974.

WKCC   *Wu Ch'ao-tsung hsien-sheng wen-kuo chai chi* 吳朝宗先生聞過齋集, by Wu Hai 吳海. Ts'ung-shu chi-ch'eng ed.

WKCL   *Wen-kung chia-li* 文公家禮, attr. Chu Hsi 朱熹. Ts'ui-ch'ing t'ang ed., 1589 preface.

WS   *Wei shu* 魏書, by Wei Shou 魏收. Peking: Chung-hua shu-chü ed.

WSHSWC   *Wen Shan hsien-sheng wen-chi* 文山先生全集, by Wen T'ien-hsiang 文天祥. Wan-yu wen-k'u ed.

WSTP   *Wang shih tsu-p'u* 王氏族譜, by Wang Jen-yuan 王仁元. 1625 ed.

YIIML   *Yen-i i-mou lu* 燕翼詒謀錄, by Wang Yung 王栐. Peking: Chung-hua shu-chü ed.

YTC   *Yuan-tu chi* 綠督集, by Tseng Feng 曾丰. Ssu-k'u chen-pen ed.

YYC   *Yen-yuan chi* 剡源集, by Tai Piao-yuan 戴表元. Ts'ung-shu chi-ch'eng ed.

Secondary Works

Ahern, Emily M. 1976. "Segmentation in Chinese Lineages: A View from Written Genealogies." *American Ethnologist* 3:1–16.

Anderson, E. N., Jr. 1970. "Lineage Atrophy in Chinese Society." *American Anthropologist* 72:363–65.

Baker, Hugh D. R. 1979. *Chinese Family and Kinship*. New York: Columbia University Press.

Ch'en, Kenneth K. S. 1973. *The Chinese Transformation of Buddhism*. Princeton: Princeton University Press.

Chikusa Masaaki 竺沙雅章. 1956. "Sōdai Fukken no shakai to jiin" 宋代福建の社會と寺院 [Buddhist institutions and the society of Fukien in the Sung], *Tōyōshi kenkyū* 15:170–96.

Cohen, Myron L. 1976. *House United, House Divided: The Chinese Family in Taiwan*. New York: Columbia University Press.

Ch'ü, T'ung-tsu. 1972. *Han Social Structure*. Ed. Jack L. Dull. Seattle: University of Washington Press.

Dardess, John W. 1974. "The Cheng Communal Family: Social Organization and Neo-Confucianism in Yuan and Early Ming China." *Harvard Journal of Asiatic Studies* 34:7–52.

De Groot, J. J. M. 1892–1910. *The Religious System of China*, 6 vols. Taipei: Ch'eng-wen reprint, 1972.

Dull, Jack. 1978. "Marriage and Divorce in Han China: A Glimpse at Pre-Confucian Society." In *Chinese Family Law in Historical Perspective*, ed. David Buxbaum. Seattle: University of Washington Press.

Ebrey, Patricia Buckley. 1974. "Estate and Family Management in the Later Han as Seen in the *Monthly Instructions for the Four Classes of People*." *Journal of the Economic and Social History of the Orient* 17:173–205.

———. 1978. *The Aristocratic Families of Early Imperial China: A Case Study of the Po-ling Ts'ui Family*. Cambridge: Cambridge University Press.

———. 1980. "Later Han Stone Inscriptions." *Harvard Journal of Asiatic Studies* 40. 325–53.

———. 1981. "Women in the Kinship System of the Southern Song Upper Class." *Historical Reflections* 8:113–28.

———. 1983. "Types of Lineages in Ch'ing China: A Re-examination of the Chang Lineage of T'ung-ch'eng." *Ch'ing-shih wen-t'i* 4.9:1–20.

———. 1984a. "Conceptions of the Family in the Sung Dynasty." *Journal of Asian Studies* 43:219–45.

———. 1984b. *Family and Property in Sung China: Yuan Ts'ai's Precepts for Social Life*. Princeton: Princeton University Press.

———. 1986. "Economic and Social History of the Later Han." In *Cambridge History of China*, vol. 1, ed. Michael Loewe and Denis Twitchett. Cambridge: Cambridge University Press.

Freedman, Maurice, 1958. *Lineage Organization in Southeastern China*. London: Athlone Press.

———. 1966. *Chinese Lineage and Society: Fukien and Kwangtung*. London: Athlone Press.

Fried, Morton. 1970. "Clans and Lineages: How to Tell Them Apart and Why— With Special Reference to Chinese Society." *Bulletin of the Institute of Ethnology, Academia Sinica* 29:11–36.

Gamble, Sidney D. 1963. *North China Villages: Social, Political, and Economic Activities before 1933*. Berkeley: University of California Press.

Gernet, Jacques. 1970. *Daily Life in China on the Eve of the Mongol Invasion, 1250–1276*. Trans. H. M. Wright. Stanford: Stanford University Press.

Grafflin, Dennis. 1983. "The Onomastics of Medieval South China: Patterned Naming in the Lang-yeh and T'ai-yuan Wang." *Journal of the American Oriental Society* 103:383–98.

Hartwell, Robert M. 1982. "Demographic, Political, and Social Transformations of China, 750–1550." *Harvard Journal of Asiatic Studies* 42:365–442.

Hu, Hsien Chin. 1948. *The Common Descent Group in China and Its Functions*. New York: Viking Fund.

Johnson, David G. 1977a. "The Last Years of a Great Clan: The Li Family of Chao Chün in Late T'ang and Early Sung." *Harvard Journal of Asiatic Studies* 37:5–102.

———. 1977b. *The Medieval Chinese Oligarchy*. Boulder: Westview Press.

———. 1983. "Comment: Chinese Kinship Reconsidered." *China Quarterly* 94:362–65.

Kobayashi Yoshihiro 小林義廣. 1980. "Ōyō Shū ni okeru zokufu hensan no igi" 欧陽脩における族譜編纂の意義 [The significance of Ou-yang Hsiu's compiling a genealogy]. *Nagoya daigaku Tōyōshi kenkyū hōkoku* 6:189–216.

Kyō Heinan 喬炳南. 1976. "Sōdai no gisō seido" 宋代の義荘制度 [The institution of the charitable estate in the Sung dynasty]. *Tezukayama daigaku ronshū* 11:74–98.

Langlois, John D., Jr. 1981. "Authority in Family Legislation: The Cheng Family Rules." In *State and Law in East Asia: Festschrift Karl Bunger*. Weisbaden: Otto Harrassowitz.

Liu, Hui-chen Wang. 1959. *The Traditional Chinese Clan Rules*. Locust Valley: J. J.

Augustin.

McDermott, Joseph P. 1984. "Charting Blank Spaces and Disputed Regions: The Problems of Sung Land Tenure," *Journal of Asian Studies* 4:13–41.

McKnight, Brian E. 1971. *Village and Bureaucracy in Southern Sung China*. Chicago: University of Chicago Press.

Makino Tatsumi 牧野巽. 1939. "Sōshi to sono hattatsu" 宗祠と其の發達 [Ancestral shrines and their development]. *Tōyō gakuhō* 9:173–250.

———. 1949. *Kinsei Chūgoku sōzoku kenkyū* 近世中國宗族研究 [Studies of descent groups in modern China]. Tokyo: Nikkō.

Matsui Shūichi 松井秀一. 1968. "Hokusō shoki kanryō no ichi tenkei—Seki Kai to sono keifu o chūshin ni—" 北宋初期官僚の一典型—石介とその系譜を中心に —[A model of the early Northern Sung official, concentrating on Shih Chieh and his ancestry]. *Tōyō gakuhō* 51.1:44–92.

Meskill, Johanna M. 1970. "The Chinese Genealogy as a Research Source." In *Family and Kinship in Chinese Society*, ed. Maurice Freedman. Stanford: Stanford University Press.

Morita Kenji 森田憲司. 1979. "Sō-Gen jidai ni okeru shūfu" 宋元時代における修譜 [Genealogies during the Sung and Yuan periods]. *Tōyōshi kenkyū* 37:509–35.

Niida Noboru 仁井田陞. 1937. *Tō-Sō hōritsu bunsho no kenkyū* 唐宋法律文書の研究 [A study of T'ang and Sung legal documents]. Tokyo: Daian 1967 reprint.

———. 1942. *Shina mibunhōshi* 支那身分法史 [A history of status law in China]. Tokyo: Zayūhō kankōkai.

Pasternak, Burton. 1968. "Agnatic Atrophy in a Formosan Village." *American Anthropologist* 70:93–96.

———. 1969. "The Role of the Frontier in Chinese Lineage Development." *Journal of Asian Studies* 28:551–61.

Sangren, P. Steven. 1984. "Traditional Chinese Corporations: Beyond Kinship." *Journal of Asian Studies* 43:391–415.

Satake Yasuhiko 佐竹靖彦. 1973. "Tō-Sō henkakki ni okeru Kōnan tosai ro no tochi shoyū to tochi seisaku—gimon no seichō o tegakari ni" 唐宋變革期における江南東西路の土地所有と土地政策—義門の成長を手がかりに —[Landownership and land policies in the Chiang-nan circuits during the T'ang-Sung transition—based on the development of communal families]. *Tōyōshi kenkyū* 31.4:503–36.

Shang Ping-ho 尚秉和. 1941. *Li-tai she-hui feng-su shih-wu k'ao* 歷代社會風俗事物考 [An investigation of social customs over the ages]. Taiwan Commercial Press reprint.

Shimizu Morimitsu 清水盛光. 1949. *Chūgoku zokusan seido kō* 中國族產制度攷 [A study of clan property in China]. Tokyo: Iwanami.

Tai Yen-hui 戴炎輝. 1936. "Saiden mata wa saishi kōgyō" 祭田又は祭祀公業 [Sacrificial fields or sacrificial corporations]. *Hōgaku kyōkai zasshi* 54.10:93–122; 54.11:99–113.

T'ang Chang-ju 唐長孺. 1959. "Men-fa ti hsing-ch'eng chi ch'i shuai-lo" 門閥的形成及其衰落 [The formation and decline of aristocratic families]. *Wuhan ta-hsueh jen-wen-k'o hsueh pao* 1959.8:1–24.

Tso Yun-p'eng 左云鵬. 1964. "Tz'u-t'ang tsu-chang tsu-ch'uan ti hsing-ch'eng chi ch'i tso-yung shih-shuo" 祠堂族長族權的形成及其作用試說 [On the nature and functions of the lineage power of heads of lineage ancestral halls]. *Li-shih yen-chiu* 1964.5–6:97–116.

Twitchett, Denis. 1959. "The Fan Clan's Charitable Estate, 1050–1760." In *Confucianism in Action*, ed. David S. Nivison and Arthur F. Wright. Stanford: Stanford University Press.

———. 1960. "Documents on Clan Administration I: The Rules of Administration of the Charitable Estate of the Fan Clan." *Asia Major*, ser. 3, 8:1–35.

———. 1973. "The Composition of the T'ang Ruling Class: New Evidence from Tunhuang." In *Perspectives on the T'ang*, ed. Arthur F. Wright and Denis Twitchett. New Haven: Yale University Press, pp. 47–85.

———. 1982. "Comment on J. L. Watson's Article." *China Quarterly* 92:623–27.

Uchida Tomoo 内田智雄. 1950. "Kahoku nōson kazoku ni okeru sosen saishi no igi" 華北農村家族に於ける祖先祭祀の意義 [The significance of ancestral rites to farming families of North China]. *Dōshisha hōgaku* 6:1–22.

———. 1953. "Kahoku nōson ni okeru dōzoku no saiso gyōji ni tsuite" 華北農村における同族の祭祖行事について [On annual rites of agnates in North China villages]. *Tōhō gakuhō* (Kyoto) 22:59–64.

Ueyama Shunpei 上山春平. 1982. "Shushi no 'Karei' to 'Girei kyōden tsūkai'" 朱子の「家礼」と「儀礼経伝通解」. *Tōhō gakuhō* 54(1982), 173–256.

Watson, James L. 1982. "Chinese Kinship Reconsidered: Anthropological Perspectives on Historical Research." *China Quarterly* 92:589–622.

Watson, Rubie S. 1982. "The Creation of a Chinese Lineage: The Teng of Ha Tsuen, 1669–1751." *Modern Asian Studies* 16:69–100.

———. 1985. *Inequality among Brothers: Class and Kinship in South China*. Cambridge: Cambridge University Press.

Xu, Yangjie. 1980. "The Feudal Clan System Inherited from the Sung and Ming Periods." *Chinese Social Science* 3:29–82. Chinese original in *Chung-kuo k'o-hsueh* 1980. 4:99–122.

Yang, Martin. 1945. *A Chinese Village*. New York: Columbia University Press.

Yang Shu-ta 楊樹達. 1933. *Han-tai hun-sang li-su k'ao* 漢代婚喪禮俗考 [An investigation of marriage and funerary customs in the Han period]. Taipei: Hua-shih ch'u-pan she reprint, 1976.

Zurndorfer, Harriet T. 1981. "The *Hsin-an ta-tsu-chih* and the Development of Chinese Gentry Society, 800–1600." *T'oung Pao* 68:154–215.

THREE

Political Success and the Growth of Descent Groups: The Shih of Ming-chou during the Sung

Richard L. Davis

When, in the early years of the dynasty, the Sung (960–1279) government set out to make examination success the chief criterion in its selection of civil servants, it paved the way for profound social change. The hereditary elite of the past, commonly referred to as the "aristocratic families" or "medieval oligarchy," in time gave way to a class of professional bureaucrats, men whose social status derived largely from bureaucratic service and not vice versa. The government's objective was to have a civil service founded upon individual merit, in which the loyalty of its bureaucrats could be firmly secured. The influence of family background on career success, therefore, had to be minimized. To this end, the government strove to make education widely accessible by developing an empire-wide network of public and private schools. Massive expansion of the bureaucracy and the size of the educated class, a surge in the number and size of urban areas where the highly educated and the scarcely educated could interact, the wealth generated by an unprecedented level of commercial activity, and the challenge this represented to the former dominance of land as a source of economic security and political influence—these were but a few of the many factors that made the Sung elite far more diverse and the Sung civil service far less of an oligarchy than in the past.

On the other hand, the Sung political system was hardly "open." Although individual merit and bureaucratic diversity may have been the goal, one of the realities of the time was that family background could have a much greater impact upon political success. Probably the two factors contributing most to this phenomenon were "protection" and imperial favor, privileges afforded only those from accomplished families. The principal objective of this essay is to explore how these two factors influenced the fortunes of one descent group in the Sung dynasty, a descent group whose unusual political achievements theoretically should have enabled it to exploit "protection" and imperial favor far better than most others around it. A second objective is to explore the relationship between political privilege and group cohesion. Did "protection," one aspect of state policy, effectively encourage or impede the growth of organized descent groups? For reasons that will soon become apparent, the focus here is not on the whole elite, or upper class, but on its most privileged sector—those who penetrated the highest echelons of the bureaucracy.

Hereditary Privilege versus Individual Merit

The assignment of bureaucratic rank to descendants of accomplished officials was hardly new to the Sung. In the past this was commonly referred to as the "employment of sons" (*jen-tzu*), a term which suggests that the privilege was not designed to extend much beyond the nuclear family (Yang 1976:370–77; WHTK 34:323ff). Thus, while fostering the transmission of official status along the patriline from father to son, "protection" in those periods did not necessarily encourage cohesion or unity among collateral agnates or the formation of descent groups. Under Sung rule, to the extent that the privilege came to be more broadly shared by the larger kinship unit (albeit in a limited fashion), "protection" may have given kinsmen a greater incentive to stay together.

During the Sung, the practice of *yin-pu*, or "protection," permitted a restricted number of persons to gain access to the civil service merely by virtue of their personal ties to ranking scholar-officials or prominent court personalities.[1] With rank, of course, came the multitude of privileges commonly afforded scholar-officials, including government stipends, various tax exemptions, and no small measure of social prestige. The practice of "protection" had numerous functions. First, it provided the throne an important nonmonetary means with which to reward meritorious service or to confer special favor; it was, in effect, a means of repaying a political debt by providing employment to offspring. Second, there was the assumption that the close relatives of accomplished scholar-officials represented an important source of talent, as they had learned a good deal about bureaucracy and state simply by observing those around them. This talent, quite understandably, the government was anxious to tap. Third, both scholars in the service of the government and the government itself were concerned about maintaining some level of political and social stability. As recruitment examinations become more competitive and access to education is enhanced, the

1. Relating to the practice of *yin-pu*, there exists a sizable body of material. Among the more useful primary materials are CYTFSL *ch.* 12; SHHSC *ch.* 3; SS 159:3723–35, 170:4096–99; WHTK 34:323c–27a; NESCC *ch.* 25. Modern analyses include Kracke 1953:73–75; Umehara 1980:501–36; Yang 1976:370–77; Chang 1977:111–15.

future of accomplished families becomes progressively less certain, for the offspring of even the most meritorious of officials might not succeed at the examinations. The practice of *yin*, therefore, enabled the government to achieve some measure of bureaucratic continuity at the same time that it helped reduce anxiety among statesmen concerned about the long-term impact of competitive examinations upon family fortunes.

As many modern scholars have noted, hereditary privilege is fundamentally at odds with both the time-honored Confucian ideal of merit and the Sung government's commitment to bureaucratic recruitment based upon ability. The contradiction was nonetheless of no great concern at the dynasty's outset, when the demand for educated men to staff the civil service quite exceeded supply. The new government confronted far more pressing issues, chief among them being the sensitive job of dismantling regional military machines that had long stood in defiance of central authority and replacing military officials with civilians—a chore that necessitated rapid expansion of the civilian bureaucracy. "Protection" was, no doubt, an important means of achieving this expansion, and the court had little time to worry about the long-term impact of the practice upon the size, quality, or morale of the civil service. Thus, during the early years of the dynasty, the number of individuals taking advantage of the privilege was not carefully monitored, nor were the criteria by which officials gained access for their families clearly defined. A single high-level executive might well be responsible for bringing into the bureaucracy twenty or more kinsmen (Umehara 1980:505; NESCC *ch*. 25). Some concern about the "protection" system did emerge toward the end of the reign of T'ai-tsung (r. 976–97). In large part due to pressure from the bureaucracy itself, the court then placed modest restrictions on the number of "protected" slots available to each official. With the eleventh-century obsession with bureaucratic reform, most notably the efforts of Fan Chung-yen and Wang An-shih, progressively more stringent measures were taken further to limit the size of this privileged group. The trend continued into the Southern Sung (1127–1279), receiving special attention under emperors Kao-tsung (r. 1127–62) and Hsiao-tsung (r. 1162–89), both of whom were gravely concerned about the growing size and worsening morale of the bureaucracy.

Such efforts notwithstanding, we know that in the mid-eleventh century one highly favored official still managed to bring some twenty kinsmen into the civil service (SS 283:9563), and this had far-ranging implications for the composition of the bureaucracy. Under Kao-tsung, for example, it is reported that an ordinary examination candidate could often expect to wait ten years after earning his degree to receive an official appointment, this due to the proliferation of "protected" individuals in the bureaucracy (SS 159:3733). One modern historian concludes that "protected" bureaucrats without degrees represented nearly 40 percent of the civil service of 1213

(Chaffee 1979:40), a time when the privileges of "protection" were much less accessible than they had been during the first two centuries of Sung rule. That the pool of privileged candidates should be so large is quite understandable in light of the fact that, even in the mid-Southern Sung, riding on the coattails of just one chief councillor could be as many as ten "protected" bureaucrats, while officials with rank as low as seven (on a scale of nine) were afforded as many as three "protected" slots—and retirement promised modest supplements (CYTFSL 12:162–63; SS 159:3734).[2]

Admittedly, a simple reading of the documents can be deceptive. The fact that a chief councillor was afforded ten protected slots does not really mean that he was *entitled* to all ten; ten merely represents the theoretical ceiling, to rise above which required special imperial action. Most chief councillors probably never reached their quota. For example, on the occasion of a major imperial sacrifice, chief councillors could petition for the advancement of only one kinsman at a time, and eventually it became unacceptable to submit petitions more than once every several years (Umehara 1980). It turns out that most councillors held onto their posts for only two or three years, so there were definite limits to the number of kinsmen they could draw into the civil service on these occasions. Upon retirement, three additional slots became available to them; but with the retirement age being seventy *sui*, with life expectancy for the thirteenth century being what it was, and with an early retirement granted only under highly unusual circumstances, it is safe to assume that a good many councillors never got around to enjoying the benefits of this retirement supplement. In effect, it was necessary both to hold onto power for a great many years *and* to enjoy considerable longevity in order to make full use of the "protection" scheme. Allowing for such factors, it may still be concluded that, for every individual who succeeded in the recruitment examinations and performed modestly in the civil service, there may have been several without such credentials who gained access to public office simply through family ties.

2. According to the mid-Southern Sung source, CYTFSL (12:162–63), limits on the number of "protected" slots afforded one official were as follows: chief councillors and others with rank of 1a–1b, 10 persons; assisting councillors (rank 2a) and other civilian executives, 8 persons; grand marshals (rank 2a) and other comparable military officials, 8 persons; civilian officials from *tai-chung tai-fu* (rank 4b) to general censor (7a), 6 persons; military officials from *chieh-tu-shih* (2b) to *kuan-ch'a-shih* (5a), 6 persons; civilian officials from *chung tai-fu* (5a) to *chung-san tai-fu* (5b), 4 persons; military officials from *t'ung-shih tai-fu* (5a) to *yu wu tai-fu* (6a), 4 persons; civilian officials from *ch'ao-yi tai-fu* (6a) to *ch'ao-feng-lang* (7a), 3 persons; military officials from *wu-kung tai-fu* (7a) to *wu-yi tai-fu* (7a), 3 persons.

This list is far from complete (note the ambiguity pertaining to those directly beneath the chief councillor) and was apparently intended to be a simple summary. Then again, "protection" was initially administered in a highly informal way—it did, after all, originate as an expression of imperial goodwill. No doubt, there were as many exceptions to the rule as there were confirmations.

In defining access to *yin* privilege, the Sung government was quite liberal. Sons and grandsons most commonly benefited from the privilege, yet close agnatic relatives (*ch'i-ch'in*), relatives of different surnames (chiefly affines), and occasionally household retainers (*men-k'o*) might also represent beneficiaries (SS 159:3733, 170:4096). On one occasion the merit of Shih Hao resulted in official appointments for a younger brother, a son, and two sons-in-law (YTLK 7:5b–6a). This inclusion of affines apparently happened because, at this time, Shih Hao had few mature sons or other close agnates. Under ordinary circumstances, priority in the "protection" scheme was related to the "five grades of mourning" (*wu-fu*).[3] Sons and grandsons tended to benefit most frequently. Distant kin, in fact, were customarily required to take eligibility examinations before exploiting "protection" (SS 159:3733). This was not expected of sons and grandsons, and the requirement suggests that the government discouraged sharing of the privilege much beyond the immediate family. Then again, most "protection" candidates had to meet minimum age requirements (usually twenty-five *sui*), and this must have made it difficult to confer the privilege on kinsmen more than one generation removed from the favoured official, including legal grandsons (CYTFSL *ch.* 12). Thus, even though grandsons may have had closer lineal ties to the official, they were in fact probably often bypassed in favor of more mature collateral agnates.

The practice of "protection," which had been quite informal in the early Sung, became rigidly institutionalized later on. Upon an official's retirement, or sometimes upon his death, the privilege was made accessible to his kinsmen; this also occurred on the occasion of "great ceremonies" such as a state sacrifice or imperial accessions and birthdays (Umehara 1980:503). With access regularized, "protection" came to be viewed by officials as more of a right than a privilege, a prerogative of one's office and not merely an act of imperial goodwill. The government, meanwhile, found itself locked into a system that was determined more by the calendar than by the personnel requirements of the civil service, one that everyone recognized as detrimental to the vitality of the bureaucracy but few were willing to overhaul drastically. This development, combined with the enormous size of the "protection" pool, suggests that family background became as important

3. Umehara (1980:505) illustrates how "protection" is related to mourning grades. In theory, the meritorious official's father (assuming that he was still alive) and the eldest son of the principal wife were afforded first priority; grandfather, paternal uncles, brothers, additional sons, and grandsons received second priority (grade two); then came paternal cousins (the offspring of uncles), paternal nephews, and various other agnates (grade three); finally, secondary nephews (grandsons of paternal uncles) and grandnephews (grandsons of brothers), representing grade four, were followed by great-grandsons (the eldest followed by others), great-great-grandsons, great-grandnephews, and secondary grandnephews (great-grandsons of paternal uncles), who represented grade five.

as individual merit in providing access to the Sung civil service, and that hereditary privilege was no less a part of Sung tradition than it had been in the past.[4]

Nonetheless, access to government posts did not ensure career success. At the same time that the government welcomed non-degree-holders into its civil service, it almost uniformly assigned them low rank, conducted regular evaluations to eliminate those deemed unfit, and customarily reserved mid-to-high level administrative and executive posts for those with degrees (Chang 1977:166–69). The Sung government had no intention of permitting its civil service to degenerate into an hereditary institution controlled by elite families and not the court. The vast majority of "protected" recruits thus entered and remained in the lower echelons of the civil service where, in the absence of demonstrated ability and bureaucratic advancement, their influence would be limited and, more importantly, they would be unable to exploit "protection" to the benefit of their own sons and grandsons.[5] "Protection," therefore, was designed to retard downward political mobility and to foster social stability within the elite, not to promote upward mobility for the unworthy or to encourage bureaucratic nepotism. An examination of the experience of the Ming-chou Shih in Southern Sung times serves to illustrate these several points.

A House on the Rise

For those familiar with Sung history, no house stands out as more politically accomplished or more perennially controversial than the Shih of Ming-chou (modern Ning-po). These Shih were descended from one couple in the eleventh century, Shih Chien (1034?–58) and his wife, née Yeh (1033–1118). All that is known about Shih Chien is that he once worked for the local government, probably as a flogger, and died an untimely and humiliating death at the hands of an irate sheriff. The menial character of his employment leaves little doubt that the founder of the lineage was of humble back-

---

4. It is, of course, important to distinguish the kinds of advantages sons and other close agnates had in the Sung and the privileges enjoyed by aristocrats in earlier periods. In the Sung the advantages were related to specific attainments, albeit of the senior agnate. Under the Nine Rank system in use from the Three Kingdoms until the Sui, a man whose father died in an entry-level post, but whose descent group was ranked as an illustrious one, would enter the bureaucracy easily and at an elevated rank. This sort of facilitated entry for *generalized* descent line status (not the official rank of the current family head) did not exist in the Sung, nor had it in the T'ang (see Johnson 1977b:19–32).

5. "Protection" recruits, like those entering the civil service through examination, were generally assigned rank 9b or 9a. Further advancement commonly rested upon both success at special "promotion examinations" and a good record as a minor official. An individual, in turn, would then have to climb to *ch'ao-feng-lang* to become eligible to exploit "protection" for his own offspring.

ground. There is no indication of either previous civil service involvement or regional prominence (Davis 1980:chap. 2; PCSMC 9:28a–29a; HSSSTP 8:10b–12b).[6] Weaving in her home to keep the family fed, the widow Yeh eventually earned enough to secure a reasonably good education for her only surviving son, Shih Chao (1058–1130). In time, Shih Chao became an esteemed member of the community, allegedly due to the extraordinary filial piety with which he served his self-denying mother. This reputation subsequently resulted in a recommendation by local officials that he be allowed to enter the Imperial University under the "eight virtues of conduct" program, a program designed to recruit for government service moral exemplars, men of no particular wealth or standing yet respected by the community for their internalization of Confucian virtue. He declined the opportunity, reportedly out of devotion to his mother, but the recommendation alone was sufficient to bolster his status and help the next generation to make the leap more easily from local exemplar to civil servant.

Although Shih Chao could not be induced to leave home, even to attend the Imperial University, his offspring were not so politically aloof. Two sons were eventually promoted to the University, with Shih Ts'ai (d. 1162) graduating from the institution in 1118 and earning the coveted *chin-shih* degree (CCTC 45:20a–22b; HHYHC 14:27a–b; HSSSTP 5:11a–12a). He was the first degree-holder of the family—a family with no history of civil service involvement nor, apparently, with any of the resources or connections that are often considered vital to social and political advancement. As it was, thirty-five years after this novice entered the bureaucracy, and late into the reign of Kao-tsung, Shih Ts'ai catapulted to the post of assistant chief councillor. A generation later, Shih Hao (1106–94), son of Shih Ts'ai's elder brother, earned a *chin-shih* degree through the regular examination process and rose to chief councillor under Hsiao-tsung. In the end, neither uncle nor nephew held onto power for long before falling victim to factional politics. Shih Ts'ai appears to have had little contact with the throne, access to which

6. More sources on the history of the Shih are given in Davis 1980. Much of the information on official ranks given below comes from a nineteenth-century genealogy. Contemporary historical documents suggest that the Ming-chou Shih had no genealogy, at least not prior to the thirteenth century (KKC 74:1a–1b); genealogical writings did appear later, however, and apparently survived into the late Ch'ing (YHTC 940–48). Unfortunately, none of the Ming-chou documents are extant. The genealogy used here, along with more authoritative historical records, to reconstruct the kin group is HSSSTP. It was compiled in 1892 by the Hsiao-shan Shih, who claim to have descended from the Ming-chou house when, in late Yuan times, one Shih Kung-heng migrated to Hsiao-shan county, near modern Shaohsing. The genealogy's removal, both in time and space, from the Ming-chou Shih of Sung and Yuan times perhaps raises questions about its reliability; yet the detail that it provides suggests that its author had access to reasonably authoritative writings of an earlier date, probably including documents from Ming-chou. Moreover, a comparison of the genealogy with standard historical works has demonstrated a high level of accuracy.

was carefully guarded by a jealous chief councillor, and consequently enjoyed no special favor. In the case of Shih Hao, on the other hand, a relatively short political career did not preclude lasting influence at court.

Prior to the accession of Hsiao-tsung in 1162, Shih Hao served as his lecturer and chief adviser. As a distinguished professor at the Imperial University, Shih Hao had already won the emperor's respect, and he retained it for the remainder of their lives. Although he held onto the chief councillor's post for less than two years in total, the favor that the emperor conferred on him was truly exceptional (KKC 93:1a–19b; PCSMC9:3a–17b; SS 396:12065-69). His honorary titles included those of Grand Preceptor (*T'ai-shih*) and duke. The emperor held court banquets in honor of his former teacher and regularly sent him birthday gifts of gold, fine silk, and exquisite teas (Davis 1980:113–14). In 1175 Shih Hao received from the throne a mansion that occupied a prominent section of his native place, and several years later he was presented with a "family shrine" (*chia miao* or *tsung-miao*), also at Ming-chou (SHY, L 62:80b, 12:6a).[7]

As former councillor, Shih Hao was allotted ten "protection" slots and he clearly wasted none: All four of his younger brothers, his four sons, and his two sons-in-law are known to have received official rank through his merit, and there were probably other nominations above and beyond the normal quota that have evaded historical note (HSSTP 5:30b–31a, 15a–b, 26a–27a, 35a–36a, 37a–b; HHYHC 14:26b–34a, 27:37b; YTLK 7:5b–6a). It did not take long before Shih kinsmen, once bureaucratic outsiders, came to enjoy the privileges of the established and influential few; yet this was just the beginning of what would become an unusually close relationship between the Shih and the Sung court.

Surpassing Shih Hao, in terms of both political achievements and imperial favor, was his third son Shih Mi-yuan (1164–1233). This son entered the civil service through "protection," but he soon proved his own erudition by placing at the top of the Ministry of Personnel's "promotion examination" at seventeen and passing the *chin-shih* examination at twenty-three (Davis 1980: chap. 4; YYSMC 5:10b–12a; SS 414:124515–18). After serving in a variety of high-level executive posts during the early years of Ning-tsung's reign (1194–1224), the throne appointed Shih Mi-yuan chief councillor at the end of 1208. For the next quarter century, he would remain bureaucratic chief (a record-breaking tenure by Sung standards), thus becoming among the most awesomely powerful councillors of the dynasty. His grip on the bureaucracy was firm and the throne's confidence in him was unshakable.

---

7. High officials had been allowed to maintain family shrines for centuries, and detailed rules for such structures were elaborated in the T'ang. At these shrines offerings were made to the canonical four generations only, which means that they did not become the focus of great genealogical depth (see Johnson 1977b:94–96).

Although as chief councillor he was not without fault, in troubled times he managed to steer the empire along a course of relative stability and thus won the court's lasting goodwill.

The favor enjoyed by Shih Mi-yuan was also unprecedented. His father's noble rank was advanced to prince and Shih Hao became one of only two ministers to be honored with a tablet in the temple of Hsiao-tsung (SHY, L 11:1b, 11:12a). Ning-tsung once favored Shih Mi-yuan by giving him a mansion and, in 1221, providing an ancestral shrine for his household; these were both located in the capital, unlike those given to Shih Hao. Following the Hsiao-tsung precedent, the second shrine was built and maintained at government expense (SHY L 12:14a). Shortly before the chief councillor's death, in a special act of grace, Emperor Li-tsung (r. 1224–64) conferred *chin-shih* degrees upon Shih Mi-yuan's two surviving sons. Furthermore, the two youths were immediately appointed to executive posts in the bureaucracy, a highly unusual act in Southern Sung times (SS 41:798–99; SSCW 32:8b–9a). The court also conferred civil service status on some fifteen "grandsons" (including some grandnephews), several times the number ordinarily afforded a chief councillor's family upon his death (HHYHC 14:34a). Shih Hao and his son Shih Mi-yuan represent perhaps the most illustrious members of the line descended from Shih Chao, but political success and regional prominence were not confined to their own so-called Branch A (see figure 3.1). There were four other branches, which produced dozens of civil servants and erudite scholars, not to mention the Shih's third chief councillor. Limits of space, unfortunately, preclude discussion of these other branches here.

The Shih were extremely privileged, and one might assume that the most privileged houses within the elite would have been the most effective at maintaining their privileges. With reference to Branch A, it is apparent that the Shih were at the height of their influence and prestige at the time of Shih Mi-yuan's death. Enjoying the fullest measure of bureaucratic privilege and imperial favor, the branch should have proven particularly adept at exploiting "protection" and imperial favor, thus ensuring that later generations could maintain a similar level of prominence and security.

Continuing the Line

Descendants of Shih Mi-ta

The eldest son of Shih Hao, Shih Mi-ta (fl. 1169–85), earned a *chin-shih* degree in 1169 and rose to a high-level post as executive at the Ministry of Rites (KKC 93:16a; HHYHC 27:37b; HSSSTP 5:14a)(see figure 3.2). Although he possessed examination credentials, his career is also known to have been furthered significantly by his father's standing at court (YTLK

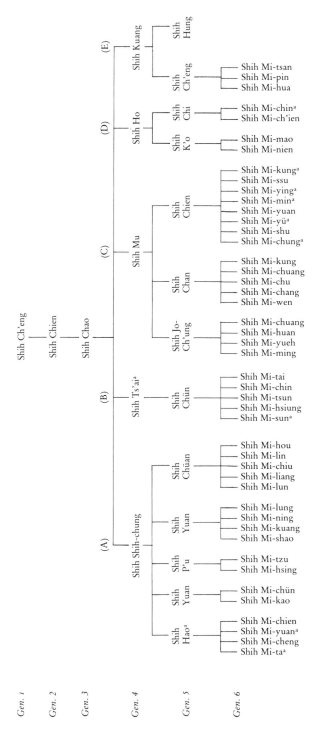

FIGURE 3.1 Genealogy of the Shih, Generations 1 to 6

Gen. 1

Gen. 2

Gen. 3

Gen. 4

Gen. 5

Gen. 6

This chart is based chiefly on the HSSSTP, with some modifications.

[a] *Chin-shih* recipients.

7:5b–6a). Shih Mi-ta's only surviving son, Shih Shou-chih, similarly entered
the bureaucracy through "protection" and quite effortlessly achieved the
civil service rank of 5a, despite a very short official career (HHYHC 30:17a–
b; HSSSTP 5:14a–b). The emperor once favored this moderately prominent
thinker with a piece of his own calligraphy. On the other hand, "protection"
did not work so well for his son, Shih Ssu-ch'ing, whose bureaucratic career
failed to carry him beyond rank 8a, and Ssu-ch'ing's own son did even less
well (HSSTP 5:14a–b). At this point, information on the line diminishes, but
it may well be concluded that the descendants of Shih Mi-ta produced no
other officials. Interestingly, this was the senior line, Shih Mi-ta being the
eldest son of an eldest son, yet there is no evidence to suggest that kinsmen
in other lines made any effort to rescue it from impending decline.

Descendants of Shih Mi-cheng

The second son of Shih Hao, Shih Mi-cheng, lacked the examination
credentials of his elder brother, but he managed nonetheless to rise to a
prestigious rank 4b post (HHYHC 27:37b; HSSSTP 5:15a–b)(see figure
3.2). In theory, the post he held only entitled him to three "protection"
slots, yet all of Mi-cheng's seven sons entered the civil service without *chin-shih* degrees, which probably represents either special imperial favor or a
share of someone else's privilege. His eldest son, Shih Tsung-chih, an official
of no great accomplishment, held a rank 7a post. This was enough to entitle
his offspring to enter the bureaucracy through "protection," and, in this
way, his son Shih Hsia-ch'ing managed to surpass his father and to secure a
mid-level (5a) administrative appointment (HSSSTP 5:15a). Hsia-ch'ing's
brother Shih Han-ch'ing did not fare as well, failing to rise above 8b, and his
grandsons were also confined to the bureaucracy's lower level—effectively
denying to their offspring access to "protection."

The second son of Shih Mi-cheng, Shih I-chih (fl. 1194–1229), enjoyed a
reasonably successful career, having served in mid-level administrative posts
both in and away from the capital and holding the title of baron (HHYHC
30:18b; HSSSTP 5:15b–16a). One of I-chin's sons held the respectable post
of prefectural vice-administrator (7b); but in the next generation no one
advanced beyond the bureaucracy's lowest entry level (HSSSTP 5:15b).

Shih Shih-chih, another of Shih Mi-cheng's sons, only held the rank of
8b, yet the merit of an uncle in Branch C enabled his son, Shih Hsien-ch'ing,
to surpass him by securing a mid-level administrative post (CJCSC 30:24a–
25a; HSSSTP 5:17a–b). Shih Hui-sun (1234–1306), heir to Shih Hsien-ch'ing, was never promoted beyond minor police inspector, but his sons
probably still enjoyed the "protection" privileges afforded their grandfather.

Shih Mi-cheng's fourth son, Shih An-chih, a conscientious local administrator, eventually won the rank of 5a. Although An-chih's sons never
rose above the entry level of 9b, one of his grandsons fared much better:

FIGURE 3.2 Descendants of Shih Mi-cheng

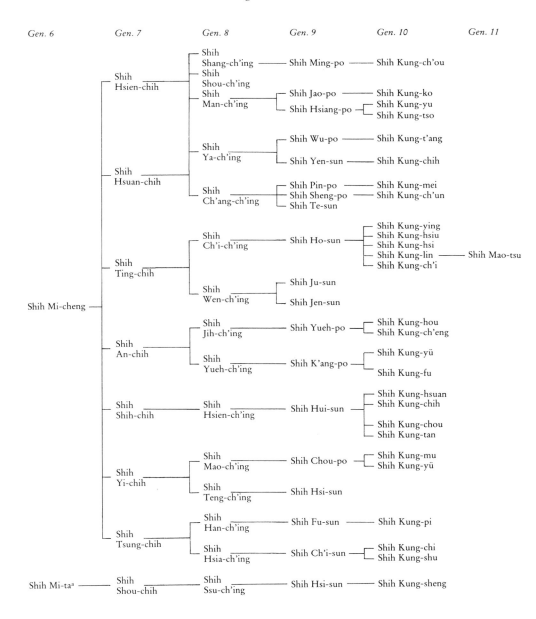

Shih K'ang-po became prefectural vice-administrator, with a rank of 5b (HHYHC 30:28b–29a; HSSSTP 5:16b–17a).

Another son of Shih Mi-cheng to do well as a civil servant was Shih Ting-chih (fl. 1191–1207). On one occasion in 1191 he is reported to have accompanied his aging grandfather, Shih Hao, to court and was favored by the throne with gifts (SHY, L 59:10b). Later, his conscientious service won for him the rank of 5b and ennoblement as baron (HHYHC 30: 17b–18b; HSSSTP 5:16a–b). His two sons, in turn, were equally successful: Both served as prefects, a mid-level post (HSSSTP 5:16a; HHYHC 30:18b). For three consecutive generations of men without degrees to maintain a high level of prominence is quite exceptional and can only be explained in terms of unusual imperial favor. Such good fortune, however, could not be maintained, and none of the three grandsons rose above rank 8a (HSSSTP 5:16a–b). One of them, Shih Ho-sun, had five sons, none of whom entered the civil service, and a grandson Shih Mao-tsu is known to have fallen into slavery during the Yuan (HSSSTP 5:16a–b; IPCK 34:2b–4a). In addition, we know that the landholdings of Shih Ho-sun, representing some eight thousand *mou*, were seized by "bullies" from the Hangchow region. The line thus found itself not only without office, but also without land to see it through hard times. Prior to the ninth generation, this had been one of the most politically successful lines to emanate from Shih Mi-cheng.

Another highly prosperous line of descendants is that of Shih Hsuan-chih, one of the younger sons of Shih Mi-cheng. He personally held rank of 6a and a post at the Imperial Archives (HSSSTP 5:17b–18a). His son Shih Ch'ang-ch'ing, taking advantage of the merit accrued by his cousin Shih Mao-ch'ing, entered the civil service and eventually came to hold the rank of 6a; Shih Ya-ch'ing became prefect, and Shih Man-ch'ing was ranked 6a. Then again, despite the accomplishments of the seventh and eighth generations, the ninth generation performed with far less distinction. Only three of the seven heirs are known to have held civil service rank and those three never made it beyond the entry level of 9b (HSSSTP 5:17b–18a).

The final son of Shih Mi-cheng, Shih Hsien-chih, was once a staff supervisor (8b). His son, Shih Shang-ch'ing, was ranked 9b, and his grandson, Shih Ming-po, received the rank of 8b in a special act of grace on the occasion of an imperial sacrifice to Shih Hao (HSSSTP 5:18b–19a). Under ordinary circumstances, "protection" would not have been available to Shih Ming-po.

Descendants of Shih Mi-yuan

The most politically successful Shih, Shih Mi-yuan, also had the most descendants (see figure 3.3). Eldest son Shih K'uan-chih appears to have died rather young, thus explaining his failure to rise above rank 7a; his two adopted sons only attained rank 9a, perhaps due to early deaths as well

(HHYHC 14:34a, 30:27a; HSSSTP 5:19a–b, 8:18a–19a), and their offspring seem to have had neither political office nor civil service rank. Thus, again, the Shih had no policy of giving priority to the senior line, for more successful lines clearly failed to share their privilege with the less fortunate. Yet the waning of this line was surely compensated for by the waxing of others.

Shih Mi-yuan's second son, Shih Chai-chih, appears to have been politically quite astute, and many years after his father's death he rose to become coadministrator at the Bureau of Military Affairs, ranked 2a (CCTC 45:22b–24a; HHYHC 14:39b–40b; HSSSTP 5:19b–22b). All seven of his sons held civil service rank, but five of the seven appear not to have gone beyond the low entry level of 8b. Son Shih Chou-ch'ing was among the more successful, having received the special conferral of *chin-shih* status in 1275 and serving in the metropolitan bureaucracy with rank of 6a; of Shih Chou-ch'ing's eight sons, however, only one held civil service status, and this was quite low (HSSSTP 5:20a–21a). The other son of Shih Chai-chih to rise above the lower bureaucracy was Shih Ch'ang-ch'ing, who served as military adviser with rank of 6b; none of his own four sons were involved in the civil service. Shih Chai-chih had a total of nineteen known grandsons, only four of whom held bureaucratic status. One of these, Shih Chi-sun, reportedly served in an administrative capacity as prefect in the distant south; the others were low-level officials. The only descendant of Shih Chai-chih to hold *chin-shih* examination credentials was Shih T'ang-ch'ing, who with the rank of 8b served as prefectural vice-administrator. His son, in turn, held the rank of 8a and his career seems not to have gone very far.

Shih Yü-chih, the youngest of Shih Mi-yuan's sons, may have been less active than his brother in national politics, yet he succeeded in producing a far more durable line of descendants. He personally received a long succession of bureaucratic assignments, most being away from the capital; the court nevertheless confirmed its special favor by honoring him with the high rank of 3a. This afforded Shih Yü-chih several "protection" slots, and three of his five sons appear to have taken advantage of the privilege (HYWWSC 37:19a–21a; SMWHC 5:41b–46a; HHYHC 30:26b–27b; HSSSTP 5:22b–23b). Eldest son Shih Chi-ch'ing was a highly successful regional official whose career culminated in an appointment as prefect (mid-level). In turn, his son, Shih Chen-sun, held the rank of only 8b (apparently without holding office), but a grandson emerged in Yuan times to serve the alien government as regional instructor.

Another unusually resilient line was that starting with Shih Hsi-ch'ing. Both he and his son, Shih I-sun, held low-level civil service status under the Sung, but grandson Shih Kung-ching refused to serve the Mongol Yuan dynasty. Even so, a tradition of learning must have been preserved in the line, for in early Ming times his great-grandson Shih Ting-tsu emerged as a mid-level official and Shih Ting-tsu's son, Shih Sui, served the Ming in a similar

FIGURE 3.3 Descendants of Shih Mi-yuan

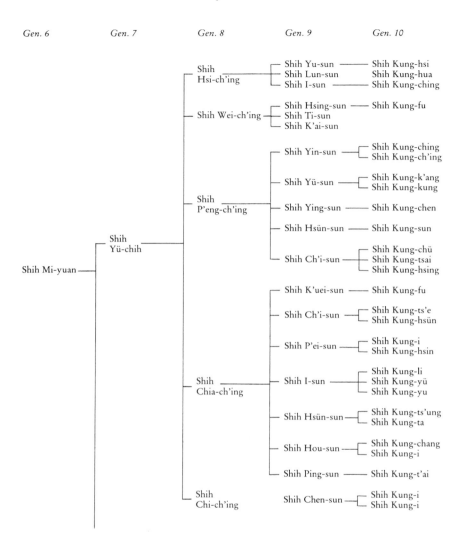

FIGURE 3.3 (continued)

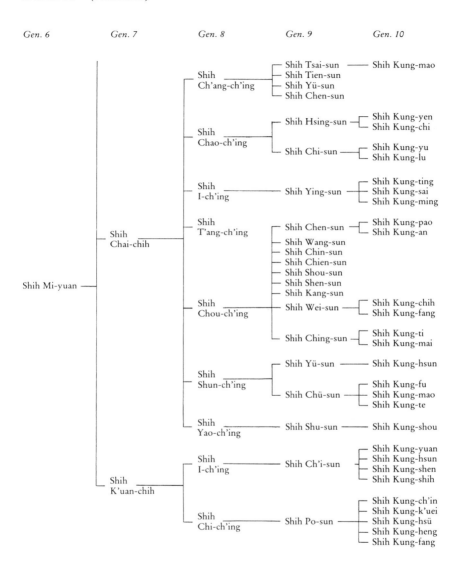

capacity (SWHKCC 23:11a–12a). These two are the only individuals clearly descended from the once-prominent Branch A who are known to have entered the Ming bureaucracy. By this time, of course, the "protection" privileges and imperial favor of the Sung court were hardly of use to Ming descendants, so this can only be explained as a special act of grace for a formerly distinguished line. Descendants of Shih Yü-chih, on the whole, fared poorly in the ninth and tenth generations: Of nineteen known grandsons, only two managed to secure even low-level official status. Even less is known about his twenty-eight great-grandsons, most of whom lived under Yuan rule.

Descendants of Shih Mi-chien

Although the youngest son of Shih Hao, Shih Mi-chien, lacked *chin-shih* credentials, the combination of favor enjoyed by both father and brother and a strong record as metropolitan and regional official enabled him to retire with the high rank of 2b (YYSMC 5:22a–23a; HHYHC 29:26b–30a; HSSSTP 5:26a–30b) (see figure 3.4). His offspring did not earn degrees either, but this did not impede their advancement. Eldest son Shih Sui-chih rose to the post of prefect (mid-level) and his son, Shih Yeh-ch'ing, became staff supervisor with rank of 8a. This did not mean that the line was in decline: ninth-generation Shih Ang-sun, served as a low-level military adviser and Shih Ch'ang-sun was ranked 5b, which suggests that he enjoyed a reasonably successful career. Through the merit of Shih Ch'ang-sun, "protection" would have been available to members of the tenth generation, although there exists no information on their careers.

The second son of Shih Mi-chien fathered a relatively resilient line as well. Shih Ch'ung-chih served for awhile as prefect and ended his career at rank 7a (HSSSTP 5:26b–27b). Ultimately he was surpassed by his eldest son, Shih Sung-ch'ing, who held low-level bureaucratic rank. Shih Sung-ch'ing's younger brother served as a regional military leader (mid-level), and two of his four heirs, like their cousins, held low-level civil service status. In this way, the two senior lines to descend from Shih Mi-chien realized a good measure of success in maintaining civil service involvement through the ninth generation.

The most eminent heir to Shih Mi-chien was nonetheless his younger son Shih Pin-chih (1190–1251). Through "protection," he entered the civil service while still a teenager and held an impressive succession of regional posts (including a half dozen stints as prefect) before serving briefly in the capital as executive at the Ministry of Finance, ranked 3b (HTHSC 67: 8a–b; HHYHC 29:28b–30a; HSSSTP 5:27b–30b). He was later ennobled as baron. The eldest son of Shih Pin-chih once served as prefectural vice-administrator of Lin-an with rank of 5a. Two of his offspring, enjoying the privileges of "protection," similarly entered the bureaucracy: Shih Sheng-

FIGURE 3.4   Descendants of Shih Mi-chien

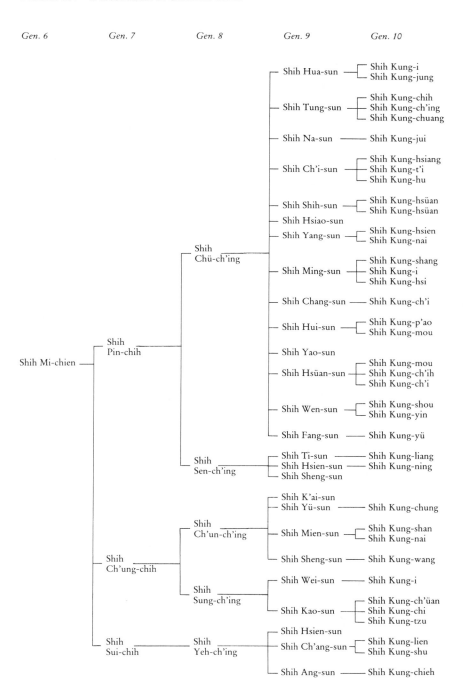

Gen. 6   Gen. 7   Gen. 8   Gen. 9   Gen. 10

sun was named subprefectural registrar (8b), and Shih Ti-sun held rank
9b, both entry-level positions. Shih Pin-chih's second son, Shih Chü-ch'ing
(fl. 1266–1313), was perhaps somewhat less accomplished than his brother
Shih Sen-ch'ing, having served only as a subprefect (8b) under the Sung, yet
he could hardly be matched in the realm of paternity—he sired fourteen
sons! None of his many heirs held Sung civil service rank, but three became
officials in the Yuan: Shih Hsüan-sun accepted an appointment as regional
instructor, while the two remaining brothers held lesser posts (HSSSTP
5:28a–30a). As it was, by identifying with the new dynasty they were hardly
breaking with a family tradition; after the demise of Sung rule, their father
Shih Chü-ch'ing himself elected to serve the Mongol government, ironically
in the same capacity as earlier. Similarly, cousin Shih Hsien-sun served the
Yuan as a minor official (HSSSTP 5:27b). Among the descendants of Shih
Hao, the only other ninth-generation kinsmen known to have entered the
Yuan civil service are two of the eight sons of Shih Chou-ch'ing (great-
grandsons of Shih Mi-yuan), Shih Ching-sun and Shih Wei-sun, both of
whom became regional instructors (HSSSTP 5:20a). That the willingness to
accommodate to alien rule should be so prevalent among the descendants of
Shih Pin-chih, and especially the household of Shih Chü-ch'ing, might con-
ceivably represent an unusual response to the economic pressures created by
an exceptionally large family—Shih Chü-ch'ing did, after all, have fourteen
sons and twenty-five grandsons. Interestingly, despite their accommodation,
none of those associated with the Mongol government managed to earn
promotions beyond low-level regional posts.

Prosperity and Its Dangers

The rise and decline of the Shih as a descent group cannot be separated
from the political success of key individuals and the wealth they came to
acquire. There is little question that the Shih of the mid-to-late eleventh
century were penniless, for the widow Yeh is known to have supported her
son and daughter by selling her services as a seamstress (YYSMC 5:33a–
34a). It was only with the rise of Shih Hao to political prominence that the
Shih began to prosper and multiply.

One sign of that prosperity was the acquisition of concubines. Shih Hao
appears to have been the first to take one; yet other kinsmen, at winning the
security that accompanies political success, followed suit. Additional
spouses, in turn, enabled kinsmen to spawn large families. Shih Mi-cheng
had seven sons, fourteen grandsons, nineteen great-grandsons, and twenty-
seven great-great-grandsons. Shih Mi-yuan had an issue of only three;
however, with one son having seven male heirs and another having five, he
had a total of fourteen grandsons, forty great-grandsons, and fifty-six great-
great-grandsons. Shih Mi-chien, like his brother, started with three sons, but

his great-great-grandsons numbered thirty-eight. Thus, by the tenth generation, the descendants of Shih Hao included 122 males and probably an equal
number of women—and this represents just one segment of Branch A,
not the entire group. Kinsmen in other branches, although they fell somewhat short of Shih Hao's attainments in this regard, nonetheless did enjoy
a healthy measure of fecundity: Shih Hao's cousin in Branch C, Shih
Chien, for example, was great-great-grandfather of seventy-eight males.
Meanwhile, there is good reason to assume an underreporting of the actual
number of kinsmen, for the names of children who die early often go
unreported. Keeping this in mind, genealogical sources give a total of approximately 160 males in Branch A and another 100 in the other branches—
twenty times the size of the Shih group five generations earlier.

This begs the question of why so many sons. Some might argue that
expansion of the descent group in this way represents a strategy for maintaining elite membership, men of the time being convinced that having more
sons would thereby enhance the possibility that one or several would win
degrees and penetrate the civil service. Consistent with this hypothesis is the
fact that the rapid growth of the sixth to ninth generations tended to taper
off (or at least stabilize) in the tenth generation, by which time a new dynasty had emerged and the prospects for official employment had declined.
Then again, there is also a human dimension. To the extent that every male
needed an heir for purposes of ritual, those individuals fortunate enough to
have several sons were frequently expected to offer one or two for adoption
to brothers and cousins without heirs. This allowed unbridled growth, the
assumption being that surplus sons would eventually be cared for by someone else. The wealth derived from public office initially made such growth
possible; yet, to the extent that a greater percentage of kinsmen were excluded from the civil service by the tenth generation, it may well be that the
Shih simply could not afford continued growth at the earlier pace. Having
been subjected to prolonged official unemployment, not only under the
Yuan but later as well, simply to provide every male with an heir would have
represented an unbearable strain on dwindling resources. By this time, there
must have been every incentive for the group to disband.

In light of the unusual political prominence of Branch A and its phenomenal growth in Southern Sung times, it is astounding that so few kinsmen emerged in Yuan and Ming times as civil servants. It is equally surprising that there exist so few references to the activities, political or otherwise,
of kinsmen of the post-Sung period in general, a phenomenon almost
reminiscent of the disappearance of prominent T'ang aristocrats prior to the
Sung (cf. Ebrey 1978:112–15). The descent group's unwieldy size and the
growing economic burden that this represented must have been partially
responsible for its decline. No less important, it would seem, is the limited
effect of "protection" and imperial favor in prolonging the life of the house.

FIGURE 3.5   Descendants of Shih Hao

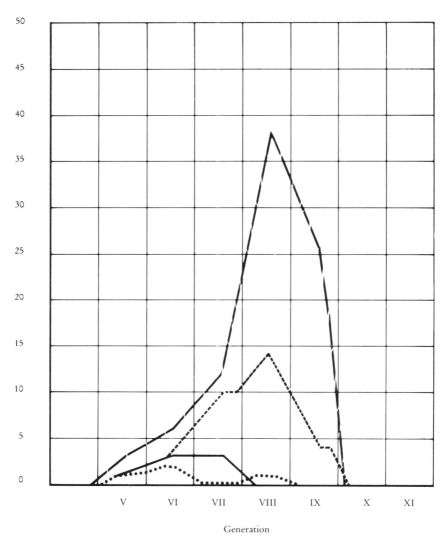

Generation

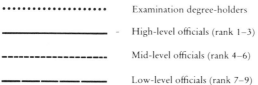

Examination degree-holders

High-level officials (rank 1–3)

Mid-level officials (rank 4–6)

Low-level officials (rank 7–9)

TABLE 3.1
Summary of Civil Service Attainments of the Descendants of Shih Hao

Generation	Total number of male kinsmen	Number entering Civil Service	Civil servants with chin-shih credentials	Civil servants without chin-shih credentials[a]
6	4	4(100%)	2	2
7	14	14 (100%)	0	14
8	35	28 (77%)	1	27
9	85	32 (38%)	0	32[b]
10	122	c	0	c

a. This group chiefly represents those who availed themselves of "protection" privilege, although some may have entered the civil service through special acts of imperial favor or through promotion from the Imperial University.

b. This includes those who served the Yuan dynasty.

c. Genealogical sources do not provide this information and historical sources (which are also quite scant at this point) reveal only one civil servant in Generation 10, Shih Kung-i, who served the Yuan as regional instructor.

This is illustrated by figure 3.5 and table 3.1. Assuming that officials lacking *chin-shih* degrees entered the civil service through "protection," several trends become apparent. First, the line of Shih Hao produced regular *chin-shih* degree-holders for only three generations and the total number was actually quite small: one in generation five, two in generation six, none in generation seven, and one in generation eight. While Shih Hao initially penetrated and later prospered in the civil service through examination success, a larger number of descendants did not translate into more degree winners: Subsequent generations relied heavily upon bureaucratic privilege to penetrate the political realm. It was, undeniably, through the special favor enjoyed by individuals such as Shih Hao and Shih Mi-yuan that the line's total number of officials swelled from just over four in the sixth generation to thirty-two in the ninth. The civil service attainments of individuals in other lines and branches was somewhat less stunning, yet hardly insignificant—they produced several high officials and dozens of mid-level bureaucrats as well (see figure 3.5). Such an enormous increase in the ranks of kinsmen with official status nonetheless brought career success to only a few; the vast majority of Shih recruits remained at the lower end of the bureaucracy. In addition, the total number of high officials never rose above three and remained closely related to *chin-shih* output. This suggests that "protection" and imperial favor, while frequently inflating the ranks of the bureaucracy's lower and to a lesser extent middle levels, had a negligible impact on the highest level. In effect, advancement to the higher echelons was still chiefly a function of individual merit.[8]

8. It is remarkable how much the Shih in the Southern Sung resemble the so-called "old families" of the T'ang. In both cases, an extraordinarily high proportion of known agnates became officials, although the majority remained in lower-level posts. In both cases, those who

A second observation relates to the political demise of the Shih. That the eighth and ninth generation peaks should be followed by a precipitous drop in the tenth generation, from a high of thirty-two officials to nothing in the course of one generation, would seem to imply that "protection" and imperial favor only affected descendants for one generation. This is not quite true. Dynastic change also occurred as members of the ninth and tenth generations matured, and there is no question that this played a crucial role in accelerating a decline that might otherwise have been more gradual. Moreover, even if the new dynasty chose to recognize the privileges afforded scholar-official houses under the old regime—and there is some indication that it was indeed so inclined—social pressure against serving the alien government prevented all but a few from taking advantage of this. Such pressure was, no doubt, especially severe for the Shih, whose identification with the Sung court had been so close and lasting. The change of dynasties, and especially the difficult adjustment to the extension of alien rule to South China for the first time in history, certainly cannot be disregarded in an assessment of collective fortunes.

In the final analysis, however, the Shih group was doomed long before the Sung dynasty ended, and at the source of its ruin was political success. Shih Mi-yuan's quarter-century tenure brought unbridled imperial favor, yet it was also beset with unending controversy. Rising to the chief councillorship following the assassination of special military councillor Han T'o-chou, an incident in which he had the dubious distinction of playing a prominent role, Shih Mi-yuan began with a stained reputation. Even more damning was a controversial imperial succession some fifteen years later, one that resulted in the death of an imperial son and allegations that the chief councillor had acted illicitly in replacing that son with someone more to his own liking. These suspicions, combined with a weak and seemingly irresponsible foreign policy, had left him thoroughly discredited by the time death came in 1233 (Davis 1980: chap. 4). Shih Mi-yuan's politically involved second son, Shih Chai-chih, would win no popularity contest among his colleagues either. Not only had he been perhaps too closely associated as a youth with his father's administration, but his own record as regional official was hardly honorable—rumor had it that he was unabashedly corrupt (CCTC 45:22b–

---

attained high posts were much more likely to have held *chin-shih* credentials. Another similarity concerns the way in which bureaucratic service tended to take men away from their native homes, often for years on end, which served to weaken ties to home and to the kin left behind (see Ebrey 1978:87–115). And the more politically successful the individual the more bureaucracy demanded of his time and allegiance. Hartwell (1982) similarly discusses the many features of T'ang aristocratic "families" that can be found among professional bureaucrats of the Northern Sung. Yet, contrary to Hartwell's assumptions, the Shih case demonstrates that the "professional bureaucrat" type of the Northern Sung did to some extent persist into the Southern Sung.

24a). Several cousins in Branch C, one of whom became the Shih group's third chief councillor, were similarly accused of highly improper official conduct, which ranged from cowardice in the face of enemy invasion to political assassination. Although allegations of this sort were often unsubstantiated, they still served to sully the reputation of the entire group and would have negatively affected its political fortunes quite independent of dynastic turns. Reacting to the pervasive influence of the Shih at court, Chief Councillor Chia Ssu-tao (1213–75), a native of southern Chekiang, reportedly went so far in late Sung times as uniformly to block the advancement to metropolitan posts of most Ming-chou natives (CCTC 45:23b). Success for the Shih had, in effect, made them a prominent target for the politically ambitious.

Political controversy also generated vicious tensions within the descent group. Shih Mi-yuan's growing unpopularity in the capital came to be reflected within his own immediate family. Toward the end of his first decade in power, his younger brother Shih Mi-chien urged him to step down, and when he refused, Shih Mi-chien himself withdrew from the civil service to spend his remaining fourteen years in retirement (YYSMC 5:22a–23a; HHYHC 29:26b–30a). Shih Shou-chih, the son of Shih Mi-yuan's eldest brother, reacted similarly to his uncle's dominance (HHYHC 30:17a–b). This took place even before the succession controversy of 1224, an event which must have confirmed the conviction of Shih kinsmen that the chief councillor's long tenure would ruin both his own personal reputation and that of the Shih as a group. Even more critical of Shih Mi-yuan were cousins in other branches. Although beyond the scope of this paper, it should be noted that the interaction between the various branches of the descent group (and especially between the rivals, Branch A and Branch C) was as much negative as positive after 1224. One cousin in Branch C, having failed repeatedly at the *chin-shih* examination, blamed all upon Shih Mi-yuan, who appears not to have gotten on very well with him (SS 423:12637–38; HHYHC 30:14a–15b). Later, another kinsman even less popular than Shih Mi-yuan was accused of assassinating his own nephew for political reasons (SS 414:12426–27; HHYHC 30:27b–29a). Moreover, the passage of time, which often helps to heal old wounds and add luster to a once-tarnished name, was not so generous to the Shih. In the Ming dynasty, the writings of more than one prominent historian would cast Shih Mi-yuan in the mold of a wicked official and trace the decline of Sung rule to his marathon tenure (SSC 27:21, 81:42; SSHP 151:1; NSS 49:10a–11b).

The Shih as a Corporate Descent Group

A major question to ask of any descent group is its degree of corporateness: To what extent did kinsmen share resources, human and material, for the purpose of prolonging the life and welfare of the group as a whole? Were they united simply by ritual, coming together only on the occasion of funerals and ancestral sacrifices, or did they have a corporate base represented by common landholdings or comparable tangibles? The absence of any sense of "corporateness," according to many anthropologists (Fried 1970:15–16; Watson 1982:594), would imply that the Shih merely constituted several lines of descent, rather than a self-consciously organized kin group. Perhaps this principle is in need of reassessment.

In the late twelfth and early thirteenth century, the Shih were definitely more than a loose collection of agnates or related lines held together merely by the knowledge of common descent. There did exist a sense of community beyond a superficial recognition of shared blood. Thus, beginning with generation five, the Shih chose to order the personal names of all kinsmen so that each individual could be readily identified with a given generation and branch, an undertaking that even entailed the posthumous alteration of some names (KKC 74:12a–14b; HSSSTP 2:10a–b).[9] This practice, commonly referred to as *p'ai-ming*, was uniformly observed through the eleventh generation. In consequence, all members of generation five have one-syllable personal names with the "water" radical, those in generation six have two-syllable names containing the character *mi*, those in the seventh generation share a common *chih*, and so forth. Moreover, the variant in the two-syllable generational name often contains branch and subbranch identifiers: The grandsons of Shih Hao, for example, share a common *mien* radical in their variant name; this distinguishes them not only from cousins in other branches, but also from cousins within their own Branch A who descended from brothers of Shih Hao. Implicit in the universal adoption of and strict adherence to a scheme of generational names is, at the very least, close identification of members of the larger descent group. Naming patterns provided the adhesive needed to cement the group together, to define the relationship of one kinsman to another, even to create an easily recognizable generational hierarchy within the group. If the Shih began as a loose collection of agnates, they had clearly adopted a good deal of structure by the fifth generation.

Although historical and genealogical sources contain no references to communal landholdings in the form of charitable estates, there did occur a sharing of *yin* privileges. As mentioned earlier, the merit of Shih Hao was responsible for the official advancement of not only a son, but also brothers and sons-in-law.[10] The merit of Shih Mi-yuan resulted in the conferral of

---

9. It is for this reason that the names of some kinsmen in generations four and five are not consistent with the general pattern.

10. More work needs to be done to determine the extent of *yin* privileges to affines (e.g., sons-in-law) among the Sung elite. If affines regularly shared in the political advantages, they would have done so at the expense of agnates and, hence, the corporateness of the agnatic groups might have been diluted.

civil service status upon his own sons and grandsons as well as in-laws and descendants of brothers (SSCW 32:8b; HHYHC 14:34a). Meanwhile, genealogical sources frequently allude to "advancement through the *favor of an ancestor*" *(tsu-tse)*, which is often contrasted with "the favor of a father" or grandfather (HSSSTP *ch*. 5). This may well mean that "protection" was sometimes used as a communal resource that kinsmen drew upon in times of need, much like a charitable estate except that the common property represented political privilege and not land. It is also known that other types of political favors were extended to kinsmen outside one's immediate line or even branch. Shih Mi-yuan, for example, is known to have repeatedly interceded on behalf of a younger kinsman in Branch C whose promising career might otherwise have taken a very different turn (HHYHC 14:35a).

Some degree of solidarity among the Ming-chou Shih is also suggested by adoption practices within the group.[11] From generations five to ten, and for the line descended from Shih Hao alone, some twenty-one adoptions are mentioned in genealogical sources (HSSSTP 5:14a–30b). The overwhelming majority of these adoptions (at least fifteen) occurred among the closest agnates, where the fortunate individual with several sons offered one of these to a brother; yet a limited number of adoptions did occur among more distant agnates. For example, Shih Ch'ang-sun, originally the son of Shih Ch'un-ch'ing and great-grandson of Shih Mi-chien, was adopted by Shih Yeh-ch'ing, his father's first cousin (see figure 3.4; HSSSTP 5:26a, 27a). Among the descendants of Shih Mi-cheng, Shih Kung-mu and Shih Kung-yü similarly represent adoptions among cousins of the same line (see figure 3.2; HSSSTP 5:15b, 17b–18a). Going one step further, Shih Ch'i-sun, son of Shih Hsi-ch'ing, was adopted as heir to a second cousin of his father (see figure 3.2; HSSSTP 5:19b, 25b). The most remote adoption in this group occurred in the case of Shih Ang-sun: Born a descendant of Shih Mi-cheng (son of Shih Ya-ch'ing), he was named heir to the line of Shih Mi-chien (son of Shih Yeh-ch'ing), an adoption among third cousins (HSSSTP 5:18a, 26a). Among descendants of Shih Hao, there is no instance of an adoption crossing the still higher barrier of "branch," that is, those outside of the Shih Shih-chung/Shih Hao line (see figure 3.1); yet it does occur in subbranches sired by Shih Hao's brothers. On the whole, adoption practices among the descendants of Shih Hao suggest limited interaction between lines, especially as genealogical distance increases; but lines never become totally irrelevant to one another.

11. A question of importance here—which, however, would require a comparative analysis to answer—is whether or not the Shih were at all exceptional in this regard. Perhaps whenever close agnates lived near one another they came to each other's aid in providing heirs. There is, at any rate, no evidence that appropriate heirs were especially hard to find; furthermore, there is some evidence that implies that men were often eager to see their sons adopted out (see Ebrey 1984:106–10).

Given the distribution of *yin* privileges and the patterns of naming and adoption, it is difficult to deny that some degree of "corporateness" existed among the Shih. On the other hand, there is little to suggest the organization of a "lineage" as defined in chapter 1. There is no indication of corporate property that might have generated income for the Shih as a group; there existed no strict rules governing the inheritance of property; no set of elders were vested with ritual authority for the larger kinship group. Moreover, the Shih appear to have had a negligible sense of community in the early years of their development. When the tomb inscription for the widow Yeh was drafted by Lou Yueh (1137–1213) at the turn of the thirteenth century, we know that the Shih still lacked a genealogy, and information on ancestors just a few generations removed was scant at best (KKC 74:12a–14b). A spirit of corporateness or group consciousness did develop with time, but without the concomitant drive to manifest that spirit through something tangible like a communal home. There were no lineage schools, and all property was owned individually. Sung dynasty maps of Ming-chou refer to the "home of Shih Hao" and the "home of Shih Mi-yuan"; there is no "Shih estate," save for a sizable garden outside the city walls that was given to the "family" (*chia*) of Shih Hao by Emperor Hsiao-tsung (PCSMC 1227 edition). The Shih emerged from an urban base and remained urban oriented. They did not begin with a sprawling country estate and perhaps for this reason never bothered to establish one later on. Nor was there a common burial ground to serve as a focus of ritual unity. Shih Chien and Shih Chao were buried in the same general area, but subsequent sons were buried in entirely different districts, sometimes even in different counties (HSSSTP *ch.* 8). Only the wives were matched with the men in this regard. The Shih possessed such extraordinary wealth that it was certainly not for financial reasons that they had no common gravesite; we can only conclude that they saw no need to organize in this way.

Also mitigating against descent group solidarity and community spirit was the Shih's political involvement. Public service, whether in the capital or in the provinces, inevitably entailed years away from home. The standard tenure of office for an administrative post such as prefect was three years, and there are many cases of Shih kinsmen spending ten or more years in service away from Ming-chou. Although many served in areas not far from home, there are cases of some individuals being posted in distant Szechwan and Kwangtung. For the politically influential, time away from Ming-chou could be lengthier. Shih Mi-yuan spent his last twenty-five years at his official residence in the capital, most of the time accompanied by his wife and sons. Although Ming-chou was relatively near, there is nothing to indicate that he visited there frequently. The Shih's third chief councillor, Shih Sung-chih, spent a total of about twenty years in one high-level post or another, and, for much of the five years that he was councillor, his father

is believed to have joined him in the capital (Davis 1980:chap. 5). Other kinsmen, being less prominent, may have spent more time at home, but a surprisingly large number were separated from family and friends for at least a
few years.

Meanwhile, the wealth that accompanied political success must have enabled many to own secondary homes away from their native place. The
second son of Shih Mi-yuan, for example, is reported to have owned a home
on the "Western Lake" of Hangchow (HSSSTP 8:18b–19a). This dispersal
inevitably took its toll on descent group solidarity. The more kinsmen
moved about the less they interacted with one another. For example, it
seems not unlikely that most Shih kinsmen of the early thirteenth century
never managed to meet Shih Mi-yuan (SJISHP 18:90ff), the busy councillor
who spent nearly all of his time in the capital. Contact may have been rather
intimate through the fifth generation, but as the group expanded in size and
more kinsmen spent more time elsewhere, intimacy inevitably became difficult to sustain. It is perhaps for this reason that members of the sixth and
seventh generations did not hesitate to attack the policies of influential relatives in high office—after all, they were little more than strangers.

The deterioration of relations among kinsmen prompted many to migrate
elsewhere. Interestingly, such migration occurred first in the eighth generation, as the political fortunes of the Shih began to wane, and it was confined
to two individuals in Branch A who descended not from Shih Hao but from
a brother (HSSSTP 5:35b, 37b–38a). By the next generation, the total number of emigrants from Branch A had risen to nine, some of whom settled in
nearby subprefectures while others moved as far away as Fukien (HSSSTP
5:16a–b, 22b, 29a–b, 30a, 35b, 39b, 47a–b, 63a). Among later emigrants
were descendants of Shih Mi-yuan and Shih Mi-chien. Some were from
relatively prosperous lines, others from less accomplished ones; some fled
Ming-chou out of poverty, others, perhaps less destitute, fled out of choice
and established new lineages or descent groups in their adopted homes. Most
such emigrants were never heard of again, and they probably disappeared
into the common masses. The widespread official unemployment accompanying alien rule may have been responsible for certain migrations, yet
three emigrants in the ninth generation were sons of Shih Chü-ch'ing, one of
the few kinsmen who chose to serve the Mongol dynasty. Although employment was probably not at issue in this case, finances may well have been—
we can only imagine how difficult it was for the moderately successful
household of Shih Chü-ch'ing to support fourteen sons and twenty-five
grandsons. As they settled in new areas, the few emigrants for whom we
have information appear to have abandoned the generational naming scheme
of the Ming-chou main line (HSSSTP *ch.* 6); many reverted to one-syllable
names. By the twelfth generation, even those remaining in Ming-chou
adopted unrelated, one-syllable names (SWHKCC 23:11b–12a), thus for-

mally recognizing the disintegration of corporate practices inherited from Sung ancestors.

By the fourteenth century, after two generations of alien rule, one of the wealthiest and most politically influential descent groups of Sung times found itself not only weak, but largely bankrupt. There were reports of numerous kinsmen becoming impoverished or falling to the status of commoners (SWHKCC 23:11a–12a; SYC 11:13b–14a). Even with migrations, the group remaining behind must have been sizable; yet only a few appear to have succeeded in maintaining a regional "presence," and only a few emerged in Ming and Ch'ing times as degree-holders and officials. What happened to the many others is a mystery. We know that the local prestige of the Shih suffered noticeably after a generation or two of official unemployment. Thus, in Yuan times "bullies" from the outside were not the least bit timid about seizing some eight thousand *mou* of land from a descendant of Shih Mi-cheng in the ninth generation (IPCK 34:2b–4a). Interestingly, in his study of the Fan and their decline after Sung rule, Denis Twitchett also speaks of property being threatened in Yuan times (1959:122–23). Perhaps it was common for the landholdings of the once-prominent to come under attack following a change in dynasty. Fortunately for the Fan, their overall image in post-Sung times remained positive, and this undoubtedly served to ward off a good many pernicious tax-collectors and land-grabbers. The legacy of the Shih, in contrast, was far less esteemed. However daring, no one would have risked entanglement with the Shih under the Sung. That they should do so later on suggests that economic security in traditional China was extremely difficult to maintain without a handsome measure of political influence; wealth alone was nearly useless.

Some might argue that the decline of a family is related to the division of family property among a growing body of sons at precisely the time that office-related income was declining (cf. Ebrey 1984:263–64). The Sung government itself seems to have encouraged this pattern of family dissolution. To its highly meritorious and favored officials the court could be most generous in providing homes, gardens, "fiefs of maintenance" (*shih-feng*), family shrines, and exquisite birthday gifts of gold and jade. Beyond prestige, such gifts also gave their recipients a sense of security, so much so that they must not have been especially pressed to be frugal or careful to invest their easily acquired wealth in such stable enterprises as land and corporate property. Yet such pervasive lack of reckoning was quite unwarranted. Fiefs of maintenance and government domiciles were given to the individual official on a temporary basis and generally returned to the court upon the individual's retirement or death. Such expressions of imperial goodwill were not considered family, much less descent group, property. Shih Mi-yuan's home in the capital, therefore, was officially returned to the court following his death, but through a special act of grace the court decided that it should remain in the "family" (*chia*) (SS 41:799). Nonetheless, even temporary use of government homes enabled the politically involved to concern themselves less with property holdings and concentrate instead on more "important" matters, such as affairs of state. Other government policies also discouraged thrift and cooperative endeavors within the descent group. The shrines given by the court in honor of Shih Hao and later Shih Mi-yuan were both built and maintained with government funds. Less favored lines might set aside "sacrificial lands" (*chi-t'ien*) to pay for the shrines and the various sacrificial apparati; not so for the Shih. Meanwhile, official status entitled the sons and grandsons of many Shih kinsmen to receive advanced education at the Imperial University or Directorate of Education; thus less had to be invested in the education of Shih youth. The Shih remained in the good graces of the court for the duration of the Sung, yet the emergence of a new dynasty brought an abrupt end to both political privilege and the steady flow of gifts from the capital. Shih kinsmen, many of them accustomed to a sumptuous life-style and seemingly limitless court favor, had never properly prepared themselves for its termination. In this respect, as successful bureaucrats they were far more vulnerable to the insecurities accompanying a change in dynasty than those of less prominence, for their dependency on the court was quite complete.

Conclusion

The experience of the Shih, their sudden leaps from obscurity to extreme prominence and back to obscurity again, can hardly be generalized for scholar-officialdom as a whole during Sung times, yet their experience was not simply an aberration. For those lines that distinguished themselves in the political arena, for the "super-elite," fortunes could be equally unpredictable. The Lü of Northern Sung times, the only descent group of the dynasty to produce three consecutive generations of chief councilors, also experienced a precipitous fall in the transition from Northern to Southern Sung (Kinugawa 1973). One might think that the wealth accompanying political success would ensure security, but as Chinese commentators have noted for centuries, the more accomplished the house the more fragile its existence. As seen in the chapters by Hymes and Dennerline in this volume, the less privileged were not so vulnerable. Their descendants were not likely to grow in number at the same astonishing rate as the Shih, nor to find themselves dependent upon generous gifts from the court or salary supplements, nor to become plagued by a bitter divisiveness stemming from political conflicts in the capital, nor to become a popular target of seemingly every ambitious politician to come along. Having fewer resources, they were likely to be more pressed to invest those resources wisely and, being smaller in size, their communal efforts had a greater chance of being successful. All things considered, the moderately privileged probably enjoyed far greater stability than the eminent few.

For the super-elite, those most successful at playing the high-stakes civil service game, the prospects for maintaining kinship solidarity were not very good. In the early stages of development, the Shih appear to have developed a definite sense of collective identity. Shih Hao, the senior member of the fifth generation, was a popular figure who willingly shared *yin* privilege with his kinsmen, and the scheme he devised for ordering the personal names of the entire Shih line was destined to remain in use for the next six generations and thereby reinforce a corporate identity. Also suggesting cohesiveness was the pattern of adopting among second and third cousins. There exists enough evidence of corporate identity and group consciousness to conclude that the Shih indeed represented a "group" and not merely a loose collection of agnates; yet there was no communally owned property, no charitable estate or sacrificial land. The sense of insecurity that the establishment of such lands implied simply did not exist among the prosperous Shih. As the bonds of agnatic kinship grew more distant, there tended to be less sharing and individual lines became more insular, although not entirely independent of one another. After the death of Shih Hao, the political attainments of men such as Shih Mi-yuan and Shih Sung-chih were as much a curse as a blessing, at least in terms of the welfare of the descent group as a whole. Differences of opinion on court policy served to strain relations among kinsmen in general, even among brothers. If the number of male heirs had not grown so rapidly from the fifth to seventh generations, or if Shih Mi-yuan's tenure had been shorter in duration and less controversial, or if the descent group had produced in subsequent generations an individual like Shih Hao—whose popularity could draw together its various centrifugal forces—then perhaps there might have emerged some inspiration for community action.

In analyzing kinship organization in China, anthropologists (and historians following in their footsteps) have stressed the importance of group unity as manifested in charitable estates or similar forms of corporate property (Fried 1970:16; Watson 1982:594–96). I would propose that the Shih example demonstrates the need to reconsider this view. For the early imperial period, when the socially and politically prominent represented an oligarchy of regional influential houses with a strong base in land, such stress on landholdings and their communal use may be appropriate. Starting with the Sung dynasty, however, cities prospered throughout China as centers of economic and intellectual activity, producing a fair number of civil service recruits who lacked ties to the countryside. To the extent that many within the professional elite of Sung times did not emerge from rural estates but from an urban diaspora, it is understandable that they should not necessarily be inclined later to establish communally owned estates. For a group such as the Shih, corporate identity instead manifested itself in naming patterns, adoption practices, or the sharing of political privileges such as "protection." Shared landholdings, therefore, may be *one* criterion, but it should not be the *only* criterion for defining corporate descent groups.

REFERENCES

Primary Sources

CCTC   *Chieh-ch'i t'ing-chi* [*wai-pien*]   鮚埼亭集, 外編,   by Ch'üan Tsu-wang 全祖望. Ssu-pu ts'ung-k'an ed.

CJCSC   *Ch'ing-jung chü-shih chi* 清容居士集, by Yuan Chueh 袁桷. Ssu-pu ts'ung-k'an ed.

CTS   *Chiu t'ang shu* 舊唐書, by Liu Hsu 劉昫 et al. Peking: Chung-hua shu-chü, 1975.

CYTFSL   *Ch'ing-yuan t'iao-fa shih lei* 慶元條法事類, by Hsieh Shen-fu 謝深甫. Rpt. Tokyo, 1968.

HHYHC   [*Hsin-hsiu*] *Yin-hsien chih* 新修鄞縣志, comp. by Tai Mei 戴枚 et al. 1887.

HSSSTP   *Hsiao-shan shih-shih tsung-p'u* 蕭山史氏宗譜. 1892 ed.

HTC   *Hsu-tzu-chih t'ung-chien* 續資治通鑑, by Pi Yuan 畢沅. Peking: Ku-chi, 1958.

HTHSC   *Hou-ts'un hsien-sheng ta ch'üan-chi* 後村先生大全集, by Liu K'o-chuang 劉克莊. Ssu-pu ts'ung-k'an ed.

HTS   *Hsin T'ang Shu* 新唐書, comp. by Ou-yang Hsiu 歐陽修. Peking: Chung-hua, 1975.

HYWSC   *Hsing-yang wai-shih chi* 滎陽外史集, by Cheng Chen 鄭真. Ssu-k'u ch'üan-shu chen-pen ed.

IPCK   *I-pai chai-kao* 夷白齋藁, by Ch'en Chi 陳基. Ssu-pu ts'ung-k'an ed.

KKC   *Kung-k'uei chi* 攻媿集, by Lou Yueh 樓鑰. Ssu-pu ts'ung-k'an ed.

NESCC   *Nien-erh shih cha-chi* 廿二史箚記, by Chao I 趙翼. Rpt. Taipei: Ting-wen, 1978.

NSS   *Nan Sung shu* 南宋書, by Ch'ien Shih-sheng 錢士升. In *Sung Liao Chin Yuan pieh-shih.*

PCSMC   [*Pao-ch'ing*] *Ssu-ming chih* 寶慶四明志, by Lo Chün 羅濬 et al. Taipei: Sung-Yuan ti-fang-chih ts'ung-shu, 1978.

SHHSC   *Shui-hsin hsien-sheng chi* 水心先生集, by Yeh Shih 葉適. Ssu-pu ts'ung-k'an ed.

SHY   *Sung hui-yao chi-kao* 宋會要輯稿. Rpt. Taipei: Hsin-wen-feng, 1976.

SJISHP   *Sung-jen i-shih hui-pien* 宋人軼事彙編, by Ting Ch'uan-ching 丁傳靖. Peking: Shang-wu, 1958.

SMWHC   *Ssu-ming wen-hsien chi* 四明文獻集, by Wang Ying-lin 王應麟. In *Ssu-ming ts'ung-shu.* Taipei: 1964–66.

SS   *Sung shih* 宋史, by T'o T'o 脫脫 et al. Peking: Chung-hua, 1977.

SSC   *Sung shih chih* 宋史質, by Wang Chu 王洙. Rpt. Taipei: Hsin-wen-feng, 1977.

SSCW   *Sung-shih ch'üan-wen hsu tzu-chih t'ung-chien* 宋史全文續資治通鑑. In *Sung-shih tzu-liao ts'ui-pien.*

SSHP   *Sung-shih hsin-pien* 宋史新編, by K'o Wei-ch'i 柯維騏. Rpt. Taipei: Hsin-wen-feng, 1974.

SWHKCC   *Shan wen-hsien-kung ch'üan-chi* 宋文憲公全集, by Sung Lien 宋濂. Ssu-pu pei-yao ed.

SYC *Shan-yuan chi* 剡源集, Tai Piao-yuan 戴表元. Pai-pu ts'ung-shu chi-ch'eng
  ed.
WHTK *Wen-hsien t'ung-k'ao* 文獻通考, by Ma Tuan-lin 馬端臨. Rpt. Taipei:
  Shang-wu, 1964.
YHTC *Yin-hsien t'ung-chih* 鄞縣通志. 1935. Rpt. Taipei: Ch'eng-wen, 1974.
YYSMC *[Yen-yu] Ssu-ming chih* 延祐四明志, by Yuan Chueh 袁桷. Sung-Yuan
  ti-fang-chih ts'ung-shu ed.

Secondary Sources
Beattie, Hilary J. 1979. *Land and Lineage in China: A Study of T'ung-ch'en County,
  Anhwei, in the Ming and Ch'ing Dynasties*. Cambridge: Cambridge University
  Press.
Chaffee, John W. 1979. "Education and Examinations in Sung Society (960–1279)."
  Ph.D. dissertation, The University of Chicago.
Chang Chin-chien 張金鑑. 1977. *Chung-kuo wen-kuan chih-tu shih* 中國文官
  制度史 [A history of China's civil service system]. Taipei: Hua-kang.
Davis, Richard L. 1980. "The Shih Lineage at the Southern Sung Court." Ph.D.
  dissertation, Princeton University.
Ebrey, Patricia Buckley. 1978. *The Aristocratic Families of Early Imperial China: A
  Case Study of the Po-ling Ts'ui Family*. Cambridge: Cambridge University Press.
———. 1984. *Family and Property in Sung China: Yuan Ts'ai's Precepts for Social
  Life*. Princeton: Princeton University Press.
Franke, Herbert, ed. 1976. *Sung Biographies*. Wiesbaden: Steiner.
Freedman, Maurice. 1958. *Lineage Organization in Southeastern China*. London:
  Athlone Press.
Fried, Morton. 1970. "Clans and Lineages: How to Tell Them Apart and Why."
  Bulletin of the Institute of Ethnology, Academia Sinica 29.1:11–36.
Hartwell, Robert M. 1982. "Demographic, Political, and Social Transformations of
  China, 750–1550." *Harvard Journal of Asiatic Studies* 42:365–442.
Johnson, David. G. 1977a. "The Last Years of a Great Clan: The Li Family of Chao
  Chün in Late T'ang and Early Sung." *Harvard Journal of Asiatic Studies* 37.1:5–
  102.
———. 1977b. *The Medieval Chinese Oligarchy*. Boulder: Westview.
Kinugawa Tsuyoshi 衣川強. 1973. "Sōdai no meizoku: Kanan Roshi no baai"
  宋代の名族;河南呂氏の場合 [A famous house of the Sung dynasty: the case of
  the Lü house of Honan]. *Chūgoku kankei ronsetsu shiryō* 15.3a:37–53.
Kracke, E. A., Jr. 1953. *Civil Service in Early Sung China, 960–1067*. Cambridge,
  Mass.: Harvard University Press.
Twitchett, Denis. 1959. "The Fan Clan's Charitable Estate, 1050–1760." In *Confucianism in Action*, ed. David S. Nivison and Arthur F. Wright. Stanford: Stanford University Press.
Umehara Kaoru 梅原郁. 1980. "Sōdai no on'in seido" 宋代の恩蔭制度 [The Sung
  dynasty's system of favor and protection]. *Tōhō gakuhō* (Kyoto) 52:501–36.
Watson, James L. 1982. "Chinese Kinship Reconsidered: Anthropological Perspectives on Historical Research." *The China Quarterly* 92:589–622.
Yang Shu-fan 楊樹藩. 1976. *Chung-kuo wen-kuan chih-tu shih* 中國文官
  制度史 [A history of China's civil service system]. Taipei: San-min.

FOUR

Marriage, Descent Groups, and the Localist Strategy in Sung and Yuan Fu-chou

Robert P. Hymes

Marriage and descent have sometimes been seen as competing, even contradictory, principles in the organization of societies. The classic instance, surely, is the dispute in anthropology between "alliance theory" and "descent theory," which in their purest expressions have treated marriage or descent respectively as the fundamental principle around which the whole of a society constructs and defines itself (Schneider 1965). This radical form of the distinction has perhaps been largely superseded. Still, the notion that strong ties to affines and to agnates must in some sense be in conflict, that an emphasis on one must in part be at the expense of the other, retains common currency. J. L. Watson, in a review of recent work in Chinese history, has suggested that the transition from the T'ang dynasty (618–906) to the Sung (960–1278) appeared to encompass a shift "from alliance to descent" in Chinese kinship practices and conceptions (Watson 1982:617). It is surely true that commitment to affines may sometimes conflict with commitment to agnates. Social circumstances, momentary or persistent, may compel more or less permanent choices by individuals, groups, or perhaps even whole societies for one at the expense of the other. I will try here, however, to argue quite a different case: That in a crucial period of Chinese history— broadly, the Sung and Yuan dynasties—marriage ties and agnatic commitments among the elite shifted, not in complementary or reciprocal fashion, but in parallel directions; that similar changes in both can be explained as parts of a larger shift in elite strategies and self-conceptions. Marriage and descent, far from being in tension, were used in tandem by elite households to serve parallel ends.

That forms and strategies of kinship changed in the Sung is hardly a new idea. At least since the work of Denis Twitchett on the invention of the charitable estate by the Northern Sung statesman Fan Chung-yen (989–

1052), it has seemed clear that certain elements of later Chinese lineage organization have their roots in Sung (Twitchett 1959). There has been some tendency among scholars to go further and see "the" Chinese lineage, as reconstructed from nineteenth- and twentieth-century evidence by Maurice Freedman, as a Sung creation. Twitchett himself has recently cautioned against drawing this inference from his own work (Twitchett 1982:624–26). It will be clear from all the papers in this volume, I think, that "the" Chinese lineage is a notion of questionable value; and from this essay and others it should become clear too that to place Freedman's fully formed (and perhaps stereotyped) institution in the Sung is to go beyond the sources. Evidence on what in Chinese agnatic organization began in the Sung is discussed in Patricia Ebrey's chapter in this volume (chapter 2). What is of immediate concern for my purposes here are the strategic ends to which elite members put the new forms. Both Fan's charitable estate and the revival of genealogy writing by Su Hsun and Ou-yang Hsiu are, of course, phenomena of Northern Sung (960–1126), promoted by men of the national elite. In Ebrey's terms, these developments added to the repertoire available to those who wanted to organize their kinsmen, but they did not necessarily cause men to organize. Their timing, however, would seem at first to set them apart sharply from major changes that recent work has found in elite marriage: The new marriage patterns emerge not in Northern but in Southern Sung (1127–1278). I will argue, however, that a new concern on the part of educated men to form and strengthen ties to their locality—a concern whose expression in the agnatic sphere I call the "lineage orientation"—was at least as crucial an element in the development of lineages in China as the invention of the charitable estate. This orientation, like the new marriage patterns, became common in Southern, not Northern, Sung. Both are aspects of a single broader transformation of the elite.

This essay falls into three parts. In the first I review the recent work that has found a major reorientation of the elite between Northern and Southern Sung. In the second I present new findings from my own research in Yuan local history to show that Yuan marriage patterns are fundamentally continuous with those of Southern Sung. In the third, working again from the vantage of local history, I turn to agnatic strategies and the problem of descent groups (*tsu*) in Sung and Yuan.

The Sung Elite Transformation: Previous Research

Elite marriage patterns changed dramatically between Northern and Southern Sung. This conclusion has emerged from work done in the last ten years, quite independently and from different starting points, by two historians of China, one Japanese and one American: Ihara Hiroshi and Robert Hartwell. Their work and its implications are crucial to the focus of the present study.

Ihara's contribution to the problem developed through work on the marriages of late Northern and early Southern Sung office-holding families of Ming-chou, home of the Shih lineage discussed in Richard Davis's essay in this volume, and its neighbor Wu-chou (Ihara 1972 and 1974), and culminated in a general treatment of the "meaning of marriage" for Sung bureaucrats (Ihara 1976). Here Ihara noted that Northern Sung officials—especially high officials—seem to have married preferentially with others of similar rank regardless of place of origin, and to have used their marriages chiefly as a prop for their families' bureaucratic position and secondarily as a basis for factional alignment. This, he pointed out, contrasts sharply with the local or regional marriage pattern of Southern Sung officials of comparable rank, such as Shih Mi-yuan of Ming-chou or Wei Liao-weng of Ch'eng-tu-fu in Szechwan. This more locally focused pattern, he suggested, had even in Northern Sung been characteristic of low-ranking officials or of families who reached office for only a single generation; now it was adopted by the most successful and enduring families in the Southern Sung bureaucracy.

In the same study, and at greater length in a later article (Ihara 1977), Ihara drew attention to another change. The peculiar tendency of famous Sung officials such as Wang An-shih, Su Shih, and Ou-yang Hsiu—all men of Northern Sung—to move permanently from their original residences to new homes far away has been pointed out by more than one commentator. Ihara called attention to the quite different behavior of men like Shih Mi-yuan and Wei Liao-weng and their affines, who remained all their lives—and whose descendants stayed on after them—in their places of origin. This too, Ihara suggested, represented a general Northern/Southern Sung shift: The changes in marriage and in residence were somehow connected. This suggestion has been borne out abundantly in other research. Ihara's work as a whole is of great importance, and too little noticed in the West.

Hartwell's work on the marriage problem had its roots in different concerns—most generally in the problem of economic development in T'ang and Sung China, and more specifically in questions of central economic policy and decision-making in Sung, which led him into research on the nature of the Sung and post-Sung bureaucratic elite. For Hartwell the change in marriage is one aspect of a general transformation of the political elite, which in turn holds a pivotal place in a many-stranded process of demographic, economic, political, and social change reaching from the eighth to the sixteenth centuries (Hartwell 1982). Here I will outline only his findings on the political elite and its strategies, in which marriage held a central place; these findings derive from prosopographic study of several thousand central officials in the policy-making organs and the agencies of financial administration during Northern and Southern Sung.

For Hartwell, the crucial fact of Northern Sung political history, after the early decades in which power was concentrated in the hands of the personal staffs and longtime associates of the Sung founders, is the rise to dominance of a "professional elite" of office-holding families who specialized in government service for generations and shaped their family strategies accordingly. Such families eventually established main residences in the primary or auxiliary Sung capitals, often far from home, and from the start married preferentially among themselves without regard to place of origin. "Preferentially" does not mean exclusively: Standing alongside the professional elite, and throughout Northern Sung holding (in absolute terms) a higher proportion of policy-making and financial posts, was a much larger number of families whom Hartwell calls "local gentry" or simply "gentry." These families did not specialize in government service but pursued a more diversified, locally centered strategy, sending a son into office when possible but others into teaching, commerce, farming, perhaps military service, and so on. Gentry families married extensively with one another, generally—though not always—within a single locality; but families of the professional elite too formed periodic affinal connections with gentry families, especially with those in their own place of origin. For Hartwell such marriages are either a trade of "social prestige and political opportunity for economic advantage" (p. 417) or, especially in the middle and late eleventh century, a means by which professional elite members recruited new support and aid in factional conflict (p. 421).

The shift in marriage strategies that Ihara points out reflects, for Hartwell, the disappearance of the professional elite between late Northern and early Southern Sung—not primarily through physical extinction but through the abandonment of bureaucratic specialization in favor of the more diversified strategy of the gentry: in effect, through *absorption into* the gentry. (The Shihs of Ming-chou, despite their local marriages, seem to be an exception to the general trend, concentrating on an office-holding strategy through the Southern Sung.)[1] For this transformation Hartwell offers two

1. Two possible interpretations of their position are consistent with the general picture of the Southern Sung elite developed in Ihara's and Hartwell's work and, for Fu-chou, confirmed in my own. One of these would treat the Shihs as a thoroughgoing exception, a Southern Sung family pursuing in isolation the capital-focused strategy of the Northern Sung elite, and able to succeed at it through luck and/or strategic positioning. The other would absorb the Shihs into the Southern Sung strategy, but as a special case. Most families, one might argue, did not (and perhaps could not realistically) plan for continuous high office and for massive representation in the bureaucracy as they once had done. But if a son or two happened to reach the top, it made perfect sense, even in the localist strategy, to use as fully as possible the opportunities that high office brought with it. Offices were, after all, sources of income, and they added to the prestige of the descent group as a whole; wealth and prestige could be exploited locally as well as nationally. On this reading, the evidence that the Shihs were in fact ultimately concerned with local position is precisely their marriage pattern. These two interpretations are clearly in direct contradiction to one another, but both are consistent with the evidence on the Shihs as it stands. Perhaps only new data could decide between them. That the Shihs were in many respects *not* typical of their time is, I think, beyond question.

primary reasons: first, that the intense bureaucratic factionalism of late Northern Sung ultimately made long-term specialization in office an unreliable strategy, since one was almost certain to be "out" periodically and so unable to exploit hereditary privilege and bureaucratic connections to ensure the next generation's entry; second, that the increasing number of *chin-shih* degrees in late Northern and Southern Sung gradually made the locally-based strategy a reliable foundation for periodic—though not necessarily continuous—access to office.

My own study of the elite of Fu-chou in Chiang-hsi circuit (modern Kiangsi) during the Sung is in part an exploration, confirmation, and elaboration of Hartwell's findings *at the local level* (Hymes 1986). Fu-chou, a regular prefecture of the upper grade, comprised an area about the size of the island of Puerto Rico lying along the middle course of the Ju River in the eastern region of the P'o-yang Lake basin. Six counties fell under its jurisdiction at various times in Sung and Yuan: Lin-ch'uan, Ch'ung-jen, I-huang, Nan-feng, Chin-ch'i, and Lo-an. Its population, which grew from a few hundred thousand at the beginning of Sung to slightly over a million in Southern Sung and Yuan, was supported by a flourishing economy centered chiefly on the production, and export to other prefectures, of rice and rice products. Local industries in paper-making, bronze-casting, porcelain manufacture, and hemp and kudzu textiles were also of some importance, though a quantitative assessment is impossible. Fu-chou first became an important producer of officials in the Sung, when well over six hundred local men achieved the highest civil service degree, the *chin-shih*. Among these were such figures of national importance as Wang An-shih, Tseng Kung, and Lu Chiu-yuan. In population and in the successes of its sons, Fu-chou ranked among the leading thirty or so prefectures of the Sung empire. It is thus not strictly a "typical" case, but it is reasonably typical at least of the relatively advanced regions of the empire from which virtually all our knowledge of Sung China comes.

In my work on Fu-chou I focus not simply on office-holders and their kin but on a "local elite" identified by a broad range of criteria, all in some way involving privileged access to wealth, power, or prestige.[2] On two points my findings directly confirm Hartwell's (and Ihara's as well). First, marriage

---

2. Specifically, I count as a local elite member a man who does any of the following: (1) holds office; (2) passes the prefectural examination or another examination of the qualifying level; (3) contributes significantly to Fu-chou Buddhist or Taoist temples; (4) organizes or contributes to the founding or building of schools, academies, libraries, bridges, waterworks, or gardens; (5) organizes or leads local defense activities or local programs of charity or famine relief; (6) maintains ties, through friendship, master-student relations, or common membership in academic or poetic societies or cliques, to members of categories 1 through 5; (7) is affinal kinsman to members of categories 1 through 5. For detailed discussion of these categories, see Hymes 1986: Introduction.

outside Fu-chou or its surrounding region, common in Northern Sung, especially among the eight or so Fu-chou families most successful in office, virtually ceases in Southern Sung (Hymes 1986:chap. 3). Second, these same Northern Sung families share a striking tendency to move away from Fu-chou to the region of the capital (especially in the first half of the eleventh century) or (in the second half) to the economically focal Yangtze delta region. By the end of the Northern Sung most of the emigrant families have apparently severed all ties with Fu-chou, though some members return after the loss of North China. In Southern Sung not a single elite family can be shown to have left Fu-chou (Hymes 1986:chap. 3).

Other, seemingly parallel changes, not detectable in a study of national scope, emerge when one's focus is local. In Fu-chou, families of particular prominence in office distinguish themselves not only by marrying far from Fu-chou but also, within Fu-chou, by marrying with each other across county lines and physiographic boundaries. In Southern Sung even the most prominent local families do not intermarry unless their residences are fairly close together on the local scale. For two of the Northern Sung families, data are adequate to plot multiple residences and involvement in building projects (temples, gardens, studios, etc.) within Fu-chou. Both of these display a pattern that, like their marriages, extends well across county lines and covers a significant proportion of the prefecture. In Southern Sung the residences, edifices, and donations of elite families cluster—perhaps even more closely than their marriages—around a single local center. Finally, the inclusion of nonofficials makes it possible to say with fair confidence that, although in most spheres of elite social interaction the line between office-holder and "commoner" was of little discernible significance, the geographically extended marriage pattern was available *only to office-holders or their close patrilineal kin*. This is clear when one examines the marriages of certain men who had extensive nonmarital connections far from Fu-chou and nonofficial claims to national prominence: As far as the evidence will show, these men (and their kin) did not marry far from home (Hymes 1986: chap. 3).

All of these findings lend further support to an interpretation very much along Hartwell's lines: that the shift in marriage patterns reflects the replacement of a strategy centering almost exclusively on office and bureaucratic achievement—a strategy available in the first place only to families already represented in office, most easily and fully exploited by those with a considerable record of success, and thus never universally adopted by the elite even in Northern Sung—by one focusing on local position, in which periodic office for a son or two is only one of a number of important components. The reasons for this change itself were surely rather complex. As we have seen, Hartwell proposes two main causes: the effects of bitter factionalism on the chances for a continuous bureaucratic presence, and the increasing opportunities to convert local position into occasional office through the *chin-shih* system. I am certain that each of these played some part, but my own emphasis would be somewhat different. I suspect that the level of *chin-shih* quotas was already high enough by the middle of the eleventh century to make the localist strategy feasible; yet the other was not abandoned for another six or seven decades. One must consider, I think, not only the feasibility of the national strategy—which surely was reduced by factional struggles—but its inherent desirability as well. The value of central office to a family's interests in Southern Sung, perhaps, was simply much less than it had been in Northern Sung: The control of the central government over events and processes in the country at large, even in the region of the new capital, was greatly reduced; central office did not offer the sort of wide-ranging power that it once had offered (Hymes 1986: chap. 3).

The Fu-chou evidence suggests as well that, whatever the particular concatenation of causes that led to the shift in strategies, that shift was reflected, paralleled, reinforced, or in part provoked by separate changes in what one may broadly call the "cultural" or "ideological" sphere. First, the kinds of activities recorded in the biographies and other records of elite lives and in the literary remains of elite authors themselves in Northern and Southern Sung respectively seem to show that local elite intervention in government on behalf of purely local concerns and interests was newly respectable, even laudable, in Southern Sung.[3] Second, the sacrificial altars of figures of "local" importance erected and maintained by the state, which in Northern Sung seem devoted to the glorification of the state and its local agents, in Southern Sung come to celebrate the achievements of Fu-chou men themselves, most strikingly the purely *local* achievements of men with no connection to the state. Here then, in the ideal sphere, local commitments and contributions seem to have become, in Southern Sung, at least as highly valued as action in official capacities and on the national scale. The congruence of this more or less demonstrable shift in ideals with the—largely inferred—change in practical strategies is striking. Just what place each may hold in a proper explanation of the other is a question it would be premature to try to answer. That a shift from national and bureaucratic toward local and nonofficial concerns has its resonances in many aspects of Southern Sung elite life, however, seems undeniable. The drastic change in marriage is only this shift's most obvious practical expression.

It must be stressed again that much of the change in family strategies is an

3. Hymes 1986: chap. 4. Here I show that records of such elite intervention—as represented for example by Lu Chiu-yuan's numerous surviving letters to county, prefectural, and circuit officials on behalf of local interests—are almost wholly confined to Southern Sung. I argue that this more probably reflects changes in the principles of selection of material for inclusion in collected works or discussion in biographies than quite so drastic changes in elite behavior itself; hence that it is evidence of cultural or ideological change.

inference: a theoretical creation that makes a whole cluster of observed changes intelligible. We have very little direct testimony from Sung men on the reasons for their marriage choices, and none at all (so far as I know) on the particular aspect of marriage—its geographical range—at issue here. Nor are any of the other changes mentioned so far directly commented on in Sung sources. One useful practical test of an explanation of this kind is the extent to which later developments in the same sphere are intelligible or explicable in the same terms. For instance: Does the notion, applied here to Sung, that marriage patterns are controlled by broader strategies of status and social position, and that the relative importance of office-holding in such strategies is crucial, help us at all in dealing with later changes in elite marriage? I move in the section that follows to examine in this light my own more recent findings from Fu-chou under the Yuan.

Marriage in Yuan Fu-chou

The data on local elite marriage in Fu-chou under Yuan, though not all that one might wish, are on the whole not inferior to those of Southern Sung. Overall, considerably fewer marriages are recorded for Yuan; but the proportion for which the residences of both parties can be identified is actually higher. Enough remains from each period to make a comparison possible and useful.

Table 4.1 displays the Fu-chou elite marriages of Northern Sung, Southern Sung, and Yuan for which the county of origin of both partners is known.[4] One fact is immediately clear: The national marriage network that had flourished in Northern Sung but vanished after the Chin conquest did not reemerge under Yuan. Among the Fu-chou elite only one Yuan marriage is recorded in which one partner lived farther away than the nearest counties of immediately neighboring prefectures. This is hardly surprising. The basis of the Northern Sung network had been office-holding and a strategy of bureaucratic advancement; the Yuan discriminated so vigorously against Chinese in office that to rise to any height was very difficult, and outside of academic service (for Southern Chinese at least) almost impossible. One can imagine other hypothetical bases for a national marriage network under the Yuan (ethnic cooperation among local leading groups in the face of Mongol administration, for example); but on the Fu-chou evidence, at least, these did not emerge.

The table, which measures residence fairly roughly, suggests that Fu-

---

4. For the sake of simplicity of presentation I exclude from the Southern Sung marriages tabulated here those involving Fu-chou elite members whose families or immediate ancestors had recently migrated from other prefectures. On the anomalous character of these marriages see Hymes 1986:chap. 3.

TABLE 4.1
Residences of Partners in Fu-chou Marriages

	Northern Sung		Southern Sung		Yuan	
(A) Same county	22	30.6%	60	65.9%	57	60.6%
(B) Adjacent county: same prefecture	11	15.3%	14	15.4%	15	16%
(C) Adjacent county: different prefecture	2	2.8%	11	12.1%	14	14.9%
(D) Non-adjacent county: same prefecture	4	5.6%	0	0%	4	4.3%
(E) Non-adjacent county: adjacent prefecture	2	2.8%	1	1.1%	1	1.1%
(F) Non-adjacent prefecture	31	43%	3	3.3%	0	0%
(Same circuit)	(0)	(0%)	(1)	(1.1%)		
(Adjacent circuit)	(6)	(8.3%)	(2)	(2.2%)		
(Non-adjacent circuit)	(25)	(34.7%)	(0)	(0%)		
Total	72	100%	89	100%	91	100%

chou marriage patterns hardly changed between Southern Sung and Yuan. Apart from three Southern Sung marriages to partners from prefectures not bordering Fu-chou—perhaps at most a vestigial survival of Northern Sung patterns—only one difference strikes the eye: four Yuan marriages, matched against none in Southern Sung, joining partners from nonadjacent counties within Fu-chou. The difference is, at this level of measurement, not statistically significant. It is, however, a clue to a significant change that emerges when the data are treated in a more refined way. For about 40 percent of the Southern Sung and Yuan marriages in table 4.1, it is possible to map precisely the residences of both partners. (Limitations in my sources confine these marriages within the borders of Fu-chou.) Maps 4.1 and 4.2 show the patterns that then emerge. The Southern Sung pattern is clearly localized in a fairly drastic way. Only six of the thirty-three marriages join partners in different counties; in five of these, one partner's home lies just across the county border. (On the exception, marked A, more below.) Local elite families of special prominence—the Lus of Chin-ch'i county, the Lis of Ch'ung-jen county, the T'us of I-huang county—are not connected by marriage, as they would probably have been in Northern Sung, but find their sons- and

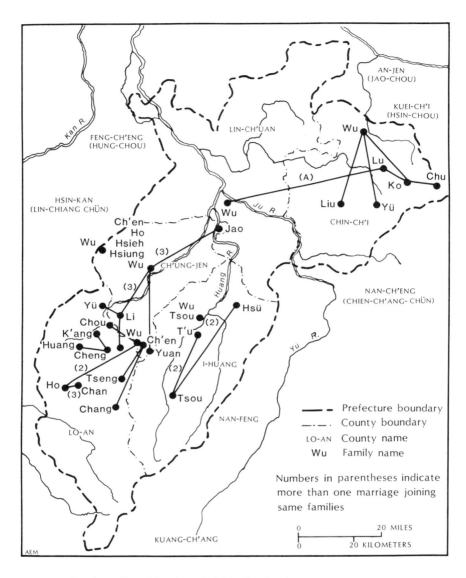

MAP 4.1   Southern Sung Marriages (within Fu-chou)
Numbers in parentheses indicate more than one marriage joining same families.

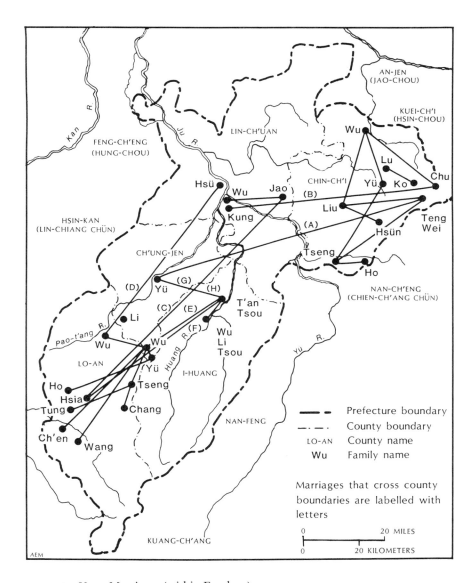

MAP 4.2   Yuan Marriages (within Fu-chou)

daughters-in-law well within their own county or their own physiographic micro-region. Marriages that cross both a county line and a clear physio-graphic boundary—as for instance a major local watershed—are particularly unusual. Only the marriage marked A clearly qualifies here; and this, it seems, is a rather special case. We learn from a funerary inscription that the Wus of Lin-ch'uan county (who provided a wife for Lu Chiu-yuan of Chin-ch'i), on first settling in Lin-ch'uan, had bought land in Chin-ch'i. This reference to the location of property in a funerary inscription is so unusual that it seems likely that the author saw the pattern—home in one county, fields in another—as, in Fu-chou at least, anomalous. The Wus may thus have been neighbors of the Lus in property though not in residence; and even if they were not, an anomalous landowning pattern makes an anoma-lous marriage less surprising. The Wus, then, have all the earmarks of an exception. Exclude them, and the Southern Sung pattern collapses into a disconnected assemblage of local marriage clusters.

Similar clusters appear in map 4.2, for Yuan: Consider Chin-ch'i county and Lo-an county in particular. But these are overlain by a significant few marriages that span much longer distances or seem wholly to disregard counties and physiographic divisions. Seven of the thirty-four—as com-pared to one of thirty-three in Southern Sung (marriage A again)—cross both a county line and an important local physiographic boundary. For sam-ples of the given sizes, this difference in proportions can be expected by chance only about thirteen times out of a thousand: It is, in other words, statistically significant to a reasonably high degree.[5] The data, then, despite their small numbers, suggest a change, and perhaps a change of some impor-tance. To place this beyond doubt would require confirming evidence from other prefectures; for the moment, I will treat the change as given and seek an explanation.

One cannot explain change, surely, except by change. If the Fu-chou

---

5. To be precise, the difference of proportions has a level of significance of between .0132 and .0135. Another way to test the significance of the difference between the Southern Sung and Yuan data is to measure actual distances between marriage partners' residences and compare the respective means. This method is, I think, less satisfactory, since physical, as-the-crow-flies distance seems a less adequate measure of *social* distance than the presence or absence of signi-ficant political or physiographic (hence probably economic) boundaries between the two resi-dences. I have, however, performed a difference-of-means test for the mean distance for South-ern Sung and Yuan respectively. For the Southern Sung marriages, the mean distance is 17.503 kilometers; for Yuan it is 29.104 kilometers. This difference is significant at a level of roughly .02—less impressive than by the other method, but still representing only a 2 percent likelihood that a disparity of such magnitude could be the result simply of chance. The difference in mean distance is virtually entirely accounted for by the seven marriages singled out in the difference-of-proportions test: without these seven the mean distance in Yuan becomes 18.809 kilometers. For the difference-of-means and difference-of-proportions tests used here I follow Blalock 1972:219–39.

elite, or some part of it, married differently in Yuan than in Southern Sung, what had changed to make it do so? Some things had changed very little: The local elite itself, for example, had weathered the transition rather impressively (Hymes 1981). Of the sixty-eight marriage partners represented in map 4.2, sixty were descended from men already prominent in the Southern Sung elite; several others represented not new Yuan families but Sung elite migrants from other parts of China. The local militia organization that first resisted the Mongols, then went over to their side, and in the 1350s, with the Yuan collapsing, took up arms again to maintain local "order," did all of this under the leadership of the same family—the Tengs of Chin-ch'i county—that had commanded it against the Chin in 1126 and against marauding bandits in 1230. A great many temples, academies, schools—much of the semi-public framework of elite life—survived the conquest unaltered.

What, then, had changed? Primarily, of course, the relationship of the local elite to the state. Here two aspects are particularly obvious and, I think, particularly crucial. First, the local representatives of the state in Fu-chou were no longer Chinese but Mongols and Central Asians, men who—especially in the early years of Yuan—had little knowledge of South China and few if any personal ties to the Fu-chou elite. Second, from the conquest to 1315 no Sung-style system of civil examinations channeled local elite men constantly into office. Even after the exams were restored, the number of degrees was so small that their effect was slight. Insofar as the Fu-chou local elite hoped to cooperate with the new state or to preserve the way of life and the place in society that had belonged to it in Sung, the problem of routes to office was critical. These changes and these issues, I think, offer the basis of an explanation of the new Yuan marriage pattern; but the explanation I propose rests on a picture of Yuan recruitment and household classification that requires some elaboration here.

In a recent article Hsiao Ch'i-ch'ing has made what seems to me the most important contribution thus far to an understanding of the institutional position of the Chinese elite in the Yuan state (Hsiao 1978).[6] Hsiao is as far as I know the first to explore adequately the Yuan institution of the *ju-hu* or "Confucian household." This was only one of a number of special occupational and religious census classes introduced under Yuan; oddly enough, it was in the "religious" category that the *ju-hu* fell. The Mongols, as is well known, took a tolerant and even eclectic approach to the religions they encountered in their conquests, and from early on undertook to identify religious specialists in subject populations and extend to them the fiscal privileges enjoyed by their own shamans. In North China special status

---

6. The treatment of *ju-hu* and of routes to office in Yuan that follows relies heavily on Hsiao's article. I have, however, checked his findings against the major sources he has used. The most important documents are to be found in MHTL *ch*. 1, 2, 3, 4, and 6, passim.

had been granted both to Taoist priests and to Buddhist monks by the 1230s. Under Ögödei, "Confucians" acquired the same status for the first time: In 1238 the state organized special examinations for Buddhist and Taoist clergy and for self-declared Confucian scholars as a basis for their assignment to special registers and certification for privileges. Some four thousand North Chinese were reclassified as members of *ju-hu* as a result of this exam: not an unimpressive number but, as Hsiao points out, surely only a rather small proportion of the North Chinese with a background of classical education and Chin official service or degreeholding. Several reexaminations of households or reinvestigations of registers followed in the next few decades. The last, in 1276, reduced the number of *ju-hu* by two hundred or so. After this, Hsiao believes, the numbers in the North remained more or less unchanged.

In the South the new classification was applied virtually from the moment of the conquest. The first southern Confucian registers were established in 1277, not by examination but on the basis of reports by village officers and other locals. In theory the status belonged to any who had been degreeholders, prefectural graduates, "great scholars," officials, or "*shih-ta-fu*" under Sung. Thus in the South from the outset the new system acted to preserve and reinforce established status of certain kinds from the previous dynasty. The earliest registers, however, were not at once stabilized: Local school officials were expected to make adjustments and additions as necessary. In 1290 and 1291 extensive discussions at court dealt with the problem of the southern Confucian registers and how their membership should be determined; it was finally decided that the self-reports made in the census of 1290 should be the basis. With this, it seems, the southern registers were fixed: Families excluded as of 1290, whatever their true background, were excluded forever. Hsiao estimates that nearly fourteen thousand households may have qualified.

Of the privileges of *ju-hu* status, two were chief: The *ju-jen* himself—the man by whose talents or position the household qualified as *ju-hu*—was entitled to a permanent stipend, which however varied by locality and was influenced by need; and the lands of the household as a whole were exempted from consideration and valuation in the assessment of virtually all service duties. Apart from this, the members of *ju-hu* were entitled, in sharp contrast to the population at large, to ride horses; and their horses were until 1328 never included in the periodic appropriations of private livestock for military purposes. To maintain these privileges through the generations a household, once classified as *ju-hu*, had only to keep one member in attendance at an official local school. Even this requirement was waived for households with a school of their own or whose elder members instructed the younger, or for households without a son to spare from the duties of earning a living and helping run the household.

The Yuan, then, granted to *ju-hu* automatically many of the privileges granted in Sung only to the households of current or recently deceased officials or of prefectural exam graduates. Yuan was unique among the dynasties of the last thousand years in making the right to such privileges a matter of ascription, not achievement—in making a permanently privileged caste of the households of Sung office-holders, degree-holders, and the like (or of those who somehow managed to find a place on the special registers). At the same time, however, the Yuan did not exclude sons of other families from attending school or, most important, from serving in office: Here the *ju-hu* had, at least in principle, no special advantage. Entry into office was thus a separate problem for *ju-hu* and others alike. Hsiao explores this problem as well.

Two main routes to office were regularly available to Chinese local elites in Yuan. One was appointment as clerk (*pu-li*) in central organs via "yearly send-up" (*sui-kung*): Each year a prefecture was expected to forward the names of one or two men, either currently serving as local clerks or registered *ju-jen* (members of a *ju-hu* or students at an official school), for appointment to central clerical posts. The men sent up were to be selected by examination, partly in classics and history, partly in clerical skills. From a central clerk's post a man might with time advance into regular ranked office. The second route was entry through a post in an official prefectural or county school. Here Sung *chin-shih* were to be given first access; other candidates, again, were to be tested locally in classics and poetry before being recommended by their prefectures for appointment. Then they might begin as recorder or corrector of an official school, move up in the school ranks gradually, and ultimately reach a regular, ranked appointment with broader responsibilities. In Fu-chou this seems the preferred route to office: Only one or two men are recorded to have entered through clerkships, while a great many are known to have begun (and often ended) in school posts.

It seems clear that the "testing" to which local candidates were subject before being sent up for central clerkships or recommended for school posts resembled very little the old Sung prefectural examination. Such testing finds no mention whatever in the extensive Yuan sources on the Fu-chou elite— no funerary inscription, for example, points with pride to its subject's excellent performance in a local examination; and no source that Hsiao uses suggests a process even nearly so regular, public, and extensive in scope as the Sung exam. Indeed Hsiao cites one contemporary complaint that those sent up for clerkships had not as a rule undergone examination at all (1978:176). In effect, I would suggest, the system of send-up for clerkships and of recommendation for school posts functioned as a form of direct and essentially unconditioned recommendation by local officials, especially the preceptor of the prefectural school and the prefectural administrator. For about the first two decades of Yuan, both of these men would have been Northerners and more often than not non-Chinese. Later, Southerners and even men from Chiang-hsi itself began to move in significant numbers into the school posts of Fu-chou and neighboring prefectures; but these were still nonnatives and subject to the supervision of the prefectual administrator, whose post remained the province of Mongols, Central Asians, and North Chinese throughout the dynasty.

How, under these circumstances, could local officials choose reliable and promising Fu-chou men for recommendation? Perhaps at least in part by relying on the advice and suggestions of other Fu-chou men who had already, by various means, formed strong connections with the Yuan state and its agents. In an earlier study of Yuan Fu-chou I have discussed what seems to have been the crucial role of several local men who in the first decade or so of Mongol rule—a good deal earlier than most of their neighbors—acquired Yuan office or were drawn into close association with the new state (Hymes 1981:1–4, 8–12). Two of these were leaders of local military forces under Sung, who seem to have gained their new positions chiefly by quickness on their feet. One, Teng Hsi-yen, took over the leadership of the old Teng militia of Chin-ch'i county as it was defending the Fu-chou prefectural city against the Mongols in 1273 and, after a brief silence in the sources, is found a few years later holding Yuan military office and leading his forces on the new government's behalf; later he moves into regular office (TCCC 22a:1a–5a; WWC 79:10a–11b; HSCC 2:3b). The other, Hsia Hsiung, the last of a family line of minor military officers who command a fort in Lo-an county under the Sung, turns up in early Yuan as general commander of the same county's official troops and one of the richest men in Fu-chou (WWC 75:6b–8a; 74:8b–10b; 47:7b–8a).

Two other men come to special prominence in early Yuan in quite a different way: Tseng Ch'ung-tzu of Chin-ch'i and Wu Ch'eng of Ch'ung-jen were recruited in 1287 by the court official Ch'eng Chü-fu on a trip south to gather "neglected" talent for the dynasty. Tseng accepted office; Wu did not, but traveled north with Ch'eng, visited the new capital, and afterward maintained close personal ties to Ch'eng and several other major Yuan officials for years before he finally accepted office in 1323. Both Tseng and Wu had preconquest connections to Ch'eng Chü-fu through a local academy in Fu-chou at which Wu and Ch'eng had studied in their youth (Hymes 1981:1–4). A fifth Fu-chou man gained his position in early Yuan by means now unclear: This was Wu K'o-sun of Chin-ch'i, who had been a Sung *chin-shih* in 1274 but took Yuan office as a school preceptor some time before 1280 (CHLWC 16:12a–13b). Wu's family too had connections to Ch'eng Chü-fu dating back to his years at the academy in Sung; but his early access to office may reflect some role he or his kinsmen played in the crossover militia along with the Tengs: They had done so earlier in Southern Sung.

What makes these men so important is not simply their early involvement with the Yuan state, but a separate and remarkable phenomenon in the later sources for Fu-chou: If one looks at the men who reach office under Yuan from about 1290 on, one almost always finds earlier personal connections, often predating Yuan, to Wu Ch'eng, to Tseng Ch'ung-tzu, to the Tengs and their militia, to Hsia Hsiung and his immediate personal network, or to the family of Wu K'o-sun. Two especially good examples, but only two among many, are Yü Chi and Wei Su, the most famous and, in office, the most successful Fu-chou men of middle and late Yuan. Both had been Wu Ch'eng's students. Yü Chi was indirectly connected to Hsia Hsiung by marriage; Wei Su's family had Sung connections, both affinal and scholarly, to Tseng Ch'ung-tzu, and Yuan affinal connections to the Tengs (Hymes 1981:11).

Men like Wu Ch'eng, the Tengs, Hsia Hsiung, and Tseng Ch'ung-tzu, I would suggest, were because of their close and early association with the Yuan state precisely those on whom local officials unfamiliar with Fu-chou were most likely to rely in choosing local men for recommendation to office. The evidence on the abundant social connections of later office-holders to just these men suggests that their role as, in effect, brokers between local elite and officialdom was not merely potential, but actual. In their turn men like Yü Chi and Wei Su, whose success in office gave them strong ties of their own to the state and its representatives, would later come to play the same role. It is here, I think, that one finds the basis for the long-distance and cross-county marriages of Yuan. Men or families in a position to play the broker's role might reasonably hope to firm up their influence over routes of access to office by forming alliances among themselves; others, not in the same position, might seek connections, direct or indirect, to those who were and so help their own chances for recommendation. This would be a particularly useful strategy for those whose own prospects were in other respects weak or for those seeking to "rise." Here a second look at the new-style marriages in Map 4.2 proves enlightening. One of these (marked A) connected the kin of two potential brokers, Yü Chi and Wei Su. Another (B) joined a family of relatively minor Sung official pedigree and with no apparent advantages of its own in Yuan (the Kungs) to one whose personal and affinal connections to both the Tengs and the Wus dated back into Sung (the Chus). The family of Jao Meng-chih again had little or no Sung pedigree and no known early Yuan connections: Marriage C joined them to the family of potential broker Hsia Hsiung. The Hsus of Lin-ch'uan county were another newcomer family in Yuan, unrecorded in the Sung local elite; we are told that Hsu Ching-jui's father had grown wealthy through commerce. Ching-jui's marriage to the sister of Wu Ti (D) brought his family into alliance with men who in turn had affinal connections to Wu Ch'eng. The T'ans of I-huang county were very prominent in the local scheme of things but seem to have been resisters (or at least withdrawers) at the start of Yuan and so presumably began with certain disadvantages in the hunt for offices. Their four recorded long-distance or intercounty marriages in Yuan joined them (E) to Wu Ch'eng (through his granddaughter), (F) to Hsia Hsiung (through his daughter), and (G, H) to Yü Chi (through his father and his daughter). The marriage to Hsia Hsiung's daughter was in fact uxorilocal, which further suggests the dependent position of the T'ans here. Marriages like these, perhaps, cleansed the T'ans of associations with their earlier loyalist role in the eyes of Yuan local officials. In all but the Wei/Yü marriage, then, a family of shaky position or of relatively new prominence formed connections with one especially well situated in relation to the Yuan state.

The marriages recorded here took place, for the most part, in middle or late Yuan; still, the broader pattern may have had its origin much earlier. Here one is reduced to speculation. Local officials may have faced much the same problem in drawing up registers of *ju-hu* that they would later face in recommending locals for office. *Ju-hu* status depended on Sung achievement or on descent from Sung achievers; how was the Mongol or North Chinese who sat in the administrator's seat to know who had really done what in Sung, who was descended from whom? In theory the system rested on self-reporting, but this, unchecked, might have yielded a population of nothing but *ju-hu*. Some form of confirmation must have been required, if only to limit the numbers of privileged households. Did Teng Hsi-yen, Hsia Hsiung, and the like play some role here? There is no direct evidence, but remarkably we know that the very creation of the Fu-chou *ju-hu* registers was owing to the efforts of a man from one of the "potential broker" families. This was Wu K'o, kinsman to Wu K'o-sun. Early in Yuan he complained that the edicts on *ju-hu* registration were being ignored, and evidently gained the attention of local officials (TCTH 13c:11b–12a; see also SAC 23:18a–21b). From prompting the creation of registers to influencing their content does not seem too large or too implausible a step. The consolidation of the registers took fifteen years; if certain local men or families exerted especial influence over the process, they may very soon have become attractive affines for those not as close to the new state.

In all this, one point is crucial: The new pattern was not the overthrow of the older localist strategy, but its preservation—in changed circumstances to be sure—and confirmation. Occasional access to office, after all, had been one of the essential elements of the localist strategy in Southern Sung, precisely because office, with its prestige, its fiscal and legal privileges, and its income, could be an important factor in a family's local position. In Southern Sung—as probably already in Northern Sung—periodic access to low-ranking office could nearly be guaranteed, certainly made likely, by concentration on the exam system. This meant educating sons, which in turn required a firm economic base and strong connections to the local elite. In

Yuan, with the examinations discarded in favor of a system that amounted to direct recommendation, to pursue the same strategy required connections, not simply to the broader elite around one, but to specific men in a position to influence recommendation at the prefectural level. One way to form such connections—though by no means the only way—was through marriage; and marriage planned on this basis would, inevitably, sometimes disregard local geography. But nothing in the Yuan pattern suggests that Fu-chou families once again, as in Northern Sung, aimed more at national than at local position, planned for bureaucratic success above all. All other evidence—in temple-building, in local defense, in famine relief, in schools and academies—suggests instead that the Yuan local elite worked, as in Southern Sung, primarily to strengthen its *local* position and, at times, to serve the wider interest of its neighborhood, its locality, or its county. New institutional surroundings demanded new tactics; but broad strategies were unchanged.

Paradoxically, then, I see in the partly new Yuan marriage pattern a symptom, not of broader change, but of fundamental stability. In the Northern Sung/Southern Sung shift that Ihara and Hartwell were the first to identify, we must expand the second term to include the Yuan.

The Localist Strategy and the "Lineage Orientation"

It is hard to survey the new localist strategy in Southern Sung, and its continuation with adjustments in Yuan, without thinking of lineage organization. Consider the head of an ideal-typical Southern Sung elite household, a man (sometimes a woman) whose energies were focused on the maintenance and improvement of his (or her) family's local position, who was involved, perhaps, in the defense and welfare of the surrounding neighborhood and county, and who cultivated marriage ties within the local elite, in part to create or expand a sort of pool of potential allies in these same involvements and projects. It is easy to imagine the same man or woman striving to build up strong agnatic ties as well—to develop another pool of potential local allies, supporters, or clients, this one among patrilineal kin—and so working to found or strengthen an organized, corporate lineage, centered on a common geographic base, as one element of a firm local foundation. Easy to imagine; but imagination must not run too far. Evidence in Southern Sung and even Yuan for prime elements of the corporate lineage, as we know it in, say, Freedman's nineteenth-century Kwangtung and Fukien—in particular for the lineage ancestral hall and the common charitable estate or ancestral trust—is, in Fu-chou at least, extremely rare. Patricia Ebrey's historical overview, in tracing the appearance between the eleventh and fourteenth centuries of a number of the institutions and practices commonly associated with later corporate lineages, suggests that the elements of

Freedman's model were not available as a complete or nearly complete assemblage much before 1350. There is certainly no evidence of lineages with all these features in Fu-chou in Sung or Yuan.

Corporateness, of course, is a matter of degree: To exclude Freedman's full-blown model is not to exclude, at least as a possibility, lineage-like descent groups in some less (or differently) developed form. But the state of the sources, again, makes it impossible to judge in any general sort of way just how corporate Fu-chou's agnatic groupings may have been in Sung or Yuan, or whether all were similar. Thus I cannot say how far or in what spheres the descent groups I will be treating here acted together as units; whether they regularly worshiped together or shared property. The same would be true for nearly all parts of Sung and Yuan China: The questions can sometimes be answered for single groups, but rarely if ever for whole localities. Corporateness, in all its possible meanings, would be a plausible goal for the localist strategy. But to what extent it was achieved, or indeed how far it was pursued, must remain a matter for speculation. Because of these problems, the argument I will make here must be more limited. I argue as follows: that the elite household strategists of Southern Sung and Yuan who cultivated marriage connections as a foundation for local position treated agnatic kin in a similar way, by working to strengthen connections (or potential connections) with a relatively broad but distinctly *local* circle of patrilineal kin; and that a prime means to this end was the promotion of common identity through the creation, definition, and celebration, at least in theory, of a group they called the *tsu* (which I gloss below as "descent group"). A fundamental aspect of *tsu* identity in this strategy was the association of its members, through a common founding ancestor, with a specific place below the county level (the common *tsu* "residence," in principle and often in fact the place at or near which most members still made their homes); membership in a local *tsu* became an increasingly important and defining aspect of elite identity during Southern Sung and Yuan. This way of defining both descent groups and elite identity—like other aspects of the localist strategy—represented a departure, for the most part, from the practices and notions of Northern Sung. The strategy, and the ideas of identity and membership it embodied, I will call the "lineage orientation." To what degree the formal lineage was or became a real group, a functioning organization, again is a question that has no discoverable general answer; undoubtedly the answer varied from case to case. Since the issue here is primarily one of strategies, it is enough for my purposes if elite household heads *believed* that proclaiming the idea of common identity, promoting knowledge of a relationship, defining people as a group (and perhaps, in many cases, embodying it in some common ritual) would itself create or strengthen real, practical ties. This notion was of course virtually a commonplace of Chinese thinking about identity and human relations since long before the Sung.

Even in this more limited form, the argument must confront two difficulties. First, as we have already seen, the Northern Sung inventor of the charitable estate (Fan Chung-yen) and recreators of the written genealogy (preeminently Su Hsun and Ou-yang Hsiu) were, in Hartwell's terms, clearly men of the "professional elite": men who married nationally, who (with their descendants) served in office across two generations or more, and who (in the cases of the Ou-yangs and the Sus) moved far away from their original homes. Surely the cultural forms they created had, at the outset, little to do with any "localist" strategy. Second, in the sources for Fu-chou and, I believe, for much of the rest of China, groups called *tsu* most clearly emerge as a focus of elite concern not in Sung but in Yuan. In what follows, I will try to address these two problems: The thesis they seem to contradict is, I think, essentially sound.

To deal with the second problem first: Perhaps the prime written evidence one might hope to find for a *tsu* as a group with common identity is a genealogy. It is well known that hardly any Chinese genealogies survive from before the Ming dynasty; but we do have two hundred or so *prefaces* (or postfaces) to genealogies, preserved in Sung and Yuan collected works. Of these, as Morita Kenji has recently shown, the overwhelming majority—all but nineteen—date from Yuan (Morita 1979:27–53). This is all the more surprising as our source base—the number of collected works that have survived—is considerably larger for Sung than for Yuan. The imbalance is just as clear in the Fu-chou sources: Here four genealogy prefaces survive in whole or in part from Sung (one from Northern, three from Southern Sung), twenty-eight from Yuan. To judge from this evidence alone, there was an unprecedented flowering of genealogy-writing (and so presumably of the "lineage orientation") in the Yuan.

Very much the same impression emerges from the most important Sung and Yuan genre of biographical writing: the funerary inscription. In Yuan Fu-chou this fairly bristles with references to *tsu*.[7] According to the inscrip-

---

7. The word *tsu* in funerary inscriptions and elsewhere must of course be approached with some caution, as the term could have many referents (see chapter 1). The compound *tsu-jen*, for instance, when context indicates it is used in the singular, will often mean little more than "agnate beyond the household and apart from immediate collaterals" (since a closer collateral will usually be called by a specific kin term), and as a plural may refer to the whole set of agnatic kin taken together, with no implication of any—even theoretical or ideal—group of which the agnates are members. The same can be true of *tsu* itself. But in certain other usages, *tsu* refers to agnates taken as a group with common or corporate identity. This is clearest when some trait is attributed to the *tsu* as a unit: *wang-tsu* "a prominent *tsu*," *ta-tsu* "a great or large *tsu*," *kuan-tsu* "an office-holding *tsu*," *shih-tsu* "a gentlemanly *tsu*." To translate *tsu* simply as "agnates" here would generally miss the sense of the term. The traits are not necessarily ascribed distributively to each "agnate," but to the unit of which each is a part. Thus a *kuan-tsu* is a *tsu* that has or has had *kuan*, office-holders; not every member need be a *kuan*. (Indeed if this were required the term would be virtually unusable in Southern Sung: One would search almost in vain for an

tion of a woman of Chin-ch'i county, surnamed Ko, who died in 1317 at the age of eighty-one, "The Ko are a prominent *tsu* of Chin-ch'i.... A daughter married into the Chu of the same district. The Chu too are a prominent *tsu*" (WWC 79:8b). In the inscription of Yü Tou-hsiang (1234–1312) of Chin-ch'i we read: "Where his *tsu* was gathered was called Ta-yuan; ... his mother was the lady Chang, of the prominent *tsu* at Tsung-ch'i" (WWC 74:5b, 6b–7a). And the inscription of Tseng Yeh of Lo-an county tells us:

> The area west of Hua-kai Mountain first belonged to Yung-feng [county] in Chi-chou, then to Lo-an [county] in Fu-chou. The canton is called Yun-kai, the township Wang-hsien ["looking out for immortals"], named for the mountain and its immortals. Wang-hsien's land is very broad and flat, ringed in by mountains and streams. Since long ago those who dwell here have often been prominent and prosperous. The Tseng are the leading *tsu*. (WWC 78:6a–b)

In the last two inscriptions the stress on *location*, on a particular place with which the group is associated, is especially striking. This is in fact typical of Yuan inscriptions. Commonly one finds an account of the moves and divisions of founders and branches. Wu Ch'eng wrote of Wu En: "As to the Wu of Wu Pond in Chin-ch'i, those who live at Tung-ch'i or at Hsin-t'ien are branches that have split off. The son of the An-yuan magistrate Wei-hsin, named Ch'u-li, split off again from Tung-ch'i to live at Kuei-t'ien" (WWC 81:8a–8b. Cf. CHLWC 16:12b–13a). The places mentioned here—Wu Pond, Hsin-t'ien, etc.—can still be found on modern topographic maps; they lie very close together in what was then Chin-ch'i's northeastern corner. The passages remind one inevitably of a higher-order lineage settlement and branch residences of a kind familiar from more recent dynasties (see Freedman 1966:21–25; J. Watson 1982:608–9). Along the same lines is Yü Chi's account of the (unrelated) Yü of Ch'ung-jen county: "South of the mountain there is a stream called Chu-ch'i. The Yü *tsu* has lived there for generations. I do not know in what period they began; there have never been other *tsu* among them" (TYHKL 38:12a).

---

extended set of male agnates all of whom were officeholders.) A *ta-tsu* is not simply a number of "great agnates," whatever those might be; and the word *wang* as an attributive is, I believe, virtually never used of individuals, but only of groups (or, to be absolutely precise, of sets of people who are being *spoken of as* groups, and who may also *be* groups). The case seems to me much the same when the word *tsu* appears in connection with a specific place of residence, spoken of as common to the *tsu*; in many cases the place name applies to a fairly small geographic unit, and one knows or may presume that some of the households covered by the term *tsu* must actually live at a certain distance from it; it is the focal point of an assemblage that the sources are treating as a *unit*. It is these usages of *tsu* that I translate as "descent group" throughout this section. Here *tsu* is being used *as if* it named a corporate group, whatever the practical facts of the matter; and one may say at least that the members share, or are being said or encouraged to share, a corporate identity.

Such attention to *tsu* is rare in the funerary inscriptions of Sung. These do, as in Yuan, customarily touch on their subjects' ancestry or family background but rarely do much more than list the three ascending ancestors in the direct line. If the first migrant ancestor—the first to come to Fu-chou, or to the specific place the subject now lives at—is mentioned, we are told when he arrived, but rarely if ever precisely where he settled; the crucial sense of *place* that in Yuan inscriptions (as in later dynasties) goes hand in hand with descent group identity is little present, if at all.[8] Yuan inscriptions make it their business to locate their subjects precisely both in space and—what often amounts to the same thing—within a community of elite descent groups; Sung inscriptions, for the most part, do not.

Are we to conclude that the *tsu*, even as idea, as corporate identity, was a rarity in Sung—even in localist Southern Sung—and blossomed suddenly in Yuan? Perhaps; but other interpretations need to be explored. One of these emerges, again, from the work of Morita Kenji. The genealogy prefaces of Yuan differ from those of Sung not only in number, but in character as well. A Sung genealogy preface almost always introduces the genealogy of its author: Like the genealogy itself it is an internal product of the group. (This is true of three of the four Fu-chou prefaces from Sung.) Yuan prefaces are overwhelmingly the work of outsiders. Certain famous men in Yuan virtually mass-produced prefaces for the genealogies of friends, neighbors, and bare acquaintances. This is perhaps clearest of all in Fu-chou. Here the twenty-eight Yuan genealogy prefaces come to us from just four men: Five are by Wei Su, three each by Yü Chi and Liu Hsun, and seventeen by Wu Ch'eng. To Morita this phenomenon, along with a new tendency in Yuan (judging by the prefaces themselves) for genealogies to be printed—not merely held in manuscript—suggests that genealogy-writing had become a more public enterprise, "no longer a thing of the inner circle" (Morita 1979:40–41).

It seems clear that this shift in preface-writing alone might account for the apparent blossoming of genealogies in Yuan even without any change in the number of descent groups for whom genealogies were written. So long as men wrote prefaces almost exclusively for their own genealogies, a preface would not survive unless (a) the writings of the particular member who authored it were later brought together in a collected works, and (b) that man's collected works survived. Any surviving collected works can in turn contribute at most one preface to our present corpus. But when one man writes prefaces for many genealogies not his own, and particularly if people solicit prefaces from the most prominent men and the most brilliant writers of their

---

8. This does not mean it is difficult to discover from inscriptions where a Southern Sung man lived: It is often very easy. We may, for instance, be given a man's place of burial and then told that it is "next to" his residence.

time—those whose works are most likely to be collected and to survive—
then the corpus may expand dramatically while the number of genealogies
remains stable. Similarly, if genealogy and corporate identity in general
emerge from the private into the public domain, one might expect other elite
documentary forms—funerary inscriptions, for example—to show a new
concern for the descent group. This would be an especially natural development where, as in Fu-chou, the author of the largest number of genealogy
prefaces (Wu Ch'eng) produces a disproportionate share of the surviving
funerary inscriptions as well.

It is surely not giving much away to say that I favor this argument. Still,
one would like positive evidence that corporate identity was already well
developed in (at latest Southern) Sung. Oddly enough the Yuan sources
themselves may offer the best point of departure here. Yuan men, it seems,
recognized no "blossoming" of *tsu* in their own time, no major change in
patterns of kinship since the Sung. What they saw instead in the Sung-Yuan
transition was extensive destruction of *specific descent groups*. Wu Ch'eng
remarked of the "hereditary descent groups" (*shih-tsu*) of Chin-ch'i county
that "No less than several dozen of them began and ended together with the
Sung throne" (WWC 46:12b). Ho Chung noted that of the descent groups
in Lo-an county who had genealogies before the county's founding, "only
the Chan and the Huang are still thriving" (CFTK 4:18a). And Yü Chi
wrote: "Of the tall and stately trees that were our old families, some now are
prominent, some obscure; of their genealogies some still survive and some
do not" (TYHKL 40:6a). Here we read of old "families" (*chia*), but the
reference to their genealogies suggests that these, or some of them, were
broader descent groups. The three passages together picture a Sung countryside perhaps as filled with eminent *tsu* as in Yuan.

Accounts of particular descent groups written in Yuan suggest much the
same picture. According to Yü Chi again: "The Ch'en have been a prominent *tsu* of this county [Ch'ung-jen] ever since Ch'en Yuan-chin passed the
chin-shih examination [in 1211] and lifted up his family" (TYHKL 20:2a). And
Wu Ch'eng provides three other examples:

> The Ts'ao *tsu* had [in Sung] three *chin-shih*; three students at the National
> University; thirteen or fourteen sent up by the prefecture; and their entrants into
> office, whether through the exams, through hereditary privilege, or through
> honor from their sons' office, followed one upon the other. There was good
> reason why late in Sung they were celebrated as an official *tsu* and a scholar *tsu*, and
> were prominent in their county. (WWC 32:16a–b)
>
> In a remote canton of a subordinate county of Lu-ling [Lo-an county] there
> was a Tung *tsu* who, from the beginning of Sung to the end, produced seventy or
> eighty men who distinguished themselves in scholarship and culture. (WWC
> 24:13a)
>
> In the beginning one Wu of Chien-ch'ang was registrar of Ch'ung-jen [coun-
> ty], became son-in-law to one Chang of Ch'ing-yun canton, and made his home

there. The place was called Hsiao-chia-kang, its name later changed to Shih-ch'iao. They gradually became numerous, and under Sung, in the *ting-yu, keng-tzu,* and *kuei-mao* years of Ch'un-hsi [1177, 1180, and 1183], Ju-shan, Ju-ling, and Li-i were sent up in succession by the prefecture. In the *wu-hsu* year of Chia-hsi [1238] Fang-shu entered the National University, and subsequently, in the *i-ssu* year of Ch'un-yu [1245], reached office through the *chin-shih* exam. The *tsu*'s reputation for culture flourished greatly. (WWC 32:8b–9a)

All of this, of course, is rather vague; if there were nothing else one might argue that Yuan authors simply projected into an earlier time the social conceptions and terminology of their own. But the Yuan prefaces offer more specific testimony. Wu Ch'eng gives this account of the Huangs of Pa-t'ang in Lo-an:

At the end of Ch'un-hsi [ca. 1189] one Huang Yun made a genealogy of the *tsu*; in the *keng-yin* year of Shao-ting [1230] it was destroyed by bandits. In Pao-yu [1253–59] Huang K'ua remade it, and Huang Ch'ung-shih planned to carve it on blocks [for printing]; but in the end he did not. During Ching-ting [1260–64] Huang K'ai enlarged and continued the one made by K'ua, and Huang San-chieh wrote a preface. Under Yuan, in Chih-ta [1308–11] Huang Shao-fu embellished the old genealogy and had it carved for transmission. (WWC 32:18a)

Similarly, here is Wei Su on the Lius of Chin-ch'i:

One member was sent up first in the National University exam and, after serving as Professor, became vice-administrator of Lung-hsing: this was Liu Yao-fu.... In Ch'un-hsi [1174–89] he had his genealogy carved in stone at the Hsiu-chen [Taoist] Temple. In the thirteenth generation [during Yuan], Liu Chieh went to live with his wife's family, the Hsun of Wu-kang, and, fearing that his descendants might with time forget their ancestors, checked and corrected his genealogy and entrusted me with writing a preface. (TPC hsu-chi 1:12b–13a)

These two Yuan genealogies, then, were simply reeditions of works already compiled during Sung. This may in fact be typical of the Yuan prefaces that survive. Of the twenty-eight, only seven introduce a genealogy definitely composed in Yuan and mention no earlier version. Fifteen are for genealogies composed at an earlier date or for new Yuan revisions of older editions. Of these, seven provide or imply dates for the earlier version: All fall within Sung. Apart from two prefaces for continuations of a Nan-feng Tseng genealogy first composed in 1080 (thus in Northern Sung), the dates range from the 1180s to the 1260s. The other eight in this group give no exact dates but refer to "old" editions that seem also to belong to Sung. Six remaining prefaces give no indication of the age of the genealogy; if these were for new works, one would expect at least some mention of the author. On this evidence, I very much doubt that even as many as a third of the Yuan prefaces represent genealogies first composed (and descent groups first conceived) in Yuan. The Yuan image of Sung as a time of flourishing *tsu* seems to find some support here.

What of the Sung sources? Again, one cannot expect to find evidence as striking as for Yuan; yet here too there are at least scattered indications that descent group formation was not something exceptional. One of the three genealogy prefaces surviving from Southern Sung, dated 1166, is the work of the Lo-an county scholar and official Tseng Feng. The genealogy, as was typical of the period, is his own: He belonged to the Sung-chiang Tsengs of Yung-feng county, whence he and his father had moved to neighboring Lo-an. One point is of especial interest: Tseng Feng's own is not the only Tseng *tsu* he recognizes locally. He begins by tracing the (certainly mythical) descent of all Tsengs from the Chou dynasty via Confucius's disciple Tseng Tzu in the state of Lu, down to the Five Dynasties.

> The branches (*p'ai*) in Fu-chou were two: one in Nan-feng county, with the first migrant ancestor Tseng Lueh; one at Hsien-ch'i, with the first migrant ancestor Tseng Chiu. Now my eighth-generation ancestor, named Tseng Ts'ai, was of the Hsien-ch'i *tsu*. He later moved to Sung-chiang in Chi-shui county; later Chi-shui was split to make Yung-feng county. Since Great Sung arose, the *tsu* in Nan-feng and the one in Wen-ling [Chin-chiang in Fukien] have had some who by their writings and their careers have become well known; but *my* ancestor's posterity have not had great renown in the world. (YTC 17:1a–2b)

Thus according to Tseng Feng there were currently descent groups of the same surname in Nan-feng county and at Hsien-ch'i in Ch'ung-jen county. Both of these can be confirmed in other sources. The Nan-feng Tsengs are the subject both of the only surviving Northern Sung genealogy preface (a fragment) from Fu-chou and of another of the Southern Sung prefaces. The Hsien-ch'i group is attested for the Yuan by Wu Ch'eng's preface for yet another Tseng descent group in Lo-an county (WWC 32:5a–6b). Here, as of Southern Sung, are three coexisting Fu-chou descent groups of one surname alone.

In Sung funerary inscriptions references to *tsu*, as we have seen, are rare, but they do occasionally appear. The inscription of Lo Tien (1150–94) refers to branch residences within the Lo *tsu*'s larger territory (CCC 12:1a–b). We read of Tung Kuan (1080–1166) that "his *tsu* is numerous and prolific, regularly producing men of note" (LCWC 44:3a–b); of Wu Hao (1150–1227) that his "*tsu* is great and cultured" (YSLK 6:17b); of Fu Shou (1056–1139) that "the Fu of Nan-feng [county] are a famous *tsu* of the present day" (PSWC 15:189). We are told that Meng Tse (1118–81) "built a mansion and gathered his agnates (*tsu*), numbering over a hundred; his neighborhood celebrated their harmony and concord" (NCCIK 21:12a). All of these inscriptions were written, and honor men who died, in Southern Sung; in Northern Sung Fu-chou inscriptions no similar reference survives.

The funerary inscription is a rather formal genre—naturally enough, given its function; if descent groups were already a commonplace in Southern Sung one might expect to find better evidence, perhaps, in sources less bound by etiquette and tradition. The *I-chien chih* of Hung Mai, a collection of anecdotes on occult subjects, often dwells at length on details of everyday life—disease, dreams, ambitions, "popular" religion—little touched on elsewhere. A fair number of the pieces deal with Fu-chou; here is one:

> T'u Cheng-sheng of I-huang county, whose courtesy name was Shih-piao, attained a degree and became administrator of Hsiang-t'an. He dreamed that at his ancestral residence, Upon-the-Plain, there was a yellow dragon that flew up and passed over two places separated by a stream, called Deer Pond and White Tea, before stopping. The T'u were an office-holding *tsu*. When Shih-piao awoke he was not pleased. He reported the dream to others and said: "The official successes of Upon-the-Plain are to be interrupted by the rise of White Tea." In the next year T'u Ssu-yu passed the exam: he was precisely of the White Tea branch (*p'ai*). (ICC *san-jen* 4:3a–b)

Much of the sheer factual matter in this tale is easily confirmed. T'u Cheng-sheng was indeed a *chin-shih*, passing in 1121; T'u Ssu-yu, his second cousin, passed in 1151. The two were descendants of the same great-grandfather; their grandfathers had been brothers, so it is reasonable that they should be called members of different "branches." All the places mentioned can be found in gazetteers and on modern topographic maps close by the site that Ch'ing gazetteers identify as the T'u descent group residence. The anecdote was collected in 1193, published in 1198; but contemporaries had called the T'us a *tsu* much earlier—at least by 1142, when their neighbor Tsou Fei-hsiung, in an inscriptional record for a pagoda, identified its builder, T'u Cheng-sheng's kinsman T'u Chung, as a member of a "leading descent group" (*chia-tsu*) (TCIH 45b:35a–b). A fragmentary Ming genealogy of the same group records its earliest edition as the work of T'u Cheng-sheng himself, completed in 1144, and preserves Cheng-sheng's own preface (TSTP 33). Hung Mai, writing in the 1190s, evidently thought easily in terms of *tsu* whose common identity (as "office-holding descent groups") might span "branches" with separate (though clustered) subresidences and, as in this case, potentially separate fates.

Some of the Sung sources cited here are more suggestive than conclusive. By way of taking stock, it is worth reviewing here what is hardest of the evidence seen so far: the testimony of dates. Of the four Sung genealogy prefaces that survive, one, again, dates from Northern Sung: the fragmentary preface to the Nan-feng Tseng genealogy, composed around 1080. The three others are all from Southern Sung: T'u Cheng-sheng's preface, dated 1144; Tseng Feng's, dated 1166; and Hsieh O's preface to a Southern Sung version of the Nan-feng Tseng genealogy, dated 1188. From Yuan prefaces, as we have seen, one may draw a list of five Sung genealogies (leaving aside the Nan-feng Tseng work, which we meet here again) whose dates of first compilation range from the 1180s to about the 1260s. To these we must add the genealogies of the Chans and Huangs (mentioned in Ho Chung's funerary inscription above), which antedated the founding of Lo-an county in 1149. Clearly the bulk of this material—of the eleven dated genealogies, no fewer than eight and perhaps as many as ten—falls in Southern Sung. As we have seen, the few Sung funerary inscriptions for Fu-chou men that refer to groups called *tsu* all come, similarly, from Southern Sung: the death dates of their subjects are 1139, 1166, 1181, 1194, and 1227. The material as a whole seems to justify two tentative conclusions. First, the "lineage orientation"— judging at least by the composition of genealogies—was by no means a Yuan innovation: As we have seen, only seven of the total of thirty-two prefaces are for genealogies definitely first compiled in Yuan. Second, the tendency toward descent group formation, apparently well established in Southern Sung, was—on the Fu-chou evidence—at best embryonic in Northern Sung. I will return to the second point further on; the first requires a bit more discussion.

The "lineage orientation," I have suggested, fit into the locally focused strategy of elite householders in Southern Sung because they could see it as a means for forming or strengthening useful social relationships. Where common descent and common association with a particular nearby place were known, proclaimed, recorded, and perhaps ritually celebrated, they might become the basis for alliance, clientship, control, or mutual support and aid. The strategy made sense, potentially, even where no corporate group, with real and continuous cooperative activities and common properties, emerged on the foundation of ideal common identity. It might be enough, for an elite household's purposes, to carve out of the local population an agnatic *pool* of potential allies and clients: Of the many relationships established or reestablished in theory by the formal affirmation of *tsu*-hood, only a few might ever be made real. Pierre Bourdieu's distinction between "official" and "practical" kinship is relevant here (Bourdieu 1977:33–43). Genealogy-writing was in part an attempt to establish and define official relationships that could, when needed, be turned into practical ones. It may often have been accompanied by immediate efforts to establish the entire unit as a practical group (especially through common ritual) but need not always have been. We may agree with Bourdieu that to convert the official into the practical, and keep it so, needs constant effort and regular joint action, that without this the official tends even to fade from awareness. But it is surely also true that relationships once proclaimed officially may have, at least in the short term, a potential for realization and for occasional renewal that they would not have otherwise. This was perhaps all the more true in Sung China, a society that, on the one hand, made the written word itself an object of some reverence— common descent displayed on a written page was surely more salient than common descent merely asserted—and where, on the other hand, a long tradition encouraged the literate elite in particular to identify the official with the practical.

These considerations, I think, justify treating genealogy-writing as in itself a strategic act, even without further evidence of corporation. Still, if one hopes to show that the "lineage orientation" was both largely a Southern Sung innovation and a part of the localist strategy, one would like some evidence that the sorts of broader agnatic relationships traced and affirmed by genealogies *were* sometimes, in Southern Sung, made real and practical: that the orientation expressed itself not only on paper but in action. For Fu-chou such evidence, though rare, does appear, chiefly in local defense.

The Chin-ch'i county militia of Southern Sung, which served as the mainstay of Fu-chou local defense from its founding at the Northern Sung/Southern Sung transition in 1127 down to the fall of Sung in 1278 and on into Yuan, was at the outset an amalgam of two militia organizations, which were in turn the respective creations of two "surnames": the Tengs and the Fus. Other Chin-ch'i men joined them, apparently as their subordinates, but the central position of the two leading groups is clear in the descriptions left by contemporaries (Hymes 1986: chap. 5). In 1175 Chou Pi-ta gave this account:

> The tea bandits have gone unpacified for a long time. Several days ago, the leading graduate of the Upper Hall of the National University, Liu Yao-fu, came and told me: "The great surnames of Chin-ch'i in Fu-chou, the Tengs and the Fus, have several thousand militiamen each.... They are feared far and wide and are called the Two Societies of the Teng and Fu." (CWCKWC 20:16b)

At the beginning, Chou noted, men of a third surname, the Lus, had held the supreme command. Sung sources refer to the Tengs and Fus, and to the Lus, only as "great surnames" (*ta-hsing*) or "great families" (*ta-chia*), and the like. The two societies, however—in their connection to specific descent groups, in their general independence of state authority, and in their long persistence—look very much like the lineage militias (and the Chin-ch'i militia as a whole like the multi-lineage defense federations) of later dynasties (cf. Kuhn 1970). In this connection the transmission of leadership positions is of some interest. The post of commander of the Teng society passed, between 1127 and 1278, three times from father to son (not all in one line), twice from brother to brother, twice from uncle to nephew, and once between cousins more distant than first: more often across descent lines, in other words, than along them. As of the early 1200s the three leading officers came from two separate lines no closer than second cousin; later officers were drawn from each of these lines, down to 1278 (TCCC 22a:1a–5a; WWC 79:10a–11b).[9]

---

9. Lower officers of the Teng surname in the same period cannot be placed with confidence in either line. Teng Yuan-kuan, who dealt on the militia's behalf with Hsieh Fang-te in the 1260s when Hsieh was trying to organize regional defense against the Mongols, seems not to have been an immediate kinsman of any of the current officers.

Evidently the militia was not the affair of a single household, or even of a single line. It is tempting to imagine the Tengs as a corporate lineage with a military specialization. In fact, we cannot be sure just in what respects, and from when, they were corporate. A genealogy preface exists from Yuan, with no indication that the genealogy itself is new (WWC 79:10a–11b). Of common property we learn nothing, though as of 1230 a pair of "charitable granaries" (*i-ts'ang*), established by officers out of their own funds, were maintained for provisioning of the militia's troops. All this is suggestive at best. The militia itself is a corporate group, certainly. What we cannot know is whether that group was coterminous with "the Tengs" as a whole. Still, common action and organization among agnates of different descent lines, lines that by Yuan at latest were to be charted in a single genealogy, is certain and striking.[10]

Another major figure in local defense in Southern Sung was Hou Ting of I-huang county, who after a bandit outbreak in 1230 built a fort in the mountains near his home, stocked it with troops, and took steps to assure their constant provisioning. The inscriptional record for the fort's construction gives details: "He disbursed over three-thousand *shih* of his own rice, and got those among his agnates who had resources (*tsu chih yu-li-che*) to give aid. This was granaried in the fort solely for the payment of troops, and was called the Charitable Granary" (PCKL 4:10b).

Militia organization and support may thus have been a frequent focus of common agnatic action. This is by no means to say that it was the only one. The sources for Fu-chou provide only occasional insight into the ground-level processes of mutual aid, alliance, patronage, and conflict for which a pool of potential ties might have been useful. Some material is available in surviving legal judgments. As often as not these show agnates themselves in contention; but a phenomenon of some interest is the sometimes crucial role of men called *tsu-chang*. The term is familiar from later dynasties in its application to the formal head of an organized lineage. In Sung sources we probably cannot assume it has more than its literal content: "an elder among the agnates."

Three Fu-chou judgments mention *tsu-chang*. In 1272 Huang Chen, then prefectural administrator, judged the case of one Sheriff Yueh, who had died

10. Similarly, the supervisory position held by the Lu passed from Lu O in 1127 to his "agnate" (tsu-jen) Lu Chiu-ling in 1175: If the relationship had been a close one, a more specific term would surely have been used (CWKCW 20:16b–17b). In fact in Lu Chiu-ling's funerary inscription (LHSCC 27:2b–3a) the term is not *tsu-jen* but *tsu-tzu*, which if taken literally would mean *son* of a collateral kinsman of the same generation, hence a man one generation *below* Chiu-ling in genealogical terms. To precede Chiu-ling in the leadership position by fifty years and yet be of a generation one below Chiu-ling's, this man would have to be of quite a distant collateral line. The term, however, is perhaps not used so literally here: It may simply mean "son of an agnate" without regard to generation.

without heir and whose estate was now in dispute. Huang chose Yueh's kinsman Wen-ping as heir, but made a lesser concession to the claim of another, not chosen, whom he then instructed to bring the guarantee of a *tsu-chang* (HSJC 78:38a).[11] The context suggests strongly that the unnamed elder was outside the mourning circle of the deceased, since all those within have already appeared as contenders in the case. In a second case, judged by the Ch'ung-jen county administrator Fan Ying-ling in the 1220s, a dead man's former servant challenges the right to inherit of the man's adoptive son, and claims to be the man's son himself, by a maidservant. Fan proposes asking a *tsu-chang* to resolve the issue by testifying, and speculates that the servant's suit—which he takes to be frivolous—is being abetted by the man's own *tsu* (agnates? descent group?), who he thinks are dissatisfied over the adoption (MKSPCMC 143–46). A third judgment, also by Fan Ying-ling, reads, in part:

> Liu Ching and his brothers, four men in all, had long since divided, each occupying his allotted portion in the registers; there had never been any suits. The three elder brothers all having died, there are now in all four nephews [of Liu Ching]. On the day Ching died, as his property alone was rich and his son was young, and as his four nephews were poor, he gave each of them ten thousand cash in aid, and wrote it down on paper to be a regular yearly [arrangement]. Now it has been only five years or so, and Ching's son and wife have gone back on the agreement. The nephews have sued, seeking the extraction [of the money]. I have obtained from the *tsu-chang* the deed, which was written by Ching personally. (MKSPCMC 139–41)

Here the *tsu-chang* clearly stands (stand?) outside the circle of kin immediately at issue—he (they) cannot be related to the contending son and nephews more closely than through their great-grandfather—yet is in possession of the deed written by their father/uncle Liu Ching and, once again, is treated as someone in a position to provide evidence binding on his collateral kinsmen. Again there is no reason necessarily to see organized descent groups or lineages in these cases: The point is simply the reality and practical significance, in legal matters, of relatively distant agnatic ties. This in itself was not necessarily a reflection of the "lineage orientation"—it was agents of the state who gave this role to *tsu-chang*—but rather, I would argue, part of the context from which the "lineage orientation" derived its sense and purpose. An elite household head interested in the maintenance of his property and its orderly transmission to his heirs had good reason to affirm and

---

11. This passage is somewhat problematic. An alternative possible reading is: "As future *tsu-chang* and guarantor he has [or will] come to the authorities together with Wen-ping." On this interpretation a formal position of lineage head would seem to be involved. The construction (*tang lai tsu-chang pao-ming yü Wen-ping t'ung tao kuan*) is rather odd no matter which reading is chosen.

strengthen ties to local kin who might at some point be asked by magistrates to play the role that *tsu-chang* played here; or indeed, perhaps, reason to aspire to the same role himself.

In sum, then, we have four kinds of evidence for Fu-chou in Southern Sung. First, Yuan men in general depict a Sung community of elite descent groups not as a whole different (though different in its particular members) from their own. Second, many, perhaps most of the genealogy prefaces of Yuan by their own testimony represent genealogies first compiled in Southern Sung. Third, Southern Sung sources themselves, however occasionally, do mention *tsu* in terms that imply common identity as groups. Finally, there is evidence of organized cooperation among agnates of separate households and across descent lines in the sphere of local defense. Moreover, the role in litigation of men called *tsu-chang* confirms from another aspect the salience of collateral agnatic ties, sometimes of considerable distance, in real social interaction at the local level. Taken together, this evidence persuades me that what I have called the "lineage orientation," though still little discussed in formal genres of writing, was already a well-established part of elite strategies by late Southern Sung. This implies that both the sudden flood of genealogy prefaces in Yuan—written by outsiders, not only by members—and the new attention given to *tsu* in funerary inscriptions reflect, as Morita has suggested, a movement of extended kinship into the public domain of cultivated literary discourse, and not the first emergence of a new sort of descent group.

In one sense, then, what had changed in Yuan was purely "cultural" (taking culture in its narrow, literary/cultivated sense): Certain social facts were talked about in contexts they had not appeared in before, and one form of writing—the genealogy preface—changed from a mainly private artifact of kinship to a public literary genre, solicited, like funerary inscriptions, prefaces, and poems, from figures of scholarly or literary note regardless of kin ties. But this change itself, I would argue, had larger social meaning. On the one hand, perhaps, it was the culmination of a process of cultural and ideological change that had begun, as I have already suggested, in Southern Sung: a process in which local, "private," and now familial concerns came more and more to be respectable topics of cultivated discussion, even objects of praise and celebration. The change in the kinds of activities recorded in biographical genres and the transformation of the function of state altars to local heroes, both mentioned in the first section, are examples of this process in Southern Sung. Descent group identity, then, was simply one more private and fundamentally *local* sphere of action that was now a matter for public discussion, note, and celebration. It is interesting in this connection that the change in preface-writing seems already to have begun in late Southern Sung. Morita notes that three men of Southern Sung authored as many as three genealogy prefaces (so at least two not their own): Ou-yang Shou-tao, *chin-shih* 1241;

Wen T'ien-hsiang, *chin-shih* 1256; and Liu Ch'en-weng, *chin-shih* 1267. In Fu-chou, Hsieh O had prefaced the Nan-feng Tseng genealogy as early as 1188, while Wei Su's preface to his own genealogy mentions three prefaces by nonkinsmen in Sung, all falling between the 1230s and 1278 (TPC 6:1a–2a). Even in this sphere, then, the Yuan may have carried further a trend already begun at the end of Southern Sung.

And yet the change is surely too striking to be *only* a continuation of earlier trends. It is a far cry from the three genealogy prefaces of Ou-yang Shou-tao to the dozens written by Wu Ch'eng. Why did *so many* Yuan men invite Wu Ch'eng, and later his students Wei Su and Yü Chi, to read and preface their genealogies? We have already seen, in the previous section, the apparently strategic position of just these men in relation to the Yuan state. I would suggest that the reading and prefacing of genealogies became, in Yuan, in part a medium of acquaintance and social connection, especially with local men of note and influence. Men who hoped to make themselves known to potential teachers, sponsors, or protectors had long used their own writings to introduce or advertise themselves: The young scholar presenting himself at a great man's gate, sending in a sheaf of poems or essays, and hoping to be invited to follow them in was a familiar figure in Chinese society long before the Sung. Perhaps in Yuan the same man, having gained admission and having asked his host to visit in turn his own home, might there invite him to peruse his genealogy and to grant the favor of a preface. (Prefaces often tell us that such-and-such a man "took out and showed me his genealogy.")

The same Yuan political conditions that made long-distance marriage a new element in the old localist strategy made the genealogy an especially apt medium of contact, for two reasons. First, the Yuan—unlike the Sung—expressly recognized descent as a permanent criterion of formal status: This was an important part of the meaning of the *ju-hu* system. But second, and I suspect more important, the "great man" might now be one of only a few direct conduits to the attention of the authorities, hence to an appointment; and the man who gained his presence was obliged, perhaps, to stand in for a host of kinsmen as eager for preferment as he. A genealogy was at once evidence of descent (and of honorable and cultivated position in the society of one's own day) and a list of living kinsmen, all candidates in their own right for the patron's attention. Poems and essays introduced the man; a genealogy introduced both his pedigree and his kin.[12]

The new way of prefacing genealogies, then, has two aspects. On the one

---

12. The display of pedigree itself cannot have been the only motive, as several of the Yuan prefaces from Fu-chou are for descent groups without officials, famous scholars, or indeed any unusually important men among their ancestors: This is sometimes noted in the preface, and a shining future is predicted.

hand it was the culmination of a process of change in ideas about a gentle-
man's private and local roles that was deeply rooted in Southern Sung, and
that must have both reflected and supported the transformation of household strategies in the same period. As such it had already begun to emerge
before Sung fell. On the other hand it was an ideal medium for making
important connections in the new political climate of Mongol rule. As such
it blossomed in Yuan as never before.

All of this, however, has dealt only with the second of the two "difficulties" I raised at the beginning of this section. The issue of Northern Sung
predecessors remains to be addressed. If descent group formation went hand
in hand with the localism of Southern Sung and Yuan, why were its institutional foundations, seemingly, first laid by men—Ou-yang Hsiu, Su Hsun,
Fan Chung-yen—who, far from localist, were the very types of the Northern Sung *national* professional elite? There is no question that the role of
agnatic groupings in Northern Sung needs more thorough exploration than
it has previously received or than I can give it here. But here again, at least as
to genealogies, it may be well to take a cue from Morita Kenji. As he has
pointed out, the genealogies of Ou-yang Hsiu and Su Hsun, though in spirit
the models for all that were to follow, differed in crucial ways from those of
Southern Sung (judging from prefaces), Yuan, and after (Morita 1979:35–
36). As Patricia Ebrey's chapter details, Su and Ou-yang began the genealogy proper (as distinct from the prefatory matter that traced the earlier history of the line's ancestors) with the great-great-grandfather—in accord
with the ritual system of mourning grades—rather than with the "first migrant ancestor" (or "first ancestor") who so often heads the genealogies of
later periods and whose posterity in principle defines and constitutes the
descent group itself. Both emphasized a single main line of descent and gave
less attention to collateral lines, in contrast to later genealogies, which sometimes embrace dozens of lines or *fang* and may treat all or several in equal
detail. In short, the special traits of the genealogies of Ou-yang and Su in
effect *limited*, in size, depth of descent, and complexity, the ritual and social
body that made up the descent group (Morita 1979:35–36). Quite apart from
its foundations in classical views of ritual, this surely made a great deal of
sense for men whose world, commitments, and ambitions were far more
national than local. To concentrate their energies and resources on this larger
world they needed, perhaps, to limit their ties and commitments to distant
kin whose aid and support, however valuable in purely local terms, were of
little use on a larger scale.[13]

---

13. Indeed, if the descent group was in fact limited to the mourning circle, it could not, in
the long term, continue as a "group" at all. It would have to redefine itself in each generation by
excluding what had been the highest ancestral generation along with any kin tied only through
ancestors of that level. More or less the same argument on the purpose of Ou-yang Hsiu's

In Southern Sung and afterward, on the other hand, when the agnatic group (as I am arguing) became part of a strategy that focused precisely on local position, it made no sense to limit at the outset—by setting one's "first ancestor" too low or by concentrating on one line—the range of local kin with whom, on a foundation of common identity, one might form ties of cooperation, of alliance, or of control. Rather than do so, the compilers of Southern Sung and after were evidently willing to abandon the model, and with it perhaps a part of the reflected glory, of the founding Northern Sung genealogists. The contrast Morita draws between Northern Sung and later styles of genealogy is well supported by the Fu-chou evidence.[14] The rise of the localist strategy, then, seems to be reflected directly in methods of genealogy-writing.

The role of Fan Chung-yen in the creation of the charitable estate as a model for later lineages may be harder to explain. (On Fan and his estate see Twitchett 1959; on Sung charitable estates in general see Kyō 1976.) One cannot underestimate the importance of purely personal factors: as Michael Freeman has shown, Fan's own life history and relation to his kinsmen were highly unusual, even bizarre (Freeman n.d.). But Fan's charitable estate was imitated in Northern Sung by men, also of the national professional elite, whose personal positions were by no means so atypical. Within Fu-chou at least two of the most illustrious Northern Sung families founded charitable estates. How did an estate providing aid and support equally to an entire lineage fit with a Northern Sung strategy focused on bureaucratic success and national position? At the outset it may be said that, insofar as a lineage's membership was limited by the choices made in compiling its genealogy, the range of beneficiaries of the charitable estate too would be limited. Fan's lineage was, in fact, defined in the same way as Ou-yang Hsiu's or Su

---

genealogy has been made by Yoshiro Kobayashi in an article published in 1980. I have not as yet had access to this article (Kobayashi 1980). See the citation in Patricia Ebrey's essay in this volume (chapter 2).

14. In Southern Sung, the cases are the genealogies written by Tseng Feng and T'u Cheng-sheng, which reached back eight generations, and the Nan-feng Tseng genealogy prefaced by Hsieh O, which included at least six and more probably eight generations of ancestors (YTC 17:1a–b; TSTP13;YFLK front matter). In Yuan, though not all prefaces specify their genealogies' depth in generations, those that do almost without exception far exceed the four-generation limit for ancestors imposed by Ou-yang Hsiu and Su Hsun. The prefaces occasionally comment on the detailed treatment of large numbers of branches; somewhat more often, they simply mention, in tones of praise, the large numbers of present descendants. Size in itself is, it seems, something to be proud of for the genealogists of the Yuan. The only Northern Sung genealogy represented by surviving prefaces, the work of Tseng Chao, completed in 1080, included a total of six generations. In 1080 Tseng was thirty-three and had sons but no grandsons. Assuming he charted his own and his sons' generations in the genealogy, the earliest ancestor included would have been, again, his great-grandfather. For the surviving fragment of the work see TYHKL 35:2b–3a, and for its date see SYTK 7:37b.

Hsun's: as the descendants of his great-grandfather. Still his estate involved a very considerable expenditure of funds and effort for the benefit of local kinsmen of, in many cases, a fair genealogical distance.

The problem may have no neat solution. But it does seem reasonable to argue that Fan's charitable estate was a rather flexible institution that could answer different needs in different circumstances. Assuming a generous original grant of land or periodic additional gifts, a charitable estate might serve to promote lineage well-being and—through dependence—lineage solidarity on a very broad scale, and so strengthen an elite family's local foundation along Southern Sung lines. But perhaps for a Northern Sung man with more far-flung aims and concerns the value of the charitable estate was that, by *defining* his obligations to his local kin—to endow an estate and make provision for its long-term management—it also *limited* them. It was thus consistent at once with the demands of morality (that a man must care for those with legitimate claims on him) and with the imperatives of bureaucratic striving (that legitimate claims ought not to be unlimited). A man who had provided for his agnates in this way, perhaps, could move away permanently from his original home without feeling that he had abandoned his kin or failed in his obligations. Thus the founders of both known Fu-chou charitable estates, for instance, emigrated from Fu-chou before the end of Northern Sung. Of one we learn that by late Northern Sung (the founders having left, long since, for Lo-yang) it had fallen into disuse and so had been confiscated by the state.[15] When things changed in Southern Sung, an institution that had served in part to resolve the tension between national ambitions and local obligations proved to be equally well suited to a strategy in which that tension was no longer an issue, in which obligations and ambitions came together at the local level. The charitable estate, in other words, may have had a useful role to play in either strategy. There is no insuperable difficulty here, any more than in the genealogical productions of Ou-yang and Su, for the notion that the "lineage orientation" had its first real flowering under Southern Sung, and that this flowering reflected the particularly good "fit" of the notion of the localized *tsu*, defined in genealogically inclusive terms, with the new localist strategy of the Southern Sung elite.

I have seemed in all this to treat the descent group and lineage purely as a project of the elite, as something made from the top down. In fact this reflects my general concern here with elite strategies and their transformation—in marriage as well as in the agnatic sphere—more than any belief in the elite's omnipotence. For the local descent group to develop and survive as a corporate entity of any size, surely, required the assent and

15. For the charitable estates founded by Tseng Kung of Nan-feng in Lin-ch'uan and Chin-ch'i, see TYHKL 35:2b–3a. For the charitable estate of the Yuehs of I-huang, see TCIH 14:23a–b; on the Yueh and their emigration to Lo-yang see Hymes 1986:chap. 3.

cooperation of kinsmen who were not, in the sense of the word used here, of the elite, and who had reasons of their own for what they did. Even if, in Southern Sung, the agnatic group sometimes shared nothing more real than common identity, common identity could not, if it was to be real, simply be proclaimed by elite genealogists. The interests, motives, indeed the actions, of those outside the elite are, for Sung and Yuan Fu-chou, largely inaccessible; this does not make them irrelevant. The argument I have made is in fact perfectly consistent with the notion, argued by Patricia Ebrey in chapter 2, that the *tsu* of these periods was in many cases a de facto group before an elite member decided, for instance, to chart its descent in a genealogy. Local clusterings of people of common descent, even of a considerable size, were surely a very old phenomenon in China: In Sung they are demonstrable from the beginning of the dynasty (e.g. Otagi 1974). Some of them may have shared occasionally or regularly in common activities, especially group worship. It is not necessarily the existence of such groups or quasi groups that is new in Southern Sung. What is new is the role of the elite—at even its highest bureaucratic levels—in their promotion, celebration, and, in some cases, creation. It is this role—viewed in another way, the new impulse of the elite to define themselves as members of the same group as (in principle) all their local agnates—that I have tried to explain. To explain this is not to explain "the rise of the lineage"—perhaps too variegated a creature to admit a single explanation. Still, the position of the bureaucratic and literate elite as leaders, organizers, promoters, and controllers of large localized descent groups is surely one of the more important phenomena of Chinese (at least South Chinese) society in later periods (see Hazelton's chapter in this volume). If, as I argue, that position was first staked out, at least in the sphere of "official" kinship, in Southern Sung, this is no small development.

This raises, however, the issue of continuity. Given that one cannot know whether the descent groups of Southern Sung and Yuan were corporate groups on the model of, say, Ch'ing lineages, is there any reason to see the earlier form as ancestral, or in any way related, to the later? The problem of the later development of descent groups in Fu-chou is a complex one. As my own research has been almost wholly limited to Sung, Yuan, and early Ming, I cannot propose definitive answers here. Some clues, however, do emerge from even a quick scan of the sources for later periods. In the first place, there seems no question that corporate lineages were commonplace in Kiangsi by Ch'ing times. Philip Kuhn has described the role of the Liu lineage of Nan-ch'ang, to Fu-chou's immediate northwest, in the organization of the Kiangsi army in the 1850s (Kuhn 1970:157–60). James Polachek has discussed the functions of the "clans" and "clan-villages" of the Fu-chou region in late Ch'ing and Republican times as "risk-sharing communities" and organizations for the minimization and arbitration of conflict among member households. The "individual clan branches" of these organizations, at least, were owners, and their heads the managers, of corporate estates (Polachek 1983).

At least three genealogies of Ch'ing date survive from Fu-chou or immediately surrounding counties. One, for a Huang lineage of Pei-shan in I-huang county, includes along with its tables of descent an engraving of the common ancestral hall and a long list of lineage contributors to its construction; lists of field lots and amounts of stored grain assigned for use in the sacrifices to specific lineage ancestors; and a list of contributors to the compilation of the genealogy itself. Material of the same sort appears in two other genealogies, for the T'an lineage of Nan-feng county and the Wei lineage of Nan-ch'eng county (IHHSP, last volume; CHTSTP, last volume; NCWSCP, first volume).

Further study might well show that these lineages were of the looser, more purely elite-centered, "T'ung-ch'eng" type recently proposed by Patricia Ebrey, rather than of the more tightly organized closed type described by Freedman for Kwangtung; but that they were corporate groups with common property and ritual organization seems beyond question (Ebrey 1983).

None of these lineages, of course, is itself the descendant of one of the Sung/Yuan descent groups I have identified from genealogy prefaces. Their example shows only that the corporate lineage was an established organizational form in Fu-chou, as elsewhere in South China, under the Ch'ing. The problem can be approached, however, from the other side: Specific Sung or Yuan descent groups can be traced without difficulty into the Ch'ing, though through sources that again leave the question of corporateness in principle open. The Ch'ing local histories for three of Fu-chou's counties, Lo-an, I-huang, and Chin-ch'i, consistently append place names to the names of successful examination candidates listed in the chapters on degree-holders; the same place names very often appear as well in the biographies of individual men of note. A glance through the exam lists will show that these places are something other than individual residences: The same place names recur for dozens, sometimes hundreds, of men of a single surname. The inference that these are lineage residences is a natural one; and indeed in the lists for the Sung one finds a good number of the place names that appear in genealogy prefaces or in Yuan funerary inscriptions as descent group residences for men of the corresponding surname: the Wus of Hsin-t'ien in Chin-ch'i for example, or the Huangs of Pa-t'ang in Lo-an. A number of these place name/surname combinations, which demonstrably represent descent groups in Sung and/or Yuan, can be followed in the exam lists and biographies right through Ming and Ch'ing.[16] Certain Sung/Yuan descent

16. This continuity is most notable in Lo-an. The county produced only four *chin-shih* degree-holders in the Ch'ing: two Chans of Ya-pei in 1691 and 1772; a Tseng of Lo-shan in

groups, in sum, continue as identifiable social entities, important enough to be noted in examination lists and biographies, deep into the Ch'ing dynasty, when other sources show that corporate lineages were an established form in Fu-chou. It does not seem unreasonable to suppose that the Lo-shan Tsengs or the Kung-fang Kungs were, as of this late date, themselves corporate lineages. If so, then in Fu-chou at least, Sung/Yuan descent groups are indeed, quite literally, the ancestors of the lineages of the Ch'ing. There may then be more than metaphoric force in the claim that the Sung/Yuan descent group *as an institution* was similarly ancestral to the Ch'ing corporate lineage. The emergence of the "lineage orientation" among the elite of Southern Sung was, on this interpretation, a crucial first step.

The two major sections of this paper make arguments that are in many respects parallel. I have tried to show for both marriage and agnatic ties that what seem innovations in the Yuan are in fact continuations of practices and notions already well established in Southern Sung; and, for agnatic ties, that apparent Northern Sung predecessors may actually represent quite different tendencies. The result is to unite in time new marriage patterns and new agnatic groupings and so to make both intelligible as parts of a single larger shift in the strategies and self-conceptions of the elite. The argument, founded on work in one prefecture, must of course be taken as tentative, as a hypothesis for testing and elaboration elsewhere. The timing of change may well prove to vary from place to place; for my hypothesis to stand, however, change in marriage and in agnatic strategies must, in any one place, coincide at least roughly in time.

How does one sort out, in all this, the relative positions of alliance and descent? From one angle, if a broader, more inclusive conception of agnatic kin emerged, expressed in the notion of common lineage identity, then descent would seem to have become more important. It had begun to organize, at least potentially, a greater part of the social world. Yet it would be a serious mistake, I think, to suppose that as descent advanced, "alliance" (a preoccupation with marriage ties) receded. There is no reason to suppose that the local network of marriages constructed by the elite householders of Southern Sung was less important to their strategies of status maintenance and mobility than the national network had been for their Northern Sung

---

1737; and a Kung of Kung-fang in 1754 (TCLA 7:16a–b). All of these were in Yuan descent groups whose genealogies were prefaced by Wu Ch'eng. The last *chin-shih* in Ming was a Huang of Pa-t'ang in 1634; the Pa-t'ang Huangs' first genealogy, it may be recalled, had been compiled in 1189 (TCLA 7:16a; WWC 32:17a–18b). The *en-kung* list for late Ch'ing ends with the three reigns of Tao-kuang, Hsien-feng, and T'ung-chih (1821–74): Here there are four Ya-pei Chans and one Lo-shan Tseng (TCLA 7:49a). The phenomenon holds true, though not as spectacularly, for I-huang and Chin-ch'i as well. In I-huang, for example, a T'u of Shih-lu received a *chin-shih* degree in 1705 (TCIH 27:10a); the first genealogy for the Shih-lu T'u was T'u Cheng-sheng's work compiled, as we have seen, in 1144 (TSTP 13 and 33).

predecessors. It must be clear from the discussion so far that I would describe what happened in quite different terms. What had changed was, above all, the stage on which both alliance and descent were acted out: This had once, at least for the bureaucratically successful, been the empire at large; now it was the county and the subcounty locality. Alliance and descent, as mediating principles for social relationships, were for the elite of Fu-chou two arrows from the same quiver. The target had simply moved closer.

REFERENCES

Primary Sources

CCC   *Chieh-chai chi* 絜齋集, by Yuan Hsieh 袁燮. Ssu-k'u chen-pen ed.

CFTK   *Chih-fei-t'ang kao* 知非堂稿, by Ho Chung 何中. Ch'ing printed edition.

CHLWC *Ch'eng hsueh-lou wen-chi* 程雪樓文集, by Ch'eng Chü-fu 程鉅夫. Taipei: Kuo-li Chung-yang t'u-shu kuan, 1969.

CHTSTP *Ch'ung-hsiu T'an-shih tsu-p'u* 重修譚氏族譜. Preface 1920.

CKC   *Ch'ang-ku chi* 昌谷集, by Ts'ao Yen-yueh 曹彥約. Ssu-k'u chen-pen ed.

CWCKWC *Wen-chung chi* 文忠集, by Chou Pi-ta 周必大. Ssu-k'u chen-pen ed.

HSCC   *Hsueh-shuo-chai chi* 學說齋集, by Wei Su 危素. Ssu-k'u chen-pen ed.

HSJC   *Huang-shih jih-ch'ao* 黃氏日鈔, by Huang Chen 黃震. Ssu-k'u chen-pen ed.

HTTCC *Hou-ts'un hsien-sheng ta ch'üan-chi* 後村先生大全集, by Liu K'o-chuang 劉克莊. Ssu-pu ts'ung-k'an ed.

ICC   *I-chien chih* 夷堅志, by Hung Mai 洪邁. Kyoto: Chūbun shuppansha, 1975.

IHHSP *Chiang-hsi I-huang Pei-shan Huang-shih shih-i hsiu p'u* 江西宜黃北山黃氏十一修譜. Preface 1899.

KHNF   *Nan-feng hsien chih* 南豐縣志, by Cheng I 鄭釴 et al. K'ang-hsi ed., 1899.

LCWC   *Lu-ch'i wen-chi* 盧溪文集, by Wang T'ing-kuei 王庭珪. Ssu-k'u chen-pen ed.

LHSCC *Hsiang-shan ch'üan-chi* 象山全集, by Lu Chiu-yuan 陸九淵. Ssu-pu pei-yao ed.

MCC   *Mien-chai chi* 勉齋集, by Huang Kan 黃榦. Ssu-k'u chen-pen ed.

MHTL   *Miao-hsueh tien-li* 廟學典禮. Ssu-k'u chen-pen ed.

MKSPCMC *Ming-kung shu-p'an ch'ing-ming chi* 名公書判清明集. Tokyo: Koten kenkyūkai, 1964.

NCCIK *Nan-chien chia-i kao* 南澗甲乙稿, by Han Yuan-chi 韓元吉. Ssu-k'u chen-pen ed.

NCWSCP *Nan-ch'eng hsien Wei-shih chia-p'u* 南城縣危氏家譜. 3d. ed.

PCKL   *Pi-chou kao-lueh* 敝帚稿略, by Pao Hui 包恢. Ssu-k'u chen-pen ed.

PSWC   *Pei-shan wen-chi* 北山文集, by Cheng Kang-chung 鄭剛中. Ssu-pu pei-yao ed.

SAC   *Ssu-an chi* 俟菴集, by Li Ts'un 李村. Ssu-k'u chen-pen ed.

SYTK   *Shui-yun-ts'un kao* 水雲村稿, by Liu Hsun 劉壎. Ssu-k'u chen-pen ed.

TCCC   *Chin-ch'i hsien chih* 金溪縣志, by Ch'eng Fang 程芳 et al. T'ung-chih, 1870 ed.

TCIH   *I-huang hsien chih* 宜黃縣志, by Chang Hsing-yen 張興言 et al. T'ung-chih, 1871 ed.

TCLA   *Lo-an hsien chih* 樂安縣志, by Chu Kuei-chang 朱奎章 et al. T'ung-chih, 1871 ed.

TCTH   *Tung-hsiang hsien chih* 東鄉縣志, by Li Shih et al. T'ung-chih, 1869 ed.

TCTS   *Tseng-shih tsu-p'u* 曾氏族譜. Taichung, 1966.

TPC   *T'ai-p'u Yun-lin chi* 太樸雲林集, by Wei Su 危素. Republican ed.

TSTP   *T'u-shih tsu-p'u* 涂氏族譜. Taipei, 1974.

TYHKL   *Tao-yuan hsueh-ku lu* 道園學古錄, by Yü Chi 虞集. Ssu-pu ts'ung-k'an ed.

WNWC   *Wei-nan wen-chi* 渭南文集, by Lu Yu 陸游. Ssu-pu ts'ung-k'an ed.

WWC   *Wen-chung kung chi* 文忠公集, by Wu Ch'eng 吳澄. Ssu-k'u chen-pen ed.

YCTI   *Yin-chü t'ung-i* 隱居通議, by Liu Hsun 劉壎. Ts'ung-shu chi-ch'eng ed.

YFLK   *Yuan-feng lei-kao* 元豐類稿, by Tseng Kung 曾鞏. Ssu-pu pei-yao ed.

YSLK   *Yü-shu lei-kao* 漁墅類稿, by Ch'en Yuan-chin 陳元晉. Ssu-k'u chen-pen ed.

YTC   *Yuan-tu chi* 緣督集, by Tseng Feng 曾丰. Ssu-k'u chen-pen ed.

Secondary Works

Blalock, Hubert M., Jr. 1972. *Social Statistics.* New York: McGraw-Hill.

Bourdieu, Pierre. 1977. *Outline of a Theory of Practice.* Cambridge: Cambridge University Press.

Ebrey, Patricia Buckley. 1983. "Types of Lineages in Ch'ing China: A Reexamination of the Chang Lineage of T'ung-ch'eng." *Ch'ing-shih wen-t'i* 4.9: 1–20.

Freedman, Maurice. 1966. *Chinese Lineage and Society: Fukien and Kwangtung.* London: Athlone Press.

Freeman, Michael. N.d. "The Fan Clan of Suzhou: I. The Early Life of Fan Zhongyan." Unpublished paper.

Hartwell, Robert M. 1982. "Demographic, Political, and Social Transformations of China, 750–1550." *Harvard Journal of Asiatic Studies* 42.2:365–442.

Hsiao Ch'i-ch'ing 蕭啓慶. 1978. "Yuan-tai ti ju-hu: Ju-shih ti-wei yen-chin shih ti i-chang" 元代的儒戶儒士地位沿進史的一章 [The Confucian household of the Yuan dynasty: An essay on the development of the status of Confucian scholars]. *Tung-fang wen-hua* 16.1–2:151–78.

Hymes, Robert. 1981. "From Sung to Yuan: Continuities in the Local Elite of Fu-chou, Chiang-hsi." Paper presented at the Association for Asian Studies meetings.

———. 1986. *Elite, State, and Locality in Sung China: A Study of Fu-chou, Chiang-hsi.* Cambridge: Cambridge University Press.

Ihara Hiroshi 伊原弘. 1972. "Sōdai Meishū ni okeru kanko no kon'in kankei" 宋代明州における官戶の婚姻関係 [Marriage relations of official households in Ming-chou in the Sung dynasty]. *Chūō daigaku daigakuin kenkyū nenpō* 1:157–68.

———. 1974. "Sōdai bushū ni okeru kanko no kon'in kankei" 宋代婺州における官戶の婚姻関係 [Marriage relations of official households in Wu-chou in the Sung dynasty]. *Chūō daigaku daigakuin ronkyū* 6.1:33–42.

———. 1976. "Sōdai kanryō no kon'in no imi ni tsuite" 宋代官僚の婚姻の意味について [On the meaning of marriage for Sung dynasty bureaucrats]. *Rekishi to chiri* 254:12–19.

————. 1977. "Nan-Sō Shisen ni okeru teikyo shijin—Seidofuro Shishuro o chūshin to shite" 南宋四川における定居士人成都府路梓州路を中心として [The fixed-residence gentryman in Southern Sung Szechwan: Focusing on Ch'eng-tu-fu circuit and Tzu-chou circuit]. *Tōhōgaku* 54.

Kobayashi Yoshihiro 小林義廣. 1980. "Ōyō Shū ni okeru zokufu hensan no igi" 歐陽修における族譜編纂の意義 [The significance of Ou-yang Hsiu's compiling a genealogy]. *Nagoya daigaku Tōyōshi kenkyū hōkoku* 6:189–216.

Kuhn, Philip. 1970. *Rebellion and Its Enemies in Late Imperial China*. Cambridge, Mass.: Harvard University Press.

Kyō Heinan 喬炳南. 1976. "Sōdai no gisō seido" 宋代の義莊制度 [The institution of the charitable estate in the Sung dynasty]. *Tezukayama daigaku ronshū* 11:74–98.

Morita Kenji 森田憲司. 1979. "Sō-Gen jidai ni okeru shūfu" 宋元時代における修譜 [The compilation of genealogies in the Sung-Yuan period]. *Tōyōshi kenkyū* 37.4:27–53.

Otagi Hajime 愛宕元. 1974. "Godai-Sōsho shinkō kanryō: Rinshi no Bashi o chūshin to shite" 五代宋初新興官僚臨淄の麻氏を中心として [The newly risen bureaucrats of Five Dynasties and Sung: Focusing on the Lin-tzu Ma]. *Shirin* 57.4:57–105.

Polachek, James M. 1983. "The 'Moral Economy' of the Kiangsi Soviet (1928–1934)." *Journal of Asian Studies* 42:805–29.

Schneider, David M. 1965. "Some Muddles in the Models: or, How the System Really Works." In *The Relevance of Models for Social Anthropology*, ed. Michael Banton. London: Tavistock.

Twitchett, Denis. 1959. "The Fan Clan's Charitable Estate, 1050–1760." In *Confucianism in Action*, ed. David S. Nivison and Arthur F. Wright. Stanford: Stanford University Press.

————. 1982. "Comment on J. L. Watson's Article." *The China Quarterly* 92:623–27.

Watson, James L. 1982. "Chinese Kinship Reconsidered: Anthropological Perspectives on Historical Research." *The China Quarterly* 92:589–622.

FIVE

Patrilines and the Development of Localized Lineages: The Wu of Hsiu-ning City, Hui-chou, to 1528

Keith Hazelton

Hui-chou prefecture, situated in the Anhwei highlands south of the Yangtze River, is an area with unique advantages for the study of descent groups and their social context. It lies just outside the great economic and cultural heartland of late imperial China, the Lower Yangtze region, and shares with that area the distinction of being one of the most richly documented regions of China. The Southern Sung (1127–1279) witnessed a remarkable acceleration of commercial development in Hui-chou. Social and economic disruptions at the end of the Mongol Yuan dynasty (1279–1368) gravely eroded these gains, but a new surge of growth in the Ming (1368–1644) and early in the Ch'ing (1644–1911) period gave the prefecture one of the most advanced economies in the late empire. The mainstays of commerce were the export of tea and lumber and the import of food grains. However, the mountainous terrain and white-water rivers of Hui-chou effectively prevented it from becoming a major transshipment point for interregional trade. Rather, local entrepreneurs spread out over the empire, gradually elevating the reputation of the "Hsin-an merchants" to the first rank of regional trading groups by the late sixteenth century. Due to the energy and wealth expended by these rich merchants to foster corporate descent organizations and activities, more Ming-period genealogies survive from Hui-chou than from any other area. Moreover, the three extant late imperial "Gazetteers of Renowned Lineages" all came from that prefecture (Zurndorfer 1981:154–57).

Until quite recently, the large, segmented Kwangtung lineage with extensive corporate landholdings provided the explicit or implicit model for most studies of patrilineal descent groups in China (see, e.g., Freedman 1958, 1966; Baker 1968; Potter 1970). The universal applicability of this model has now been seriously questioned by a number of historians and anthropologists (see, e.g., Ebrey 1983; Sangren 1984). The chapters of this book provide several graphic illustrations of the high degree of variability in the forms of kinship organization in different times and places in China. Even a single locale could be the site of a wide variety of contemporaneous descent groups. But to move beyond the mere cataloging of individual case studies it will be necessary to define generalized subtypes applicable to broad groupings of individual lineages. The lineage of the Hsiu-ning City Wu, the subject of the present study, differs from the Kwangtung model in several important respects, and I would argue that it represents a subtype of lineage common throughout large parts of the Middle and Lower Yangtze regions in Ming and Ch'ing times. In the course of outlining the origin and development of the Wu lineage, I will pay particular attention to features characteristic of this proposed lineage subtype.[1]

History of the Hsiu-ning City Wu

The primary source of information for the Wu lineage of Hsiu-ning City is the 1528 woodblock print edition of their genealogy (HSWS). When that work was compiled, the lineage was a small group with about two hundred male members divided among three branches or segments (*fang*): the North (*Ch'eng-pei*), Front (*Hsien-ch'ien*), and South (*Ch'eng-nan*) branches. The group's members resided, for the most part, in or just outside the city of Hsiu-ning.[2]

The "first ancestor" (*shih tsu*) of the Hsiu-ning Wu, the T'ang (618–907) censor Wu Shao-wei (*chin-shih* 701), was also the first ancestor of twenty-five other Wu-surname groups in She and Hsiu-ning counties. A total of forty-four Wu-surname descent groups were recorded in the *Hsin-an ming-tsu chih* ("The Gazetteer of Renowned Lineages of Hui-chou," published in 1551), the greatest number for any surname in the two-county area (CTS 190.2:5013–14; HCFC 1566:13:281; HAMTC 2:8a–30b).

---

1. The present study builds on material presented in the third chapter of my dissertation, "Lineages and Local Elites in Hui-chou, 1500–1800," (Princeton University, 1984). An earlier chapter of that work explores the historical and economic geography of Hui-chou prefecture. Another traces the history of two individuals of early imperial times who came to be revered as apical ancestors by an extensive network of descent groups, and who also took on the guise of tutelary deities, receiving the prayers and offerings of the prefectural population at large. In a final chapter, entries in the "Gazetteer of Renowned Lineages" (*Hsin-an ming-tsu chih*) were correlated with lists of upper-degree holders. This led to the identification of a small number of descent groups that successfully maintained membership in the top stratum of the prefectural elite over long periods of late imperial history.

2. Each branch was a true descent group associated with one of the three choronyms. All lineage members who received copies of the 1528 edition of the genealogy are listed in the work's final chapter. Because they are explicitly grouped by branch in this list, it is possible to check the tables of descent lines (*shih-hsi*) to confirm that the segments were membership groups composed of agnatic descendants of particular individuals.

Shao-wei was buried on Feng-huang mountain, just west of Hsiu-ning City, where his son is reported to have dwelt (HSWS 2:1a; HNHC 8:1393). Information beyond the names of ancestors in the direct line and occasional close collaterals is extremely rare for several generations after Shao-wei's time. Only in Southern Sung times is there a marked improvement in detail. Wu Chin of the ninth generation and his grandson were buried on Feng-huang mountain, suggesting that the group retained close ties to that area. Another Wu Chin of the thirteenth generation (tenth–eleventh century), was the first to be buried in Feng-lin park, just south of the city, a site that became the single most favored location for burial of subsequent generations of Hsiu-ning City Wu (HCFC 1699:1:279).

Two of Wu Chin's six sons had special significance for the later segmentation of the descent group: Wu Wen-tso was an ancestor held in common by the North and Front branches, while the South branch traced descent from Wu Wen-ku, who resided in the southern part of Hsiu-ning City, as did many of his descendants. The South residential grouping was thus by far the oldest of the three.

The Ascendancy of the South Branch during the Yuan Dynasty

Five of the total of fourteen office-holders in the recorded history of the group came from a striking three-generation cluster within the South branch. Their story spans the whole period of Mongol rule over South China. Wu Fu was an associate administrator of Ho-chien in the late 1200s. Two of his sons served in office as did two grandsons. The elder son, Li (1278–1359), held a series of posts in the late Yuan: scribe in the Chiang-che Branch Secretariat, clerk in the Chiang-hsi Branch Secretariat and senior clerk of Ching-chiang Route. In 1350 he received appointment as prefectural judge of Lien-chou on the far south coast of modern Kwangtung province. In the face of military uprisings in neighboring coastal prefectures, Wu Li trained local troops in defense tactics and thereby managed to keep the peace. For this success he was promoted to general administrator of neighboring Ch'in-chou and commander of the northern and southern seaways. Li's brother Hsuan-yu became deputy commissioner of the Che-chiang Salt Transport Commission. His brother's son, Wu Yen-t'ung, was a deputy chief clerk in Chen-chiang prefecture (HSWS 2:8a–10a; HHCCC 1:1542).

Wu Li's own son, Wu Na (1330?–57), learned the military arts accompanying his father on campaigns in Kwangtung. He later served as commissioner of records in Chien-te Route (which bordered Hui-chou on the southeast) and myriarch of the local defense forces. Under commander Li K'o-lu, he helped drive the rebel army of Hsu Shou-hui's T'ien-wan regime out of Hui-chou during the height of the late Yuan chaos of competing regional overlords.

On 24 July 1357, forces under Hu Ta-hai (d. 1362) wrested control of

FIGURE 5.1   Abridged Genealogy of the South Branch

Generation

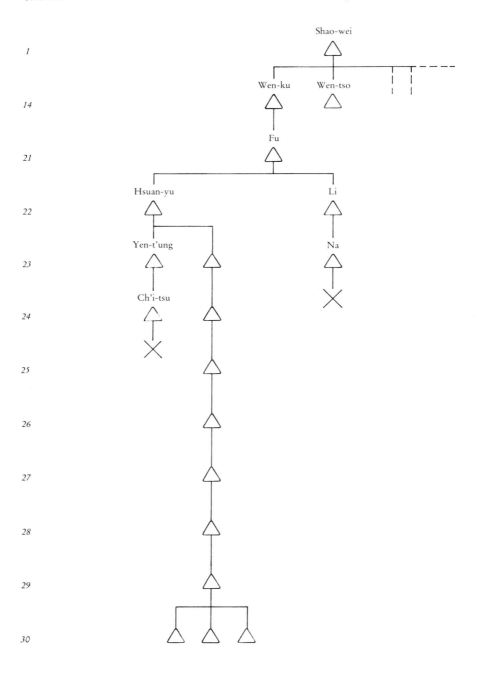

Ning-kuo from the Mongols and then advanced southwestward into Hui-chou, incorporating both prefectures into the expanding territorial base of Chu Yuan-chang, who, after eleven more years of fighting, would found the Ming dynasty. When the defense led by Wu Na and Mongol commander Pa-ssu-erh-pu-hua (Bars Bukha) broke down, Na and two garrison officers, A-lu-hui (Alghui) and Li K'o-lu, retreated into Sui-an county. Hu Ta-hai pursued them, inflicting a final defeat at Pai-chi ling, a range of mountains along the border between Hui-chou and Chien-te Route. Rather than submit to Ta-hai, Wu Na cut his own throat.[3] His suicide brought to an end the family's remarkable record of official service. His nephew Wu Ch'i-tsu compiled a genealogy for their branch of the lineage. The 1431 preface to that work praises all five of these illustrious forebears. Subsequent to this, the line was maintained only by collaterals, and according to the tables of descent in the 1528 genealogy, it was preserved by a fragile thread of only sons for six successive generations between the twenty-fourth and the twenty-ninth generations. The group of individuals discussed here is so small and closely related as to be better described as a line rather than a branch or lineage segment. What has just been related, then, is the story of one patriline in relation to the larger political and military events in the empire and in relation to the larger descent group of which it formed a part. This line's close association with Yuan rule may go far to account for the fact that they shared the fortunes of that conquest dynasty. Even so, the decisive and irrevocable eclipse of that family after Wu Na's death is a dramatic and remarkable segment of the history of the lineage.

The Flourishing of the North Branch in the Fifteenth Century

The North branch was the last to take up residence in the city, but it quickly rose to prominence, soon outshining the other two branches in both numbers and wealth. Wu Hsuan-nu (1382–1429) and a distant cousin, Wu Shan-ming (1379–1466), moved from Mi-ts'un village in the suburbs of Hsiu-ning city into the northern part of the city along the main north-south avenue. Shan-ming had amassed a fortune as a merchant, and the largesse attributed to Hsuan-nu in his biography and epitaph suggest that he too was a man of considerable means (HSWS "Hsu":4b, 3:14b–16a, 7:6b–7b).

---

3. HSWS 2:9b, 4:9b. See also Na's biographies in HCFC 1502 9:12b–13a, and HNHC 6:17b, and the account of his campaign against Hu Ta-hai found in MTTSL 5:55; in the latter source, the commander Wu Na accompanied in retreat is identified as Li K'o-yung. For Hsu Shou-hui, see Goodrich and Fang 1976:600–602. For Hu Ta-hai, see Goodrich and Fang 1976:629–31; MS 133:3878–80; and KCHCL 6:201–3. The name Pa-ssu-erh-pu-hua is being read as a metathesis for Pa-erh-ssu-bu-hua. In the latter form, it yields the quite common Yuan-period name, Bars Bukha. The character *ssu* when used to transcribe Mongol or Turkic names occurs as a final, and should not be followed by a vowel. On this basis, Pa-ssu-erh is properly Pa-erh-ssu.

The prosperity of these lines seems to have antedated the founders of the North branch proper. The two cousins who migrated to the city shared a common great-great-grandfather, Wu Fo (1275–1332), who saved his line from a decline into poverty. He opened new paddy and mountain lands, set aside land to pay expenses of the ancestral rites (*chi t'ien*), and conferred it upon his descendants with the injunction that it be held by them in perpetuity. He counted the locally eminent Neo-Confucian writer and teacher Ch'en Li (1252–1334) as a good friend.[4] Wu Ch'ing (1335–87), one of Wu Fo's grandsons and the grandfather of Wu Hsuan-nu, was also renowned for his wealth (HSWS 2:12b–13a).[5]

A prosperity based on mercantile ventures continued to characterize this line after Hsuan-nu's move to the county seat. His son Wu Shou-t'ung (1407–69) traded along the Lower Yangtze and the southeast coast as well as in Hunan, Hupei, Shantung, and Hopei, building a thriving business. At home he reclaimed mountain land belonging to the lineage, planting trees and creating paddy to provide for the ancestral tombs. He brought the members of the lineage together to draw up a compact to preserve these common lands in perpetuity. Shou-t'ung's son Tsung-chih (1440–1512) prevailed upon Hui-chou's most illustrious official of the fifteenth century, Ch'eng Min-cheng (1445–99), to write a joint epitaph for Shou-t'ung and his wife, née Hsieh (HSWS 2:17a, 7:8b–10a, 12a). It was at this time that the North branch finally achieved the coveted honor of seeing one of its members serve in office. After repeated failures in the provincial examinations, Tsung-chih was made a tribute student in the National Academy in 1480, and subsequently granted an appointment as assistant magistrate of Jao-yang county, in Pao-ting prefecture (HSWS 2:20b–21a). His brother Tsung-jen, who was held in high esteem by the county magistrate, participated in the commercial ventures of his father and eventually succeeded in making his family the richest in their locale. He was also remembered for works of charity such as helping families meet the expenses of marriage. He opened several additional

4. Ch'en Li, in the last year of his own life, wrote an epitaph for Wu Fo in which he praised Fo's conduct in both the poverty of his youth and the affluence of his later years, HSWS 2:10b, 7:2a–3a. On Ch'en Li, see his biography in YS 189:4321, and see his *Ting-yü chi* (TYC), which was copied into the *Ssu-k'u ch'üan-shu* compendium. Ch'en Li is also important here as the compiler of the *Hsin-an ta-tsu chih* (1316), the first of the three surviving composite gazetteers of prominent families or lineages of Hui-chou and Hsiu-ning (see Zurndorfer 1981).

5. There are problems with the dates given for Wu Ch'ing; they would imply that two of his sons were born when he was between six and eight years of age. In turn, the date of death of one of those sons, Wu Lü, is given as the seventeenth of the third month of 1380, while according to another entry, Wu Lü's son Hsuan-nu was born two and one-half years later, on the seventeenth of the eleventh month of 1382. Moreover, it is related in Hsuan-nu's biography that he lost his father at the age of two *sui* (that is, in late 1382 or early 1383). These discrepancies could easily be the result of errors of transcription, but they are nonetheless cautionary reminders that even in matters of significance for ritual observances, such as the dates of birth and death, the genealogical record contains some obvious flaws.

FIGURE 5.2 Abridged Genealogy of the North Branch

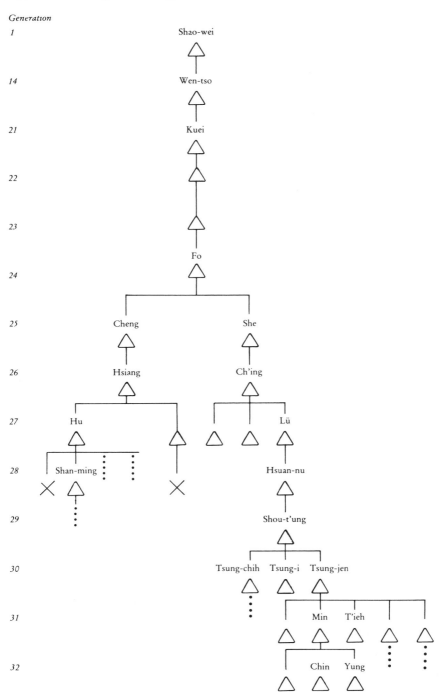

FIGURE 5.2 Abridged Genealogy of the North Branch

mou of paddy at Chia-yuan to provide a permanent source of funds with which to defray expenses of the ancestral rites. His three wives and one concubine gave him a total of five surviving sons and three daughters whose marriages or betrothals are recorded. Of the eight marriages contracted by his sons and daughters, four were to descent groups included in the 1551 gazetteer of prominent lineages of Hui-chou, such as the Lan-tu Ch'en and the Chu-tzu fang Chin. Another daughter married the son of a county magistrate. Eighteen grandsons followed, one of whom, Wu Chin, became the compiler of the 1528 genealogy. At the end of the fifteenth century, then, this branch represented established wealth and its members were regularly arranging marriages with other prominent families of the county.

The history of the lineage from the thirteenth through the fifteenth century can thus be divided into two major phases. In the first phase, the South branch (never more than a few lines in width) dominated through an unexcelled record in producing office-holders. The eclipse of this group at the end of the Yuan dynasty was followed shortly by the rise of the North branch. In this phase, one line within the branch was especially successful in commercial ventures and especially prominent in lineage-building activities. In fact, from the twenty-fifth to the twenty-ninth generation, this line was maintained by an unbroken sequence of eldest surviving sons.

In both phases, the period of greatest success was followed by the compilation of a branch genealogy (see the section on genealogies below), a fact of the greatest importance for understanding the nature of this type of lineage. The genealogy, as the historian's primary source for studying the lineage in premodern times, lends itself to the impression that the successes recorded there are the corporate achievement, so to speak, of the whole lineage. When examined more closely, however, it becomes clear that the "lineage as a whole" is in large part the creation of a few lines within the group whose successes mark them off from their lineage brethren. What appears at first as the flourishing of a lineage is, in fact, a reflection of the rise of a few patrilines and their close collaterals. Such a view reverses the balance between family and lineage characteristic of the Kwangtung model. There the member families often look to the lineage for help in maintaining their livelihoods. In this respect, the Wu, and many similar lineages in Hui-chou, better fit Patricia Ebrey's description of lineages in T'ung-ch'eng, Anhwei, where "the economic benefits of lineage membership are slight [and] ... the activists within the lineage are upper-class, educated men, mostly falling within the lines of such men" (Ebrey 1983:15).

The Lineage in the Sixteenth Century

When members of the lineage helped put down a local rebellion in the early sixteenth century, it marked the first time since the end of the Yuan that the group gave active support to official military campaigns.

In mid-May 1513 a detachment of the Yao-yuan rebels under Yang Luan-erh invaded Wu-yuan and threatened Hsiu-ning. Several members of the lineage responded to the call of county magistrate T'ang Hsun to launch a counterattack. The call-up of local forces had been authorized at the request of the supervising secretary for the Ministry of War, Wang Hsuan-hsi (*chin-shih* 1511), a prefectural native acting in his official capacity as monitor of the court's ongoing efforts to put down this hydra-headed uprising (MS 203:5354–56). If Hsuan-hsi was not already familiar with the Hsiu-ning City Wu lineage, their participation in the battles to follow brought them to his attention. Fifteen years later, when their new genealogy was completed, he graced it with a highly complimentary preface (HSWS "Hsu":1a–6a).

The main body of the rebel forces was at that time based in K'ai-hua, Chekiang, which shared a common border with Wu-yuan and Hsiu-ning. In Wu-yuan the bandits had killed more than thirty local militiamen and had captured large numbers of people. Some of the female captives had jumped from riverbanks, drowning themselves rather than suffer rape and dishonor. The magistrate T'ang Hsun had been traveling on official duties when he heard that the rebels were advancing on the county's southern border. He returned at once to lead the defense effort, successfully turning back Yang Luan-erh and his forces at Ta-ling.[6] A number of Hsiu-ning Wu took part in this defense. Wu Ch'i and Wu Hsi, who were both thirty-one that year, served honorably in the campaign. Wu Ch'i had been a devotee of martial arts and was known as a good rider and archer. He was called into service by the magistrate and acquitted himself well in the face of the enemy. His uncle was honored for his own meritorious service in helping T'ang Hsun drive off the rebels. Wu Hsi's first cousin contributed to the defense plans but, at fifty-eight, did not himself actively campaign. These four men were all members of the North branch. Wu Kuei-min (1460–1521) of the South branch was also called on by the magistrate to oversee aspects of the mobilization (HSWS 2:22b, 26a, 27b, 30b, 34b; KC 49:3042–51; MWTSL 91:1939–41, 96–104:2023–2138).

Military service is one of the few kinds of deeds that genealogists deemed worthy of inclusion in the collective record of the group's history. Why were martial exploits held in such high regard? In planning and carrying out military campaigns, members of the lineage forged closer ties with officials of the imperial bureaucracy, a benefit of lasting value. Added to this was the aura of glory attendant on valorous service in the cause of the common good. Through these actions the Wu took on the role of protectors of the populace, a role quite attractive for a group seeking recognition as a leading element of local society.

---

6. These hills were renamed Te-sheng ling ("Attaining Victory Range") in honor of that battle.

What became of the Hsiu-ning City Wu after 1528? There is very little to report and there were certainly no great bursts of glory. Yet the group did not entirely sink from view. According to Wu Ch'ien, a distantly related kinsman who consulted the 1528 genealogy in the course of compiling one for his own lineage, no new editions of the work had appeared between 1528 and 1793. However, the old lineage hall standing outside Hsiu-ning's north gate was an imposing sight which convinced him that the lineage "still did not lack for descendants who respected the ancestral line and brought the lineage together" (*ching tsung shou tsu*).[7] None of the Hsiu-ning City Wu earned a *chin-shih* degree in Ming or early Ch'ing times, so their long-term survival must have depended on a deeply rooted local social base and very likely on a continued involvement in commerce as well.

The Hsiu-ning City Wu as a Lineage

The Hsiu-ning City Wu of the early sixteenth century meet the definitional requirements for categorization as a lineage as used in this book. They were a ritual group possessing corporate assets, membership in which was based on demonstrated descent. Their ritual unity was expressed in the group rites conducted at graveside and at the ancestral temple dedicated to the Hsiu-ning first ancestor, Wu Shao-wei, as well as in the distribution of copies of the 1528 genealogy to members of nearly every family in the group. Their corporate holdings included the temple itself and "ritual fields" (*chi-t'ien*) bringing in an annual rental income of 183.5 piculs (*tan*) of grain (something over twelve tons) that was set aside to pay for the expense of the rites and maintenance of the hall and gravesites, plus an additional twenty-five *mou* (about four acres) of mountain land (HSWS 10:21b–22a).[8] There were most probably other corporate estates held by the lineage as a whole or by segments within it, but the genealogy reveals nothing of their existence. The tables of descent lines (*shih-hsi*) in its first chapter are the recognized and authoritative source for demonstrating one's descent from the "first ancestor" and thereby establishing claim to membership in the lineage.[9]

---

7. HSWS, an unpaginated addendum to the first *ts'e*, following chapter 1.

8. The yield in piculs can be used to make a very rough estimate of the total area of land in the estate. Figures of 1.5 to 2 piculs of husked rice per *mou* (about one-sixth of an acre), a rough rule for computing yields of this region and time, would suggest that the total paddy holdings were on the order of 100 *mou*.

9. These definitional attributes can be traced back as far as the late Southern Sung. Wu Tzu-chih (d. 1255), identified as the head of the lineage (*tsung-chang*), was credited with contributing regulations for rites and with writing a preface on the old "stone Buddha" ancestral tomb for the first known edition of the Hsiu-ning city Wu genealogy. These items imply the fulfillment of each of the definitional requirements of a lineage—ritual unity, corporate assets, and a basis for demonstrating descent (HSWS 2:6b, 10:26b). The "stone Buddha" (*shih-fo*) tomb almost certainly refers to the tomb of Wu Ch'eng (fl. tenth century?), the only Hsiu-ning city Wu known to be buried at that location.

Residential Concentration

The mention of a specific local place in the title of a genealogy is not enough to establish that the individuals recorded there were near neighbors. Such confirmation can come only from an accumulation of bits of evidence. In the case of the Hsiu-ning City Wu, it seems clear that a large and significant core group did reside within the city, at least during the generations after the arrival of the most prominent lines of the North branch Wu in the early 1400s (other lines within that branch remained behind in the Hsiu-ning suburban village of Mi-ts'un). Indirect support for this contention comes from the numerous cases in which emigration from the city is noted: Descendants of the emigrants are never included in the genealogy, a practice implying that the lineage was conceived as a residentially localized group that readily excluded even close agnates who permanently left the home base. Further, many of the more heavily used Wu tomb sites are located in the subcounty divisions (*tu*) immediately outside Hsiu-ning City.[10] Group participation in the Ch'ing-ming grave-sweeping rites as stipulated in the genealogy implies that the members resided close enough to the tomb sites to make this practical. Of course it was not uncommon for individuals to travel long distances to participate in such rites, but continuity of ritual practice depended on the consistent participation of a strong, local core group. Finally, as will be seen in the section on marriage below, the majority of wives and sons-in-law whose local place can be identified came from the city or its vicinity.

The Compilation of Lineage and Branch Genealogies

A residential concentration of agnates in and of itself does not constitute a lineage. What follows is an examination of those activities, predominantly concerning matters of ritual, that shaped the Hsiu-ning City Wu into a lineage. The first known genealogy for the Wu descent group of Hsiu-ning City was compiled in the late Southern Sung by Wu Tzu-chih and Wu Jih-ch'i (d. 1295). A preface and postface for this work by Wu Jih-ch'i dated 1267 are preserved in the surviving 1528 edition (HSWS "Hsu":1a–1b; 10:26b–27a). Wu Jih-ch'i was a *chin-shih* of 1265 whose official career included appointments as prefect of Chi-chou, general of the Yu-ling Guard and military governor of Chen-chou. He had also been granted a patent of nobility as Baron of Hsiu-ning (HSWS 2:8a; HCFC 1827:9.2:37a; 12.1:45a). Wu Tzu-chih showed Jih-ch'i a draft genealogy he had prepared, but it was

10. The Feng-lin yuan cemetery contains tombs for members of the Wu lineage and their wives from the thirteenth and fourteenth generations and from all but four of the fourteen generations from the nineteenth to the thirty-second generation. Feng-lin yuan is located in the second *tu* of Hsiu-ning county, immediately south of the city. Other common burial sites in neighboring *tu* are Mi-ts'un (second *tu*), Chien-ch'u ssu (second *tu*), and Chan-ch'iao (in the fifth *tu*, north-northwest of the city).

left to the latter to see the work through to completion. Tzu-chih contributed regulations for ancestral rites, thus suggesting that a descent group with common ritual practices had come into existence at least by this time.[11] A manuscript copy of this Sung genealogy was passed down through the generations of the South branch at least into the mid-fifteenth century (HSWS "Hsu":6a).

In 1334 another edition of the genealogy was prepared by Wu Lei, who served as assistant instructor in the Nan-ch'ang prefectural school. In his preface, he takes special pains to narrate geographical shifts in the Wu descent group subsequent to their settlement in Hsiu-ning in T'ang times. According to this account, all members of the group in Ming times shared descent from Wu Chin, a thirteenth-generation descendant of the first Hsiu-ning Wu. Two brothers of Chin's grandfather had moved away from Hsiu-ning, leaving the grandfather as the group's only tie to the old home area. Moves by other county-seat Wu within the city were also noted (HSWS "Hsu":1b–2b; 2:10b–11a).

The next preface, dated 1431, was written for a genealogy of the South branch. It was compiled by Wu Ch'i-tsu, whose father, uncle, grandfather, great-uncle and great-grandfather had all served in office during the period of Mongol rule. He was also a lineal descendant in the fourth generation of one of the compilers of the 1267 edition. The preface is noteworthy in that it marks the first time someone outside the Wu descent group was called on to contribute to the genealogy. The author here was a local student, Ch'eng Shun-tao (HSWS "Hsu":6b–7b).

A new genealogy for the whole lineage was compiled around 1485 by Wu Tsung-jen (1427–87), grandfather of the compiler of the 1528 edition used here. Tsung-jen enjoyed a privileged position in local society. The magistrate of the county, Ch'en Yü, gave Tsung-jen a place of honor at official banquets, consulted him on matters of local concern, and even deputed him to settle suits brought before the county yamen (HSWS "Hsu":3a–4a; 10:19b–20a; 7:13b–15a; HCFC 1827:7.2:488; 8.2:574). As in the previous example, this preface was the work of an outsider. In this case, the author was K'ang Yung-shao (*chü-jen* 1450) of Ch'i-men county, Hui-chou, a retired official who had served in the Censorate and the Ministry of Rites (HCFC 1827:9.3:660, 12.2:1002, MS 180:4774–75). By this time, prefaces by outsiders were becoming a standard feature of Hui-chou genealogies. This trend gives support to the hypothesis that, from Sung to Ming times, private genealogies came increasingly to have public functions as well, a process to

11. One difficulty with this version of the events is that according to a biographical note, Tzu-chih died in 1255, some ten years before Jih-ch'i won his *chin-shih* degree, yet the account has the two discussing the genealogy during Jih-ch'i's tenure as military governor of Chen-chou (HSWS 2:6b, 10:26b).

which Morita Kenji (1979) has drawn attention, and which Robert Hymes discusses in his chapter here in relation to Fu-chou, Kiangsi.

A year earlier Tsung-jen's younger brother had commissioned a preface for a branch genealogy of the North segment.[12] Subsequently another genealogist in the same generation as Tsung-jen and his brother supplemented an earlier edition to produce a genealogy for the Front branch in 1491. The compiler, Wu Yen (1442–1503), was the direct sixth-generation descendant of Wu Lei, the editor associated with the 1334 edition.

While the South branch genealogy of 1431 was done in a certain sense to mark that group off from the other branches, the North and Front genealogies were, as will be seen below, conceived from the start as part of a larger project to revise the genealogy of the whole lineage and to reinforce group cohesion. At that juncture, the North and Front groups could have opted to define the group so as to exclude the much-diminished South branch, but they chose not to. The North and Front groups shared common ancestors for several generations after their line split with that of the South group. They could have set up one of their later common ancestors as the focus of a new, shallower lineage while retaining their interest in the corporate property of the old group as members of the "higher-order lineage" stemming from Wu Shao-wei. The main argument against such a move would seem to have been that by writing out the South branch they would lose the patina of prestige associated with the five Yuan-period officials from that branch. In effect, the surviving members of a now much-reduced segment were invited to retain a place of honor in the revitalized lineage organization by virtue of the achievements of their distant ancestors. This goes directly to the question of the ways in which the institution of the lineage could work to translate the transitory achievements of individual degree winners and office-holders into an enduring elevation of the status of their line and segment, even in the absence of significant lineage landholdings.

The 1528 edition of the Hsiu-ning City Wu genealogy was compiled by Wu Chin, scion of the elite patriline within the North branch. This work is best understood as the culmination of an ambitious editorial project begun two generations earlier in the closing years of the fifteenth century. As noted above, those years saw the preparation of North and Front branch genealogies, and a new edition for the lineage as a whole. Wu Chin's grandfather and great-uncle had been two of the chief contributors to this project, and his father and uncle had continued to work on it. His father called on him and his elder brother to see to the completion and printing of the genealogy and

12. This preface was written by a putative distant relative, Wu Le, an erudite in the Nanking National Academy. He claimed to be related to the Hsiu-ning Wu through the common ancestor Wu Jui, a Ch'in period prefect of P'o (modern P'o-yang, Kiangsi) (HSWS "Hsu":4b, 1:3b–4a).

the restoration of the ancestral hall. In Wu Chin's postface to this edition, he recalls:

> I spoke of this to my father and elder brother, and then to the lineage members at large. They all immediately said, "You really have struck what was on our minds," even saying, "You possess talent and energy adequate to the task." Moreover, they said I should plan with urgency and not be slow in this project. All the elders of the lineage brought out old genealogies stored away by past generations and we edited them. The miscellaneous literary pieces were appended and the corporate estates of the ancestral tombs were recorded. It can be considered fully complete. I asked Mr. Chüeh-chai [Ch'eng Tseng] to collate and correct the work. He was to preserve the trustworthy, supplement the incomplete, and edit out complications, without phrasing a single expression carelessly or writing vaguely about a single incident. Thus the conduct of men of former times could be clearly seen again in the present day, and would not be utterly lost from sight. After several years of collation and correction, the genealogy was finally brought to completion in the fifth month of 1528. It will be distributed by cutting wood blocks with which to print copies. (HSWS "Hou hsu":2b–4a; cf. HSWS "Hsu":2a–4b)

The final product was thus the result of three generations' work by men from both the North and the Front branches, with assistance from a "specialist" outsider (HSWS "Shih-te hsu":5b–6a). The complete work required the cutting of 262 printing blocks. One hundred and fourteen copies were distributed to members of the group at a total cost of eight catties (128 taels) of silver.

The genealogies were widely distributed throughout the group so that typically either an adult male would possess a copy himself, or his father or brothers would have one. Few lineage members would have had to go outside their immediate family to see a copy, and, in those cases, one of their paternal uncles or first cousins would certainly have had one (HSWS 1:7b–17a, 10:24a–26a). Each copy also included a page identifying to whom that particular copy had been given. The copy used here is known to be one of a set of three given to Wu Yung, elder brother of the chief compiler, Wu Chin (HSWS 10:26a).

The Association of Office-holding with the Compilation of Genealogies

For the Hsiu-ning City Wu, the compilation of a genealogy was always closely associated with office-holding. The 1267 edition was largely the work of the *chin-shih* and later military governor of Chen-chou, Wu Jih-ch'i; the 1334 preface was written by Wu Lei, assistant instructor of the Nan-ch'ang prefectural school in the early fourteenth century. The 1431 branch genealogy was compiled by Wu Ch'i-tsu, scion of the remarkable group of South-branch officials in the Yuan dynasty. The 1491 genealogy of the Front Wu was the work of Wu Yen, one of only two men to attain office after the decline of the South group. The other official, Wu Tsung-chih, was responsible for the 1484 edition of the North branch genealogy. At the same time, his brother Tsung-jen was working on a genealogy for the whole lineage. The only known edition not linked as immediately as these to office-holding is the surviving 1528 edition by Wu Chin, but as noted above, he saw his task as carrying to completion the project begun by his grandfather and others in the late fifteenth century. It is especially striking that this correlation holds even for a lineage like the Hsiu-ning City Wu where there were relatively few officials among the members, and where most of those officials held only low positions obtained through channels other than the examination system.

If editions of genealogies had been compiled with less regard for the social position of the descent group's current representatives, it would be easier to see the production of a genealogy as motivated by some purely internal dynamic such as a need to update records with the passage of time and demographic expansion, or a perceived need to bolster declining standards of conduct and a waning group identity. Instead, this quite regular pairing of an individual's rise to official position with the subsequent compilation of a genealogy suggests a more externally oriented concern with relative social status and the attempt to consolidate gains won through the prestige of an official career.[13] Of course, it also suggests the obvious point that the compilation of genealogies was an occupation of the literati, one of the cultural pursuits that was coming to be considered appropriate to men of that status. But this association worked both ways. One could put forth a claim to membership in the literati stratum by performing deeds thought characteristic of that group, and the compilation of a genealogy lent a convincing substantiality to the claim.

Rites, Lands, and Hall

Rites for sacrifice and ancestor worship had been formulated by Wu Tzu-chih (d. 1255) and included in the first known edition of the Wu genealogy. Beyond that bare fact, nothing is known of the lineage's early ritual practices. Wo Fo (1275–1332) is said to have *once again* purchased ritual land, charging his descendants to protect it, a phrasing that suggests that even before his time land had been set aside to defray expenses of the lineage sacrifices. The possession of corporate ritual lands that was to become a hallmark of well-developed late-imperial descent groups was at this time still something of a mark of distinction. Wu Fo's fifth-generation descendant, Wu Shou-t'ung (1407–69), made further additions to the ritual land trust as

---

13. This again calls to mind the point made by Robert Hymes that the manifest concern with local nonagnates was part of the general trend to a localist strategy for status preservation that he sees operating in Southern Sung and Yuan times.

did his son Wu Tsung-jen (1427–87) (HSWS 2:10b, 2:17a, 7:8b–10a, 7:11b–13a). These three contributors to the corporate ritual land holdings represent a single patriline within the dominant North branch, the same line that includes the compiler of this edition of the genealogy. Of course it is likely that the information on the compiler's direct forebears would tend to be fuller, but there can be little question about the pivotal role played by this line in the activities of the lineage at large.

Materials on ritual practices, graves, ancestral halls, and ritual lands were included as a final chapter of the 1528 genealogy. Their content reveals a growing interest in matters of ritual during the years leading up to the production of the 1528 edition of the genealogy. New rules for group worship had been instituted some forty-three years earlier by Wu Tsung-jen, just mentioned for his donations of land to the lineage trust, and Wu Yen, one of the two Wu office-holders in Ming times and a member of the Front branch (HSWS 2:25a–25b, 10:14a). These rites were to be conducted in the ancestral hall or the home of the ritually senior member of the lineage (the *tsung-tzu*) at the New Year festival. Other rites on the same occasion were conducted in accord with the general customs in Hsiu-ning, but the Hsiu-ning City Wu claimed to excel in the performance of ancestral rites: "While other eminent *tsung* and great *tsu* occasionally conduct rites with rich and pure sacrificial goods, neat and respectful attire, with a gravity of ritual and demeanor and with harmony and joy of words and mood, we Wu are especially outstanding and far surpass the ordinary" (HSWS 10:13b–14a).

As discussed in Ebrey's chapter, during the Sung-Yuan period, Ch'ing-ming became an important part of the repertoire of ways to express and strengthen agnatic kinship ties. The practices of the Hsiu-ning City Wu on the occasion of the Ch'ing-ming festival are portrayed in detail in the final chapter of the genealogy, in texts that convey a vivid sense of the contemporary meaning of the rites.

Three days prior to Ch'ing-ming, the whole group of agnates assembled at the grave of the first ancestor, Wu Shao-wei, where sacrifices were offered and the grave-sweeping ceremony was performed. All members, old and young alike, partook of the feast that followed: "There are mutual toasts and exchanges of felicities. The proprieties of superior and inferior and the observances of distinctions of generational rank are also orderly, harmonious, and reverential. No one offends against the rites through boisterous behavior." One day prior to the Ch'ing-ming festival, the four headmen of the lineage (selected on a rotational basis) fasted and lodged overnight in the ancestral hall (*tz'u*). On the next day, sacrifices were offered before the ancestors as represented by their tablets in the main room of the hall. Everyone over fifteen and under sixty years of age was then to go to their various branch grave sites to sweep and decorate them.

Ch'ing-ming was also the occasion of the clearing of lineage accounts and

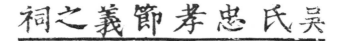

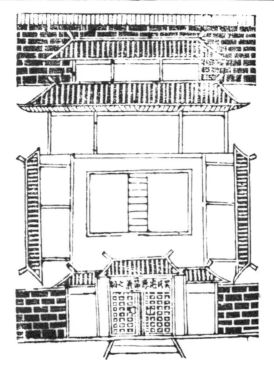

PLATE 5.1   The Hsiu-ning City Wu Ancestral Hall

the transfer of the books to the manager serving for the next annual term. One of the rules governing the Ch'ing-ming observances contains evidence that some of the capital held to meet ritual expenses was invested in commercial ventures:

> As for profits from kinsmen's shops, descendants in the various branches of the lineage must not be dilatory in the transfer of funds. This would work harm on the conduct of the sacrifices. In many great lineages (*tsu*) of the present time, this has led to the disruption of harmony and concord. It must be perpetually guarded against. (HSWS 10:16a)

Several other regulations concerned the management of ritual fields (*chi-t'ien*) and other corporately held assets. The location and boundaries of all

the plots "bought or opened since Sung and Yuan times, and additional
fields purchased subsequently" were recorded in an appendix to the genealogy. Moreover, the headmen were charged with making an annual personal
inspection of these plots "not only to mutually encourage awareness of the
plots, but also to avoid suffering the harms of encroachment and fraud committed by outsiders." The headmen were also charged to survey the various
lineage grave sites: If any of them were "run-down or in disrepair," the
headmen were "to give a first-hand report in the presence of all lineage
members, and to make timely repairs" (HSWS 10:15b–16a).

Grave Sites

Recording the location of grave sites seems to have been one of the
genealogists' main concerns. Just under a quarter of the 274 male members
of the Hsiu-ning City Wu who lived and died in the first thirty generations
had their grave locations recorded. The record of grave sites is, as one would
expect, much more complete in later times: Grave sites were identified for all
but two of the thirty-two members of the thirtieth generation who had died
by the time of the compilation of the 1528 edition.

Ancestors in generations one through thirteen were held in common by
all of the Hsiu-ning City Wu. Generation fourteen is the point at which lines
that later found expression as branches first began to diverge. Thus, insofar
as rites served to symbolize the unity of the lineage and its major structural
divisions, the grave sites of these early ancestors held a particular importance. This importance is reflected in the fact that grave sites were recorded
for nine of the thirty-four men in the earliest generations.

By contrast, only six grave sites were recorded between the fifteenth and
twenty-third generations. Four of the six were ancestors or close collaterals
of Wu Ch'i-tsu, the twenty-fourth generation compiler of the 1431 South
branch genealogy. As noted above, the careers of Ch'i-tsu's immediate
ancestors and their close collaterals defined the high point of the fortunes of
their branch. One man and four of his ten sons and grandsons held official
posts, a record unequaled in the whole lineage before or after that time. This
shows, once again, that the quality of data in a genealogy reflects in part the
relative stature of its component subgroups. More successful lines tended to
keep fuller records of their history. More specifically, whole blocks of information from earlier editions of a genealogy may have been carried over
into later ones, with a resulting unevenness of coverage. Outside of this
distinguished line, for example, there is an almost complete lack of information: Only two grave sites are recorded for the other 123 men in those
generations.

It is only during the late Yuan dynasty that most of the Hsiu-ning City
Wu began taking greater care to record this information. More significantly,
however, information on grave sites is concentrated within those lines that

survive into the later generations: With few exceptions, all of the known grave sites for generations one through twenty-nine are in the direct lines of members of the thirtieth generation. That is, lines that had died out before the thirtieth generation had only a slight chance of having their grave sites recorded. The likeliest explanation for this fact is that information on the location of grave sites of ancestors of present members was considered vitally important since Ch'ing-ming rites were conducted at graveside (see Ebrey's chapter in this volume). The same logic could justify the omission of this information for extinguished lines.

To a certain extent, branch affiliations were reflected in the choice of burial sites (see table 5.1). The South branch is clearly distinguishable from the other two on the basis of favored grave sites. With one exception, the South group shared no locations in common with either of the other two groups. The single exception was Feng-lin park. This park was the single most favored site for the burial of Hsiu-ning City Wu, and it had the longest history of continued use, spanning the thirteenth to the thirty-second generation. The South group had six ancestors buried at Lung-wang t'an, while the North and Front groups had between them eleven graves situated in Mi-ts'un and eighteen in a "park behind the great Buddhist temple" (*Ta ssu hou yuan*).[14] The North group buried six of their members at Chan-ch'iao and five at the Chien-ch'u temple, sites seemingly reserved for their exclusive use.

Fully twenty grave sites were located in spots where there were no other known Wu graves. The groups thus reveal a mixed pattern of clustered and isolated grave sites. The distribution of burial sites shows how the tension between lineage and family interests was played out in case after case over a period of centuries. The nature of this *tsung–chia* tension has recently been investigated by Patricia Ebrey (1984a). In her chapter in this volume, she identifies the source of this tension: It was in the interest of descent-group cohesiveness for the burial sites of agnates to be clustered in one locale so that graves of a larger group of agnates could be visited together on ritual occasions. An individual family, on the other hand, might seek to improve its fortunes by burying its immediate ancestors in sites chosen solely with a view to their favorable geomantic properties (*feng-shui*).[15]

As noted above, Wu burial sites were most numerous in Hsiu-ning's suburban areas. Ten of the thirteen known grave sites for South branch men were located in the first or second of the county's thirty-three subdistricts, or *tu*—the regions closest to Hsiu-ning City. Twenty-three of the fifty

14. I am interpreting several variants of this designation as referring to the same site. Thus I equate *ta ssu hou yuan* with *ta ssu hou, ssu hou yuan, ssu hou*, and *hou yuan*. It may be that the temple referred to is the Chien-ch'u ssu, in which case there would be a total of twenty-three Wu grave sites at this one location.

15. See chapter 4 of my dissertation for a fuller treatment of this topic.

TABLE 5.1
Distribution of Grave Sites by Lineage Branch

	Feng-lin park	Chan-ch'iao	Chien-ch'u temple	Mi-ts'un	Temple park	Lung-wang t'an
North	10	6	5	8	9	–
Front	10	–	–	3	9	–
South	3	–	–	–	–	6

North sites are in these two suburban *tu*, and, if the various sites described as "in the park behind the Buddhist temple" refer, in fact, to the Chien-ch'u temple, the total becomes thirty-two of fifty. If grave sites in the fifth and ninth *tu*, in the second ring of subdistricts outside the city are included, then it can be said that thirty-eight of fifty sites were in near proximity to the city. The corresponding figure for Front grave sites in the first, second, fifth, and ninth *tu* is twenty-five out of a total of thirty-four.[16]

Conjoint burial (*ho tsang*)[17] was a common practice, but far from an exclusive one: Of the 104 known cases, 45 percent were conjoint burials. As might be expected from ritual considerations, second and third wives were seldom given conjoint burial.

For the most part, wives were buried in sites used by male members of their husband's lineage branch. Thus the restriction of such sites as the suburban Lung-wang t'an to members of the South branch, and the Chan-ch'iao site in the fifth *tu* to members of the North branch, applied with equal force to the wives.

Motives for the Formation and Maintenance of the Lineage

The relatively meager collection of rent-producing property (yielding an annual rent less than two hundred piculs) held corporately by the Hsiu-ning City Wu would seem too weak a force to hold the group together by itself. If

16. It is possible that even more of the listed grave sites were near the city, for, with very few exceptions, the location of the remaining sites cannot be identified. In light of this, the figures above would tend, if anything, to underestimate the concentration of grave sites in the vicinity of the city. The location of an individual's grave cannot, of course, be taken as proof that the deceased was a resident of the immediate area. The custom of returning coffins of those who died elsewhere for burial in the "old home" was practiced here as elsewhere in China, as the following examples show: Wu Fo died in Ku-shu in 1332 (Shu-chou is a T'ang- and Sung-period name for An-ch'ing prefecture, Anhwei province, and the appellation Ku-shu probably refers to this prefecture), and his son, She, brought his coffin back to Hsiu-ning for burial behind the Chien-ch'u temple (HSWS 2:10b). The well-traveled Wu Ch'eng-tsu (1408–?) of the North branch died in Lin-ch'ing, Shantung, but his remains were finally brought home for interment in the traditionally favored site at Feng-lin yuan (HSWS 2:17b).

17. See Chao I's discussion of this term in KYTK 32:677–78. By late imperial times, the custom no longer implied, as it had in antiquity, two inner coffins buried in a single outer coffin (*kuo*), but merely burial of the coffins of husband and wife in the same excavation or burial vault.

the records in the genealogy represent anything like the whole of the corporate estate, there can be little doubt that the real wealth of the group was held
by its constituent families, or in estates shared by smaller groups of agnates.
In this respect, they present similarities with the Ma descent group of Yang-
chia-kou discussed in Rawski's chapter, and with the T'ung-ch'eng type of
lineage discussed by Ebrey (1983). Conversely, they offer a sharp contrast to
many of the well-studied Kwangtung lineages. Since no considerable economic gains appear to have accompanied lineage membership, the question
arises: What motives did lie behind the efforts to organize the lineage and the
commitment to maintain it?

As shown above, the key figures behind the efforts to create, support, and
revitalize the Wu lineage came nearly exclusively from a few lines of descent
within the larger group. This puts a finer point to the question: What were
these particular individuals about when they built up the lineage, and what
kept the group alive once it was set up?

Looking first at the motives of the architects of the lineage, it seems advis-
able to begin by examining the reasons they themselves gave for their actions, reasons often enunciated in prefaces and postfaces to various editions
of the genealogy. The classical justification invoked in nearly all examples of
such action was to revere one's ancestors, honor the *tsung*, and bring the
agnates together.[18] K'ang Yung-shao, in a preface written for the 1485
genealogy, explained: "To revere one's ancestors and honor the *tsung* is to
esteem the ancestral hall by manifesting a concern with seasonal sacrifices
and to protect the graves by being conscientious in sequestering the body
and the earthly soul. To gather the agnates is to perpetuate the old genealogies and record the names of the newly born" (HSWS "Hsu":3b–4a). In this
interpretation, the first two terms of the triad are closely related expressions
of the moral obligations towards one's ancestors, while the third concerns
the maintenance of desent-group identity and cohesion.

Certainly a feeling that the compilation of a genealogy and the consolidation of a lineage were a proper way to meet moral obligations toward ancestors and agnates should be recognized as a significant motive for those activities. To say that there may have been self-serving motives in addition to the
self-proclaimed ones is not to deny the sincerity of the latter. For the men
who took on the responsibility, more narrowly personal interests may also
have played a part. The responsibility for administering the annual rites was
rotated among four "headmen," and at least for them, there was some financial return for their labors, but this was not likely to be a primary motivation.

---

18. The most common variant of this stock expression is *tsun tsu ching tsung shou tsu*, the
locus classicus for which is the "Great Treatise" of the *Book of Rites*: CTLCIS 47:50a. For an
English translation of this section, see Legge 1967 2:66–67.

Especially in a region like Hui-chou with a tradition of strong descent groupings, the creation or revitalization of a lineage was a public as well as a private act. The moving forces behind such enterprises would expect the approbation of the larger community not only for belonging to one of the area's well-organized lineages—in itself a mark of distinction—but also for being men of vision and means, capable of translating moral desiderata into living social forms. As shown above, the Wu men who undertook these actions typically held elevated positions in local society by virtue of education or government service. For someone of that stratum in Hui-chou, an active role in a strong lineage may well have been de rigueur.

For the membership at large, participation in lineage activities was made attractive in part because through that participation, each individual could lay claim, to a certain extent, to the prestige and protection of the lineage as a whole—and especially of its more powerful and well-connected members—in his personal dealings with those outside the group. Moreover, as described above, the rites had the character of a celebratory family gathering, an event with a great deal of popular appeal. Indeed, the injunctions to observe the proprieties and refrain from overindulgence during the feast after the ritual observances give a sense that the organizers were concerned that the event could all too easily degenerate into merely an enjoyable social occasion.

"External Relations" of the Hsiu-ning City Wu Lineage

The focus now shifts to a discussion of two facets of the Wu lineage's "external relations": their marriage network and their relations with other Wu-surname groups in the two counties of She and Hsiu-ning.

Marriage Networks

It is sometimes possible to recast the scattered references to women in genealogies and literary collections so as to give a richer sense of their experiences and of the multiplicity of roles they actually played (e.g., Ebrey 1984b). In the Wu genealogy, however, women tend to figure only as wives, mothers, and daughters of the male members of the patrilineal descent group. It is perhaps to be expected that the compilers of a genealogy would discuss women only in their relation to matters of great significance for the lineage. This perspective is perhaps nowhere more clearly exemplified than in the treatment accorded to daughters. In no case are the daughters' names given. Rather, the total number born to a particular wife is mentioned, and for married daughters, their husband's surname and local place may be listed, in order of seniority. In other cases, the entry may merely note that the several daughters "all married into notable families" (*chü shih ming chia*).

TABLE 5.2
Affinal Surnames

Wife's father's			Daughter's husband's		
Surname	*%*	*Rank*	*Surname*	*%*	*Rank*
Wang	14.2	1	Wang	17.7	1
Chin	13.1	2	Chin	12.5	2
Ch'eng	9.3	3	Ch'eng	11.5	3
Wang²	6.9	4	Wang²	7.3	(4, 5, 6)
Liu	5.2	5	Shao	7.3	(4, 5, 6)
Chang	4.5	6	Yeh	7.3	(4, 5, 6)
Shao	3.8	7	Chang	5.2	7
Chu	3.5	(8, 9)	Liu	4.2	(8, 9)
Hsia	3.5	(8, 9)	Ch'en	4.2	(8, 9)
Ch'en	3.1	10	Hsia	3.1	10

The genealogy lists the father's surname for all but three of the 292 wives and concubines mentioned. The wives came from a total of forty-eight surnames, but Wu men preferentially married into nine surnames: Nearly two-thirds of the wives (183) came from one of these nine. As one of the premier surname groups in the county, it is not surprising that a good proportion of Wu marriages (over one-fifth) were contracted with women from Hui-chou's two other most notable surnames, the Wang and the Ch'eng, 41 (14 percent) and 27 (9.3 percent) respectively. The Wang and Ch'eng take first and third place in a ranking of most frequent affinal surnames. Wives whose father's surname was Chin held second place, with thirty-eight cases.[19] Daughters of the Wu lineage married predominantly into the same surname groups from which wives were taken. In fact, a very tight pattern of continued intermarriage seems to be indicated by the fact that the first-, second-, and third-ranked surnames for married daughters match exactly the corresponding rankings of surnames of wives: 41.7 percent of the Wu daughters married Wang, Chin, or Ch'eng men.[20] Table 5.2 shows the ten most frequently occuring maiden names of wives and married names of daughters ranked in decreasing order of frequency. The percentage of the total is given in each case.

The son-in-law's local place is indicated for fifty-eight of the ninety-six daughters mentioned. Marriages to men from Hsiu-ning City were most

19. The natal home of wives is given much less frequently than that of daughters, but of the fourteen Chin wives whose home is known, eight came from two urban Hsiu-ning places—the "central market" (*chung shih*) and the Chu-tzu ward (*Chu-tzu fang*)—so the prevalence of Chin wives may reflect a pattern of intermarriage between two primarily urban-dwelling descent groups.

20. The single exception to this parallel pattern is the ten cases of wives coming from the Chu surname: There are no corresponding cases of Wu daughters marrying Chu men.

common: Forty-two of the locations mentioned (nearly three-fourths of the total) are unmistakably urban Hsiu-ning locales. This is similar to the pattern for wives: forty-two (64 percent) of the sixty-six wives whose local place is identified were also from urban Hsiu-ning locations.

Changes in the kinds of information about marriage given in the genealogy reveal shifts over time in what the compilers considered important. The surnames of wives were recorded, at least sporadically, from the very first: We know that Wu Shao-wei married a Wang. But it is only in the very late generations, the twenty-sixth to the twenty-ninth, that the information begins to be recorded with any great frequency. Before the twenty-seventh generation, daughter's married surnames were never recorded, but the practice had been generally adopted by the thirtieth generation. There is no mention of concubines before the twenty-ninth generation, and altogether only eighteen were mentioned, all but three of whom belonged to men in the dominant North branch. The increase in the attention being paid to women in the genealogy reflects, more than anything, a growing concern with the lineage's "external relations." It is in this sense another indication of the increasingly public nature of lineages over this period. The three branches are hardly distinguishable from one another with respect to their choice of affines. If this is not merely a false impression engendered by a shortage of detailed information, it suggests that in the external relations of the Wu lineage, internal segmentation was of little consequence.

The existence of these enduring, geographically restricted marriage networks calls to mind the pattern of intermarriage between the Ch'ien and the Hua of Wu-hsi treated in Jerry Dennerline's chapter. There is a crucial difference between the two, however, making it unlikely that the process at work in Wu-hsi operated here. There is no evidence that the Wu had a charitable estate with which to guarantee the security of widows and orphans. Rather, the pattern of Wu marriages may reflect a version of the "localist strategy" that Robert Hymes identifies in his chapter on Sung and Yuan Fu-chou. In his view, marriage ties to other families in the local elite were used to build a "pool of potential allies."

Links to Other Hui-chou Wu

Of the numerous descent groups claiming descent from Wu Shao-wei, the Hsiu-ning City Wu lived closest to Shao-wei's home area and that of the earliest generations of his descendants. Other such groups could be found in all directions from the base area in and around Hsiu-ning City, although the greater number of settlements were concentrated in the south-central part of the county. Of the fifteen Wu groups with identifiable locations in She county, all but three were offspring of Wu Shao-wei groups in Hsiu-ning.

Maps 5.1 and 5.2 of Hsiu-ning and She counties show the distribution and filiation of Wu descent groups based on data provided in the *Hsin-an ming-tsu chih* (HAMTC). Each surname-choronym entry in the sections for the two counties was assigned a numeric code, and this numeric code appears on the map at the approximate location of the settlement.[21] Parent groups (those from which other groups are known to have split off) are enclosed in hexagons on the map. Filiation of groups is indicated by arrows from the parent group to the offspring group. The initials within the parent group hexagons refer to the home region of their predecessors. The one dotted line represents a case in which the link was mentioned in the 1528 Wu genealogy, but not in the *Hsin-an ming-tsu chih*. The editors of that work were not particularly assiduous about recording the date of founding of these groups, but in those cases where the information is given, or can be estimated from other data, the century of foundation is given in roman numerals under or alongside the group's numeric code.

Map 5.1 shows only those groups tracing their descent ultimately from Wu Shao-wei. Note the strong concentration in the immediate vicinity of Hsiu-ning City, and to the south and east; also note the cluster of tertiary offspring groups in west-central She county: There is a dense cluster of nine sites centered about fifteen kilometers west of She City, in the direction of the Hsiu-ning border. Strikingly, seven of them are offspring of an eighth group that had emerged, in turn, from an eleventh-generation descendant of Wu Shao-wei. These seven thus represent a second level of migration and settlement formation, a pattern that might be considered characteristic of a large and long-established descent group.

As for Wu settlements of other origin (see map 5.2), five groups in Hsiu-ning and She traced their origins to Ya-shan in K'ai-hua, Chekiang, just across Hsiu-ning's southeast border. The first group left Ya-shan during the turmoil of the first half of the tenth century between the end of the T'ang and the reunification of the empire by the Sung. They settled in Wu-t'ien in the twenty-third *tu*, fifteen to twenty kilometers south of the county seat. Eventually four other groups split off from this original settlement, one nearby in the tenth generation, one each just outside Hsiu-ning and She cities and one near the border of the two counties on a line between the two cities.

Another unrelated Wu group arrived from P'ing-chiang prefecture in northeastern Hunan in the late ninth century, supposedly in flight from the depredations of Huang Ch'ao's rebels (875–84; raids in this area 879–80). They settled in Ta-hsi in western Hsiu-ning and eventually spawned two offspring settlements, one in the immediate vicinity of the original site in the early thirteenth century, another at Shang-hsi-k'ou, some twenty kilometers

---

21. The placement of settlements is based on the very rough information provided by the *Hsin-an ming-tsu chih*, where the location of most groups is given as so many *li* in a specified compass heading from the county seat.

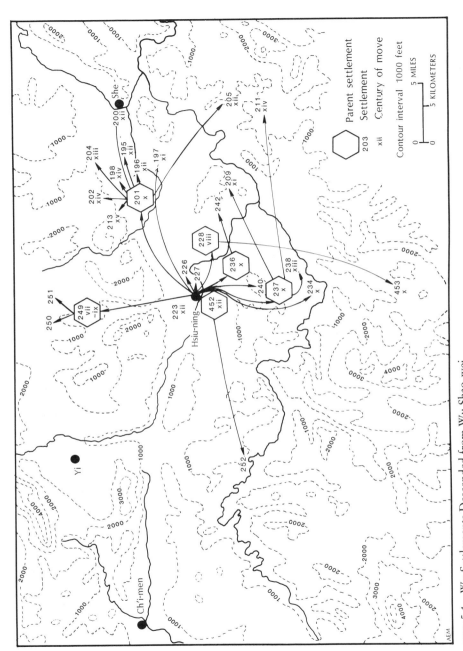

MAP 5.1 Wu Settlements Descended from Wu Shao-wei

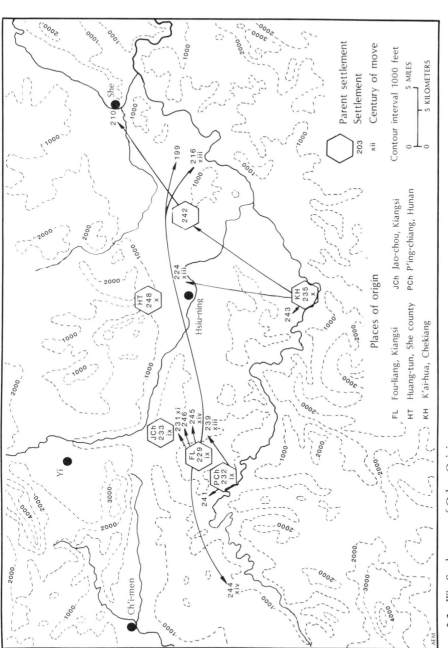

MAP 5.2 Wu Settlements of Other Origin

Parent settlement

Settlement

xii Century of move

203

Contour interval 1000 feet

0   5 MILES

0   5 KILOMETERS

Places of origin

FL   Fou-liang, Kiangsi   JCh   Jao-chou, Kiangsi

HT   Huang-tun, She county   PCh   P'ing-chiang, Hunan

KH   K'ai-hua, Chekiang

west-southwest of the county seat. The Wu of Lang-ssu, a lone settlement a few kilometers north of Hsiu-ning City, claimed they were established in the early Sung by a former resident of Huang-tun in She county, but no other information survives that would show a Wu group at the latter location.

Two Wu groups not descended from Wu Shao-wei, but sharing some ancestors in common with him, came from his ancestral home area in Jao-chou, Kiangsi, across Hui-chou's southwestern border. Both came to Hui-chou at the time of the Huang Ch'ao rebellion, one settling in the western part of the county at Ch'ang-feng and the other in nearby Chiang-t'an, both in the thirtieth *tu*. The latter settlement gave rise, over time, to several offspring settlements, four in western Hsiu-ning and two in southwestern She county.

In general, there was a tendency for offspring groups to emerge in relatively close proximity to the parent group, but there was no shortage of cases involving lengthy intra- or inter-county moves. All of the parent groups except one were established by the tenth century, and several of them continued to spawn offspring groups for several centuries. Only one new Wu settlement was established after the fourteenth century, but there was a relatively steady rate of formation from the tenth through the fourteenth century: On average, between five and six new groups emerged per century. Of course, nothing is known about the internal structure of these groups beyond the fact that they—or at least their reputation—endured into the sixteenth century, and that enough of their members held official posts or honors to win them the status of "renowned *tsu*."[22]

From these data in the *Hsin-an ming-tsu chih*, it can be seen that the Hsiu-ning City Wu had kinship ties to many other Wu settlements in Hui-chou. In addition to the twenty-five groups claiming descent from Wu Shao-wei, a good number claimed to come from the P'o-yang area of Kiangsi from lines that in remote times included ancestors of Shao-wei himself. Thus, all but a handful of Wu groups in these two counties could consider themselves members of a larger grouping of kin of the sort that occasionally found expression as a higher-order lineage. Although the existence of many of those links is acknowledged in the 1528 genealogy, there is no evidence of a higher-order lineage for Wu descent groups in this area in the mid-sixteenth century, the time of compilation of the *Hsin-an ming-tsu chih*. It is worth noting that the shared traditions of common agnatic ties necessary to create one had been preserved independently by numerous widely scattered groups. In light of the later trend toward the definition of descent groups of increasingly wide geographical scope, the fact that there was a preexisting

22. The preceding discussion is based primarily on the HAMTC entries for Wu surname groups in She and Hsiu-ning counties (see 2:8a–30b).

account of origin and descent which linked many of the "Chiang-nan Wu" is quite significant. In this case, at least, the tradition of common descent from a single ancestor was shared long before the emergence of county- or prefecture-wide "clans" or higher-order lineages. This suggests the hypothesis that the emergence of higher-order lineages in such cases could proceed smoothly and, to all appearances, quite naturally, since it required only that representatives of the constituent groups meet to compare traditions and reconcile gross contradictions between them. A likely preliminary step would have been the compilation of a comprehensive genealogy or *t'ung-tsung shih-p'u*. This possibility was in the minds of the compilers of the 1528 Hsiu-ning City Wu genealogy when they noted in passing a discrepancy in traditions about the founder of the first She county branch with the comment that its resolution would have to await someone's calling a gathering of the whole *tsung* (*hui t'ung tsung*; HSWS 2:1b).[23]

Conclusion

The significance of the Hsiu-ning City Wu for the history of kinship organization is, I would argue, that their group can stand as an early representative of an important subclass of lineages in late imperial China. For convenience, this subclass might be designated "Lower Yangtze" lineages, since the groups sharing this set of defining characteristics have up to now mostly been found in that region of China (see Zurndorfer 1981; Ebrey 1983; Beattie 1979; Dennerline's chapter in this volume; and Yeh 1983). Lower Yangtze lineages are thus to be distinguished both from "Kwangtung" lineages, and from "unincorporated" descent groups like those from North China examined by Naquin and Rawski in this volume. Examples of each type might certainly be found outside the area with which they are most closely identified, but as provisional labels, these regional designations seem useful. Using the example of the Hsiu-ning City Wu, the identifying and distinguishing features of Lower Yangtze lineages can be listed as follows:

23. Ch'eng surname groups had gone through just such a process in the late fifteenth century under the direction of Ch'eng Min-cheng (1445–99, *chin-shih* 1466). See his 1482 preface to the *Hsin-an Ch'eng-shih t'ung-tsung shih-p'u* (SKCS "chiu p'u hsu":21a–23b), and his remarks on the desirability of such a general genealogy of the Ch'eng (*Ch'eng-shih tsung-p'u*) in his collected writings: HTWC 12:35b–36a. For biographies of Min-cheng, see MS 286:7343–44, and HNHC 1693 6:800–802. Such comprehensive genealogies were not without their critics. Ku Yen-wu bore a particular animus toward this enterprise. When done privately, without official checks and approval, he felt that it led to a proliferation of errors and excesses. He proposed setting up an administrative procedure for handling applications by groups wishing to compile such works, and suggested that the families of those who proceeded without official approval be barred from office for generations (see Ku Yen-wu, JCLCS 23:534–35).

(1) Rent from corporately held property in Lower Yangtze lineages was often sufficient only to meet the expenses of the group's annual cycle of rituals and of the maintenance of ancestral halls and grave sites. This is the sharpest point of distinction from the Kwangtung lineage. For the latter, vast corporate landholdings in and of themselves give the lineage a powerful influence over member households (see, e.g., Freedman 1958, 1966; Baker 1968; Potter 1970). There may, however, be an underlying historical trend to be taken into account. In his chapter, Dennerline shows that substantial and enduring "charitable estates" became a common feature of the Wu-hsi region in the eighteenth and nineteenth centuries. A tabulation of lineage properties in Hui-chou drawn up by Yeh Hsien-en reveals that estates in the Ming rarely exceeded one hundred *mou* (comparable to the holdings of the Hsiu-ning City Wu). In the Ch'ing period, however, holdings of several hundred to over a thousand *mou* were not unusual (Yeh 1983:48–51). However, even modest amounts of property together with the group ritual observances supported by those assets serve to distinguish Lower Yangtze lineages from groups like the Ma of Yang-chia-kou, and the Lang-yeh Wang of Yung-p'ing prefecture, discussed in the chapters by Rawski and Naquin. These descent groups possessed no corporately held estates, and there is no evidence that they took part as a group in joint ritual observances.

(2) The active figures in the history of the Hsiu-ning City Wu lineage came consistently from a small number of patrilines within the larger group. These same lines accounted for the majority of officials to have come from the lineage, and these officials and their immediate descendants bore almost sole responsibility for preparing various editions of lineage and branch genealogies. In the conclusion to chapter 4, Hymes stresses that what was new in Southern Sung times was not co-residential descent groups per se, already at that time a venerable feature of Chinese social organization, but the self-chosen role of "the bureaucratic and literate elite as leaders, organizers, promoters, and controllers of large localized descent groups." The existence of an elite core of activists is also a feature of what Patricia Ebrey has identified as the "T'ung-ch'eng type" lineage (1983:12–17). Studies of the structure and activities of such lineages must therefore look first at the question of the motives and interests of this elite element within the larger group.

(3) Behind these lineages is a social landscape composed of residentially concentrated descent groups created by the emigration of family groups from their ancestral home area. Heads of these families often became "first migrant ancestors" (*shih-ch'ien tsu*) of newly emergent descent groups. This pattern is seen with great regularity and clarity in the "Gazetteer of Renowned Lineages." The link between lineages and this underlying fabric of descent groups could be made in one of several ways, and variations in the kinds of lineages to be found within the general Lower Yangtze category

stem primarily from differences in this relationship. The most "robust" lineages were those that limited their membership to a descent group residing in a single village or village cluster. Emily Ahern (1976) was the first to argue that migration could be a more important factor than corporate estates in the emergence of new segments and lineages. Stevan Harrell subsequently focused the thesis more sharply by stating that "whereas localization seems nearly always to make a lineage into a discrete social unit, corporate property does not seem sufficient to create such solidarity unless there is enough property to bring direct economic benefit to lineage members" (Harrell 1981:140).

Alternatively, a group could be defined without regard to the place of residence of its members, giving rise to a dispersed lineage. The most important differences between the lineages of the Hsiu-ning City Wu and the Chang of T'ung-ch'eng stem, I would suggest, from just this fact: The Wu formed a true localized descent group of quite modest size whose members for the most part resided in close proximity to one another. The Chang genealogy of 1890 seems, by contrast, to define a vaguely bounded dispersed lineage. The compilers do not seem to have been in close contact with some of the remoter branches listed in the tables of descent. While the vital data in the Chang genealogy was spotty and uneven outside a few core lines, the Wu genealogy provided full information on nearly everyone (at least in the later generations), and it took more care to define the boundaries of the group, noting when particular individuals left the group through emigration, and excluding the descendants of such emigrants from the genealogical tables. The steps taken to encourage all members between fifteen and sixty years of age to take part in the ancestral rites also distinguish this group from the Chang of T'ung-ch'eng (Ebrey 1983:15). Again, this joint celebration would only be practicable for a group with both homes and graves concentrated in a relatively limited area. Finally, "higher-order" lineages could link a network of residentially concentrated lineages through common ties to a remote ancestor and shares in a corporate estate. According to the description given by Dennerline in chapter 6, the Ch'ien in the vicinity of Hung-sheng-li, Wu-hsi county, formed a classic case of this kind. Participation in lineage affairs was also conditioned by the social geography of the group. Non-elite members, by and large, found themselves able to take part only in the activities of the localized lineage to which they belonged. Involvement in matters of concern to a dispersed or higher-order lineage was the prerogative of individuals and families of wider social horizons.

The complexity of descent group organization in late imperial China is not to be denied, but if the preceding observations are borne out by further comparisons between groups in this region, the concept of a Lower Yangtze type of lineage will prove useful by helping to distinguish complexity from mere chaos.

REFERENCES

Primary Sources

CTLCIS   *Ch'in-ting li chi i-shu* 欽定禮記義疏. *Ch.* 47, "Ta chuan" 大傳. Ssu-k'u
ch'üan-shu chen-pen, pa chi ed. Taipei, 1978, vol. 48.

CTS   *Chiu T'ang shu* 舊唐書. Liu Hsu 劉昫, ed. Peking: Chung-hua, 1975.

HAMTC   *Hsin-an ming-tsu chih* (1551) 新安名族志. Ch'eng Shang-k'uan 程尚寬,
ed. Peking National Library rare book collection microfilm, r433(5).

HCFC 1502   *Hui-chou fu-chih* 徽州府志. P'eng Tse 彭澤, ed. Ming-tai fang-chih
hsuan, no. 1. Taipei: Hsueh-sheng, 1965.

HCFC 1566   *Hui-chou fu-chih* 徽州府志. Ming-tai fang-chih hsuan, no. 2. Ho
Tung-hsu 何東序 and Wang Shang-ning 汪尚寧, eds. Ming-tai fang-chih hsuan,
no. 2. Taipei: Hsueh-sheng, 1965.

HCFC 1699   *Hui-chou fu-chih* 徽州府志. Ting T'ing-chien 丁廷楗 and Chao Chi-
shih 趙吉士, eds. Chung-kuo fang-chih ts'ung-shu, 1975 photocopy of original
edition.

HCFC 1827   *Hui-chou fu-chih* 徽州府志. Ma Pu-chan 馬步蟾 and Hsia Luan 夏鑾,
eds. Chung-kuo fang-chih ts'ung-shu, 1975 photocopy of original edition.

HHCCC   *Hsi-hu chu-chih chi* 西湖竹枝記. Yang Wei-chen 楊維楨 (1296–1370).
Wu-lin chang-ku ts'ung-pien ed. Taipei, 1967.

HNHC 1693   *Hsiu-ning hsien-chih* 休寧縣志. Liao T'eng-k'uei 廖騰煃 and Wang
Chin 汪晉, eds. Chung-kuo fang-chih ts'ung-shu, 1970 photocopy of original
edition.

HSWS   *Hsiu-ning hsien-shih Wu-shih pen tsung-p'u* 休寧縣市吳氏本宗譜. 1528.
Wu Chin 吳津, ed. Peking National Library rare book collection microfilm, r354
(1).

HTWC   *Huang-tun wen-chi* 篁墩文集. Ch'eng Min-cheng 程敏政 (1445–99). Ssu-
k'u ch'üan-shu chen-pen, san chi ed. Taipei, 1972.

JCLCS   *Jih-chih lu* 日知錄. Chi-shih ed. Ku Yen-wu 顧炎武. Taipei: Shih-chieh,
1968.

KC   *Kuo Ch'üeh* 國榷. Ca. 1653. T'an Ch'ien 談遷. Reprinted Peking: Ku-chi,
1958.

KCHCL   *Kuo-ch'ao hsien-cheng lu* 國朝獻徵錄. Chiao Hung 焦竑 (1541–1620).
Facsimile of Wan-li (1573–1620) ed.; Taipei: Hsueh-sheng, 1965.

KYTK   *Kai yü ts'ung k'ao* 陔餘叢考. 1790?. Chao I 趙翼. Shanghai: Shang-wu,
1957.

MS   *Ming shih* 明史. Chang T'ing-yü 張廷玉 (1672–1755), ed. Peking: Chung-hua,
1974.

MTTSL   *Ming T'ai-tsu shih-lu* 明太祖實錄. Facsimile of the Pei-p'ing Library's
early Ch'ing edition. Taipei: Academia Sinica, 1961.

MWTSL   *Ming Wu-tsung shih-lu* 明武宗實錄. Facsimile of the Pei-p'ing Library's
early Ch'ing edition. Taipei: Academia Sinica, 1961.

SKCS   *Hsiu-ning Shuai-k'ou Ch'eng-shih hsu-pien pen-tsung-p'u* 休寧率口
程氏續編本宗譜. 1570. Ch'eng Hsu 程序 et al., eds. Taipei: National Central
Library microfilm 03011.

TYC   *Ting-yü chi* 定宇集. Ch'en Li 陳櫟. Ssu-k'u ch'üan-shu chen-pen, erh-chi,
vols. 332–34. Taipei, 1971.

YS   *Yuan shih* 元史. Sung Lien, ed. 宋濂. Peking: Chung-hua, 1976.

Secondary Works

Ahern, Emily M. 1976. "Segmentation in Chinese Lineages: A View through Written Genealogies." *American Ethnologist* 3.1:1–16.

Baker, Hugh D. R. 1968. *A Chinese Lineage Village: Sheung Shui*. Stanford: Stanford University Press.

Beattie, Hilary J. 1979. *Land and Lineage in China: A Study of T'ung-ch'eng County, Anhwei, in the Ming and Ch'ing Dynasties*. Cambridge: Cambridge University Press.

Ebrey, Patricia Buckley. 1983. "Types of Lineages in Ch'ing China: A Reexamination of the Chang Lineage of T'ung-ch'eng." *Ch'ing-shih wen-t'i* 4.9:1–20.

———. 1984a. "Conceptions of the Family in the Sung Dynasty." *Journal of Asian Studies* 43.2:219–245.

———. 1984b. "The Women in Liu Kezhuang's Family." *Modern China* 10:415–40.

Freedman, Maurice. 1958. *Lineage Organization in Southeastern China*. London: Athlone Press.

———. 1966. *Chinese Lineage and Society: Fukien and Kwangtung*. London: Athlone Press.

Goodrich, L. C., and Fang Chao-ying. 1976. *Dictionary of Ming Biography, 1368–1644*. New York: Columbia University Press.

Harrell, Stevan. 1981. "Social Organization in Hai-shan." In *The Anthropology of Taiwanese Society*, ed. Emily Ahern and Hill Gates, pp. 125–47. Stanford: Stanford University Press.

Hazelton, Keith D. 1984. "Lineages and Local Elites in Hui-chou, 1500–1800." Ph.D. dissertation, Princeton University.

Legge, James, trans. 1967. *Li Chi: Book of Rites*. New Hyde Park, N.Y.: University Books.

Morita Kenji 森田憲司. 1979. "Sō-Gen jidai ni okeru shūfu" 宋元時代における修譜 [On the Compilation of Genealogies in the Sung and Yuan Periods]. *Tōyōshi kenkyū* 東洋史研究 37.4:509–35.

Potter, Jack M. 1970. "Land and Lineage in Traditional China." In *Family and Kinship in Chinese Society*, ed. M. Freedman, pp. 121–38. Stanford: Stanford University Press.

Sangren, P. Steven. 1984. "Traditional Chinese Corporations: Beyond Kinship." *Journal of Asian Studies* 43.3:391–415.

Yeh Hsien-en 葉顯恩. 1983. *Ming-Ch'ing Hui-chou nung-ts'un she-hui yü tien-p'u chih* 明清徽州農村社會與佃僕制 [Rural Society and the Bond-Tenant System in Ming and Ch'ing Hui-chou]. Anhwei: Jen-min.

Zurndorfer, Harriet T. 1981. "The *Hsin-an ta-tsu-chih* and the Development of Chinese Gentry Society, 800–1600." *T'oung Pao* 67.3–5:154–215.

SIX

Marriage, Adoption, and Charity in the Development of Lineages in Wu-hsi from Sung to Ch'ing

Jerry Dennerline

In the southeastern corner of Wu-hsi county, about twenty kilometers north of Soochow, lies a sleepy industrial town called Tang-k'ou. About equidistant from the administrative cities of Wu-hsi, Soochow, and Ch'ang-shu, it was in the nineteenth century the center of a rural community peripheral to all three. Within the area that might be described as the hinterland of Tang-k'ou there had developed a network of scholar-gentry families, the history of which can be traced back to the early Ming period. This chapter argues that interrelated strategies of marriage arrangement, heir adoption, and charity for widows and orphans were crucial to the formation and continuous development of this network.[1]

Within a period of several months around the year 1882 there occurred three events of the sort that make family history. They were isolated but patterned events, the sort that take on significance by occurring again and again in much the same way with similar effects. Their significance is in what they demonstrate about the effectiveness of the strategies that perpetuated the scholar-gentry network. The first event was the marriage of the daughter of a relatively prosperous farmer-scholar to the son of a poor country scholar. The second was the death of a nonofficial gentryman, whose survivors were securely locked into a complex web of kinship that guaranteed their continued status as well as that of their offspring among the elite families of

1. Much of the research behind this paper was undertaken while I was Visiting Assistant Professor in the History Department at Yale University and with help of a generous grant from the American Council of Learned Societies and a grant-in-aid from the American Philosophical Society. I would like to thank all three for their support. Thanks also to H. Kaneko, curator of the East Asian collection at Yale, for assistance in procuring the genealogical sources, to Anthony Marr and to Jack Jacoby, and to Yü Ying-shih for directing me to Ch'ien Mu's memoir. I alone am responsible for the content of this paper.

the community. The third was the completion of a new ancestral temple legitimizing both the leadership status of the deceased gentryman's son in matters of lineage welfare, and the large, privileged charitable estate his family had created.

The marriage entailed some risk. A certain well-to-do scholar-farmer by the name of Ts'ai, who lived in a hamlet a kilometer northwest of the village of Hung-sheng-li, sent his daughter in marriage to a relatively poor family of the so-called Five Generations Together Hall (*Wu shih t'ung t'ang*) branch of the Ch'ien lineage in Ch'i-fang-ch'iao hamlet, about a kilometer to the east of Hung-sheng-li. The Ts'ai family—under the management of a pair of brothers who also tutored young scholars and practiced medicine—owned some land, an ox, and an acre or so of reservoir in which they raised geese and fish. Altogether it was enough to require hiring three or four men to work. The girl's father was advised that the Ch'ien family was a bad choice, as "the whole descent group lives together; their economy is in doubt but their fancy style and elegant manners just won't quit. I've heard the prospective bridegroom is a student. If so, I'm afraid he won't be very clever at doing business. If you marry your daughter to him, you'll surely reap a lot of misery for it."

According to the daughter, who related the story to her son, her father replied, "A house that lives by the *Odes* and the *Rites* doesn't count its wealth in money. I'd like my daughter to go there, where she still has some chance of practicing what the *Odes* and the *Rites* teach." Such was the justification given for marrying a daughter to a poor but pretentious country scholar household. The marriage in question produced one daughter and four sons, including the scholar and educator Ch'ien Mu, whose memoirs record his mother's description of the Ch'ien family and the village (PSISC:20).

The death occurred in the town of Tang-k'ou itself, some three kilometers farther east. Hua Ts'un-k'uan died in 1882 at the age of seventy-five. He was survived by a widow, a married son, a widowed daughter, and two grandsons. The widow was a Ch'ien from Hung-sheng-li, daughter of one of the most prominent gentry families in the area. Distant agnates of the poor country scholar the Ts'ai woman married, they managed a lineage school and charitable estate with a hundred-year history. Ts'un-k'uan's daughter was the widow of another Ch'ien from Hung-sheng-li, and one of the grandsons supported another Ch'ien woman who was the widow of Ts'un-k'uan's nephew. The grandson had been designated adoptive heir to his great-uncle's son. Ts'un-k'uan's wife thus joined a class of widows that was much in evidence among the Ch'iens and the Huas. How they were treated was one of the signs of the local scholar-gentry class. The evidence was meticulously recorded in the Hua and Ch'ien genealogies (*tsung-p'u*) compiled and printed on the Hua side by Ts'un-k'uan's son Hung-mo, and on the Ch'ien side, by the son of Hung-mo's sister, among others (HS 1881:13:376).

The new ancestral temple was the work of Hua Hung-mo. He built it primarily to provide a ritual focus for a group of some nine hundred male descendants of Hua "San-hsing" (1409–97), his thirteenth-generation ancestor, for whom no shrine had ever existed. In effect, Hung-mo was completing the process of lineage incorporation for a subbranch of the Tang-k'ou Huas that had begun in 1860 under the direction of his father and uncles. In that year, dozens of representatives of the larger descent group met and authorized the creation of a new charitable estate to supplement the one established in 1745. The new estate, finally approved by the Board of Revenue in 1875, was to provide relief for descendants of San-hsing, removing them from the rolls of the existing estate. Hung-mo compiled the new branch genealogy and built the temple, rescuing the tablets of his own immediate ancestors from the small anteroom of the family distillery where they had been forced to reside for some decades.

It was an elevation for Hung-mo's ancestors appropriate to the rising status of the family. None of Hung-mo's ancestors had passed the provincial examination, and he was the only one among the descendants of his fifth-generation ancestor to pass it, which he did in 1873. Yet the key to the family's prominence was not Hung-mo's degree. It was the charitable estate, which included more than a thousand *mou* of officially protected land, a granary, a school, and a directorate that was quite distinct from the ritual headship of the newly formed lineage branch. The process by which it was created was described in a set of documents compiled by Hung-mo and others and published by the estate (Dennerline 1981b:36).

The decision of a well-to-do scholar-farmer to marry a daughter into a poor country scholar's family, the proliferation of widows and orphans among the heavily interrelated elite families, and the dynamic presence of kin-based welfare estates in the community were part of the setting for a number of life stories. By the time of Hua Hung-mo's death in 1911, the poor Ch'ien scholar who married the Ts'ai woman had passed the county examinations, won a protracted struggle for control of a smaller charitable estate in his village, and died a victim of illness and opium at the age of thirty-two. Ts'ai, his widow, had raised the children with the help of welfare from the charitable estate. Hua Hung-mo and his son had doubled the size of their charitable estate, extended its coverage to indigent in-laws, and opened its school to poor scholars from the community. Hung-mo's grandson was by then overseeing the school's transformation into a public school as part of the educational reform. Ch'ien Mu had passed through the new Tang-k'ou community school and gone on to the new high school in Nanking on a scholarship procured for him by the directors of the Tang-k'ou school. In a word, the risk had paid off. The scholar-farmer's daughter had been loved and provided for, and her sons were on their way to promising careers.

It should be clear by now that this was a world in which patrilineal descent mattered a great deal. The history of the great surnames of Wu-hsi county goes back to the Sung period, long before corporate lineages existed there. Because the descendants of certain landed magnates of that period used the patriline to authenticate their position in society in Ming and Ch'ing times, it is possible to trace certain patterns of social practice back to these ancestors. In this chapter I shall explore four aspects of social organization: higher-order lineage organization, formation of communities of affines, charitable estate organization, and the designation of adoptive heirs. In each case, the patterns were generated by strategies followed in the continuous struggle to gain or maintain status and power in the community.[2] The patterns thus generated proliferated in an ever-expanding "scholar-gentry" stratum of the society, transforming it in the process.

The Structure of Kinship Organization among the Ch'iens

At the highest and weakest level of kinship organization, the Ch'ien family into which the Ts'ai woman married was part of a descent group that distinguished itself from other Ch'iens in the same area on the basis of demonstrated patrilineal descent from a common Sung dynasty ancestor. This group was called the Hu-t'ou Ch'iens; its members were descended from a certain Ch'ien Tzu (1099–1156), a man of hereditary title, who, following the strategic uxorilocal pattern, moved to the Grand Canal town of Hsin-an, marrying the daughter of a local family surnamed Kuo. Uxorilocal residence was a strategy common among the great surnames of the Lower Yangtze region at least since Sung times. Generally, the son of a family with relatively

---

2. The approach to elite strategies and their structural causes and effects taken in this paper reflects the influence of a number of social anthropologists who have challenged structural-functional models (especially Swartz, Turner, and Tuden 1966; Mayer 1966; Ballandier 1970; Boissevain and Mitchell 1973; Boissevain 1974). I have discussed elsewhere some of the ways their rethinking of the field might help historians of local situations of China ask more productive questions than they have in the past (Dennerline 1980). I have found it useful to conceive of elite strategies of all sorts not just as plans of action within a social system, the rules of which determine the outcomes, but as plans within a continually changing political field. The field consists of the participants together with their resources and their values (after Swartz, Turner, and Tuden 1966:7–11). As the participants compete for resources—especially land and labor—they proceed according to existing rules, and those who lose seek either to restore them or to bend the new rules to their own advantage (after Nicholas 1968; Boissevain 1974). Changes in the rules reflect a contradiction between the old rules and the new strategies, both of which are expressions of values held by the competitors. In other words, the process is not governed by a single dominant set of norms but by a shifting set of concurrently held conflicting values (after van Velson 1967).

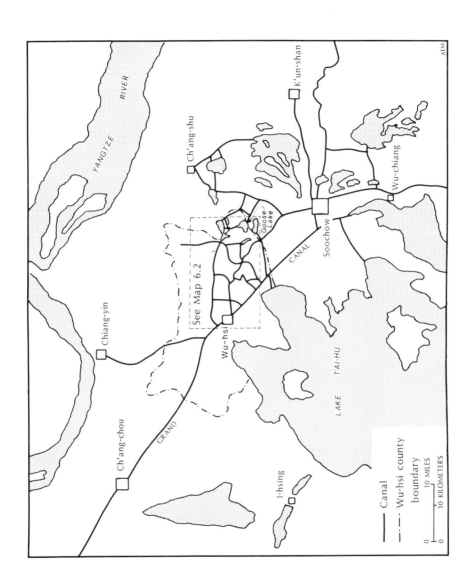

MAP 6.1 Wu-hsi and Vicinity

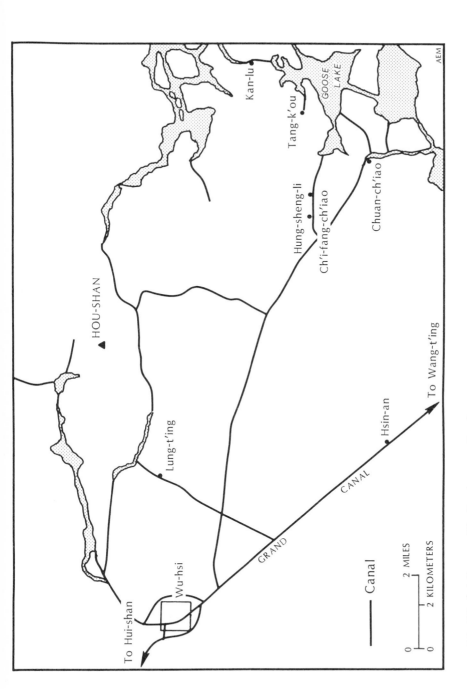

MAP 6.2 Wu-hsi County: The Southeastern Quadrant

higher status, perhaps with important political connections or perhaps with little more than a good pedigree, moved to the village of a well-to-do rural householder and married his daughter without taking her surname.[3] Ch'ien Tzu was claimed to be the great-grandson of the first Ch'ien to move to Wu-hsi county, Ch'ien Chin (998–1054), and Ch'ien Chin was a great-grandson of the third king of Wu-Yueh. The Hu-t'ou Ch'iens distinguished themselves in Southern Sung and Yuan times by continuing their hereditary rank, holding office, managing large estates and engaging in philanthropic works. Some even served as educational officials to the Mongols themselves (*Meng-ku hsueh-cheng*). With the collapse of the Yuan state, many of them settled in villages east of Hsin-an, like Chuan-ch'iao, marrying the daughters of locally prominent families while buying or receiving land. It was these refugee civil servants who became the progenitors of the various lineages and higher-order lineages that constituted the Hu-t'ou Ch'ien group in the nineteenth century (CS:*ch*. 14).[4]

At the next lower level of kinship organization, the family the Ts'ai woman married into belonged to a higher-order lineage emanating from the central town of Chuan-ch'iao. The common ancestor of this higher-order lineage was a certain Ch'ien Fa who moved to the town of Chuan-ch'iao in 1383, taking a wife from a locally prominent family surnamed Chou. Ch'ien Fa had three sons. The eldest was Chung-te, who was the first to establish corporate property for the Ch'iens in the form of a charitable estate in the mid-fifteenth century. The second was Shun-te, who had no sons but adopted his younger brother's son as an heir. The third was Cheng-te, ancestor of the progenitor of the Ch'i-fang-ch'iao lineage and father of seven sons (see figure 6.5) (CS:*ch*. 14).

In the Wan-li period of late Ming, some of the Chuan-ch'iao Ch'iens had settled in the village later called Hung-sheng-li. This move also involved the uxorilocal pattern, and Ch'ien Kuo-yao established his household with the help of a dowry (provided by his affines through his wife) of 360 *mou* of land. A great-great-grandson of this man, whose informal name was Hung-sheng, had the distinction of providing the name of this village. This man, Ch'ien Wei-yung (1665–1730), was a philanthropist, and it was his grandson

---

3. According to Hartwell (1982:405–20) the descendants of old professional elite families often pursued a strategy of uxorilocal marriage or uxorilocal residence in the Sung period. He sees the strategy as symptomatic of broader social and demographic patterns that accompanied the economic expansion of the period and led to the decline of the professional elite and the rise of the scholar-gentry to national prominence. See also Watson's chapter in this volume.

4. Although the higher-order Hu-t'ou Ch'iens were scattered over several counties and probably shared no property beyond what the Chuan-ch'iao leadership considered Hu-t'ou property, by the 1890s, they *did* have a printed genealogy and were nominally the corporate owners of the burial plots and ritual lands of the Southern Sung magnates. This shared interest distinguished them from *other* Ch'iens whose descent group identities were centered in Wu-hsi county.

who, with contributions from his widowed mother (surname Yang) and widowed sister-in-law (surname Chou) established a charitable estate of 200 *mou* in 1763 (of which more later), giving the Ch'iens of Hung-sheng-li their corporate identity (CS:*ch.* 18; CS 1922–24:4–6).

The historical link between the Ch'iens of Hung-sheng-li and Chuan-ch'iao was reinforced by this charitable estate. The founders claimed to be restoring the Chuan-ch'iao estate, which had not survived the sixteenth century. Since the original estate had been established for all the Ch'iens of Chuan-ch'iao, so should the new one aspire to provide for the widows and orphans of all the Ch'iens. By 1820, the estate had grown to nearly a thousand *mou*, supporting a sizable welfare operation and a lineage school.

The hamlet where the Ts'ai woman moved was settled entirely by families of the Ch'iens with a common ancestor probably eight generations back. Her husband's home was one of seven mansions, all built on the same pattern, comprising the hamlet of Ch'i-fang-ch'iao. According to the oral tradition described in Ch'ien Mu's memoir, all the resident males in this hamlet claimed descent from a certain Ch'ien who was said to have built seven mansions for his seven sons, who began seven branches (*ch'i-fang*) of descent, around the beginning of the Ch'ing period. Hence, the hamlet's name, Ch'i-fang-ch'iao. The person most likely to have been the progenitor, if one relies on the genealogy, was Ch'ien Ju-chang, whose dates are not known but whose eldest son was born in 1676 (see figure 6.5). The person most likely to have been the subject of the origin myth, however, was a much earlier ancestor by the name of Ch'ien Cheng-te (1402–66) (see figure 6.5). It was he who was most likely to have owned the huge estate of over ten thousand *mou* that the founder is said to have owned, and the genealogy records the birth dates of precisely seven sons. Whatever the origins of the buildings themselves, the evidence suggests that the larger descent group identified with Ch'i-fang-ch'iao at the end of the nineteenth century included only the descendants of Ch'ien Ju-chang.

According to the genealogy, compiled between 1887 and 1892, the males of Ch'eng-p'ei's generation who were descended from Ju-chang numbered exactly one hundred (CS:*ch.* 28, 29). How many families resided in the hamlet is not clear, but all were of comparable social status. There were no peasants in the hamlet and no shopkeepers. The shopkeepers were in Hung-sheng-li and the peasants were in a village a thousand paces to the east and across the creek. Yet another neighboring village continued at the end of the Ch'ing to have feudal-like obligations to the Ch'iens, in this case to provide musical entertainment on ceremonial occasions. Class differences dating back to the early Ming period were thus maintained (PSISC:3).[5]

---

5. Ch'ien Mu describes one village as the place where the "musician households for the Ch'ien surname" (*Ch'ien-hsing yueh-hu*) had lived since Ming times. Another was the place where "communal servants" (*kung-p'u*) of Ch'i-fang-ch'iao lived, a group that apparently was

By the time of Ch'eng-p'ei's marriage, there was at least one other charitable estate of 300 *mou* in Ch'i-fang-ch'iao. A third estate of 500 *mou* was
organized around that time. These estates were established on behalf of the
descendants of Ju-chang, and indicate a corporate identity for the larger descent group, regardless of the members' place of residence (CS:*ch.* 8, 28, 29).[6]

Finally, at the lowest level, the Ts'ai woman became a member of a residential group that comprised almost all the male descendants of the great-
great-grandfather of her new husband. In 1841 this domestic unit had been
honored by imperial recognition for having achieved the spectacular ideal of
five generations under one roof. The patriarch, Ch'ien Shao-lin, had distinguished himself several times by providing public relief. He had received a
scholarship from the estate in Hung-sheng-li and used it as seed money for
an estate in his own village. In 1841, he authorized the first small charitable
estate there. While Shao-lin lived, the inherited ancestral property of the
patriarch remained the common property of seventeen conjugal families in
the generation of Ch'eng-p'ei's father.

In the 1880s, this descent group claimed corporate ownership of a charitable estate of forty *mou, and*, it appears from the account in Ch'ien Mu's
memoir, corporate ownership or at least exclusive occupancy of a "mansion" (*chai*) of forty-two chambers (*chien*), fourteen anterooms (*p'ien-
hsiang*), and seven halls (*t'ing-t'ang*). According to the Ch'ien genealogy, the
descent group included thirty-four males in the generation of Ch'ien Mu's
father, Ch'eng-p'ei. The first born of that generation appeared before the
death of the common ancestor in 1846, and Ch'eng-p'ei was born in 1866.
According to Ch'ien Mu's memoir, which was based on his mother's
account, the mansion's residents included only families of descendants of her
husband's great-grandfather and great-uncle. If the memoir is accurate on
this point, then twenty-four of the thirty-four members of the descent group
actually lived there, providing the network with a residentially cohesive core
(PSISC:2–4; CS:*ch.* 28, 29).

To view this complex kinship system outward from the perspective of the
bride, her husband belonged first to a common residential unit resembling a
"communal family," a village-based lineage with a depth of eight genera-

---

at the Ch'iens' beck and call. This arrangement would seem to hark back to an early Ming
pattern. Yeh Hsien-en (1980) described dominant lineages in Hui-chou that continued to receive hereditary duties from surrounding hamlets with different surnames up to 1949, and J.
Watson (1977) describes the remnants of such a system in the New Territories. The situation in
Ch'i-fang-ch'iao differed in that the alleged original estate of ten thousand *mou* on which the
dominance was based had long since been divided up, whereas in Hui-chou and Kwangtung the
dominant lineage halls owned the land and received the services.

6. When Ch'eng-p'ei died, his family residence was in the town of Tang-k'ou. The family
received welfare payments from the charitable estate in Tang-k'ou after his death and returned
to the village some years later.

tions, a higher-order lineage with a depth of seventeen generations centered on the town of Hung-sheng-li one kilometer away but originating in Chuan-ch'iao two kilometers to the south, and, finally, her husband belonged to the Hu-t'ou Ch'iens who were a generalized descent group with a depth of twenty-five generations—the focus of which was the graves of their Sung dynasty ancestors.

Local-Level Leadership and the History of the Hua

The levels of descent group distinction mapped out above reflect a long history of concern for patrilineal authenticity. Yet, as I will show, that concern was not self-sustaining. The well-to-do scholar-farmer named Ts'ai must have been aware that the bridegroom's family was embedded in the hoary kinship networks I have described and that this was advantageous. Yet, it was advantageous *not* because the Ch'iens were descended from Wu-Yueh kings and Sung landed magnates, but because they used their kinship networks to the greatest advantage while demonstrating the qualities of social obligation and political leadership that were demanded of such families by the ideology of the *Rites* and the *Odes*.

The Hua of Tang-k'ou, whose interaction with the Chuan-ch'iao Ch'iens figures so crucially in the story of Ch'ien Mu's life, may provide the best example of how patrilineal authenticity was related to local leadership (see Dennerline 1981b).

The key figure in the early history of the Hua was a Southern Sung magnate by the name of Hua Ch'üan (1206–85), whose great-great-grandfather, a man of noble rank, had moved to Lung-t'ing, just east of Wu-hsi city, after the fall of Kaifeng in 1126. From the Lung-t'ing homestead Hua Ch'üan managed an estate that was said to have commanded 480,000 piculs in rents. He served as county registrar, ran a private county relief granary, and established a local agricultural school (HS 1905:23:5b–7).

Yet there is no evidence that Hua Ch'üan or his immediate descendants—there were fifteen fertile grandsons—were involved in any corporate lineage activity. Descendants of his continued to hold official title through the Yuan period, and when rebellion reached the area in the 1350s, they were scattered about the Yangtze delta region. One of Hua Ch'üan's great-great-grandsons stayed in Lung-t'ing until the homestead was destroyed by fire in 1353. He remained a refugee until 1372, when he moved with one of his seven sons to the western shore of Goose Lake (E-hu), where they took up residence with in-laws. The son, Hua Tsung-hua (1341–97), formally established an ancestral shrine for his own immediate ancestors and compiled a genealogy that included all the known living descendants of Hua Ch'üan. These acts marked the earliest incorporation of a Hua descent group and the beginning of the Tang-k'ou Hua line (HS 1905:24:14–19b, 25:1:9).

From the time of Hua Tsung-hua until 1504, the Tang-k'ou Hua followed Hua Ch'üan's tradition of local leadership. They served as tax chiefs (*liang-chang*) for the Ming, maintained granaries, and provided relief in times of dearth. The major difference between them and their ancestors was one of scale. Their properties appear to have been limited to the area around Goose Lake, which they were developing through irrigation projects, and their official functions remained confined to the extrabureaucratic realm of fiscal administration within the *li-chia* and *liang-chang* structure created by the Ming founder. They appear to have had no corporate lineage organization at Goose Lake beyond whatever was entailed in the management of the ancestral shrine established by Hua Tsung-hua. But the larger descent group continued to be honored with the periodic compilation of genealogies. In 1504, the Huas restored an ancient shrine at far off Hui-shan on the bank of Lake T'ai-hu and attached 500 *mou* of land for ritual expenses and charity. It was the work of the great-grandson of Hua Tsung-hua and marked the second attempt by the Tang-k'ou branch to establish a corporate group beyond the Tang-k'ou line. From then until mid-Ch'ing, activities of the higher-order descent group centered around the Hui-shan shrine and various short-lived charitable estates of considerable size.

Between 1504 and 1745 there was little to bind the smaller Hua descent groups together. Leadership in the community passed to civil service degree holders, many of whom moved to Wu-hsi city, and the tax chief system declined. Individual families managed ritual properties as they could, and those properties around which larger corporate identities might have formed were no exception. There was a hiatus in leadership between the family and the larger descent group that I have argued elsewhere was characteristic of late Ming society generally (Dennerline 1981a). The history of the estate attached to the shrine at Hui-shan shows the effects of this hiatus.

In 1504, a total of 500 *mou* was attached to the shrine for the purpose of maintaining the buildings and grounds, financing ceremonies, and providing welfare for descendants of Hua Ch'üan. By 1563, the estate had disintegrated. A certain Hua Ch'a (1526 *chin-shih*), great-grandson of the estate's founder, endowed the shrine more modestly with thirty-two *mou*—for ritual expenses only, as welfare was then the responsibility of the great charitable estates with which Hua Ch'a and others were experimenting. Even this small endowment failed to survive the Ch'ing conquest, and in 1650 a group of five families from Tang-k'ou set aside another seventy *mou* for the same purpose.

The appearance of a new charitable estate of 1,300 *mou* with its granary in Tang-k'ou in 1745 changed the situation dramatically. In 1748, representatives of the several patrilineal branches that continued to be described in the updated genealogy met and by communal agreement (*kung-i*) authorized the transfer of the Hui-shan ritual lands to corporate lineage ownership. Six years later the properties were placed under the same management as the charitable estate, where they remained in 1882.

From 1745 on, the charitable estate was the focal point of a new sort of intensified lineage organization. Ritual and relief properties remained separate, with an endowment for education being attached to the ritual properties. By the 1820s, new endowments were being designated for particular branches of the patriline. The estate that Hua Ts'un-k'uan, his brothers, and his son put together between 1860 and 1875 was the greatest of these. In 1882, when Hua Hung-mo dedicated the ancestral shrine to his ancestor—a grandson of the Tang-k'ou progenitor Hua Tsung-hua—he was completing the process by which a new lineage was created (Dennerline 1981b).

The story of the Tang-k'ou Huas demonstrates the importance of the patriline in the social and political structure of the area. In the Wu-hsi region it was not corporate lineage organization that enabled the Huas to continue among the elite from Sung times to the end of the Ch'ing. Rather it was the ability of certain families to use their kinship networks to the greatest advantage, creating in the end the institutions around which larger descent groups could be organized. The process began not with the creation of a localized corporate lineage from which other lineages were spun off through migration and segmentation, but with a tradition of local leadership based on landed estates and patronage, continuing in these certain families by virtue of the patriline (on the relationship between patrilines and lineages see Hazelton's chapter in this volume.) Not until the eighteenth century were the leaders of one branch of the patriline able to establish a durable corporate entity, and that was accomplished only with the establishment of a large welfare estate, the purpose of which was to provide relief for widows and orphans and scholarships for indigent members of the group. This was a large part of the tradition to which the well-to-do farmer-scholar Ts'ai referred when he determined to marry his daughter into a poor country scholar's family.

Marriages and the Community of Affines

If descent groups like the Chuan-ch'iao Ch'iens and Huas of Tang-k'ou only forged a corporate identity for themselves in the eighteenth century, what was it that kept the social traditions alive during the previous centuries? If the Huas and the Ch'iens were the landed magnates of the Sung, how was it that after the Mongol conquest of the thirteenth century, the popular rebellions of the mid-fourteenth, the Ming-founder's purge of the old landed elite in the late fourteenth, the decline of the tax chief system and the dominance of a new "bureaucratic elite" based on civil service examinations in the late fifteenth and sixteenth, the general commercialization of agriculture in the region, the Ch'ing conquest, and the finalization of local administrative

reforms in the Yung-cheng period—how was it that after all this, the very
descendants of those Sung magnates were the first to emerge as the leaders of
a new corporate lineage elite in the mid-eighteenth century? The answer, I
believe, is in the other side of kinship—the community of affines. The marriage network of which the Ch'i-fang-ch'iao Ch'iens were a part can be described in relation to the central place hierarchy (see Skinner 1964). In 1882
the town of Hung-sheng-li was the place where the Ch'iens carried on their
daily business. According to Ch'ien Mu's account, "As soon as the sun rose
each morning some thirty or more persons without regard for generation or
status would assemble and set out for market to drink tea and exchange
treats of noodles and dumplings, not returning until noon" (PSISC:6). The
town was also inhabited largely by Ch'iens who, it will be recalled, were
descended from a sixteenth-century progenitor. Given the scale of Ch'ien
philanthropy there, and the establishment of a charitable estate by 1763, it
seems likely that the non-Ch'ien residents included the shopkeepers and,
perhaps, the descendants of the Chin family into which the Ch'ien progenitor had married. In short, for a community of affines—families with
which the Ch'i-fang-ch'iao Ch'iens could arrange marriages—one would
have to look further up in the central place hierarchy than the town of
Hung-sheng-li.

At the next level, the town of Chuan-ch'iao has already been described as
the place to which the Ch'iens' early Ming progenitor moved. And only
slightly farther away to the east was the town of Tang-k'ou itself. Next in the
central place hierarchy came Wu-hsi city, Ch'ang-shu, and Soochow, each of
these cities being about equidistant from Tang-k'ou.

Given the prominence of the Hua surname in Tang-k'ou and the Ch'ien
surname in Chuan-ch'iao and Hung-sheng-li, it is not surprising to learn
that there was a high incidence of marriages arranged between people of the
two names. Ch'ien Ch'eng-p'ei, who married the Ts'ai woman, had two
sisters who married Hua men. His mother was a Chou, but both his grandmother and great-grandmother were Hua women, as were his matrilateral
ancestors of the fifth and seventh generations. Within the Five Generations
Together Hall group, four of seventeen males in the generation previous to
Ch'eng-p'ei's married Hua women, as did two of four in the generation
before that. These four were brothers, and they had four sisters, two of
whom also married Hua men. To complete the pattern in that generation,
one of the remaining men married a Tsou woman—the Tsou surname being
the second most prominent among Ch'ien brides generally—and the remaining two women married in the neighboring counties of Ch'ang-shu and
Ch'ang-chou (Soochow) (CS:*ch*. 29).

The pattern is clear. The Ch'iens of Five Generations Together Hall in the
nineteenth century arranged nearly one-third of their marriages, for sons
and daughters alike, with Hua families. Moreover, the pattern holds for

Ch'i-fang-ch'iao as a whole. The putative progenitor of the village's residents was Ch'ien Ju-chang (fl. 1680). Among the brides of fifteen cousins in his own generation, six were Hua women. Among the sixteen recorded brides of his great-grandsons, five were Hua women, as were eleven of thirty-one in the next generation and sixteen of fifty-two in the next. A sudden break in the pattern in the next generation, that of Ch'eng-p'ei's father, may be a result of the T'ai-p'ing occupation. But, in spite of it, eleven of sixty-six still married Hua women and the pattern held in Five Generations Together Hall (CS 1887–92:*ch.* 29).

A similar pattern emerges from Hung-sheng-li. The family of Hua Ts'un-k'uan and Hua Hung-mo, the post-T'ai-p'ing lineage segment founders, was not the only one to be so intricately intermarried with the dominant branch there as described above. So were the most prominent families of the branch that controlled the first Hua charitable estate, established in 1745. In that case, one fourth-generation descendant of the Hua estate's founder married a granddaughter of the Ch'ien estate's founder. Her brother, in turn, married his cousin, an aunt of Hua I-lun, who was commander-in-chief of the local militia in the resistance against the T'ai-p'ing (CS:*ch.* 56:76–80; HS 1872:3:45–49). In short, the Ch'iens of Hung-sheng-li, who controlled at least nine hundred *mou* of corporate welfare estate property by the turn of the century, were intermarried with both the old and the new leaders of the Hua enterprise in Tang-k'ou who controlled no less than 5,100 *mou* (see Dennerline 1981b:35–38, 43, 65n65). This pattern went back several generations. The philanthropist Ch'ien Wei-yung (1665–1730), whose progeny established the leadership core at Hung-sheng-li, married a Hua, as did his only son and his only daughter. So had his father, grandfather, and great-grandfather before him. The last was the only son of the man who had first moved to the place in the sixteenth century, marrying a daughter of the Chin family with her dowry of 360 *mou* of land.

The Hung-sheng-li line was only continuing a pattern that began in Chuan-ch'iao in the early Ming (CS:*ch.* 24). There the pattern appears to have been part of a strategy shared by the sons of the progenitor, Ch'ien Fa, who had moved to Chuan-ch'iao in the uxorilocal pattern in 1383, and the sons of his cousins. While only one of fifteen males of the generation following Ch'ien Fa's married Hua women, ten of forty in the next generation did. Another eleven married Tsou women. The pattern continued in the next generation as twenty-three of seventy-two married Hua women, twelve married Tsou women and seven married Chou women. Systematic intermarriage among certain surnames including the Ch'iens and the Huas was becoming the rule (CS:*ch.* 13).

If one considers the history of migrations of the elite families between the Yuan and the Ming, and the development of the marketing community in the area, it becomes clear that the pattern of strategic intermarriage between the Ch'iens and the Huas developed after the collapse of the old estates and the establishment of the Ming dynasty and before the development of Tang-k'ou as a central place. The original Sung in-migrants in the Ch'ien and Hua lines brought titles and privileges with them but married daughters of the local landed elite. Once settled, they seem to have divided their sons between the homestead and the frontier, as it were, continuing to intermarry with many different surnames over a broad area. The original Hua settlement at Tang-k'ou was prepared by such a policy. When the Tang-k'ou progenitor Hua Tsung-hua moved to Goose Lake as a refugee in 1372 at the age of twenty-nine it was because he had similarly uprooted affines there.

It was symptomatic of the times that families like those of Hua Tsung-hua were uprooted. Some managed to resettle as they did, but many did not. Hua Tsung-hua had six brothers who had to fare for themselves, and only three of these had any progeny. It seems clear that continuity in this case was determined by the skillful formation of a kinship alliance during a period of revolution and by the skillful development of a new bailiwick by the heirs of this alliance.

The marriage strategy of the Huas over the next four generations is difficult to document. The surname that occurs most frequently is Tsou, but it does not appear in anything like the proportions that Tsou, Hua, and Chou appear in the case of the Chuan-ch'iao Ch'iens. In the fourth generation of the three branches for which I have records, there were thirty-three males, twenty-nine of whom were known to have married. Of those twenty-nine, the genealogies record the surname of only fourteen wives, five of whom were Tsous and only one of whom was a Ch'ien woman. Since the genealogies of the local Hou-shan Ch'iens and the Chuan-ch'iao Ch'iens also survive, it seems unlikely that the unnamed wives were from either of those patrilines. The fourth generation, on the other hand, was roughly contemporaneous with the generation of Chuan-ch'iao Ch'iens who took twenty-three of seventy-two wives from Hua families in the latter part of the fifteenth century (CS:ch. 14). The evidence thus suggests that these Hua families were marrying daughters up to the Ch'iens, while other, less prominent families in the Goose Lake region were marrying their daughters up to the Huas.

If, in time, such a pattern can be shown, it would also conform to what we know about the central place hierarchy in the early Ming. Hua Tsung-hua settled not in the principal market town of Kan-lu but some three kilometers to the southwest of it where a major irrigation ditch emptied into Goose Lake. The spot was as yet undeveloped, and it lay roughly at the midpoint between Kan-lu and another developed settlement at Chuan-ch'iao. When Ch'ien Fa moved to Chuan-ch'iao in 1383 he moved to a place that was more central to a rural community than was the new Hua homestead, and he married a woman of the patriline that had dominated the area in

Sung times, the Chous (TPML 1:7). The town of Tang-k'ou grew along with the Hua fortunes until, by the end of the Ming period, it rivaled Kan-lu in wealth and population. Finally, in the Yung-cheng period (1723–35), the Ch'ing established a police commission and a public granary (*she-ts'ang*) there, a sure sign that the town had eclipsed Kan-lu in the central place hierarchy (TPML 1:8). It was only shortly thereafter that the Hua established their first charitable estate with its granary appropriately located in Tang-k'ou.

Although the particular marriages arranged between the families that directed the Ch'ien and Hua welfare estates in the nineteenth century might be explained as marriages between the most powerful families in the area at the time, the pattern of marriage reaching back into the Ming period before the establishment of the estates cannot be dismissed in that way. In fact, since the two surname groups were so heavily interrelated by marriage, an alternative hypothesis emerges. Kan-lu had been the central market town for the area in Sung and Yuan times, with Chuan-ch'iao a notch lower on the marketing scale. Ch'ien Ju-lin moved to Kan-lu to manage the branch estate established by his grandfather there. He married the daughter of a locally prominent person and served as police commissioner in Kan-lu until Chang Shih-ch'eng's rebellion brought an end to the estate system that supported the old elite and chased them from their homesteads in the north and west. Ch'ien Ju-lin moved to the least well developed part of Kan-lu's hinterland and salvaged what he could of the estate there. His father and mother, a Hua woman, joined him there and he took in a number of Hua refugees as in-laws. Over the generations, the Huas flourished. At first they married locally, and then they looked to Chuan-ch'iao, the first rung up the central place ladder, where they began to marry daughters into Ch'ien households.

The Chuan-ch'iao Ch'iens, in the meantime, had eclipsed the Chous as the dominant local surname. Like the Huas, they had been cited by the Ming for providing famine relief. Better than the Huas, they had by the mid-fifteenth century established a charitable estate for widows and orphans of Ch'ien households. In the sixteenth century, the Huas, too, worked at establishing a corporate descent group and charitable estate, and they emerged as the greatest surname in Yen-hsiang township (*hsiang*) by the late Ming. The town of Tang-k'ou developed as the Huas and others in the community reaped the benefits of agricultural development, commercialization, and the new privileges attached to scholar-official status. Eventually, Tang-k'ou eclipsed Chuan-ch'iao and Kan-lu in the central place hierarchy, but the pattern of intermarriage between the Huas and the Ch'iens continued as before.

What is most striking in this long and continuous pattern of intermarriage is that commercial development and the growth of the new town did not displace or even weaken it. On the contrary, it seems to have strengthened it.

And, to complete the picture of the complex affinal interrelationship among the directors of the nineteenth century charitable estates, the ability of the elite to provide security for widows and orphans within the descent group as well as relief for the community seems to have been at the core of this strength. At a time in the mid-fifteenth century when the memory of a past glory derived from imperial privilege and local patronage functions had not yet waned, the Chuan-ch'iao Ch'iens promised security for widows, and the Huas began to marry their daughters to the Chuan-ch'iao Ch'iens. That aspect of the relationship, which harked back to the need of the in-migrating privileged families to find women among the local landowners, did not change from the fifteenth to the nineteenth century.

The community of affines that existed in the nineteenth century was, in effect, a large network of families generated in part by the marriage strategies of earlier generations. It remains to be shown how the same strategies helped to generate charitable estates and how that process was related to the practice of designating adoptive heirs. The argument assumes as a premise that women, by virtue of their power to influence their sons, husbands, and fathers, were both resources and participants in the field of agnatic and affinal politics that the community of affines defines.[7]

The Charitable Estates

Charity in rural Wu-hsi was a part of the local political economy. The Confucianists who excelled in the rhetoric of *tsung-fa* and wrote of the lineage's obligations to its poor were not unaware of this. In an essay prais-

7. If the importance attached to strategy as a generator of social networks and political fields seems inconsistent with the findings of some anthropologists, there are two possible explanations. We may be looking at the same things through different conceptual glasses or we may be looking at different things. If in the present case the "community of affines" defines the social limits of a political field, then it also behaves like a class. It may well be that the concern for distribution and control of shared resources in this case is what distinguishes the marriage strategies of a particular political elite from the strategies of others for whom marriage involved only a simple exchange of resources. R. Watson (1981) has demonstrated that such strategic differences did produce class-based differences in affinal relations among the very southeastern lineages that Freedman (1967:6) saw as demonstrating a uniform pattern of relations based on patrilineal solidarity. Ebrey (1981) has also argued that the rights and duties of women in Sung literati society suggest patterns of affinal relations among the elite that were a greater challenge to patrilineal ideology than Freedman (1958:31) and more recently Baker (1979) would lead one to expect. I have also concluded that bureaucratic elite marriage patterns developed in another political field defined by the civil service examination system in the late Ming tended to loosen the bonds of agnatic kinship that might otherwise have tied members of the elite to their native towns (Dennerline 1981a). In sum, evidence seems to be growing that differences among local political fields and strategies reflecting class interests were part and parcel of the kinship structure of China. In other words, we are probably looking at *related* things through different conceptual glasses and, therefore, seeing the differences.

ing the poet-painter-calligrapher Hua Yun for his efforts at setting up a charitable estate in the sixteenth century, the great statecraft writer T'ang Shun-
chih asked whether charity land (*i-t'ien*) was the way of the ancients or a
symptom of the way's decline. He concluded it must be the latter, for:

> The ancients established *tsung* [descent groups] for every set of agnates (*tsu*).
> The members who had a surplus gave it to the *tsung* and those who had not
> enough took from it. They treated one another as parts of a single body....
> With the decline of the *tsung*, private property came to determine status among
> agnates.... Charity land exists only because there are men of means, whereas
> under the rules of the *tsung* (*tsung-fa*) everything, no matter how valuable, was
> shared. With charity land, it is only the benevolent man, acting as a single part
> of the body, who provides for the commonwealth, whereas under the rules of
> the *tsung* nothing, no matter how small, was hoarded. (WHCKHC 37:2–3b)

In other words, charity involved a contradiction. The rhetoric stressed
corporate welfare, while the practice confirmed the hierarchy of wealth and
power.

Managing famine relief, building orphanages, and establishing charitable
estates was the work of political leaders and brought with it political rewards. Lineage charitable estates also brought tax reductions, protection
against property disputes, and exemption from customary fees. And estate
managers derived power from the control of corporate assets. Once an estate
was established, to control the management of it was a major political
objective.[8] Charitable estates were, therefore, tools by which the most
powerful men in rural society exercised both their own influence within the
lineage and the lineage's influence within the community.

Yet unlike the lineage-owned estates described by Watson in Kwangtung
and Yeh Hsien-en in Hui-chou (J. Watson 1982; Yeh 1980), the Wu-hsi
charitable estates in the Ch'ing period were certified by the state specifically
for the purpose of providing relief for widows and orphans, funeral and
burial expenses for the poor, and scholarships for the sons of lineage members. When the Huas established their new estate in 1875 it was because the
old estate could not provide the promised income for all the widows and
orphans on the rolls. The new estate's founders had already pledged support
for 130 destitute relatives, an expense that amounted to 60 percent of the
estate's projected income. Another 10 percent was pledged for spring assistance to tenants to ensure a crop (HS 1901:1:9–11). In effect, the managers
of these estates had a constituency to please—the brothers-in-law, sons-in-
law, uncles, and cousins of the beneficiaries. Should they fail, the lineage
assembly would hear legitimate grievances voiced by contenders for power
and couched in the rhetorical terms of obligation to widows and orphans.

---

8. For a discussion of the problem in the case of the model estate established by Fan Chung-
yen, see Twitchett 1959 and 1960–61.

Since in theory the state protected charitable estates only if they were charitable, the contenders were self-interested advocates for the lineage's widows and orphans.

What, then, of the widows and orphans themselves? The point is rarely mentioned in discussions of lineage politics that charitable estates benefited women who married into the lineage. The rules of the Hua estate of 1875 gave widows and their children first priority, and the amount of rice allowed was probably sufficient to live on (HS 1901:1:9–11). Let us assume that the wife of a poor country scholar was widowed with a young son and daughter. It there was sufficient rental or interest income to support them from their own *chia* (household) property, they would still be somewhat dependent on the good will and managerial skills of the deceased's close agnates. If the *chia* income was insufficient, they would probably sacrifice the son's education and the daughter might not fare so well in the marriage market. If there was no son, the widow's in-laws might select an heir. If the heir was an adult, the widow's survival and the daughter's marriage would depend upon his good will. If there was no inheritance, or if the inheritance was large and the agnates were venal, the widow might be forced to remarry (thereby losing any claim to the estate). In such cases suicide was always an alternative.

How would the existence of a charitable estate help? It would not change much when the widow had adequate family property to use, even if she did not enjoy the good will of her husband's agnates. If she had no son and property was involved, an heir would be designated. But if there was neither son nor property, the widow with access to a charitable estate would likely pick up both an heir and welfare payments instead of being forced to remarry. Thus, a family with some education that cared about its daughters would surely consider a lineage with charitable estates to be an advantage in selecting a son-in-law.

The family that the Ts'ai woman married into in 1882 had access to a charitable estate. According to the genealogy, an estate of forty *mou* was established in 1841 by the Five Generations Together Hall progenitor for his descendants (CS:*ch.* 8, 29:29–30).The estate from which members of Ch'ien Mu's branch were eligible to receive relief, called Sea of Yearning (*huai hai*), was the oldest and the largest of three charitable estates in Ch'i-fang-ch'iao. Its granary was also the place where the kin group assembled for communal business (PSISC:9). According to the genealogy, there were at least two more estates established in Ch'i-fang-ch'iao by 1882, totaling 800 *mou*. It is possible that one of these was the Sea of Yearning estate and that the Five Generations Together Hall land had been attached to it, or that the three had been combined. Whatever the case, the land set aside for Ch'ien Mu's branch was no longer under that branch's control. That fact was to lead Ch'ien Mu's father, Ch'eng-p'ei, to challenge the lineage leadership shortly after his marriage, a story to which we shall return shortly.

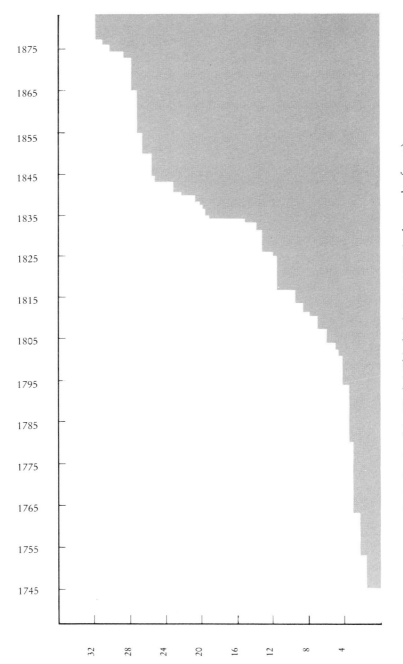

FIGURE 6.1 Lineage-Owned Charity Land in Wu-hsi/Chin-k'uei, 1745–1878 (in thousands of *mou*)

The Ch'i-fang-ch'iao estates were formed at a time when charity land was increasing dramatically in the area. The local gazetteer compiled in 1881 lists the larger charitable estates together with information on their origins. Some thirty-two thousand *mou* are included under forty-nine estates, the Hua estate of 1745 being the oldest. Figure 6.1 shows the accumulation of land recorded in the gazetteer. If what is recorded there can be taken to represent a trend, then the period from 1800 to 1845 was one of steady growth—about six hundred sixty *mou* per year entering the estates in the latter half of the period. I have argued elsewhere that the demand for tax relief—the estates paid at a fixed rate directly to revenue officials, avoiding the squeeze entailed in an increasingly 'corrupt *pao-chia* system—may help to explain the trend before 1846, and that the post-Restoration trend owed much to the fact that estate building had become a legitimate route to lineage leadership and power (Dennerline 1981b:34–44). The case of Ch'i-fang-ch'iao supports this argument, as the local estate or estates originated in the earlier period and showed a new spurt of growth after the Restoration. And, as we shall see, Ch'ien Ch'eng-p'ei established some reputation as a leader by reforming their administration. The Ch'i-fang-ch'iao case also suggests that the trend may have been more pronounced than the gazetteer listings indicate, as the 800 *mou* in question was not included in the list.

One estate that was included in the list was that of the Ch'iens in Hung-sheng-li. That estate was established in 1763, it may be recalled, with gifts of some two hundred *mou* by two widows, surnamed Yang and Chou. Their story shows how important the women could be to the process of incorporation. The Yang woman came to the Ch'iens around 1730 at the age of twenty-three from a family in the city that was down on its luck. Her father, a scholar, had died when she was fifteen, and she had worked at the family loom to support her mother and younger brothers, who were students. Her new husband, who was forty-four, had three sons (ages fifteen, twelve, and six) and two daughters still at home, their mother (a Hua woman) having died the previous year. He also had a father, Master Hung-sheng (Wei-yung, aged sixty-five), but no mother and no brothers. Yang was, in effect, brought in to take care of this family (CS:*ch.* 6, 56:41ff).

These Ch'iens had no close agnates, as Hung-sheng himself had been an only grandson. The closest relatives of the three orphaned boys were descended from a common ancestor five generations removed, by his one other son, and these were the only other descendants of the progenitor in Hung-sheng-li. But, they were wealthy. Master Hung-sheng had a reputation for his philanthropy and had lost a considerable sum of money to men who took advantage of his soft heart. Before he died that very year, he instructed his son—Yang's husband—to use his inheritance to establish a charitable estate, to restore the common property and the sense of obligation to kin that their fifteenth-century ancestors in Chuan-ch'iao had demonstrated. Hung-sheng

himself had lacked the managerial skills. To establish such an estate, one had
to have the support of a genuine corporate descent group and a number of
prominent officials, and one had to submit the titles of all the land to the
county registrar for assignment to the appropriate tax district under the special category of inalienable property. To accomplish that, one had to have
the approval of every responsible official from the county magistrate to the
Board of Revenue in Peking. Like the benevolent grandfather of the founder
of the 1745 Hua charitable estate, Hung-sheng would rather give his money
away and let someone else take care of him in his old age (CS:*ch.* 6).
Nonetheless, the instructions passed on to his son and grandsons. Five years
later, Yang found herself solely responsible for the family.

In 1735, Yang's husband died, making her a twenty-eight-year-old
widow with three unmarried stepsons and a two-year-old son of her own.
She managed to keep the family's wealth intact and arrange marriages for her
stepsons in the years that followed until, in 1740, two grandsons were
born—one each to the principal and secondary wives of the eldest stepson.
That same year, the wife of the second stepson died and a marriage was
arranged for the third to another Yang girl, the daughter of a recently
selected *po-hsueh hung-tz'u* scholar (in 1736, by special examination in hon-
or of the Ch'ien-lung Emperor's ascending the throne).

By 1750, the second stepson had died, leaving his second wife, surnamed
Chou, a childless widow. The eldest assigned his ten-year-old second son to
be the dead brother's heir. The new Yang bride having died after producing a
boy and a girl, the third son took a new wife, surnamed Hua. Yang, the
matriarch, was then forty-three years old, her own son was seventeen, and
Chou, the widow of her second stepson, was twenty-eight. By the time the
two women decided to set up the charitable estate in 1763, there were fifteen
grandsons in the family. Four more were yet to come, joining thirteen
granddaughters for a total of thirty-two cousins with an age span of at least
thirty-seven years.

It was the Chou woman who initiated the charitable estate plan by offering 160 *mou* as scholarship land for the younger boys. This she could do,
she said, because her husband's elder brother had provided her with an heir.
The offer acknowledged, in effect, the communal spirit that had prevailed
within the family under the direction of the matriarch. When the brothers
refused the offer, Chou offered the land to Yang as a contribution to the yet
unformed charitable estate. Yang matched it with forty *mou* of her own, and
her own son T'ing-mu, who was then thirty, saw it through the administrative maze (CS:*ch.* 7). A manager was then selected from the other branch of
the Hung-sheng-li patriline, and the lineage poor began to receive relief
(CS:*ch.* 56).

In this case, the widows themselves donated the land that made up the
core of the estate. However, underlying this donation is a dynamic that gives

it its significance. The sons and grandsons who eulogized them claimed it was the women who had impressed upon them the lesson that "benevolence" begins with the proper treatment of kin. Yang's life's work had been to maintain first the family of her deceased father and then the family of her deceased husband—including his two daughters, three sons, their five principal and five secondary wives, and all the grandchildren—while rearing but one child of her own. A woman like her must have been acutely aware of the predicament faced by widows who lacked the means to educate their sons, find secure places for their daughters, and deal with the economic and political pressures of the day. Yet, the land technically belonged to the men. Even if parts of it had come in as dowry, it would eventually have passed to the widows' heirs. In effect, the women were shaming the men into setting up the estate their grandfather had asked Yang's ailing husband to set up in his will, and because of this the men gave the women credit.

By the 1840s, when the first estate was created in Ch'i-fang-ch'iao, the Hung-sheng-li estate had grown to 900 *mou*. Benefits were extended to a larger descent group. The ritual properties of the Chuan-ch'iao line, the Sung dynasty grave sites, and a lineage school were attached. If the Hua estate in Tang-k'ou had served as a model for their affines in Hung-sheng-li, the Hung-sheng-li estate was a closer model for Ch'i-fang-ch'iao. And, as in the earlier case, the women were a force.

Ch'ien Mu's account of the struggle between his father and the lineage leaders in his village over the administration of charity land is based on the oral tradition he received from his mother. According to that tradition, the struggle reflected a division in the village between the "three wealthy branches"—partilines that had few descendants and much wealth—and four poorer branches that had many descendants and insufficient land. The tradition included a story that suggests how the women of the more numerous but less prosperous line could make their influence felt.

There was once a widow, the story goes, who had but one daughter and one son. The son was a wastrel but no one in the lineage had the moral authority to reform him. Finally, one of the influential men of a wealthy branch had him sent to the county jail. When the elders of the widow's branch, which happened to be Five Generations Together Hall, pleaded with the village leaders to have him released, they refused, arguing that a term in jail might help him reform.

As fate would have it, the son died in jail. After the man who had committed him to jail fell ill, the son appeared to the widow in a dream. He told her he had reported his grievance to the authorities in the underworld and they had decided in his favor. Now he needed bribe money to hasten his tormentor's death. When the daughter and several other women admitted they had had the same dream, the women of Five Generations Together Hall purchased a large sum of spirit money and burned it in a public demonstration before the mansion's great hall. As the flames receded, the wealthy branch member responsible for the transgression breathed his last. "As the story was still being told in my childhood," Ch'ien Mu wrote, "one can imagine how divisive the feelings among the branches were" (PSISC:3–5).

The story demonstrates how issues of lineage responsibility for the security of its less fortunate members affected the lives of the women and how, in turn, their control of the oral traditions and of the early socialization of the lineage members might influence decisions concerning group obligations. In this case, the oral tradition describing the nature of the political division within the village was linked in Ch'ien Mu's mother's mind to the struggle waged by her husband Ch'eng-p'ei and the lineage leaders over the charitable estates.

When Ch'eng-p'ei was still in his twenties he initiated litigation against the lineage leaders for their failure to provide adequate relief for widows and orphans in his branch. Although he had already achieved a local reputation as a scholar, having passed the county examination in first place at the age of seventeen, he was in no position to prevail over the lineage elders—all members of "the three wealthy branches"—who were twice his age and senior to him in generation. The case, which the elders of his own branch were unwilling or unable to make, was based on the grievance that Five Generations Together Hall had a relatively large number of widows and orphans who were not receiving support. Ch'ien Mu's account does not include the reasons given by "the three wealthy branches" who managed the estate for withholding relief, but it is clear that Ch'eng-p'ei's argument claimed they had a moral obligation to release provisions, being held for other purposes, to this, the poorer branch. It may be that the estate managers distinguished between the forty *mou* of land originally donated by the Five Generations Together Hall progenitor and the 800 *mou* donated by their own branches, refusing to share the wealth, but the evidence is not clear.

Only after the estate managers refused to release the provisions did Ch'eng-p'ei challenge them at the magistrate's office. The case wore on for several months, the magistrate urging a private settlement. In the end, the magistrate's mediation proved necessary, but the solution, according to Ch'ien Mu's story, was the one proposed by Ch'eng-p'ei. The three wealthy branches were allowed to continue as managers of the estate in rotation, but a fourth manager would be added as an administrative assistant. He would be the one to determine the distribution of welfare payments. The man Ch'eng-p'ei recommended for the job was one who everyone acknowledged would never have sought it for himself. Later, when the welfare recipients complained they were given low-quality rice, Ch'eng-p'ei shamed the assistant into showing them greater respect. It was through this work, Ch'ien Mu's mother told him, that Ch'eng-p'ei established his reputation as a leader (PSISC:9–12).

Not only was the charitable estate the institution around which the great surnames achieved their corporate identities after the eighteenth century, but it was also a focal point for grievances raised by the women and by opposition spokesmen on behalf of the women and orphans of branches outside the leadership core. In effect, the need of the women for security in marriage arrangements had become part of the political dynamic of the lineage.

Continuity of the Patriline and the Adoption of Heirs

The proliferation of charitable estates in the nineteenth century introduced a new institutional node into the network of elite families in Wu-hsi. On the one hand, control of the estates became a political goal for contenders within the lineage. On the other, marriage arrangements with families who had control of these resources must have become an important goal among elite families as they planned their marriage strategies. At another level, marrying a daughter into a family that had access to the resources of such an estate provided some assurance that the daughter would not be forced to remarry or produce her own income should her husband die without sufficient private property—a prospect that was increasingly likely among country scholars during the nineteenth century. In addition, it virtually guaranteed support for her son's education regardless of the husband's income. The story of the Yang woman who saw first her own brother and then her stepsons and stepdaughters through the crucial stages of education and marriage without the benefit of lineage welfare and then urged her husband's kinsmen to provide it for future generations became a part of the charter myth of the Ch'ien patriline. It symbolized a kind of power that linked the common concerns of a community of affines to the corporate properties of a patrilineal descent group.

This kind of power—political, moral, and economic—helps to explain the complex relationship among the three events that were introduced at the beginning of this essay. The well-to-do scholar-farmer had a good reason to marry his daughter to the poor country scholar. The reasons were not unrelated to those that underlay the complex pattern of intermarriage among Ch'ien and Hua families and the incorporation of yet another Hua charitable estate. The three kinds of power were indistinguishable.

Yet, as observers of lineage organization in Southern China well know, the concern for widows and orphans with all that it implies about the significance of the community of affines is not a primary one in rural patriarchal society, nor is it an essential part of the organization of patrilineal descent groups (see, e.g., J. Watson 1982). One Hua kinsman who had served in an official post in Kwangsi wrote that he saw much more lineage organization there but nothing like the charitable estates of the Hua (HS 1901:2:19). I

have argued that this concern reflects the history of the great surnames of the
area since Sung times and, in effect, the internal developments of a scholar-
gentry class.

It remains to be shown how patterns of inheritance designed to maintain
the patriline, and hence the class, helped to produce the charitable estates in
the first place. The argument is that when a designated heir was to receive a
large inheritance—one many times larger than that due to his biological
brothers and cousins—pressures were great for part of this inheritance to be
consigned to a charitable estate for the benefit of the larger descent group.
The practices of designating heirs and establishing charitable estates were
thus interrelated.

According to the oral tradition recounted by Ch'ien Mu, the seven
branches, of which Five Generations Together Hall was counted as one, had
developed unevenly since the seventeenth century. Ten thousand *mou* of
land was said to have been divided among seven heirs. By the nineteenth
century, three of the seven branches were prospering in part because there
were very few descendants among them.[9] These were the "three wealthy
branches" that provided the "gentrymen" (*shen-shih*) who monopolized
power. The other four, including Five Generations Together Hall, had proliferated to the extent that, "in my own childhood the rare family that had
one or two hundred *mou* was considered well-to-do, as the rest had only
perhaps a few tens of *mou*" (PSISC:4).

The genealogical record supports the observation that some branches had
proliferated more than others, but it is quite impossible to identify seven
separate branches that might have divided up an original estate. It seems
more likely that the seven mansions were controlled by seven groups in the
nineteenth century, each one claiming descent from a separate progenitor.
On the other hand, if Ch'ien Ju-chang was indeed the ultimate progenitor of
all the Ch'iens in Ch'i-fang-ch'iao, it is quite likely that he established himself there with a considerable landholding in the wake of the Ch'ing conquest. If so, and if the genealogy is accurate from that point on, then the
nineteenth-century Ch'iens were descended from his two sons, born in 1676
and 1683. Shao-lin, the patriarch of Five Generations Together Hall, himself
would have felt the influence of these village founders, as the second son,

9. Note the contrast to some of the other descent groups analyzed in this volume (especially
the Shihs in Davis's chapter and the Lang-yeh Wangs in Naquin's). In the cases discussed by
Davis and Naquin, wealth and official rank were associated with large sets of sons, often for
several generations in a sequence. Despite the apparent wealth and the high level of learning
among the Ch'iens, they do not seem to have been able (or willing) to produce a surplus of sons
as a resource in enhancing the standing of their descent groups. Davis argues, however, that
fecundity eventually was damaging to the cohesion of the Shih descent group. This problem was
also discussed in Rubie S. Watson's paper for the conference upon which this volume is based
(that paper is to be published elsewhere; see R. Watson n.d.).

Shao-lin's grandfather, survived until 1766 when Shao-lin was five years old. Continuity of estates is quite possible under these circumstances. The pattern of continuity, in turn, would affect the distribution of ancestral property among the group.

Only in Shao-lin's line was the pattern of distribution determined by biological proliferation. His portion of the inheritance was divided among seventeen fourth-generation descendants. But elsewhere the pattern was different. Shao-lin's grandfather had five sons, the youngest of whom was married to a Hua woman and had no son. The oldest, who had four sons, assigned one to this couple as heir. The male offspring of these five numbered fourteen in all. Of these, three had no sons. All three adopted heirs. In the next generation, four of twenty-seven were succeeded by adoptive heirs. Of forty-five married sons in the next generation, nine were succeeded by adoptive heirs. The pattern is clear: Roughly one-fifth of the lines in *each* generation were continued by adoptive heirs, and in only three cases over five generations where a marriage was recorded did a male heir fail to materialize. After the third generation, therefore, the ancestral property was divided unequally among biological descendants and designated heirs.

The Ch'ien oral tradition accounted for the uneven wealth of the various branches by emphasizing partible inheritance and political division. According to that tradition, which probably emerged among the more numerous but less affluent lines, it was the uneven division of ancestral property that made some families rich and powerful. Those families were obligated to distribute some of their inherited wealth to agnates through charity. The descendants of Ch'ien Ju-chang, the progenitor, in Ch'eng-p'ei's generation numbered one hundred. If the ancestral estate was, in fact, divided in accordance with the rules of partible inheritance through Shao-lin's generation (the fourth), the distribution of the inheritance would have looked like figure 6.2. By Ch'eng-p'ei's generation (the eighth), the population of the six branches delineated in generation three (A–F) was divided as shown in figure 6.3. Further dividing the fifth branch to distinguish between Shao-lin's descendants (E-1) in Five Generations Together Hall and those of his three brothers (E-2, 3, and 4) produces the distribution of population and inheritance in the junior branch as shown in figure 6.4. Although it cannot be said with certainty how large the ancestral heritage was at this point, an original estate of five thousand *mou* or more, depending on the actual distribution in generation four, is implied.

Ch'ien Shao-lin, it will be recalled, impressed on his descendants a strategy of direct sharing of property, while urging them to incorporate in 1841 by converting forty *mou* of the shared estate to charitable land. In 1876 the lineage leaders authorized another estate of 300 *mou* at the request of a widow surnamed Ch'in—daughter of an educational official—and her adoptive heir. The heir was one of only two males in his immediate line (E-3).

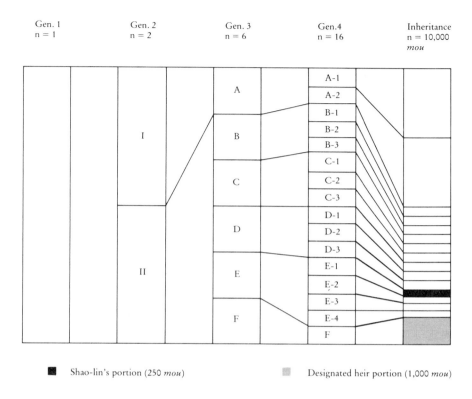

FIGURE 6.2   Distribution of Ch'ien Ju-chang's Estate among His Heirs, Generations 2 to 4

His grandfather, who died in 1849, was himself an adoptive heir, and the natal second son of Ch'ien Shao-lin (see figure 6.5). A holder of purchased degrees and brevet rank, he too had been cited for relief work, and had directed his five sons to establish a charitable estate with part of their inheritance. The T'ai-p'ing occupation intervened and by 1876 there were only the two grandsons, each of whom served as heir to a real father and an uncle, and their widows. The 300 *mou* appears to have come from the inheritance of the eldest of the five brothers who survived Shao-lin's son, the donation made possible by the adoption of a nephew who was the sole surviving son of the second brother (CS:*ch.* 29). In short, one-quarter of the inheritance of Shao-lin's father, the progenitor of branch E, which would otherwise have been divided up by more rapidly proliferating branches, was kept together through adoption over four generations until a significant portion of it was incorporated into the charitable estate.

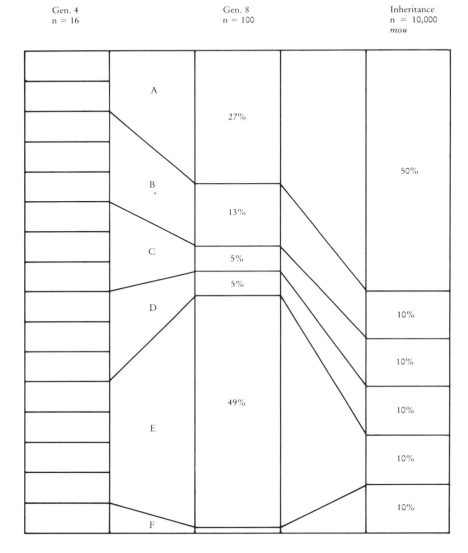

Gen. 4
n = 16

Gen. 8
n = 100

Inheritance
n = 10,000
mou

A

27%

50%

B

13%

C

5%

5%

D

10%

10%

E

49%

10%

10%

F

10%

FIGURE 6.3   Distribution of Ch'ien Ju-chang's Descendants by Branch in Generations 4 and 8, Showing Inheritance

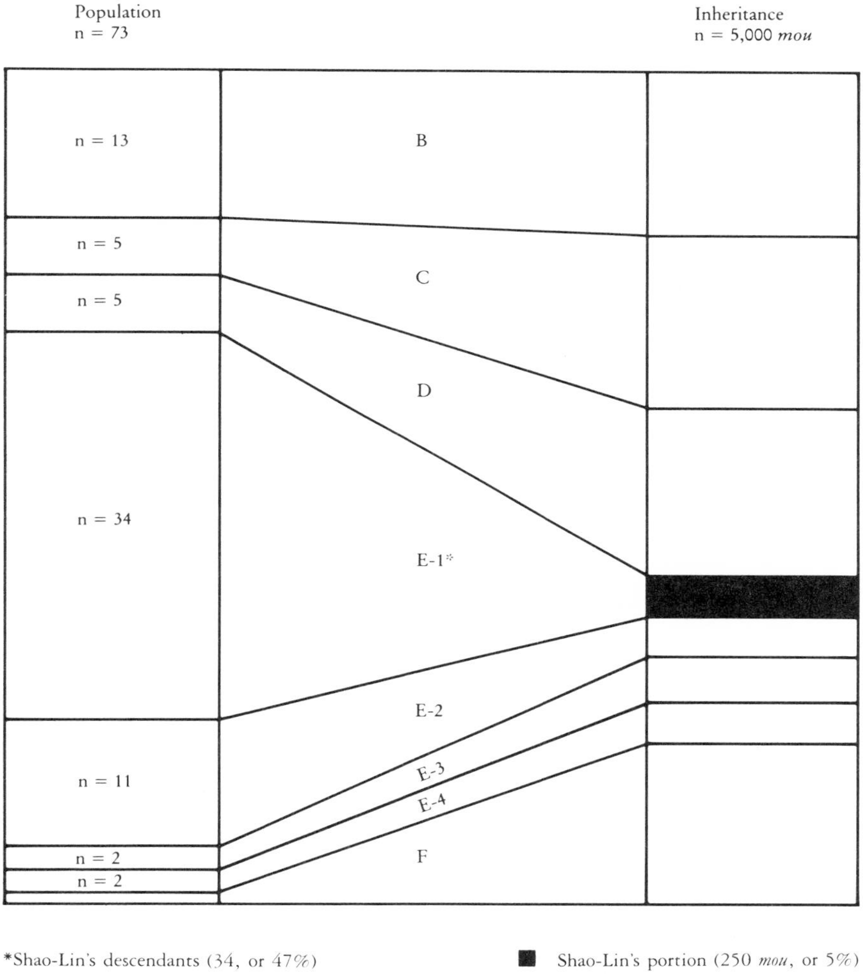

Population n = 73		Inheritance n = 5,000 mou
n = 13	B	
n = 5	C	
n = 5		
n = 34	D	
	E-1*	
	E-2	
n = 11	E-3	
	E-4	
n = 2	F	
n = 2		

*Shao-Lin's descendants (34, or 47%)   ■ Shao-Lin's portion (250 *mou*, or 5%)

FIGURE 6.4   Distribution of Inheritance among Descendants of Ch'ien Ju-chang, Branches B to F Only, in Generation 8

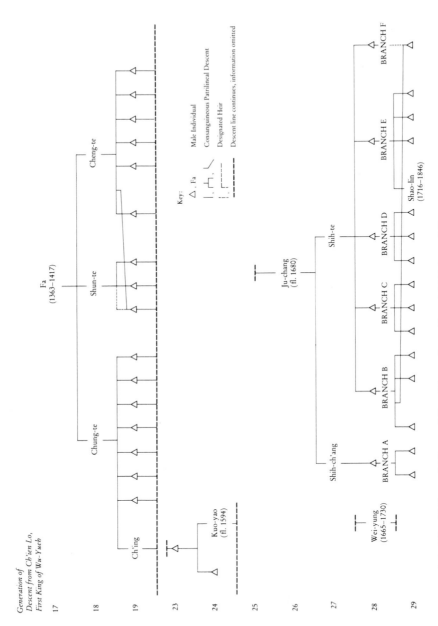

FIGURE 6.5   The Ch'iens of Chuan-ch'iao, Hung-sheng-li, and Ch'i-fang-ch'iao

Key:

△ . Fa   Male Individual
              Consanguineous Patrilineal Descent
              Designated Heir
- - - - -   Descent line continues, information omitted

Some time between 1879 and 1885, the lineage leaders authorized an additional donation of 500 *mou* and a site for additional grain storage. In this case, the donor was the only surviving male descendant of one Ch'ien Ting (1792–1866) of branch D who, together with his son, had led the local resistance against the T'ai-p'ings. The donor was but seventeen when both grandparents died in 1879. At that point the household consisted only of the boy and four women—his mother, his uncle's wife for whom he had been designated heir, and two concubines of this uncle. The mother appears to have been from the extremely prominent family of Weng T'ung-ho, the imperial counsellor from Ch'ang-shu, who entered the Han-lin Academy in 1856 (CS:28:73). The aunt was a Hua woman.

This branch, too, had managed its inheritance over several generations with a strategy of designating heirs. The entire branch of 1879 included only five households. If the ancestral property was still intact, as the oral tradition implies, it was transferred to these five households not along direct, biological descent lines but through adoptive links, as a portion of the ancestral estate. The donor (or his mother) may well have controlled between one-sixth and one-fourth of the progenitor's estate.

The crucial point in all this is that the wealthier families, like the not so wealthy, sought to continue the lines of each male who died without a son. Whether or not all the property of the adoptive father passed down to the ritual heir, the oral tradition certainly supports the conclusion that the rights to ancestral property did. The effects of this pattern, then, were threefold. The portions of ancestral estates held by heirless men tended to remain intact. The descendants of families that proliferated less tended to be identified as a wealthy group, or "branch." And women were assured of not being forced to remarry should their husbands die without sons.

The conventional reason offered by Chinese commentators on family matters for the practice of designating heirs is the imperative of continuing the line, not the need to keep one man's property intact. Keeping the property intact was an undeniably significant effect, however. The primary beneficiary was the heir. In cases where the ancestral estate was substantial, the heir and his brother both stood to gain, since the latter would likely receive a larger portion if not the whole of their father's inheritance. In the process, however, the heir took on ritual responsibilities in the ancestral cult that legitimized this gain. Why, after all, should an adoptive heir in one branch control ten times as much of the ancestral inheritance as a direct lineal heir in a different branch? This is possible only because he is responsible for keeping intact a portion of what was originally assigned to his own branch by the rule of equal division. So long as the wealthier families claimed rights to this property on the grounds of descent from Ch'ien Ju-chang, they also had obligations toward others who shared that descent. Just how strong these obligations were depended on how they were invoked. It would appear that in Ch'i-fang-ch'iao the example of Ch'ien Shao-lin was a powerful symbol in this regard.

It should be clear that, in cases where large ancestral estates were divided among heirs, the practice of designating heirs became a part of the political dynamic of the group. It should also be clear that the practice was universal in the eighteenth and nineteenth centuries. Virtually no married man who died sonless was left without an assigned heir. Furthermore, according to the genealogical records, roughly 20 percent of all married males died without sons. The fact leads to the unavoidable conclusion that women who married into the lineage faced a one-in-five chance of becoming dependent on some-one else's son in their old age. This startling statistic leads us once again to the question of how much influence the women might have exerted in this political field.

Widows might seek help in assuring that their own interests in the estates of their husbands were not ignored. The wealthier and better connected the widow, the better her chances of finding an advocate. That a widow, perhaps together with her husband before his death, might influence the choice of an heir suggests that she might also influence the disposition of the heir's estate. Where conflict among close agnates was rife, an adopted or orphaned son might well move elsewhere taking this property with him. It is not surprising, then, to learn that where there were complex patterns of adoptive heir designation there was often an effort to incorporate property into charitable estates—institutions that benefited widows and orphans, enhanced the pow-er of the estates' founders within the lineage, and prevented the alienation of landed property from the lineage as a whole.

This hypothesis gains support when we look at the experience of the Huas. Underlying both the 1745 and the 1875 estates of the Huas, there is a complex pattern of heir adoption. In the first case, of twenty-nine males in the generation preceding the founder—the great-grandsons of a common ancestor—six died without heirs. Of the remaining twenty-three, six had adoptive heirs (see figure 6.6). The founder, Hua Chin-ssu, himself adopted his brother's son as heir,and this adoptive heir was the principal developer of the estate and of the lineage school (HS 1872:ch. 3). The widow whom this adoptive heir supported was the third wife of the founder and the grand-daughter of a Han-lin academician. She and two previous wives of Chin-ssu were the only women from scholar-gentry families among the recorded wives of twenty-nine men in that generation of the descent group. As for the property, it was said that Chin-ssu's grandfather had used his own up for charitable purposes and that Chin-ssu's father had left him 500 mou with instructions to set up a charitable estate. Thirty years later, after Chin-ssu had accumulated 1,700 additional mou, he donated 1,300 to the lineage and founded the estate.

In the second case, one can trace the development of a pattern in one of

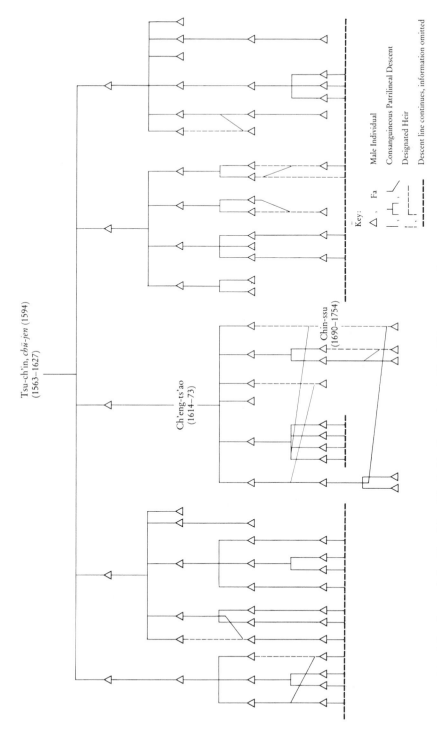

Tsu-ch'in, *chü-jen* (1594)
(1563–1627)

Ch'eng-ts'ao
(1614–73)

Chin-ssu
(1690–1754)

Key:
△ , Fa   Male Individual
| , ⊓ ,   Consanguineous Patrilineal Descent
| , ⌐   Designated Heir
▌▌   Descent line continues, information omitted

FIGURE 6.6   Adoption and the First Hua Charitable Estate (1745), Hua Chin-ssu, Founder

the two collateral lines descended from the two sons of Hua Hung-mo's sixth-generation ancestor. The first son had seven male offspring, none of whose lines survived to Hung-mo's generation. The second son had five, three of which survived to the generation of Hung-mo's father, Ts'un-k'uan, only because of adoptive heirs (see figure 6.7). Hung-mo himself was one of four grandsons, two of whom served as adoptive heirs, and Hung-mo assigned a son as adoptive heir to one of these (HS 1911:*ch.* 13). Hua Ts'un-k'uan's father had instructed his four heirs in 1841 not to divide the 375 *mou* he left them, but to add to it until there was sufficient land for a new charitable estate. The one founded in 1875 was the result.

In each of the cases presented here, the effort within one branch or one family to keep a portion of an ancestral estate intact preceded the establishment of a charitable estate for several related branches. And in each case there developed concurrently a systematic pattern of designating adoptive heirs. The intention to create a charitable estate legitimized the effort not to divide the inheritance, while the appeal to continuity of the patriline legitimized passing the inheritance of a sonless man down intact to a designated heir. Regardless of the intentions of the actors in stemming the tide of division and alienation of property, both efforts had two important social effects. They reinforced the ideology of the descent group and prevented the forced remarriage of widows.

This undeniable benefit for the women who married into the descent group may well have been crucial to the long process by which the charitable estate became the focus of elite lineage organization. As we have seen, none of the Ch'iens or Huas had charitable estates before the fifteenth century although many of them had been engaged in public philanthropic work. In those centuries many descent lines ended for want of an heir. Among the Hu-t'ou Ch'iens in the second generation preceding Ch'ien Fa's migration to Chuan-ch'iao (1383), there were twenty-three males, three of whom had no heirs and none of whom had designated heirs. Ch'ien Fa had three sons, each of whom produced his own heirs. The eldest, Chung-te (1395–1455), was the founder of the short-lived charitable estate. Of his eight sons, only four produced heirs of their own, and three were survived by adoptive heirs. The oldest, who reestablished the charitable estate, provided one of these adoptive heirs and coincidentally married his own eldest son to a Hua woman, one of ten chosen in this generation for the thirty-three great-grandsons of Ch'ien Fa. A fourth adoptive heir among the seventeen grandsons of Ch'ien Fa was assigned by the third son to the second, even before the second had a chance to produce two sons of his own.

Three of the four patterns we have set out to trace thus appear to have begun with the Ch'iens in Chuan-ch'iao between the time Ch'ien Fa's sons had established themselves in the 1430s and the time the first of the Ch'iens appeared among the provincial degree-holders in 1492. The first attempt at a

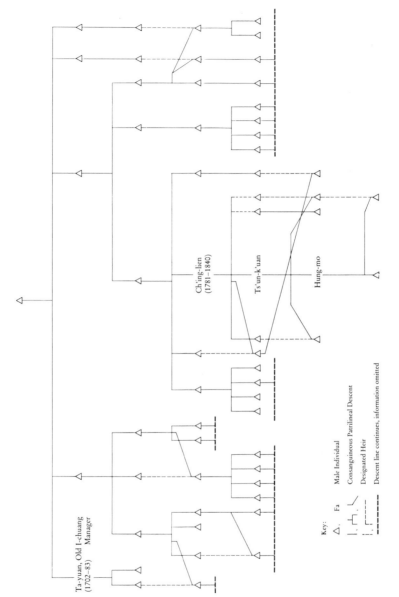

Ta-yuan, Old I-chuang
(1702–83)   Manager

Ch'ing-lien
(1781–1840)

Ts'un-k'uan

Hung-mo

Key:

△, Fa   Male Individual

│, └┴┘, ╲   Consanguineous Patrilineal Descent

- - - -   Designated Heir

┆┄┄┆   Descent line continues, information omitted

FIGURE 6.7   Adoption and the Second Hua Charitable Estate (1875), Hua Ts'un-k'uan et al., Founders

charitable estate, the first sign of systematic designation of adoptive heirs
and the first sign of systematic marriage arrangement with the Huas occurred in one generation. The managers of the strategy were the sons of the
Chou woman to whose bailiwick their father had moved in the wake of the
Ming conquest. Could they possibly not have been influenced by their
affines? It seems likely that the way they treated their women was as crucial
as their pedigree and the perquisites of their power to their survival and
ultimate prominence in the region. The fourth pattern—the development of
higher-order lineages—depended in large part on the working out of the
other three.

Conclusion

The threads that bound a marriage, a death, and the completion of a new
ancestral hall together as part of a way of life in Wu-hsi in 1881 were spun
over six centuries' time. The well-to-do scholar-farmer could marry his
daughter to a poor country scholar because the social system in which both
were embedded fixed the scholar's status above that of the farmer, regardless
of family wealth. There was nothing mystical about this. The scholar would
depend on kinship networks, both agnatic and affinal, to educate his sons,
who in turn would use them to maintain their status and to provide for their
mother in her old age. The charitable estates were a means to this end. They
provided insurance for poor scholars' families and lent prestige and power to
their gentry managers, buttressing the status of the scholar-gentry class and
authenticating its values.

Yet, it is a mistake to assume that the institutions of the lineage and its
controlling interests somehow merely constrained the lives of members. On
the contrary, as the history of marriage, adoption, and welfare practices
among the families who made up the elite community around Tang-k'ou
shows, it was those men and women who created the institutions and au-
thenticated them by their use. There is, of course, a certain irony in this. The
successful creation of a community of affines tended to isolate the poor
scholars of later generations from the poor farmers who were their neighbors. The techniques by which branches shared and incorporated ancestral
estates helped consolidate the position of their members as a class of absen-
tee landlords. The insurance provided by the lineage tended to keep the poor
scholars from taking their families' values into other kinds of work. The
security against remarriage and utter destitution tended to reinforce con-
servative preferences among the intelligent and well connected, but totally
dependent women of the scholar-gentry class. And the women, in turn,
passed these preferences on to their sons and daughters.

In a world where 20 percent of the women became widows without having produced the son that would have been requisite in a peasant family, the

story of the Chou woman in Hung-sheng-li is especially instructive. When in 1750 her husband died, a brother's son was designatd heir. She was twenty-eight at the time, and when she reached forty, the heir having grown and married, she offered to repay the brothers for their kindness by giving part of the inheritance to other brothers in the form of scholarship land for their sons. This was not allowed, of course, for the purpose of designating an heir is to keep the inheritance intact. What *was* allowed was to donate the same land to start a charitable estate, which would serve to strengthen the institutions of the patriline she had *not* helped to reproduce.

The man who married his daughter to Ch'ien Mu's father must have understood something of the process by which elite lineages absorbed their women and the women, in turn, taught the value of kinship to their sons. Ch'ien Mu's maternal grandfather showed this when he said, "I'd like my daughter to go there where she still has some chance of practicing what the *Odes* and the *Rites* teach." And Ch'ien Mu certainly understood something of it when he described the influence of his mother in his childhood:

> It seemed to me that Mother's words to the children were never instructive or reprimanding, but only idle chat about daily life. Yet, when she chatted about daily life, she would always end up talking about my grandmother and my father, invoking them as authorities on all matters pertaining to the lineage and the community. So it was as if all the talk was of trifles, idle gossip, but in truth it was always instructive and there was always something at the heart of it. (PSISC:23)

Herein lies one of the secrets of the strength of the Chinese lineage.

REFERENCES

Primary Sources
CS   *Ch'ien shih Hu-t'ou tsung p'u* 錢氏湖頭宗譜, comp. Ch'ien Shih-ping 錢士炳. Tokyo, Tōyō Bunko, 1976 reprint of 1887–92 ed.
HS 1872   *Hua shih Shan-kuei kung chih tsung-p'u* 華氏山桂公支宗譜, by Hua Wen-po 華文柏 et al. Wu-hsi, 1872.
HS 1881   *Hua shih T'ung-ssu San-hsing kung chih tsung-p'u* 華氏通四三省公支宗譜, by Hua Hung-mo 華鴻模 et al. Microfilm, Tokyo, Tōyō Bunko, 1976.
HS 1901   *Hua shih hsin i-chuang shih-lüeh* 華氏新義莊事略, by Hua Ts'un-k'uan 華存寬 et al., 1901.
HS 1905   *Kou-wu Hua shih pen shu* 勾吳華氏本書, comp. Hua Chu 華諸. Shun-chih (1644–61) ed. reprinted with introduction and appendix by Hua Hung-mo 華鴻模. Wu-hsi, 1905.
HS 1911   *Hua shih T'ung-ssu San-hsing kung chih tsung-p'u* 華氏通四三省公支宗譜, comp. Hua Hung-mo 華鴻模. Wu-hsi, 1911.
HSCS   *Hou-shan Ch'ien shih tsung-p'u* 堠山錢氏宗譜, by Ch'ien Hsi-yuan 錢熙元. Wu-hsi, 1907.

PSISC   *Pa-shih i shuang-ch'in* 八十憶雙親, by Ch'ien Mu 錢穆. Hong Kong, Chinese University, Friends of New Asia College. (Preface dated 1975).

TPML   *T'ai-po Mei-li chih* 泰伯梅里志, comp. Wu Hsi 吳熙. Wu-hsi, 1897.

WHCKHC   *Wu-hsi Chin-kuei hsien chih* 無錫金匱縣志, 1881.

Secondary Works

Baker, Hugh. 1979. *Chinese Family and Kinship*. London: Macmillan.

Ballandier, George. 1970. *Political Anthropology*. Baltimore: Penguin.

Boissevain, Jeremy. 1974. "Conflict and Change: Establishment and Opposition in Malta." In *Choice and Change: Essays in Honour of Lucy Mair*, ed. J. Davis, pp. 17–43. London: Athlone.

Boissevain, Jeremy, and J. Clyde Mitchell, eds. 1973. *Network Analysis: Studies in Human Interaction*. The Hague: Mouton.

Dennerline, Jerry. 1980. "Social Structure, Kinship, and Local Level Politics in Ming and Qing," Paper presented at the Sino-American Symposium on Chinese Social and Economic History from Sung to 1900, Academy of Social Sciences, Peking.

———. 1981a. *The Chia-ting Loyalists: Confucian Leadership and Social Change in Seventeenth-Century China*. New Haven: Yale University Press.

———. 1981b. "The New Hua Charitable Estate and Local Level Leadership in Wuxi County at the End of the Qing." In *Select Papers from the Center for Far Eastern Studies* (University of Chicago), no. 4 (1979–80):19–70.

Ebrey, Patricia Buckley. 1981. "Women in the Kinship System of the Southern Song Upper Class." In *Women in China: Current Directions in Historical Scholarship*, ed. Richard W. Guisso and Stanley Johannsen. Youngstown, N.Y.: Philo Press.

Freedman, Maurice. 1958. *Lineage Organization in Southeastern China*. London: Athlone.

———. 1967. *Rites and Duties, or Chinese Marriage: An Inaugural Lecture*. London: The London School of Economics.

Gluckman, Max. 1967. "Introduction." In *The Craft of Social Anthropology*, ed. A. L. Epstein. London: Tavistock.

Hartwell, Robert M. 1982. "Demographic, Political and Social Transformations of China, 750–1550." *Harvard Journal of Asiatic Studies* 42:365–442.

Mayer, Adrian. 1966. "The Significance of Quasi-groups in the Study of Complex Societies." In *Social Anthropology of Complex Societies*, ed. Michael Banton. New York: Praeger.

Mitchell, J. Clyde. 1966. "Theoretical Orientations in African Urban Societies." In *Social Anthropology of Complex Societies*, ed. Michael Banton. New York: Praeger.

Nicholas, Ralph. 1968. "Rules, Resources and Political Activity." In *Local-Level Politics: Social and Cultural Perspectives*, ed. Marc Swartz. Chicago: Aldine.

Skinner, G. William. 1964. "Marketing and Social Structure in Rural China." *Journal of Asian Studies* 24:3–43.

Swartz, Marc, Victor Turner, and Arthur Tuden, eds. 1966. *Political Anthropology*. Chicago: Aldine.

Twitchett, Denis. 1959. "The Fan Clan's Charitable Estate, 1050–1760." In *Confucianism in Action*, ed. D. S. Nivison and A. F. Wright, pp. 97–133. Stanford: Stanford University Press.

————. 1960–61. "Documents on Clan Administration: I., The Rules of Administration of the Charitable Estate of the Fan Clan." *Asia Major* 8:1–35.

van Velson, J. 1967. "The Extended-Case Method and Situational Analysis." In *The Craft of Social Anthropology*, ed. A. L. Epstein, pp. 129–49. London: Tavistock.

Watson, James L. 1977. "Hereditary Tenancy and Corporate Landlordism in Traditional China: A Case Study." *Modern Asian Studies* 11:161–82.

————. 1982. "Chinese Kinship Reconsidered: Anthropological Perspectives on Historical Research." *China Quarterly* 92:589–622.

Watson, Rubie S. 1981. "Class Differences and Affinal Relations in South China." *Man* n.s. 16:593–615.

————. N.d. "Illegitimacy and Strategies of Inheritance in Southeastern China." Paper presented at the Conference on Family and Kinship in Chinese History, Asilomar, 2–7 January, 1983.

Yeh Hsien-en 葉顯恩. 1980. "Kuan-yü Hui-chou Ch'i-men Ch'a-wan ho Hsiu-ning Ming-chou tien-p'u chih ti tiao-ch'a pao-kao" 關於徽州祁門查灣和休寧茗州佃僕制的調查報告 [A Report on the investigation of the tenant system in Ch'a-wan village, Ch'i-men county, and Ming-chou village, Hsiu-ning county, of Hui-chou]. Paper presented at the Sino-American Symposium on Chinese Social and Economic History from Sung to 1900. Academy of Social Sciences, Peking.

SEVEN

Two Descent Groups in North China: The Wangs of Yung-p'ing Prefecture, 1500–1800

Susan Naquin

One notable characteristic of the Chinese kinship system has been its capacity for holding together relatives who have become separated by the passage of time, movement to different residences, and changes in occupation and status. This chapter will take advantage of the coincidence of two genealogies from the same part of North China in order to examine the ways in which two descent groups became internally differentiated and geographically scattered over a period of three centuries and yet maintained some sense of common identity. By considering the extent to which these groups exhibit the characteristics of those highly organized descent groups that anthropologists term lineages (see J. Watson 1982:594), this chapter may also contribute in a preliminary way to our understanding of regional and class variations in kinship structure and organization.

Ming (1368–1644) and Ch'ing (1644–1911) genealogies from North China are comparatively rare,[1] and those covering the same place at the same

I was able to consult archival sources on the White Lotus Wangs in Taipei in 1976, while enjoying a grant from the American Council of Learned Societies, and in Peking (where the originals of the genealogical charts are located) in 1981 through the support of the Committee on Scholarly Communication with the People's Republic of China, National Academy of Sciences. I am most grateful to them both, to the staffs of the National Palace Museum and the Ming-Ch'ing Archives, and to Hideo Kaneko of the East Asian Library of Yale University, who assisted me years ago in procuring a copy of the Lang-yeh Wang genealogy.

1. Only thirty-four of the 1,228 genealogies listed in Taga (1960) are from Chihli province (present-day Hopei). Only one other comes from Yung-p'ing prefecture; it covers fifteen generations of the Sun descent group, who settled in Yü-t'ien county in the middle Ming (YTS 1926).

The Lang-yeh Wang genealogy (in eight *chüan*) consists of several prefaces; a summary of the pre-Ming history of the Wangs; a set of guiding principles (written in the twentieth century); a chart of the lines of descent through forty-nine generations; detailed genealogical data

time rarer still. The genealogies that provide the basis of this paper trace the offspring of two men who moved to Yung-p'ing prefecture in Chihli province, east of Peking on the road to Manchuria, in the middle of the Ming dynasty. Both settled in Luan department, and descendants of each later moved to nearby Lu-lung county (see map 7.1). Both descent groups have genealogies that encompass the ten generations who lived from approximately 1500 to 1800. Both had the same surname, Wang, although there is no evidence that they were related. One produced two *chin-shih*, nine *chü-jen*, many dozen *sheng-yuan*, and grew to include 118 men in the generation who were adults around 1800. Their genealogy, first compiled in 1750, was twice revised and printed in 1919 as a book of some four hundred pages (LYW 1919). The other group included only a few military officials in ten generations and was only a third as large (forty-two adult men) in 1800. Their genealogy consists of a series of charts drawn up by officials during a criminal prosecution in 1815 (TASL 3.7).

The Lang-yeh Wangs (as they chose to refer to themselves, claiming descent from the famous aristocratic line of the early medieval period, Ebrey 1978:21–22; Mao 1967), seem to be typical of the important but seldom studied strata of Ming-Ch'ing local elites whose sphere of activity and influence did not extend into the national bureaucracy. Although fully one-fourth of the men in the descent group had passed the lowest-level civil service examination, there were no holders of the highest examination degree between 1529 and 1805 and no holders of the provincial degree between 1564 and 1760. The Wangs' position apparently derived originally from wealth (whether primarily land or commercial business cannot be determined), which was translated into low-level degrees, an occasional bureaucratic post, and, probably, a life-style modeled on national elites. This status may have been used to generate patronage and influence at the prefectural level but, despite the pretentious claim to an aristocratic pedigree, could not attract the attention of higher-level elites.

The Shih-fo-k'ou Wangs (as they came to be known, in reference to the name of their village) found fame and fortune in a wider but less orthodox sphere. Throughout North and Central China, their disciples revered them as patriarchs of the White Lotus religion. This position derived from the inherited charisma of one of their ancestors and from prophecies contained in sixteenth- and seventeenth-century texts that were transmitted in oral and

---

for the last nineteen generations; brief biographies of prominent individuals; honors and titles acquired; government appointments; degrees (examination and purchase); meritorious women; and colophons. The detailed genealogical data, when available, consist of birth and death dates; degrees and posts; burial places; names and residences and distinctions of the men with whose families marriages were made. Such information exists in full only for the most successful branches and only for the middle and late Ch'ing.

written form, prophecies that the Maitreya Buddha, savior of mankind, would be reborn in their patriline. The Wangs attracted clients and supporters who hoped not just for assistance in this world but for salvation in the next. Between the 1580s and the 1810s, the Wangs enjoyed an unrivaled position among the many hereditary teachers of White Lotus sectarianism, but their religion was repeatedly scorned by literati and denounced by emperors and officials. An extensive government investigation of their sect in the early nineteenth century finally put an end to their careers and cut off the descent line.

Clearly, these two sets of Wangs lived in very different worlds, yet in fact they were contemporaries and neighbors. Let us consider each one in more detail, concentrating on how certain branches of each group specialized in certain careers, became prominent, and coordinated their activities in the sixteenth through eighteenth centuries, before drawing conclusions about their relationship to one another.

Lang-yeh Wangs

Illustrious Ancestors

According to the Wang genealogy, in the early Ming a descendant of their Han dynasty progenitor[2] moved from the Lang-yeh area (in central Shantung) first to Nanking and then to Peking. (He was probably in some form of government or princely employment.) The first reliably documented ancestor (supposedly in the thirty-second generation but here treated as the first) was a man called Wang Hsien who left Peking in 1404 and moved 200 kilometers east to settle in a small village near Luan department city. He apparently took up land there, perhaps as part of the general effort of the newly enthroned Yung-le Emperor to promote the recovery of the area that in 1421 would become the seat of the northern capital.

The Wangs lived in that village (called Ch'en-li-chuang) for the next three generations. This frontier prefecture of Yung-p'ing, which encompassed five other counties, had the advantage of good soil that was drained by the Luan River and its tributaries and was not subject to the regular flooding characteristic of the North China plain just to the south and west. We can suppose from the results that the Wangs' resources were directed toward educating their offspring in the traditional manner. Two of Wang Hsien's great-

---

2. Thirty generations are briefly charted in the genealogy, extending from the end of the Han into the Ming. It was a man of the thirtieth generation who allegedly moved from Lin-i (that is, Lang-yeh) in Shantung to Nanking in the Hung-wu reign of the Ming. Information on the thirty-first generation is suspiciously vague. Wang Cheng, the first editor of the genealogy, considered Wang Hsien, purportedly a man of the thirty-second generation, to be the founder of his line, and I have done likewise.

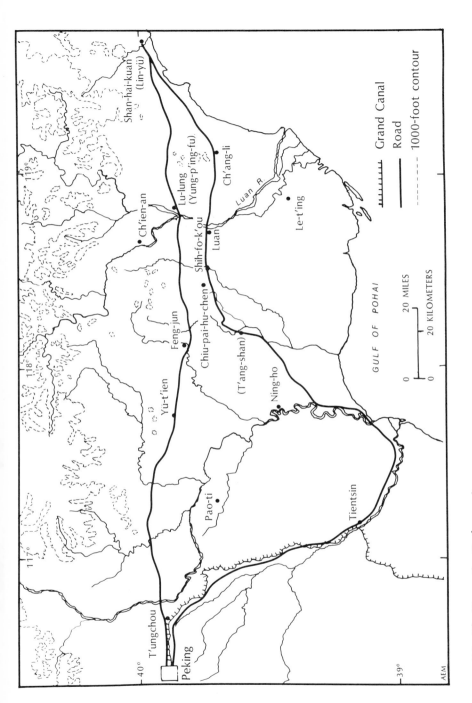

MAP 7.1   The Yung-p'ing Prefecture Area

grandsons (cousins in the fourth generation) were able to pass the provincial level *chü-jen* examinations in 1522 and 1528, and one went on to be a *chin-shih* (1529) and to serve as a second-rank official in Kansu province. (It was the descendants of this man, Wang Kao, who constituted the most successful branch of the descent group and who eventually compiled the genealogy.) In keeping with his higher status and wider network of connections, Wang Kao moved from the country village into Luan city—probably in the 1530s. When he died, his sons did not bury him with his ancestors back in that village, where a few relatives still lived, but in a newly acquired burial ground located on the prestigious slopes of Mount Heng, just north of the city. This graveyard became the most visible (and possibly the only) locus for formal association (through funerals and burial) for his descendants, and it set the pattern whereby his line became differentiated from their other relatives. (Unless otherwise noted, all information on the Wangs comes from LYW 1919.)

Wang Kao had four sons and ten grandsons—the demographic benefits of wealth and higher status (see Harrell 1985). One of his sons became a *chü-jen* (in 1564), the others were *kung-sheng* ("senior licentiates," the cream of the *sheng-yüan*), as were three grandsons. All lived in Luan city and, because only three other men from Luan besides Wang Kao won the *chin-shih* degree in the remainder of the century, surely enjoyed considerable prestige as local notables (LCC 1898:5.11–19). Unfortunately, the collapse of the Ming order in the early part of the seventeenth century, together with the accompanying violence, halted and then reversed the Wangs' mobility upward. Traditional strategies for advancement through the examination system and official bureaucracy pursued from a comfortable urban base were dependent on a stable polity and became difficult to implement during times of military crisis and social upheaval. Moreover, because of its location on the northeastern frontier near Shan-hai-kuan, the gateway to Manchuria where the Great Wall reached the sea, the Yung-p'ing area was especially threatened and increasingly militarized in this era. Warfare, military requisitions, poor harvests, and epidemic diseases began to affect all who lived there.

In the winter of 1629–30, Abahai, the commander of the expanding Manchu forces in the Northeast, marched his armies to Peking. En route through the Yung-p'ing area, they overcame local resistance and occupied four cities (including Luan and Lu-lung, the prefectural seat). One prescient Ming colonel and Lu-lung resident even took his men and joined the Manchus, becoming a Bannerman and later achieving considerable prominence.[3] Although finally expelled by Ming armies after four months, the Manchus raided the capital area again in 1636, 1638, 1639, and 1642.

---

3. He was Meng Ch'iao-fang (Hummel 1943–44:572; LL 8:5–6).

For the Wangs, these events brought near disaster. Wang Kao's grandson, P'i (1591–1644; see figure 7.1) lost two sons (whose valor was appropriately commemorated in a public shrine) in the unsuccessful defense of Luan city against the Manchus in 1630. We do not know how the others fared during the four-month occupation of that city. In the 1640s, fearing for his family and the rest of his kin—with good reason; only three of Wang Kao's thirteen grandsons lived through this turbulent era to produce male offspring— P'i decided "it is obvious that in time of great chaos one ought to live in the countryside" and therefore abandoned his city home (LYW 4.3–4).

In 1642, at the age of eighty, Wang P'i led his relatives in a major relocation. Separating into branches (that is, along descent lines), they moved to four different villages. One of Wang P'i's nephews took his son and settled very close to Luan city (perhaps to keep an eye on the family graveyard and property). The rest moved farther to the northwest, near the low mountains that backed up against the Great Wall, to a cluster of villages in adjacent Lu-lung county. Wang P'i himself, his two surviving sons, and his two grandsons settled in a place called Chiu-pai-hu-chen (Nine-hundred-household camp). Another grandson, K'un, went to nearby Min-family Village, and a nephew found a place in Huang-family Village, also not far away. Around this same time, the sole surviving member of the original Ch'en-li Village line of the Wangs also chose to follow the example of his distant but prominent cousin and move to the same part of Lu-lung county. For whatever reasons, P'i was clearly able to inspire this rough sort of collective action among his kin.

In the early summer of 1644, the rebel Li Tzu-ch'eng, fresh from his seizure of Peking and the suicide of the last Ming emperor, brought his armies to Shan-hai-kuan, where he met with defeat; the Manchus occupied Peking and established the Ch'ing dynasty. Residents of the cities of the Yung-p'ing area, already familiar with the new rulers, surrendered promptly and without resistance. The conquest was accompanied by a major reorganization of land ownership in the Peking area as Chinese lands were transferred to the conquering Bannermen. The new Manchu regent, Dorgon, set up a princely residence in the prefectural city, and at least one Chinese Bannerman apparently moved to Chiu-pai-hu. It is not clear how these events affected the Wangs' livelihood.

At this time, the relocated eighth generation of the Lang-yeh Wangs consisted of only eleven men (fewer than either of the two preceding generations) in three lines. The number and level of degrees won by the Wangs had reached its lowest point: only one *kung-sheng* and one *sheng-yuan*. The area where they were now living was still on the northeastern edge of the plain but not far from the main thoroughfares and within thirty kilometers of two major cities. The collapse of the Ming state had meant loss of life and property as well as dislocations in the social structure in which the Wangs had built

FIGURE 7.1   Outline of the Lang-yeh Wang Genealogy

Generation

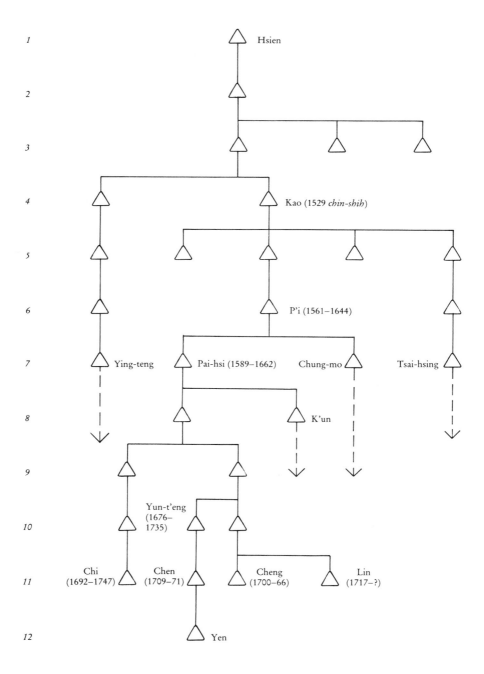

themselves a small niche. But although circumstances had forced them from their homes, they had, by choice, stayed close to one another. And some of the Wangs also remained committed to the same strategy of social advancement. When the newly installed Ch'ing rulers reestablished the examination-and-office ladder of success, the Wangs began to recover lost ground. By "plowing and studying," they gradually accumulated degrees—probably a mirror of their economic circumstances—and after six more generations were able to achieve high degrees and higher status once more.[4]

Differential Growth

Once resettled, the Wangs multiplied steadily. The four progenitors of the continuing agnatic line (two of whom were Wang P'i's sons) would produce, after a century and a half, a generation numbering more than one hundred men. (See figure 7.1) This demographic recovery is not itself surprising, for it is well known that in the century between 1680 and 1780 China as a whole experienced a dramatic and persistent population increase, and there is every indication that northeast Chihli province shared in this growth. However, Stevan Harrell's hypothesis that it was the more well-to-do who participated most actively in this population growth because the men could marry more, healthier, and younger women seems borne out by our case. Once one branch began to distinguish itself, wealth and status apparently enabled it to grow faster.

In the course of the eighteenth century, the least successful descent line was that of *chin-shih* Wang Kao's fourth son. The sole survivor of this line, Wang Tsai-hsing (seventh generation), a *sheng-yuan*, had relocated outside Luan city at the time of the Ch'ing conquest, and this was the only branch never to move to Lu-lung. We know little about them, and it seems likely that they produced no degree-holders at all, even if they had members who escaped the notice of their kinsmen genealogists, who recorded only five surviving males in the fourteenth generation (see figure 7.2 below).[5]

Somewhat more well-to-do were the descendants of Wang Ying-teng, the only survivor of the segment that had moved from the ancestral home to Min-family Village in Lu-lung. Ying-teng (in the seventh generation) had five grandsons, and this branch grew at a moderate and then declining pace during the early Ch'ing—the fourteenth generation consisted of only eighteen men. They demonstrated the ability (or resources) to win only an occa-

4. Because it was overwhelmingly the well-to-do who won examination degrees, I have worked on the assumption that an increase in number of degree-holders paralleled an increase in wealth. Direct information on the economic resources of the Wangs is nonexistent.

5. The bias of the genealogy in favor of certain lines of Wang P'i's descendants makes it difficult to judge whether other lines really died out. I do have some confidence that most successful agnates, even distantly related ones, were recorded.

sional degree (two *sheng-yuan* in six generations). The lack of data on this line in the genealogy indicates that although they lived near their more successful kin, relations were not intimate.

The offspring of Wang P'i's two sons fared considerably better, and his line far outstripped the others in numbers and honors won. At first these two segments grew at similar rates (numbering thirteen and fourteen men after four generations, that is, in the eleventh), but after seven generations it was clear that one was far more successful both socially and economically. The lesser branch had by that time produced only five *sheng-yuan*, no higher-degree holders, and numbered only twenty-four men. The first branch, on the other hand, had many generations of licentiates (an astonishing seventy in all) and eventually eight *chü-jen*; the fourteenth generation—who came to maturity in the early nineteenth century—numbered seventy-four men. As figure 7.2 indicates, moreover, within this line, it was one member of the eleventh generation (Wang Chen, 1709–71) whose descendants were far and away the most numerous and prominent. The extent to which this concentration of licentiate degrees within one descent line is typical of low-level regional elites in this period cannot presently be determined. Local gazetteers rarely record the names of civil and military *sheng-yuan* and as a result this world is very difficult for the historian to penetrate.

Although Wang P'i's second son, Chung-mo, was a licentiate and poet who lived his later years in Chiu-pai-hu Village and was buried in the family plot on Mount Heng, his descendants were not, as we have just noted, very accomplished examination-takers. His only two grandsons, one a *sheng-yuan* like his father, both left Chiu-pai-hu and moved to other villages (one not far away) where they lived and were buried. This move paralleled but does not explain the seeming decline in their fortunes. Was it lack of land, the hope of better opportunities, or conflict with relatives that motivated this separation? Here, as in the other instances when one branch became more successful and others fell away, the documents do not help us understand the process. The scarce information about this branch in the genealogy suggests the same persistent lack of contact (despite proximity) that we noted for the more distant descent lines.

It was the offspring of Wang P'i's eldest son, Pai-hsi (1589–1662), who had the greatest sense of lineage consciousness, and they were the ones who restored the Wangs' position to that of the sixteenth century; they also dominate the genealogy. Pai-hsi's eldest son lived in Chiu-pai-hu, his only brother in an adjacent village. Although one grandson left the area altogether and like many from Yung-p'ing went to Manchuria, a place of available land and work, and lost contact with his relatives, most offspring continued to live nearby. At each generation, at least one man from this line moved out of Chiu-pai-hu, but nearly all chose to settle in what may have been newly developing villages close by. In the late eighteenth century, there were twen-

FIGURE 7.2 Differential Growth of the Four Ch'ing Lines
of the Lang-yeh Wangs

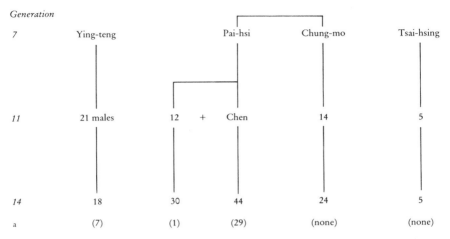

Generation

| 7 | Ying-teng | | Pai-hsi | Chung-mo | Tsai-hsing |

| 11 | 21 males | 12 + Chen | | 14 | 5 |

| 14 | 18 | 30 | 44 | 24 | 5 |
| a | (7) | (1) | (29) | (none) | (none) |

a. [Number of degree-holders in the fourteenth generation.]

ty sets of brothers (forty-nine men), all descendants of Pai-hsi in the thirteenth generation, living in Chiu-pai-hu. Eleven other sets of brothers
(eighteen men) lived in three neighboring villages.[6]

The expansion of Wang Pai-hsi's branch, as well as the intensification of
its presence in the Chiu-pai-hu area, is also illustrated by the proliferation of
grave sites. Through the middle of the eighteenth century the eldest sons of
eldest sons (the *tsung* or main line) continued to be buried in the Mount
Heng graveyard outside the departmental city—a reminder of their more glorious past and surely a focus for annual ancestral rites. Younger sons opened
up new burial grounds near their Chiu-pai-hu homes for themselves and
their descendants. These sons, displaced from the ancestral plot, then became the focus for new ritual groups. These secondary and tertiary grave
sites were clustered in the hills around Chiu-pai-hu. The last burial at Mount
Heng took place in 1763, after which time this site, which then held the
graves of nine generations (the fourth to twelfth), was abandoned and the
center of gravity shifted permanently to Chiu-pai-hu.

In the thirteenth generation, the oldest of the sites near that village held
men of four generations and was supplemented by six other graveyards nearby and nine more near neighboring villages. Ahern (1976:12) notes that the

6. Some of those men who moved to different locations were eldest sons (six out of sixteen).
New grave sites, on the other hand, were opened almost exclusively by younger sons.

physical segmentation of a lineage (which we see here reflected in both residence and cemeteries) could parallel the formation of corporate estates, but there is no evidence of ritual land being set aside when new graves were opened, and no mention at all of ancestral halls. We can only assume that at New Year's, on the *ch'ing-ming* holiday in the spring, or on the death days of recent ancestors, the graves might have been the sites of ritual activities. (See Naquin 1985b for such rites.)

The Genealogy

The revival of the Wangs' prestige in the eighteenth century came about largely through the efforts of one man, Wang Chen (1709–71), and his immediate descendants. They illustrate how the activities of a single family could transform the status of a larger descent group. It was a sign of their wealth that Wang Chen and his three elder sons began in the middle of the eighteenth century acquiring licentiate degrees by purchase (*chien-sheng*). The fourth son, Wang Yen (1742–1834), went further and earned the difficult *chü-jen* degree (in 1780), and *his* son was the Wangs' first Ch'ing *chinshih* (in 1805). Among Wang Chen's sons, grandsons, and great-grandsons were altogether twenty-nine degree-holders (see figure 7.2). Although Wang Yen never took up office, he urged his sons to follow scholarly careers: "Ten thousand pieces of gold are not as good as even a meager talent, and of the various talents, none is as great as studying" (LYW 4.11). Yen was himself the father of six sons and grandfather of eighteen, and in 1833, when he was ninety-one (by Chinese count), he celebrated the birth of two great-great-grandsons. Yen's household was said to number more than one hundred people, and the family was applauded in the local gazetteer for having "five generations living together" (LYW 4.11; LL 8.21). When Yen died the following year, his surviving son buried him in a new grave site, perhaps one with geomantic properties commensurate to his father's success (and exclusively for his line), north of Chiu-pai-hu.

It was in the middle of the eighteenth century that a member of the eleventh generation, Wang Pai-hsi's great-great-grandson Cheng (1700–66), decided to compile a genealogy. (It is likely that some records had already been kept in his line.) He tells us in his preface of 1750 that "putting together a genealogy (*tsung-p'u*) is done in order to make relatives into closer relatives … [then] if sons and grandsons are far apart, they will still not be forgotten, and although they are dispersed will still be close (*ch'in*)." Wang was a very common surname, and many relatives had already moved away and lost touch. Wang Cheng saw the genealogy as a way of holding patrilineal kin together by recording the connections between them (a function commonly performed by genealogies [see Ebrey chapter in this volume]). He therefore undertook to interview members of the descent group (he uses the term *tsu*), bring the information together in book form, and give a copy to each member. All would then know that "although they are far apart, they began with a single ancestor; although there are many descendants, they belong to one tree. Thus they will behave as proper sons and brothers and will not forget to esteem the main line (*tsung*) and be amiable toward members of the *tsu*" (LYW preface 1–2).

By appealing to a tradition of aristocratic descent, Wang Cheng was also attempting to reclaim the prestige of the Lang-yeh Wangs and to enhance his and his relatives' image in their communities as people of distinction. The genealogy anticipated (and probably contributed to) the Wangs' slow improvement in social status in the eighteenth century and had the effect of diffusing the radiated glory of the past and of the most successful members to the group as a whole. (Such efforts may have been helpful in finding higher-status marriage partners, for example.) Compilation of the genealogy does not appear to have resulted from other forms of collective action or to have paralleled the simultaneous creation of any new corporate property or institutions (as in Ebrey 1983, R. Watson 1982, or Hazelton in this volume). Its main concerns were relationships and status, not resources. Moreover, despite rhetoric about influencing behavior, the genealogy makes no mention of rules or procedures for disciplining relatives such as one finds in lineages elsewhere in China in this period (Beattie 1979:121; Liu 1959).

In reality, although the genealogy projected an image of unity, it also revealed the extent to which the larger descent group had already dispersed to separate residences and hinted at the degree of emotional distance between some branches. Even in this standardized format, the bias of the author could not be disguised, and the relatively detailed information on his line highlighted their seeming professional and demographic success. Furthermore, the genealogy was clearly already incomplete, even as it set a pattern (not systematically followed) for institutionalizing the recording of basic biographical information.[7]

One other useful indicator that the genealogy provides of the changing intensity of kinship ties among the Wang branches was generational naming. The practice of systematic generational names came into extensive use in the Sung dynasty (see Ebrey's chapter in this volume) and was commonplace among all classes in the late imperial period. Members of each generation in a descent line would be given a common character (or sometimes a common

---

7. We cannot compare Wang Cheng's 1750 genealogy with the 1919 printed version and thus cannot really tell how widely he cast his net or how much information he gathered. No great change in quality or quantity of information appears after his generation. We know only that the production of the genealogy inspired further revisions in the 1810s by Wang Yü (1775–1835), a *chü-jen* and member of the most successful segment of Wang Pai-hsi's branch, and then again in the 1910s, and that eventually (if not from the outset) all of the branches here described were included. Presumably those who cooperated were minimally sympathetic with the goals of the genealogy and willing to be a part of it.

radical, see Grafflin 1983) in their personal names as a marker of both generation and descent. These characters might even be selected from a passage of
text and assigned in sequence. The degree of adherence by relatives to such a
system of naming could constitute a kind of cooperation and express some
(albeit weak) sense of common identity.

Among the Wangs, we can see such a pattern beginning with Wang
Hsien's grandsons (third generation), all of whom were given the radical *yü*
(jade) in their names. But beginning in the next generation, a much more
ambitious system was adopted. The fourth generation (which included
the *chin-shih* Wang Kao) all had the metal radical in their names, the fifth
generation used the water radical, and the sixth wood. Thus began the not
very original practice of using in sequence these radicals representing the
Five Phases (metal, water, wood, fire, and earth) in the naming of each generation. Such a system required little coordination, but when reaffirmed by
each generation it identified relatives and indicated seniority (an important
consideration as the age difference between men of the same agnatic generation became greater with time). This system was indeed followed by every
male in the genealogy through the sixth generation (which included Wang
P'i). The end of the unified naming pattern accompanied the reversal of the
Wangs' fortunes and their dispersal from Luan city at the time of the Ch'ing
conquest.

Wang Tsai-hsing (whose offspring constituted the smallest and most remote portion of the descent group) was himself not named according to the
Five-Phases pattern, nor were any of his descendants. It may be a reflection
of a lack of aspiration to elite status, as well as distance, that for most of this
branch no generational names of any sort were given.

In Wang Ying-teng's branch, generational names were used, but the Five-
Phases radical system was not adhered to. Although this group lived near
their prominent relatives, their unwillingness to formalize their kinship in
names confirms the sense of separateness suggested by other evidence.

It was the sons of Wang P'i, as might be expected, who maintained the
naming system of their ancestors, and did so uniformly for two centuries
(through the twelfth generation). In the thirteenth generation, the increasing
gap between the most and least successful segments of Wang Pai-hsi's
branch is also reflected in their names. All five sons of Wang Chi (1692–
1747) (in the eleventh generation and main line of eldest sons) broke the
pattern in naming their sons and used a common character but without the
appropriate earth radical; thereafter, the naming of sons in this line followed
no particular system. The more successful descendants of Wang P'i, by contrast, continued to adhere closely to the Five-Phases system, and the genealogy itself notes what the appropriate radical was for each generation.

In general, consistency in naming seems to have been a function of both
aspirations to higher social status and success in achieving it. Abandonment

of this elaborate (perhaps pretentious?) naming system could represent a symbolic break with the descent group, was usually reinforced by geographic removal, and seems to have paralleled a decline in social position. Although we do not know precisely how this internal stratification among the Wangs took place or what its other consequences were, men's names provide a mirror of it.

Lineage and Locality

It is difficult to decide to what extent these Wangs can be described as belonging to a single lineage. What I have called "branches" are not called *fang* in the genealogy, and the relationship between them is not discussed. There is no evidence of the existence of any corporate property (the usual diagnostic feature of lineage organization, J. Watson 1982:593–96) and only a few hints of collective activities. The pattern of graveyards, typical of North China, suggests some corporate consciousness, as does the fact of the genealogy itself, the use of generational names, and the preference for an examination career. But in each case, it was primarily one descent line that illustrated such preferences, not the entire group. We can therefore perhaps speak only of those men descended through Wang Kao, Wang P'i, Wang Pai-hsi, and Wang Chen as belonging to a lineage.

Despite the lack of information about corporate property and joint ventures in community activities, the Wang lineage, narrowly defined, does generally conform to our expectations about the segmentation, differential growth, and cross-class character of Chinese lineages. But the Wangs resemble far more closely what Patricia Ebrey (1983) calls the T'ung-ch'eng type (typified by the Chang lineage studied by Beattie [1979]) rather than the Fukien-Kwangtung type described by Freedman (1966). But there is no evidence of the collective activities—social welfare, education, and so forth—common not only in Central China but in Yung-p'ing as well (judging from the local histories and another extant genealogy [YTS]). And even among its most self-conscious members, this Wang lineage, having few if any corporate resources, apparently exercised very little power vis-à-vis the domestic group (*chia*). They were more highly organized than the Mas studied by Rawski but less so than the Ch'iens and Huas discussed by Dennerline or the Wus studied by Hazelton (described elsewhere in this volume). Moreover, the Wangs were an inclusive, not exclusive, descent group (Barrett 1983), and in their relative lack of concern with defining boundaries or protecting property and relatively greater interest in displaying status and demonstrating an aristocratic pedigree may reflect the fluid and open society of the early and middle Ch'ing.

The patterns of residence in the Ch'ing period nevertheless do resemble those observed for demonstrably more corporate lineages in South China. In 1966 Maurice Freedman proposed that "higher-order lineages" tended to cluster within certain areas that he termed "vicinages"; these areas, he thought, were probably the same as the standard marketing communities described by G. W. Skinner within which "composite lineages" competed for dominance (Freedman 1966:23; Skinner 1964:36).

Most of the villages in which the Wangs lived were located very close together. Chiu-pai-hu was the central market town in the early twentieth century and may have been so earlier. The evidence certainly indicates a steady intensification of the Wangs' presence there that coincided with but was not limited to the rise in social status of Wang Pai-hsi's line. The other branches (who had, after all, moved there in the seventeenth century by following their most prominent kin) were less concentrated and not at all organized, but the genealogy does not suggest that they were in any way dominated by their more well-to-do relatives. We can, however, still conclude that the members of one Wang line had come to constitute a kind of lineage associated with which were smaller, less powerful related descent groups each oriented around different villages and burial sites within the market area. It may be that this preference for geographical concentration is typical of even the least organized of Chinese kin groups. The idea of the "native place" (*chia-hsiang*), where deep roots could be sunk and the patriline firmly anchored, surely encouraged this tendency, even as the quest for economic opportunity might drive individuals to leave the area.

The extent of the Wangs' "dominance" within or beyond Chiu-pai-hu is even more problematic. (On this subject, also see Rawski's chapter in this volume.) They were certainly not alone or even preeminent within the marketing area.[8] But they did try to become part of the local scholar-gentry elite. They competed for and passed the prefectural licentiate examinations from the time of the Ch'ing conquest, and early in the eighteenth century they began purchasing degrees as well as competing successfully at the provincial exams in Peking. Later in the century, successful individuals enhanced their family's status by purchasing and bestowing (often posthumous) honorary ranks on parents and grandparents. However, the Wangs did not move from their village home and achieved only a small place in the larger world of higher-degree holders in the prefecture.

Between 1644 and 1820, Yung-p'ing prefecture produced 73 *chin-shih* and 505 *chü-jen*, of whom 1 *chin-shih* and 10 *chü-jen* (about 2 percent) were

---

8. In order to know whether or not the Wangs actually dominated the marketing community, socially or economically, more information on their sources of livelihood and on other families in the neighborhood must first be located. The county gazetteer (LL 4:2) records that in the early Ch'ing a family named Li had, like the Wangs, moved to Chiu-pai-hu from Luan and resided in the center of the village. The Lis were Chinese Bannermen, and thus already members of a more privileged group; by the eighteenth century they were famous locally (as the Wangs apparently were not) for their philanthropy (in the form of charitable schools and famine relief).

Lang-yeh Wangs (YP *ch*. 11–12).[9] Looked at differently, in the Wangs' thirteenth generation (ca. 1800) there were about 24 licentiates, 5 *chü-jen*, and no *chin-shih*. In Lu-lung county at about that time, there would have been approximately 380 licentiates, 10 *chü-jen*, and 2 *chin-shih*; comparable figures for the prefecture are 2,700, 135, and 10, respectively (YP *ch*. 11–12; Chang 1955:97). The population of Lu-lung county in 1773 was about 160,000, of Yung-p'ing prefecture 1,375,000 (YP *ch*. 45). By either calculation, the Wangs were only one of a great many local gentry, some of whom did have national connections, and there is no evidence that they were in any way distinguished at this level.

Those few men who received appointments (about ten since 1644) seldom had sustained official careers, and even the *chü-jen* among the Wangs rarely held public office. There was one Wang who did find a place in the wider world of Ch'ing government. He was the first to hold office since the seventeenth century, and it may have been his success that inspired his older brother to compile the Wang genealogy. Wang Lin (eleventh generation) was born in 1717 and belonged, needless to say, to Wang Pai-hsi's branch. It is perhaps a reflection of the intensity of competition for degrees in the eighteenth century that Wang Lin's route of advancement was through the military. After passing the military licentiate exam, he contributed funds to finance river repairs (probably near home) and was rewarded with an appointment as a major (a fifth-rank post) in the Green Standard Army forces commanded by the head of the Grain Transport Administration. Lin then took up a series of successful appointments in the 1750s through 1770s in Kiangsu, Hupei, and Shantung, and must have found friends and patrons within that official world. But the impact of his career on his kin is almost impossible to discern. The career of Wang Yen (1760 *chü-jen*) was more typical: he was actually appointed county director of education (eighth-rank) but by his own decision never took up office (LYW 2.31; LL 8.21). Although Wang Lin married his son to the daughter of a military *chin-shih* from elsewhere in the empire, and Wang Yen's second son's wife was from Shensi, their other affinal relatives did not come from beyond Yung-p'ing. Indeed, the marriage patterns for the Wangs as a whole indicate that the social sphere of even the most successful branches was not much larger than the prefecture (which generally coincided with the regional trading system centered on Lu-lung). Marriages beyond this area were very rare.

Looking at the successful and best-documented Wang Pai-hsi branch, we can see evidence of a regional net of marriage partners from families of similar status. The men and women of this branch for whom there are data (116 daughters and 78 sons) married (in roughly similar proportions) into families

9. By county, these degree-holders were distributed as follows: Luan 134; Ch'ang-li 92; Lin-yü 86; Lu-lung 84; Le-t'ing 64; Ch'ien-an 63; Fu-ning 55.

from most of the nearby counties: Luan 46, Lu-lung 39, Ch'ien-an 35, Le-
t'ing 29, Feng-jun 27, Ch'ang-li 10, Yü-t'ien 5, Pao-ti 1, Ning-ho 1, Shensi
province 1. (See map 7.1.) This network was quite local, confined with a
single exception to the Yung-p'ing area.[10] The network had, however,
grown wider with time: Marriages arranged prior to the tenth generation
were confined to Lu-lung and the three adjacent counties of Luan, Feng-jun,
and Ch'ien-an. Not surprisingly, the more successful the man, the more
likely he or his children were to marry into a similarly successful family. In
general terms, most of the men married the daughters of low-level degree or
office holders. Poor information on the affines of the less successful branches
makes comparison difficult; I would guess that their marriages were made
within an even smaller area and to even less prominent people.

Marriage ties between local elites sustained as well as defined social position. The lineages studied by Beattie (1979), Dennerline, and Hazelton (both
this volume) illustrate the way in which repeated intermarriage between two
families could be extended over several generations. The connections and, to
a limited extent, the wealth of the more prominent family could be shared by
their affines; a closely knit pattern of marriage ties could also mitigate against
the fragmentation that marriage encourages. The Lang-yeh Wang genealogy
indicates that among the most successful branches, such multi-generational
marriage bonds with selected families were indeed created.

As one example, let us look at the family of Wang Chen (eleventh generation). Two of his sons married daughters of two local *sheng-yuan* of the Ho
surname (themselves brothers or cousins). At this time (the 1750s–1760s)
those Hos had produced a civil and a military *chü-jen*, and one military
chin-shih. Wang Chen's grandson Tseng, himself a *chü-jen*, married that
chin-shih's daughter. Chen's sister and two granddaughters also married
Hos from the same county who may have also been part of this group.
(Indeed, altogether nine men and fifteen women from the Wangs married
people from Lu-lung surnamed Ho.) Such marriage patterns, it could even
be said, constituted a kind of corporate activity reflective of more than
family (*chia*) interests.

All of the evidence thus suggests that the Lang-yeh Wangs were quite
local in the sphere of their activities. They resided in the countryside
throughout the Ch'ing period, never again moving into town. They did not
marry into any of the families that dominate the local gazetteer. Residences
were concentrated within a standard marketing community and marriages,
when they were not to undistinguished neighbors, were with low-level elites
from within a radius of one hundred kilometers. Although some Wangs

10. These counties go beyond Yung-p'ing prefecture and the Yung-p'ing regional trading
system and into what G. W. Skinner has defined as (in the nineteenth century at least) part of
the adjacent Tientsin trading system (1979).

passed the prefectural exams with ease and even competed effectively at the provincial and national levels, they were not professional scholars or bureaucrats. Their world was a far cry from that of the Lower Yangtze elites studied by Beattie (1979), Dennerline (1981), and Zurndorfer (1981). Their licentiate degrees seem to have been more symbols of an elite way of life than signs of an occupation or avenues of mobility beyond Yung-p'ing. Their primary income came not from the perquisites of office but probably from landowning. Nevertheless, their pursuit of higher degrees was single-minded and eventually rewarded (in the nineteenth century) with greater success, and their life-style was surely equally removed from the commoner lineages of Kwangtung for whom exams and degrees were very remote.

The Wangs sustained some sense of unity in the early and middle Ch'ing, but it was not a unity that was the basis of much collective action. The impetus for a heightened sense of kinship appears to have come from the branches or lines that were successful in the examinations: They determined residential focus, wrote the genealogy that created the lineage on paper, maintained the systematic naming patterns that could identify relatives, and intermarried regularly with families of similar status. Poorer branches may have wanted to keep up contacts with more prosperous relatives, but they were more likely to move away in search of opportunity, dispense with fancy names, fail to record vital statistics, and marry into undistinguished lower-class families. Without the initiative of the successful branches, the poorer ones alone could not possibly have created or maintained even the illusion (much less the reality) of a large lineage. For the more wealthy segments, a numerous, well-defined descent group gave the appearance of demographic success and may even have provided allies and retainers, but it also implied patronage and mutual aid and may even have been a source of embarrassment when gaps in social status between relatives became too large. Without the visible benefits that came from corporate income, family togetherness may have been a mixed blessing.

Having seen the results of the orthodox career path of one set of Wangs, let us now turn to our contrasting case, the Wangs of Stone-Buddha Village.

The Shih-fo-k'ou Wangs

Illustrious Ancestors

According to the genealogical chart reconstructed by officials in 1815, the Shih-fo-k'ou Wangs' earliest known ancestor was a man called Wang Ch'ao-feng who lived in the early fifteenth century.[11] (See TASL 3.7 from which all

11. One version (cited in Asai 1978 and Li 1983) asserts that Wang Tao-sen was originally surnamed Shih (stone) and was the second of three sons who moved to Shih-fo-k'ou and changed his name. Several versions state that he was a leather worker.

genealogical information comes unless otherwise noted, and LCC 6:38–41.)
Like the early members of the Lang-yeh Wangs, Ch'ao-feng probably found
relatively ample land in what was still a frontier of the empire (he would have
been a contemporary of the Lang-yeh Wangs' founder's great-grandson).
He had three sons, one of whom, Wang Tao-sen, was responsible for his
descendants' involvement in heterodox religion. All three sons lived in a
village along the main thoroughfare between Tientsin and Shan-hai-kuan,
about two hundred kilometers from Peking. (See map 7.1.) Shih-fo-k'ou (lit.
Stone-Buddha Wharf) was a small settlement on a river that ran south from
the mountains into the Po-hai Gulf. In 1898 the village held only 67 households, 698 people (LCC 13:26). Like many of the villages in the northern
part of Yung-p'ing prefecture, it had small hills nearby and—to the north—
mountainous terrain.

   The sketchy facts about Wang Tao-sen's leadership of a new and popular
religious movement are relatively well known, although a full and accurate
account of his life and role as a White Lotus teacher has yet to be written
(Chu 1976; Asai 1978). He was probably born in the early 1540s and began
preaching in the 1560s and 1570s. The sixteenth century had generally witnessed a widespread religious revivalism (see Yü 1981; Berling 1980; Shek
1981; Hsu 1979) that led (among other developments) to a proliferation of
sectarian teachers, the writing of White Lotus scriptures, and the emergence
of this popular religion as an important force in Chinese society. In such a
time, when orthodox values were being questioned and many felt a general
concern with matters of salvation, the teachings of Wang Tao-sen found
many converts. By the 1590s, he had a wide following in North China but
especially in the area of Peking and at the Wan-li court.[12]

   We do not have a complete picture of Wang Tao-sen's message. We know
that he preached the basic White Lotus ideas: the existence of the Eternal
Mother, adherence to correct and pious behavior as the path to salvation, the
expectation that the Buddha Maitreya (the buddha of the future) would
come to earth to teach the true way, and so forth. It seems likely that many
of his followers believed (and he himself may have claimed) that Wang Tao-
sen was himself the buddha of the future sent by the Eternal Mother with the
assurance of salvation for all who followed his teachings.

   The dislocations and crises of the late Ming thus became a source of
opportunity for Wang Tao-sen. His very successful career as a sectarian
teacher during this formative period of the religion made him one of the
handful of White Lotus patriarchs (tsu, lit. ancestor), and in his lifetime he
created a legacy of religious charisma and organizational techniques that
lasted for several centuries. Apparently, he also accumulated considerable

---

   12. Wang was the disciple of Lü P'u-sa, a nun who established the Pao-ming temple west
of Peking and was the founder of the Hsi-ta-ch'eng sect (Li 1985).

wealth and property in Peking and in the Yung-p'ing area, and despite his humble origins was far from an ordinary peasant (Li 1983).

Sectarian leadership did, however, bring with it much danger as well. Although Wang Tao-sen enjoyed a period of public preaching and imperial patronage, the heterodox and rebellious implications of White Lotus millenarianism led to its being outlawed again and repeatedly banned. Tao-sen was arrested in 1614 and eventually died in prison. Six years later his third son, Hao-hsien, organized a large-scale uprising around the claim that he was the Maitreya sent in this time of chaos to save mankind. Although the rebellion occured largely in western Shantung and central Chihli, the majority of the organizers had been from the area around Peking and particularly Yung-p'ing (Luan, Lu-lung, Ch'ien-an, Le-t'ing, and Ch'ang-li specifically) (Asai 1978; Li 1981, 1983). Debilitated though it was, the Ming state was not too weak to suppress this 1622 rising, but it did not extirpate the roots of the rebellion in Yung-p'ing.

In the spring of 1630, as Ming armies were attempting to dislodge the invading Manchus from Lu-lung, Luan, and the other occupied cities of the prefecture (to whose defense the Lang-yeh Wangs had contributed with their lives), there was a brief sectarian uprising of several thousand people in the hills of Ch'ang-li county, about thirty kilometers east of Stone-Buddha Village (YP 30:34). Many of Wang Tao-sen's followers came from Ch'ang-li, but we do not know if the family was involved in the rising.

The effect of these unsuccessful religious rebellions on the Wangs is difficult to gauge. Although Wang Hao-hsien was finally seized and executed in 1624 (YP 71:22), other members of his family were generally spared. However, they had witnessed the death of a great many of their followers in a cause they had inspired. Failure of prophecy can, of course, lead to disillusionment in some but increased devotion in others. At the same time, probably after Wang Tao-sen or Hao-hsien's death, it was asserted that not only were their offspring the "descendants" (tzu-sun) of the Maitreya, but that this buddha of the future would some day be born again as a member of their descent group.[13] "The buddha-to-come is the Maitreya Buddha," explained one Wang. "In the future he will come down to earth and be born once more (chuan-sheng) in the Stone-Buddha Village Wang family (Wang-hsing chia-nei) (TASL 3.29; KCT, NM 779.2). Such a belief gave a special and enduring potential to all descendants of Patriarch Wang, the potential for messianic leadership. Nevertheless, the Wangs appear to have preferred to use this legacy only to enhance their success as sectarian teachers, for there is no evidence that they ever again personally led any uprising.

13. In the prophecy, "Wang family" was expressed as Wang-chia (family), Wang-tsu (lineage), or Wang-hsing (surname). Speaking of their descent group in other contexts, the Wangs did occasionally call it a tsu.

Differential Growth

After the experience of the 1620s and 1630s, the Shih-fo-k'ou Wangs, like others in the Yung-p'ing area, put up no resistance to the Manchu invasion of 1644. At that time, the group consisted of the descendants of Wang Tao-sen's two brothers—who continued to live in Stone-Buddha Village but were not active in the religion—and of Tao-sen's three sons. All of his sons and their sons (with the exception noted below) carried on the religion, and their offspring formed the three major branches of this descent line. Unless otherwise noted, they will constitute the "Wangs" discussed here.

These Wangs were directly affected by the Ch'ing decision to take possession of vast tracts of land near Peking in order to support their Banner armies. Dorgon, regent for the Shun-chih Emperor, ordered the "encirclement" of land—ownerless and owned—in the vicinity of the capital, took the titles away from the Chinese owners, and assigned the land to Bannermen. Many Chinese actually facilitated this process by voluntarily surrendering their property to the Manchus in hope of deriving benefit from being part of the new ruling establishment. As we have seen, Dorgon himself had a residence in Yung-p'ing prefectural city and men from his Plain White Banner were given land nearby. Banner land assignments were confused by the political struggles at court in the 1650s–1660s, and in 1666–67 there was a massive exchange of allocations as the Bordered Yellow Banner took over the property of the Plain White. (For discussions in English, see Oxnam 1975:171–75; Kessler 1976:47–48.) It is not clear, however, how many Manchus actually took up residence in the countryside (or stayed there very long); encirclement of land may have meant little more than the appropriation of the income by Bannermen.

Two branches of the Wangs—like many other Chinese—voluntarily yielded their lands to the conquerors. But they did not physically leave their homes. Rather, the Wangs became tenants on their own land and instead of owing taxes to the local magistrate (and thus to the Board of Revenue) paid rents to a resident agent (*chuang-t'ou*) (and thus to the Imperial Household). This strategy of accommodation to the new rulers may have been a simple matter for those not burdened with a sense of obligation to a Ming state that had bestowed degrees and office on them. Surely the pursuit of this path by two of the three Wang branches suggests a calculated attention to all options.

The disorders of the conquest period even provided a time of opportunity for the Wangs in more orthodox channels. For them, as for many, a military career in the period of dynastic consolidation proved a stepping-stone to fortune. Wang Tao-sen's grandson, K'o-chiu (born in the 1610s) (see figure 7.3), had joined the Chinese Green Standard Army; because of his natural leadership ability, the 1640s saw him posted in Shantung (on the Ch'ing side), already a major (a third-rank post). His talents served him well

FIGURE 7.3   Outline of the Shih-fo-k'ou Wang Genealogy

Generation

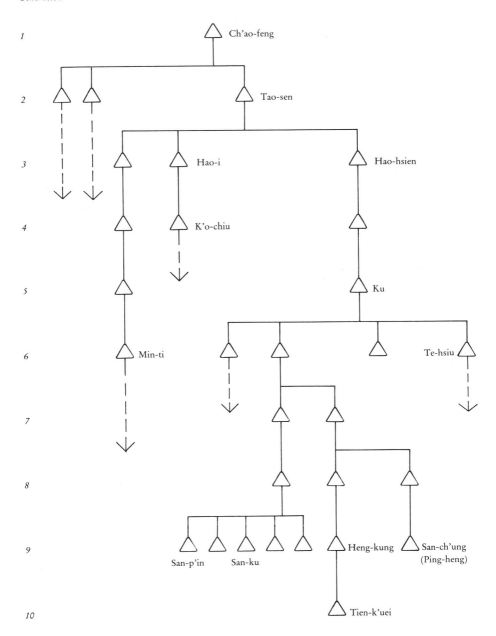

during the Manchu conquests of South China. He later served in Yunnan, Kweichow, Chekiang, and Fukien, and eventually rose to the very top of the army hierarchy, becoming a brigade-general.

Although there is no evidence of whether he believed in or transmitted the White Lotus religion, K'o-chiu's biography does reveal that part of his success as a military commander came from an ability to inspire the confidence and manipulate the beliefs of men, a talent not unlike that of his grandfather.[14] He was received by the emperor in audience and, on account of his success in defeating a rebel in the Hangchow area, was rewarded with honorary titles of the first rank. Because of his own high position, K'o-chiu's titles were extended to his father, grandfather, and great-grandfather. Thus Wang Ch'ao-feng, Wang Tao-sen, and Wang Hao-i received handsome patents in fine silk proclaiming the honor in elaborate language, and their awards were duly recorded in the same local histories where their religion was denounced (YP 65:13–15; LCC 6:38–41; Franke 1942). (Such honors far exceeded any ever won by the Lang-yeh Wangs.) When Wang K'o-chiu died during the rebellion of the Three Feudatories (1673–80), furthermore, two of his sons were then given official positions through the *yin* privilege.[15] Because of his phenomenal success and the considerable prestige it brought his relations, Wang K'o-chiu's portrait was painted and hung in the Wangs' ancestral shrine, where family (and sect members) paid it their respects (TASL 3.28).

During K'o-chiu's lifetime, the Wangs' fortunes had improved considerably. His branch was one of the two that had become tenants of Bannermen, and it was perhaps in this period that they rose to become *chuang-t'ou*, the agents who collected rents on behalf of the Imperial Household.[16] Despite their past, one would have to call the Wangs low-level elites, rather than peasants or commoners, even though they lacked prestigious civil service degrees and the classical education on which they were based. And yet, military accomplishments, imperial audiences, and service for the throne did not raise the Wangs so high that they were deterred from practicing their

14. During the campaigns against the Southern Ming in the southwest, Wang K'o-chiu was put in charge of transport and found the route slowed at a place on the Yangtze known as Chu-ko's Cave (because only a hero like Chu-ko Liang would be able to remove the huge rocks wedged in the center of the river). Wang K'o-chiu managed to "find" a stone tablet in the river with a mysterious inscription on it, one that when deciphered appeared to contain an auspicious reference to him. He used the promise of the inscription to buoy up his men's morale, and within a few weeks they had worked to move away all the rocks (YP 65:13–15).

15. It is not clear if these two sons are identical with the two who are listed in the genealogy (who have the same generational marker in their names) or are two other sons who for some reason were not listed in the genealogy.

16. In the early nineteenth century, one of Wang K'o-chiu's great-great-grandsons was *chuang-t'ou* for the estates belonging to the I Prince (the Ch'ien-lung Emperor's eighth son) (KCT, NM 476.6).

illegal heterodox sect; indeed, these may have served as useful camouflage.

Possession of religious scriptures, a claim to past and future messianic authority, knowledge of a special set of religious practices guaranteed to bring salvation, and familiarity with Wang Tao-sen's proselytizing networks—these were too valuable to give up. They came to constitute a sort of collective property for Tao-sen's descendants, and his sons and grandsons had ready-made careers as sect leaders. This profession, which they indeed followed generation after generation, brought them not only the respect and reverence of believers but also a regular income from donations. The decision (if it was a conscious one) not to encourage rebellion did not mean a reluctance to defy the law and pursue this heterodox path.

It was not long before a sixth-generation member of the first branch (Wang Min-ti) was arrested and banished. In 1650, perhaps in connection with this affair, that man's uncle from the third branch (and Brigade-General Wang K'o-chiu's nephew), Wang Ku, moved his family out of Shih-fo-k'ou to a small village only a few kilometers away over the border in Lu-lung county (close to Chiu-pai-hu), a place called An-chia-lou (An-family Tower). The decision to move could have been prompted by Banner land adjustments or simply demographic increase (four males in the fourth generation, nine in the sixth, and fifteen in the seventh), even, for all we know, by marriage ties; it did not, however, represent a break with sectarian activity (TASL 3.7).

After the move to An-chia-lou, Wang Ku fathered four sons, three of whom also continued the family religion. The fourth son, Te-hsiu, felt differently, however, and moved to a village even farther away; neither he nor his descendants were involved in White Lotus activities. (This move had probably taken place before 1700.)

Thus, by the beginning of the eighteenth century, there were three Wang lines that did not practice the sect, two of whom still lived in Stone-Buddha Village. Those who were religious teachers in that village occupied a large common residence surrounded by a stone wall, one branch living at the eastern end, one at the western (Li 1983; NYC 42:1–6). Lack of contact between sect and non-sect relatives appears to have been preferred by both parties, and to this extent internal segmentation was encouraged. Their collective religious enterprise should allow us to call those three lines that did practice the sect a lineage (or lineages).

If we look at the Shih-fo-k'ou Wangs at the time of the extensive arrests of 1815, we can try to gauge the degree of corporate unity and extent of segmentation that had taken place in the century and a half of Ch'ing rule. The genealogical chart on which this discussion is based was, it should be noted, of a wholly different order from the Lang-yeh Wang *tsung-p'u*. The goals of the official compilers of the chart were inclusive but very present-oriented. They wanted to reconstruct the past primarily to demonstrate

kinship between living Wangs, and secondarily to place earlier sect "crimi-
nals" within the family tree. They had a great many informants, and I take the
information in the chart as generally accurate but necessarily incomplete.
Both this document and the Lang-yeh Wang genealogy have, however, the
same bias, an emphasis on the professionally successful descent lines.

The use of common characters in names was also to be found among the
Shih-fo-k'ou Wangs, and it suggests both a greater degree of fragmentation
than among the other Wangs and yet a preference for the refinement that
such a system implied. Of the thirty-eight sets of brothers in the entire descent group on whom there is data (including non-sect members), twenty (52
percent) made use of a common element, usually a character, in their
names.[17] There was no discernible sequence of characters or radicals. The
least likely to use common names was the branch that had moved away and
broken with the religion, but among the others the practice was irregular but
persistent, and rarely extended beyond first cousins. But there was probably
more coordination in this practice than one would find in a smaller, poorer,
and less organized descent group.

The demographic benefits of successful sectarian careers may be reflected
in the size of the different branches of the ninth generation (who were adults
around 1800). (The interest of officials in locating and arresting all these men
should have helped promote completeness.) The sect-practicing branches
numbered five, sixteen, and twelve; those who had sworn off the religion
numbered four, two, and five. Had the descent line not been cut off, we
might have expected this process of differential growth to have increased and
for further segmentation within the White Lotus branches to have occurred.

Lineage and Sect

As we have noted, the Wangs did have an ancestral shrine (*tsu-chia-tz'u*)
that, like the descent group itself, served as a focus for both lineage and
sectarian devotions. (Unfortunately, we know nothing of their burial practices.) Followers of the Wangs' teachings would come to Shih-fo-k'ou (on
a kind of pilgrimage) and go to the shrine to pay their respects. A merging
of sect deities and lineage ancestors appears to have occurred—the word
for "patriarch" also meant "ancestor"—as believers were reminded of
Maitreya's former incarnations and told that the Wangs' ancestors were
now in heaven in charge of the religion (TASL 3.29). (Kinship terms were
not, however, generally used for relationships between individual sect
members.)[18]

17. In the eighth generation, seven sets of brothers all used single characters (no common
radical) in their names. If this also is taken as an indication of collective action, then the percentage
would rise to 71.
18. Among members of the Triad societies that emerged in the late eighteenth century in
South China, kinship terms, especially those of brotherhood, were frequently employed.

By the early nineteenth century, the Wangs had also founded a temple (*hsiang-huo-miao*) on Mount Wei-feng, just west of Shih-fo-k'ou, called Longevity-Peak Temple (Shou-feng-ssu). There they stored their sacred books and performed rites, presumably to sect deities; some income may have been produced from gifts but no mention was made of land endowments. This temple represented (and followers were encouraged to see it as) a confirmation of prophecies in sectarian scriptures. Mount Wei-feng, they were told, was the same as the Shadowless Mountain (Wu-ying-shan) so often referred to in sacred texts, the place where the true scriptures were revealed. According to the *Lung-hua ching* (Dragon flower sutra), a scripture written in 1652, a late Ming pupil of the Wangs "went to the east to get this scripture ... going to Wu-ying-shan to the Stone-Buddha region." (See NYC 42:41–45; TASL 3.28; LHC 2:22.)

The Wangs' religious activities continued in the eighteenth century. The pattern of their proselytizing had become regularized: Rebellious activities had been set aside in favor of more routinized institution building, but (also unlike the late Ming), followers were being sought not near Yung-p'ing but considerably farther afield—presumably a strategy for safeguarding the Wangs from government prosecution.

By the 1790s, the Wangs had made converts not only in central and southern Chihli, central Honan, and eastern Shansi, but in the Yangtze provinces of Anhwei, Kiangsu, and Hupei. Their pupils in Central China were located largely in urban areas, especially in prefectural and provincial capitals. Although it does not seem necessary to discuss the content of their religious teaching in detail here, it should be said that their sect was of the sort that I have elsewhere (1985a) characterized as quasi-monastic and sutra-reciting. This is also to say that the sect was directed at groups of relatively literate followers who were more likely to be urban than rural and included women as well as men.

When they traveled, the Wangs appear to have followed the routes of trade. Most of their pupils in Kiangnan were along the Yangtze, and many in Hupei were in the cities on the Yangtze or the Han River. Those in North China were located on the main roads south. The Wangs found new converts in the cities and towns through which they traveled, and in general it appears to have been their pupils who then went into the more rural areas to find followers. Many of the Wangs' pupils were, not surprisingly, city-dwellers or itinerant people: urban vegetable farmers, artisans, shop owners, barbers, Taoist priests and nuns, metalsmiths, tailors, peddlers, geomancers. One was a salt boat sailor turned Taoist priest who arranged for his teacher to travel on the salt boats in Hupei (NYC 42:27–31; TASL 3.3).

What is interesting from the point of view of the Wangs' base in Luan department is that these pupils were all located very far from home. Conversions were accomplished only after considerable traveling by the Wangs or their pupils. It became a regular practice for the men in the lineage to leave home at intervals to travel a kind of circuit, making contact with their small congregations. (See Naquin 1982 for details.) They might be away from home for years at a time, and some even set up alternative residences in distant places. Wang Ping-heng (ninth generation) had a home inside I-ch'eng city, Kiangsu; Wang San-ku (ninth generation) had a residence in Hua county, Honan, and his brother San-p'in lived and took a wife in Shansi; Wang Tien-k'uei's sons (twelfth generation) were living and working in Huai-an prefectural city in Kiangsu (NYC 42:27–31). (The fact that all of these men were from the third branch in An-chia-lou may reflect some crowding there in the late Ch'ien-lung reign—or perhaps simply a strategy of more intense involvement with pupils' communities.)

The most important part of a Wang's identity as he traveled and taught was his membership in the "Stone-Buddha Village Wang family." This identity had to be maintained, and yet it also needed to be concealed from the authorities. The Wangs routinely protected themselves with a cultivated vagueness. One said that Shih-fo-k'ou was in Lu-lung county, another placed it in Ch'ang-li; many revealed only their generation and branch but not their personal names—being addressed as Eighth Master (Pa-ta-yeh), et cetera. Although they did not have formal "courtesy names" (hao) like the Lang-yeh Wangs, most of these men had a confusing variety of given names (using two or three was common).

The nature of White Lotus organization necessitated this constant travel and routine caution. The ties between pupils and the Shih-fo-k'ou Wangs had to be renewed at each generation if sectarian bonds were to be kept alive. But one man noted that he and two other cousins who were active in Hupei "belonged to different branches (fang) and that the pupils who were taught each knew their own lines (chih-p'ai); it was not permitted to mix them up" (TASL 3.29). Members of different branches were informed about and assisted in one another's activities but proselytizing was an enterprise in which entrepreneurs tended to benefit the most and contributions were the immediate rewards.

In addition to revenue from agriculture (about which nothing is known beyond the fact that some men gave this as their occupation when interrogated by officials), small gifts were made by pupils on a regular basis and combined and passed up the chain of teachers to the Wangs. In this respect, sectarianism could differ from the career of Buddhist monk or Taoist priest where income was more unsystematized and irregular. The Wangs as a group might easily have been receiving as much as 250 taels a year from pupils in the 1810s (see Naquin 1982:348–49). When they were all arrested in 1815, their confiscated assets totaled 1,429 taels (NYC 42:46–49). (This seems too low to me, considering that it represented the possessions of eighty-five men and their families.) Although I have seen no evidence of involvement in commercial enterprise in Yung-p'ing, some of those with residences elsewhere did have supplementary income. On the other hand, information about the conspicuous consumption that great wealth might have made possible is lacking, and birth rates (as compared with the Lang-yeh Wangs, for example) do not suggest great prosperity. Resources were apparently invested in the Longevity-Peak Temple, the ancestral shrine, and the common task of proselytizing, which in turn generated new income.

Because prominence in their home community would have been a mixed blessing, not only did the Wangs concentrate their proselytizing elsewhere, they did not even attempt to make themselves dominant among other sectarians in Yung-p'ing. During the Ch'ing, they did not (that we know) interfere with the transmission of different, rival forms of the religion in their neighborhood. A number of other sects that had slightly different practices and were offshoots of patriarchs other than Wang Tao-sen were periodically discovered in the area. The largest of these was the Chin-tan (Golden Elixir) sect transmitted by a certain Chang Jung (from P'ing-ku county not far to the west); in the 1780s he distributed amulets and taught vegetarianism and sutra recitation to several thousand people in and around Yung-p'ing (CSL, CL 257 passim).

Even without active proselytizing, however, the Wangs were never quite invisible at home. Stories of their magical power persisted and set them off from their neighbors. Such tales had begun with Wang Tao-sen, who, it was said, had received from a fox spirit a magical incense whose smell had great power and from which one name of his sect was derived (Chu 1976). Two hundred years later, the story was told in the Luan area that "as the Wangs transmitted the sect, they took a fox tail and waved it about; the people who practiced their sect in all the different provinces immediately had headaches and would come from all directions to give money" (KCT, NM 453.5; also LCC 18:28–30). As P'u Sung-ling's stories (written in the late seventeenth century in Shantung) indicate, men and women suspected of having supernatural powers created their own special fields of force among their neighbors, who viewed them with a fearful respect.

Given this kind of reputation, not to mention their very real involvement in illegal activities for which arrests were routinely made and banishment a common punishment, one wonders what families would have been willing to marry these Wangs. The data on their marriage partners are, unfortunately, much too inadequate to be of much use in helping us understand their place in their home community. Although surname exogamy was preferred in China, two of the sixteen men whose wives' surnames are known married women surnamed Wang (contrast six of 108 among those in Wang Pai-hsi's branch of the Lang-yeh Wangs). More interesting are the few other indications that marriages were not easily arranged. Wang San-p'in (eighth generation), a man who traveled extensively far from home, was willing (and able!)

to pay ninety taels to acquire a woman he met in Shansi, a widow who was apparently ignorant of his heterodox activities (TASL 3.1). In another case, one Wang also took a widow in a distant place for his wife (KCT, NM 475.11). The unhappy son of a pupil of the Wangs explained his unwillingness to follow his father into the religion by stating that "the people in the village were afraid of being implicated and no one would marry into our family" (KCT, NM 493.6). Unless more data are uncovered, however, it is unlikely that we will ever know where the Wangs turned more routinely for wives and sons-in-law or what their relations with their affines were like.

While the Lang-yeh Wangs' pursuit of academic degrees was quite unexceptional in the Ch'ing, the Shih-fo-k'ou Wangs' sect represented a profession that is difficult to classify in terms of our usual understanding of Ch'ing classes. It was not unusual, however, in its behavior. G. W. Skinner has called our attention (1976) to the way in which localities specialized in certain goods and services and often engaged in the long-term export of male sojourners to carry on the business elsewhere in the empire (usually further up the central place hierarchy). The Wangs' activities were of this type, but even though the name of their village became synonymous with sectarianism only their lineage, not their local community, was involved. Like the Man lineage of Hong Kong (J. Watson 1975) that specialized in restaurant work in London in the twentieth century, the Wangs stepped into religion as their expected career. It was, in fact, this common hereditary profession that pulled and held these relatives together. The peculiar dangers of this line of work necessitated a low profile at home, rather than the enlistment of others who wanted to share in the profits. Their monopoly could not easily be transferred, moreover, and although Wang continued to be an auspicious surname for White Lotus leaders, the link with Stone-Buddha Village may have been broken after 1815.

Although more and more members of the Wang lineage were arrested in the second half of the eighteenth century, it was not until after the Eight Trigrams rebellion of 1813 that the Ch'ing government became fully aware of the Wangs' long history of subversion. In the winter of 1815, the governor-general of Chihli province, Na-yen-ch'eng, who had been in charge of the campaigns against the Trigram rebels, followed up the arrest of Wang Ping-heng in Kiangsu. He soon discovered the connections with the 1622 rebellion and, worse for the Wangs, with the recent one. The fact that pupils of the Wangs in the area of Hua county in Honan (a headquarters for the Eight Trigrams) had been found with the same inflammatory book that the rebel leader Lin Ch'ing had had in his possession gave extra impetus to Na-yen-ch'eng's investigations (Naquin 1976:102). This book clearly stated the prophecy that the Maitreya would be born in the Shih-fo-k'ou Wang family and repeated claims (with which the Wangs had also been associated previously) that at the time of the millennium even time itself would change (a year would have eighteen months, and so forth). Although the Wangs had no involvement in Lin Ch'ing's uprising, they were punished as if they were rebels.

By the spring of 1821, 136 descendants of the founder Wang Ch'ao-feng had been arrested and sentenced. Even those who had had nothing to do with the sectarian enterprise were implicated. All their property was confiscated and sold, and not a single known member of the descent group remained in Shih-fo-k'ou, An-chia-lou, or elsewhere. Those men, women, and children not executed were banished to Yunnan, Kweichow, or Sinkiang. Dozens of pupils in many provinces were arrested as well (NYC 42:46–49). Even though the millennial dimension of the White Lotus teaching had been muted by the Wangs themselves, the message was plain enough to arouse both their fellow believers and the Ch'ing state. Two hundred years after Wang Tao-sen's own death, his descendants received the punishments for which they had long been legally liable.

The survival and expansion of the Wang line from the three sons of the sixteenth-century founder to the more than fifty nuclear families arrested in 1815 had, of course, been made possible by the various benefits of their hereditary religious authority. The sect provided a natural occupation, a regular income, a network of contacts, a body of devoted retainers, the assurance of salvation, and the mystique of supernatural power. At the same time, agnatic kinship ties provided the sect with a pool of reliable manpower for proselytizing, generational continuity, a home base, and an orthodox cover for illegal activities. But sectarian activity also hampered the growth and threatened the survival of the descent group as a whole. Periodic arrests implicated relatives; suspicion from neighbors and competition from rival groups may have created tensions within the local community; and the dangerous task of conversion required that some of the men be constantly away from home. The growth of the Wangs' agnatic organization in the course of centuries simultaneously endangered the sect: Expansion reduced intimacy and security and encouraged the diversion of resources into safer and more orthodox channels, and both may have led to tensions between sectarian and non-sectarian relatives. When protected or ignored by the state, occupational specialization could be an effective tool for concentrating resources and maximizing their productivity. Among White Lotus sectarians, judicious reluctance to act on millenarian claims may have accounted for the Wangs' long survival, but ultimately more volatile fellow sectarians brought them the exposure they had avoided for so many generations.

Conclusion

In 1820 when the Stone-Buddha Village Wangs had been uprooted from their homes, the Lang-yeh Wangs were enjoying their first Ch'ing *chin-*

shih degree. Having chosen very different ladders of social mobility, the two groups had met very different fates. Yet they were really not so dissimilar.

Demographically, both cases seem to illustrate a correlation between professional success and fertility.[19] Those branches with the largest number of degree- or office-holders or sectarian teachers also had the most sons. The orthodox path (or at least the wealth and connections that underlay it) appears to have been significantly more productive. If we compare the two most successful lines, those of Wang P'i's father and of Wang Tao-sen (who were rough contemporaries), these differences become clear. This branch of the Lang-yeh Wangs grew from one to seventy men in the nine generations; Wang Tao-sen's branch grew only from one to thirty-four in the same time. But it should be remembered that the Lang-yeh Wangs had a head start as pioneers in the Yung-p'ing region. The latter had produced their Ming *chin-shih* even before Wang Tao-sen was born. The relative success of the group that followed the heterodox strategy is therefore the more remarkable. The Ming collapse and Ch'ing conquest, a cause of loss and restricted choices for the degree-holding Wangs, proved a source of considerable opportunity for the others. One group depended on the civil service status system, the other turned readily to both the Banner and army structures and to decidedly unorthodox channels.

Physically, the two descent groups not only lived within the same prefecture, in the same two counties, but very near one another. An-chia-lou, itself only a few kilometers from Stone-Buddha Village and another home for sectarians, was also located very close to Chiu-pai-hu. The relocation of one branch of the Shih-fo-k'ou Wangs in An-chia-lou occurred in 1650, not long after Wang P'i had moved his lineage to Chiu-pai-hu. By the late eighteenth century, descendants of P'i were being buried in cemeteries just outside An-chia-lou. The villages where these two Wangs lived could not have been more than ten kilometers apart.

There seems little doubt that within this world the degree-holding Wangs, with their generations of *sheng-yuan* and wider marriage networks with other lower elite families, were socially (and probably economically) the more prominent. The White Lotus Wangs do not appear to have been involved in community affairs and perhaps felt that the presence of a respectable lineage of the same surname gave them a measure of protection. It may be that the sectarians, without losing their reputation for magical power, were able to disguise the full extent of their religious activities from

19. The data in both instances are admittedly already biased in this direction; however, the extensive information on "unsuccessful" branches of the Lang-yeh Wangs does bear out this conclusion. The data for the Shih-fo-k'ou Wangs are much more skewed.

elite neighbors; it may also be that the lower-degree holders were not especially concerned about heterodoxy. In any case, they did live side by side and surely knew about one another.

Although inadequate data about corporate property and activities make generalizations dangerous, the evidence from both cases seems to confirm what James Watson (1975:203) has characterized as "the close relationship between personal profit and lineage maintenance." Those branches that were most successful in ways that were economically beneficial appear to have had the most clearly defined cooperative relationships with their relatives. But these economic benefits came not from shared property but a common profession. There appears to have been a somewhat greater degree of common endeavor and shared profits among the Stone-Buddha Village Wangs, for whom lineage specialization in sectarian activities produced a special melding of family and sect, but in both cases professional success enabled certain branches to undertake more corporate activities than was normal among the descent group as a whole. As they became professionally successful, they began to look and act like lineages.

Nevertheless, neither Wang group achieved anything like the high (and probably atypical for China as a whole) level of corporate organization that one sees along the coast of Lingnan (Freedman 1966) in the late Ch'ing period. The range of community organizations that existed beyond the lineage—a context ignored in this paper for lack of data but see Sangren (1984) and Duara (1983)—does appear to have been more extensive in North China. At the same time, there are no indications that either Wang lineage ever wanted to create any more formal institutions for corporate survival. Considerably more research needs to be done on regional variation in lineage and kinship structures before we can hope to see any systematic variations between these social forms and their environments.

One lineage had borrowed an aristocratic pedigree from the traditions of the distant past; the other invented their own choronym and made it famous throughout China. One concentrated on examinations in the classics, one on heterodoxy. One route was slow but predictable, dependent on order in government but proven viable in the long run. The other strategy was far more dangerous, born and most likely to be truly successful only when the state was weak and at considerable risk when government was strong; its rewards were great but so were the risks, and even the less dangerous path of sectarian teaching brought personal peril. In the end, one set of Wangs never became part of the national elite but survived as one of many notable local families, unlikely to be remembered except in local histories. The other Wang group was dispossessed and torn apart, yet through their religious books and the rebellions that commemorated their convictions and those of their followers achieved a wider and more lasting fame.

REFERENCES

Primary Sources

CSL, CL *Ta-Ch'ing li-ch'ao shih-lu* 大清歷朝實錄, Ch'ien-lung reign. Taipei, 1964.

KCT, NM Kung-chung-tang 宮中檔, peasant uprising file. Peking: Ming-Ch'ing Archives.

KCT, YC Kung-chung-tang 宮中檔, Yung-cheng reign. National Palace Museum, Taipei: Ch'ing Archives.

LCC *Luan-chou chih* 灤州志. 1898.

LHC *Ku-fo t'ien-chen k'ao-cheng lung-hua ching* 古佛天眞考證龍華經. 1652 (probably); 1929 reprint. Peking Library.

LL *Lu-lung hsien-chih* 盧龍縣志. 1931.

LYW *Lang-yeh Wang-shih tsung-p'u* 瑯琊王氏宗譜. 1919. Tōyō bunko.

NYC *Na-wen-i-kung tsou-i* 那文毅公奏議. 1834; Taipei reprint 1968.

TASL *Ch'ing-tai tang-an shih-liao ts'ung-pien* 清代檔案史料叢編. Peking, 1979–.

YP *Yung-p'ing fu-chih* 永平府志. 1879.

YTS *Yü-t'ien Sun-shih chia-p'u kao* 玉田孫氏家譜稿. 1926.

Secondary Sources

Ahern, Emily M. 1976. "Segmentation in Chinese Lineages: A View from Written Genealogies." *American Ethnologist* 3:1–16.

Asai Motoi 浅井紀. 1978. "Minmatsu Jo-kō-ju no ran no shiryō ni tsuite" 明末徐鴻儒の乱の史料について [Sources for the study of the Hsu Hung-ju uprising at the end of the Ming]. *Tōyōgakuhō* 60:54–91.

Barrett, Richard E. 1983. "Historical Demography and the Study of Chinese Family and Kinship: A Preliminary Reconnaissance." Paper prepared for the Conference on Family and Kinship in Chinese History.

Beattie, Hilary J. 1979. *Land and Lineage in China: A Study of T'ung-ch'eng County, Anhwei, in the Ming and Ch'ing Dynasties*. Cambridge: Cambridge University Press.

Berling, Judith. 1980. *The Syncretic Religion of Lin Chao-en*. New York: Columbia University Press.

Chang, Chung-li. 1955. *The Chinese Gentry: Studies on Their Role in Nineteenth-Century Chinese Society*. Seattle: University of Washington Press.

Chu, Richard Yung-teh. 1976. "Hsu Hung-ju." In *Dictionary of Ming Biography, 1368–1644*, ed. L. C. Goodrich and Chaoying Fang, pp. 587–89. New York: Columbia University Press.

Dennerline, Jerry. 1981. *The Chia-ting Loyalists: Confucian Leadership and Social Change in Seventeenth-Century China*. New Haven: Yale University Press.

Duara, Prasenjit. 1983. "Power in Rural Society: North China Villages, 1900–1940." Ph.D. dissertation, Harvard University.

Ebrey, Patricia Buckley. 1978. *The Aristocratic Families of Early Imperial China: A Case Study of the Po-ling Ts'ui Family*. Cambridge: Cambridge University Press.

———. 1983. "Types of Lineages in Ch'ing China: A Re-examination of the Chang Lineage of T'ung-ch'eng." *Ch'ing-shih wen-t'i* 4.9:1–20.

Franke, Wolfgang. 1942. "Patents for Hereditary Ranks and Honorary Titles during the Ch'ing Dynasty." *Monumenta Serica* 7:38–67.

Freedman, Maurice. 1966. *Chinese Lineage and Society: Fukien and Kwangtung*. New York: Humanities Press.

Grafflin, Dennis. 1983. "The Onomastics of Medieval South China: Patterned Naming in the Lang-yeh and T'ai-yuan Wang." *Journal of the American Oriental Society* 103:383–98.

Harrell, Stevan. 1985. "The Rich Get Children: Segmentation, Stratification, and Population in Three Zhejiang Lineages, 1550–1850." In *Historical Demography and Family History in East Asia*, ed. Arthur P. Wolf and Susan B. Hanley. Stanford: Stanford University Press.

Hsu, Sung-peng. 1979. *A Buddhist Leader in Ming China: The Life and Thought of Han-shan Te-ch'ing, 1546–1623*. Pennsylvania State University Press.

Hummel, Arthur, ed. 1943–44. *Eminent Chinese of the Ch'ing Period*. Washington D.C.: U.S. Government Printing Office.

Kessler, Lawrence D. 1976. *K'ang-hsi and the Consolidation of Ch'ing Rule, 1661–1684*. Chicago: University of Chicago Press.

Li Chi-hsien 李濟賢. 1981. "'Pang-ch'ui-hui' ch'i-i ch'u-t'an" 棒棰會起義初探 [Preliminary investigation of the "Cudgel Association" uprising]. *Chung-kuo nung-min chan-cheng lun-ts'ung* 3:145–79.

———. 1983. "Pai-lien chiao-chu Wang Sen Wang Hao-hsien pu-shih nung-min ch'i-i ling-hsiu" 白蓮敎主王森王好賢不是農民起義領袖 [The White Lotus masters Wang Sen and Wang Hao-hsien were not leaders of a peasant uprising]. *Wen-shih* 13:147–58.

Li Shih-yü 李世瑜. 1985. "Shun-t'ien Pao-ming-ssu k'ao" 順天保明寺考 [A study of the Pao-ming temple in Shun-t'ien]. *Pei-ching shih-yüan*, no. 3.

Liu, Hui-chen Wang. 1959. "An Analysis of Chinese Clan Rules: Confucian Theories in Action." In *Confucianism in Action*, ed. David S. Nivison and Arthur F. Wright, pp. 63–96. Stanford: Stanford University Press.

Mao Han-kuang 毛漢光. 1967. "Wo kuo chung-ku ta-shih-tsu chih ko-an yen-chiu: Lang-yeh Wang-shih" 我國中古大士族之個案研究—瑯琊王氏 [Research on a medieval Chinese lineage: the Lang-yeh Wangs]. *Chung-yang yen-chiu-yuan li-shih yü-yen yen-chiu-so chi-k'an* 37.2:577–610.

Naquin, Susan. 1976. *Millenarian Rebellion in China: The Eight Trigrams Uprising of 1813*. New Haven: Yale University Press.

———. 1982. "Connections between Rebellions: Sect Family Networks in Qing China." *Modern China* 8.3:337–60.

———. 1985a. "The Transmission of White Lotus Sectarianism in Late Imperial China." In *Popular Culture in Late Imperial China*, ed. D. Johnson, A. Nathan, and E. Rawski. Berkeley: University of California Press.

———. 1985b. "Funerals in North China: Uniformity and Variation." Paper prepared for the Conference on Ritual and the Social Significance of Death in Chinese Society, Oracle, Arizona, January 2–7.

Oxnam, Robert B. 1975. *Ruling from Horseback: Manchu Politics in the Oboi Regency, 1661–1669*. Chicago: University of Chicago Press.

Sangren, P. Steven. 1984. "Traditional Chinese Corporations: Beyond Kinship." *Journal of Asian Studies* 43.3:391–415.

Shek, Richard Hon-chun. 1980. "Religion and Society in Late Ming: Sectarianism and Popular Thought in Sixteenth and Seventeenth Century China." Ph.D. dissertation. University of California, Berkeley.

Skinner, G. William. 1964. "Marketing and Social Structure in Rural China (Part I)." *Journal of Asian Studies* 24.1:3–43.

———. 1976. "Mobility Strategies in Late Imperial China: A Regional Systems Analysis." In *Regional Analysis*, vol. 1, ed. Carol A. Smith, pp. 327–64. New York: Academic Press.

———. 1979. "Social Ecology and the Forces of Repression in North China." Paper prepared for the Workshop on Rebellion and Revolution in North China.

Taga Akigorō 多賀秋五郎. 1960. *Sōfu no kenkyū* 宗譜の研究 [A study of genealogies]. Tokyo: Tōyō bunko.

Watson, James L. 1975. *Emigration and the Chinese Lineage: The Mans in Hong Kong and London*. Berkeley: University of California Press.

———. 1982. "Chinese Kinship Reconsidered: Anthropological Perspectives on Historical Research." *China Quarterly* 92:589–622.

Watson, Rubie S. 1982. "The Creation of a Chinese Lineage: The Teng of Ha Tsuen, 1669–1751." *Modern Asian Studies* 16:69–100.

Yü, Chün-fang. 1981. *The Renewal of Buddhism in China: Chu-hung and the Late Ming Synthesis*. New York: Columbia University Press.

Zurndorfer, Harriet T. 1981. "The *Hsin-an ta-tsu-chih* and the Development of Chinese Gentry Society, 800–1600." *T'oung Pao* 68:154–215.

EIGHT

The Ma Landlords of Yang-chia-kou in Late Ch'ing and Republican China

Evelyn S. Rawski

This chapter concerns a powerful descent group in Northwest China, a macro-region at some remove from the South China environment of the dominant lineage. Its first aim is to examine the organization of this descent group, and to compare it with the lineage, which has long been identified as an effective vehicle for achieving and perpetuating local power. The exceptional features of the lineage form of organization are underlined by a study of Northwest descent groups like the Ma that achieved prominence without recourse to the lineage pattern. The second aim of this chapter is to study Ma finances, and through them to point to the importance of household (*chia*) activities in the accumulation of wealth and power. Although of obvious significance in a descent line, household activities are equally vital in lineages, yet most studies of lineages bypass this subject. A final aim of this chapter is to survey briefly the relevance of kinship in the social organization of villages. Data from North China, which like the Northwest is marked by the absence of strong lineages, show that even when entities looking like lineages exist, their ineffectiveness and subordination to the solidarity of the village set them off from their southern counterparts. In short, the social context within which most people, the powerful as well as the relatively powerless, functioned differed fundamentally from the society found in the Southeast Coast and Lingnan, where dominant lineages had carved out an important niche in the local power structure.

The Ma of Yang-chia-kou

Although bodies that conform to James Watson's (1982:594) definition of a lineage as "a *corporate group* which celebrates *ritual unity* and is based on *demonstrated descent* from a common ancestor" can be found in many parts

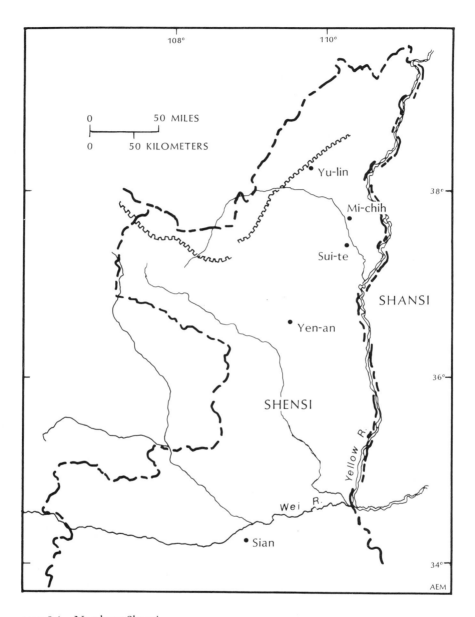

MAP 8.1   Northern Shensi

of China, there is widespread agreement that they are relatively rare in the areas of dryland cultivation such as North and Northwest China. From all accounts, Shensi province was not a place where lineages flourished. Genealogies for Shensi are rare; Taga (1960) lists only one.

Yang-chia-kou, the home of the Ma landlords, was located in the northernmost part of Shensi, in a loess area with no navigable rivers, an area that was perhaps the most backward and isolated part of the poorest region in China (SSNT:1–2). Unlike mid-Shensi, which was oriented to Yenan, the area around Yang-chia-kou was dominated by Sui-te. Sui-te, located along the eastern boundary of the province, straddled the east-west and north-south trade routes that linked Yü-lin, Shensi's northern market, with Yenan and points south as well as other routes that led eastward to T'ai-yuan and westward to Ninghsia (Pai 1926; SSZ 1918:7, 820–828). Mi-chih, the county in which Yang-chia-kou was located, was the wealthiest in the Sui-te department, thanks to its location on the alluvial plain of the Wu-ting River. Sui-te and Mi-chih were areas of relatively high population density, relatively low per capita cultivated acreage, and high tenancy (Ts'ai 1979; Hsu 1945).

One major source of information about the Ma of Yang-chia-kou is a survey conducted between 26 September and 19 November 1942 by a team of four cadres who were sent by the Yenan Rural Investigation Team (*nung-ts'un tiao-ch'a t'uan*) to conduct a survey of rural landlords. In August 1941 the Communist Party Center had decided to implement survey research, and in response the Northwest Bureau formed two divisions, one to study conditions in areas controlled by the Kuomintang (KMT), and the other to work on social conditions in the Shen-Kan-Ning Border Region (Ts'ai 1979). The Ma study was thus one of several investigative projects conducted in 1942. We have in addition to it another that examines landholding and rent arrangements in Sui-te and Mi-chih in 1942 (Ts'ai 1979).

The Ma survey, published in 1957, is over one hundred seventy pages in length. It includes genealogical and social information on the individuals in fifty-three households surnamed Ma who claimed common descent from an early nineteenth-century ancestor. Information for over four generations of males in the group is followed by detailed analysis of the landholdings and in particular of the portfolio of a "representative landlord," Ma Wei-hsin. The study presents information on the economic activities of Wei-hsin's household from the late nineteenth century to the early 1940s. A close study of tenant arrangements, changes in forms of sharecropping and rent, and the implications of each such change for tenant and landlord is included. The stated purpose of the survey was

> to investigate the conditions of exploitation of the specially concentrated Ma landlord clique, and in particular the conditions of the household of Ma Wei-hsin, who can be taken as an economic representative of this group. The book

presents materials that are a model of how land, high interest loans, and commercial exploitation are combined. The major source of materials for the book come from several decades of account books of various kinds. Further, this locality became a liberated area (*chieh-fang ch'ü*) in 1940; of the people cited in the book some have become protectors of the revolutionary regime and some early became state cadres. Our aim in publishing this book is to present materials for scholarly research and nothing else. (Survey: front matter)

How should we evaluate the biases and assumptions inherent in this survey? I would argue that the political biases are obvious ones, and that the data presented are generally internally consistent and reasonable. Moreover, the attitude of the survey team and of the Chinese Communist Party (CCP) government toward landlords was ambivalent in 1942; landlords were eligible to join in the United Front, and in the aftermath of the KMT embargo on the Border Region, they were potentially valuable allies in the struggle to raise production and reduce inflation in the CCP areas.

The Ma were also ambivalent toward the CCP. Notable landlords like Ma Wei-hsin explicitly opposed the CCP takeover of their district, and did whatever they could to prevent it. But Ma sons actually enrolled in both the KMT and CCP causes. There were Ma serving with KMT troops and other Ma who were with the Eighth Route Army. One Ma landlord, Hsin-min, was a delegate to the Border Region Congress; another, K'o-ch'en, sat on the district council and governing committee, representing Mi-chih in the regional council (Selden 1971:169). As figure 8.1 indicates, still other Ma held posts in the KMT-designated administration. Ma Wei-hsin himself was elected in 1941 to be *pao-chang*; in 1942, when the post went to his agnate Ma Jui-chang, Wei-hsin was elected chief of Ho-ch'a *ch'ü* (Survey:27). Marriage alliances tied the Ma to both political sides. Two daughters of the "representative landlord" Wei-hsin were in fact married to CCP cadres. The husband of the sixth daughter, Shu-hsing, was An Chih-wen. An went on to hold high positions in the People's Republic of China. In June 1981 he was promoted to be minister of the Sixth Ministry of Machine-Building (*Ming pao* 13 June 1981:1). Thus, the Ma were not simply excoriated villains of class struggle but partners in the United Front, who benefited from the "three-thirds" system implemented in the 1941 elections (Selden 1971:chap. 4).

The political climate in 1942 was therefore not completely hostile to the Ma. The political biases of the rural investigation team were spelled out in their opening statement of purpose, cited above: They wished to analyze the Ma as a case of landlord exploitation of peasants. The business accounts of Ma Wei-hsin that are presented, however, do not completely support this orientation. Wei-hsin's accounts show rent arrears going back for generations. In 1942 there were still unpaid rents going back to 1883–84. Since rent arrears were not charged interest, a landlord's real income and the rate of

FIGURE 8.1   Degree and Office Holders in the Yang-chia-kou Ma

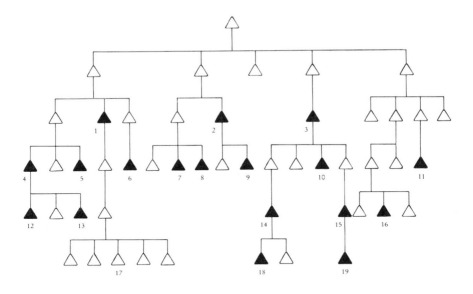

1. Kuo-shih, *fu-kung*, subprefect, Hsun-hua *t'ing* (independent subprefecture), Kansu; prefect (ca. T'ung-chih reign), An-hsi department, Kansu
2. Kuo-hua, 1885–86 *pa-kung*
3. Kuo-pin, 1862–63 *chin-shih*, district magistrate in Chiao-ch'eng and Ling-ch'uan counties, Shansi
4. Kung-hsuan, *sheng-yuan*
5. Teng-hsuan, *sheng-yuan*, magistrate, Chia county, Shensi
6. Jung-hsuan, magistrate, Ching-pien county, Shensi (1912)
7. Chu-yü, archivist, Chia county, Shensi
8. Chu-k'ang, 1889–90 *chü-jen*, brevet rank 5A, sub-director of schools, Lan-t'ien county, Shensi; director of schools, Chia department, Shensi
9. Chu-to (Hsin-min), delegate to Shen-Kan-Ning Border Region Congress (1942)
10. Ying-hsuan, education official, Nan-cheng county, Shensi
11. Wei-hsin, *sheng-yuan*, chief of Ho-ch'a *ch'ü* (1942)
12. Chung-lin (K'o-ch'en), *sheng-yuan*, deputy head, construction department, Mi-chih county (1942)
13. Chung-pi, studied two years at Peking University, in Yü-lin county office, Shensi, under KMT control (1942)
14. Shih-chou, *pa-kung* (1897–98?); "Secretary, Grand Secretariat," a title bestowed on graduates of the new schools instituted after the Boxer uprising
15. Shih-shen, *sheng-yuan*
16. Chung-hsiang, on the staff of the KMT-sponsored district magistrate of Mi-chih, Kao Chung-ch'ien (1942)
17. Hung-ch'uan, formerly in the KMT-controlled Yü-lin prefectural commissioner's office; working as an engineer in the Shen-mu county government
18. Jun-ying, a *pao-chang* before the CCP takeover
19. Jun-lien, a former *pao-chang* punished for corruption

Sources: Unless otherwise noted below, Survey: 3–14. Additional information was found for: # 1. HC *ch.* 2, 11b; # 2. CC 2, 584; # 3. CC 2, 560; # 8. CC 2, 576; # 12. Selden 1971: 169; # 14. CC 2, 584; on the title, see Brunnert and Hagelstrom (1912: # 618B, # 625).

return obtained from land were reduced by rent arrears. Wei-hsin's records show that on average there was a twenty-one month delay in payment of the rent. By permitting interest-free rent arrears, the landlord was in effect giving a free loan to a tenant. Indeed, it would have paid the landlord to give discounts of up to 86 percent to ensure prompt rent payment (Survey:71– 74).

Analysis of Wei-hsin's accounts shows that like most landlords he hedged against risk as the CCP presence in northern Shensi increased. His estate was primarily in land, at least as indicated by the survey; so were the estates of his relatives, which may help explain why they chose to remain despite the political uncertainties of a CCP administration. No doubt Wei-hsin tried to conceal and underreport his wealth, but landed wealth is rather difficult to hide, especially when investigators are free to interview tenants. The Ma could not conceal their large landholdings, which marked them as one of Shensi's richest landlords even before the CCP takeover (Kuan 1934). In 1933, KMT rural investigators had also visited Yang-chia-kou and recorded their impressions (SSNT:176). Significant evasion was probably more difficult for such a prominent group. Moreover, Ma Wei-hsin's accounts have been studied in detail by Kawachi (1963a, 1963b) and appear to be generally reliable and internally consistent.

In conclusion I would argue that the primary source for the study of the Ma is reliable despite its political biases and presents a fairly accurate picture of the structure, composition, and economic status of the Ma households.

Ma Origins

Yang-chia-kou village, known throughout northern Shensi as the home of the "Kuang-yü t'ang" Ma, was located in the sixth *hsiang* of Ho-ch'a *ch'ü*, Mi-chih county. The village was approximately forty *li* from the county seat, an equal distance from Chi-chen town, an additional forty *li* from Ssu-shih-li p'u, and fifteen *li* from T'ao-hua mao chen. Composed of six hamlets situated along a stream, the village had a total of 271 households belonging to several surnames. One of the hamlets, a walled stockade on the west bank known as Fu-feng chai, was the home of the Kuang-yü t'ang Ma. All but three of the fifty-three households in the group lived within this walled stockade. Table 8.1 presents information on the number of adult males and heads of households, by generation, as reported to the survey team in 1942.

All of the Kuang-yü t'ang Ma traced their descent from a man named Ma Chia-lo who seems to have lived in the early nineteenth century. Chia-lo began as an employee of a business firm (*p'u-tzu*) owned by a landlord and located in Sui-te town. This firm collected rents, made loans, purchased property, and engaged in trading. A hard worker, Chia-lo eventually went

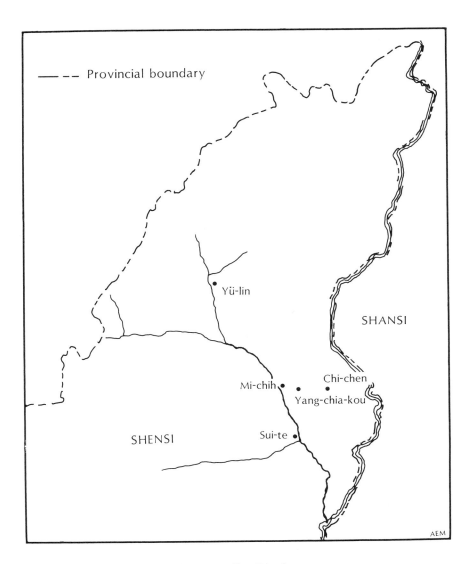

MAP 8.2   Mi-chih County and Surrounding Districts

TABLE 8.1

Adult Males in the Yang-chia-kou Ma, by Generation

Generation	Number of adult males	Number still living in 1942[a]
One (founder)	1	0
Two	5	0
Three	11	0
Four	25	7
Five	37	25
Six	19	16
Seven	1	1

SOURCE: Survey: 3–5.

a. In reality this table counts adult males who are heads of households; the CCP survey also identified other males who were married but living under their father's roof, single males ranging in age from infancy on up, and daughters. The count above is of adult males who are heads of households. In addition to the forty-nine male heads who were alive in 1942, one male head was listed who had died, and three females (two widows, one daughter) were heads of their households. The survey thus counted a total of fifty-three households.

into business for himself with a loan from his former employer. By the age of sixty he owned three *p'u-tzu* of his own in Sui-te and Mi-chih towns. Chia-lo then married and had seven children.

The move from an urban to a rural setting seems to have taken place in the second generation. According to Kuan (1934:84–85), the Ma left Sui-te to escape heavy taxation. Yang-chia-kou was a poor village inhabited by persons surnamed Yang when the Ma came and purchased land. It was the Ma who transformed the arid rural landscape by introducing irrigation works and replacing terraced plots with paddy on the banks of the stream that ran alongside the village. The Ma do not seem to have encountered any resistance as they bought up all they could. Eventually they owned 90 percent of the village land, which stood out, green and prosperous, against the brown Shensi countryside. In subsequent generations the Ma continued as traders and large landlords.

The landlord wealth of the Ma made their village an unusual place. The KMT rural investigative team's diary records a 1933 visit:

> August 20 ... at 3 P.M. we reached Kuan-chia chü village. It is under Sui-te and Mi-chih and is a village of over ninety households. A large part of the land is owned by the Ma of Yang-chia-kou, one of northern Shensi's large landlords;... we decided to visit.... We ... arrived in Yang-chia-kou in forty-five minutes. Here we saw for the first time in Shensi rich land, broad, even roads, clean clothing on the villagers, and high-ceilinged, attractive stone caves. (SSNT:176)

The diary goes on to describe a visit to Mr. Ma's cave, which was guarded by twenty to thirty men. Like the dominant lineages of the Canton delta, the Ma possessed coercive power. Mr. Ma had several tens of household servants, hired several bookkeepers, and owned over a hundred head of live-stock. The Ma holdings spread over the surrounding villages, as the team's survey shows.

The Ma began to appear in the local histories with the third generation when they produced degree-holders (see Figure 8.1). In this generation there were a *chin-shih*, Kuo-pin (degree won 1862–63); a *pa-kung*, Kuo-hua (1885–86); and a *fu-kung*, Kuo-shih. The fourth generation produced a *chü-jen*, Chu-k'ang (1889–90), three *sheng-yuan*, and a *pa-kung*. These were considerable achievements in a province that consistently ranked low in the production of degree-holders (Ho 1964:229). In the twentieth century, Ma sons were sent to the new Western-style schools. They attended universities in Shanghai, Peking, and abroad. According to Kuan (1934:85), in 1926–27 over fifty Ma sons were attending middle school and university in Peking alone. In 1942 the survey team counted sixteen Ma who were studying outside the prefecture (CC:560, 576, 584, 612; Survey:6–14). The Ma had claims to provincial if not national elite status in late Ch'ing and Republican times. Figure 8.1 indicates that Ma degree-holders and office-holders were widely distributed among the five branches; only the third branch failed to produce notables, but in the twentieth century this branch was extremely successful in sending its males abroad for study to Germany, Japan, and the United States (Survey:11). Of the four adult males in the third branch in 1942, three lived outside the village: Shih-ju, educated in Germany, was dean of the Graduate Arts Faculty at Northwest United University; Shih-liang, educated in the United States, was a professor at Szechwan University; and Shih-shang, educated in Japan, managed a textile factory in Tientsin. Only their uncle, Chu-nien, who had studied physical education for a year in Pei-p'ing Normal University, lived in Yang-chia-kou.

The Ma as a Kinship Group

The Ma presented themselves as a kinship group. They were seen by con-temporaries as a kinship group. The CCP survey team carefully differenti-ated between the Kuang-yü t'ang Ma and four other unrelated landlords whose surname was also Ma. The survey also identified peasants surnamed Ma, but these individuals did not belong to the Kuang-yü t'ang, and were not part of the descent line. Ma claims to common descent were supported by detailed information that the survey team used to draw up a genealogy of the male descendants. This genealogy shows the group was organized into five branches, each descended from one of Chia-lo's sons. Scrutiny of the personal names of Ma males reinforces the conclusion that this was a genuine descent group.

A Chinese man used many names in his lifetime, especially if he belonged to the educated and propertied elite. His *ming*, awarded by his family, was

TABLE 8.2

Common Characters in Personal Names of Males, Descended from Ma
Chia-lo, by Branch and Generation

Generation	Common character	Branch				
		One	*Two*	*Three*	*Four*	*Five*
2	ming	1	1	1	1	1
3	kuo	3	2	1	1	4
4	hsuan	5	1	0	4	2
	chu	0	4	2	0	0
	wei	0	0	0	0	7
5	chung	14	0	0	0	19
	shih	1	7	3	7	0
6	han	6	0	0	0	0
	hung	5	0	0	0	0
	jun	2	6	0	10	0
	ling	0	0	0	0	4
	other[a]	3	0	0	0	0
7	k'o	0	0	2	1	0
	other[a]	4	0	0	0	0

a. Disparate names in which no common element could be discerned were counted and placed in this category. In all other cases, 100 percent of the personal names included a common element.

the personal name by which he would be known after death. It was customary for lineages to use a character or character element in the *ming* of all its males of a given generation as a means of reinforcing the differentiation of generations. As Freedman (1958:72n) observes, the distinctiveness of the generation particles in personal names made rearrangement of past genealogical history difficult. Conversely, the existence of common elements in personal names strengthens the notion that the living members of the group conceived of themselves as a common descent group and followed the naming rules of such groups. Adherence to this naming pattern can be seen in instances as far scattered in time and space as the Shih of Sung Ming-chou (Ningpo), studied by Richard Davis, and the Lang-yeh Wang of Ming and Ch'ing Hopei analyzed by Susan Naquin in this volume.

Table 8.2 shows that the sons of Chia-lo and their sons in turn followed a naming system indicating common descent. In subsequent generations several alternative common elements were to be found in the names of males, yet in most cases such common elements cut across segments to occur in more than one branch. When disparate characters appear in personal names, as occurred in the seventh generation, they were to be found among brothers in a household in the senior branch. Nor does the use of unrelated characters in the *ming* assigned to brothers seem unusual: It also occurred among the Lins of Wu-feng (Meskill 1979:82) among brothers in the third generation.

Besides being able to demonstrate descent from a common ancestor, the

Ma also resided together in a hamlet of Yang-chia-kou. The wall enclosing Fu-feng chai, the hamlet in which most of them lived, was constructed by Kuo-shih of the third generation, to defend against the threat posed by the Muslim uprising that swept through central Shensi in 1862 and threatened the northern area in the spring of 1867. The county gazetteer (HC:2.11b) notes that Kuo-shih contributed the funds for building the walls and also coordinated local defense. As noted earlier, only three Ma households lived outside Fu-feng chai, in Ssu-kou, another of the six hamlets making up Yang-chia-kou. The rest of Yang-chia-kou's population, consisting largely of tenant farmers, seems to have resided outside Fu-feng chai.

Despite common identity and common residence, the Ma had no ancestral hall. The "Kuang-yü t'ang" by which they were identified referred to the descent line of Ma Chia-lo.[1] Since the Chinese Communists were extremely interested in tracing the "feudal" power of clans, it is difficult to see how an ancestral hall could have escaped their notice, had one existed. There is no mention of a genealogy either, although it appears that there was a printed genealogy.[2]

Did the Ma own corporate property? This question is more difficult to answer. The 1942 survey refers several times (Survey:1, 2, 14) to the Ma "Kuang-yü t'ang" and explains that this was how the Ma were known to the outside world. Did the Kuang-yü t'ang exist as a corporate estate for the descendants of Chia-lo? Although it is tempting to assume that the Kuang-yü t'ang was a corporate estate, there is absolutely no evidence either in the fairly detailed descriptions of inheritance shares or in the catalogue of the economic status of households in 1942 to support such a notion. Details on the division of Chia-lo's estate after his death suggest instead that his property was completely divided among his five sons. Each received land, some of which was owned outright and some on which the Ma held mortgages; each also received cash and apparently shares in shops or *p'u-tzu*. For example, Ma Wei-hsin held ownership rights in one of the shops founded by Chia-lo, the Ch'ung-sheng hsi, which seems to have passed to him through his grand-

1. According to Wu (1927), a *t'ang* was the name attached to the hall (i.e., residence) of an elite family, which came to be used more generally to refer to the elite household itself. It is in this sense that I interpret the use of "Kuang-yü t'ang" as a prefix for the group descended from Ma Chia-lo. The "Kuang-yü t'ang," the name of Chia-lo's estate, seems to have ceased to exist upon his death, and by 1942 there is no evidence that it owned any property or exercised any economic influence on members of the descent group.

2. After the presentation of this paper, I received part of a Ma genealogy from Professor Lawrence Ma, a descendant. It is entitled "Shan-hsi Sui-te Fu-feng Ma-shih shih-shih hsi t'ung piao" (Chart of the lines of the ten generations of Fu-feng Ma of Sui-te, Shensi). Chart 1 depicts the founder, Ma Chia-lo, as a member of the seventh generation of a larger Ma descent group; Chart 2, focusing on Chia-lo's descendants for the eighth through tenth generations, agrees in almost all details with the genealogical tables printed in Survey, and provides information, lacking in the Survey, on adoption of heirs within the Ma descent group.

father, who inherited it from Chia-lo (Survey:22). As will subsequently be
shown, shops (*p'u-tzu, tzu-hao*) were organized by individuals as share
partnerships and passed down to individual heirs, not to corporations.

Figure 8.2 presents the estates linked with male descendants in the senior
branch. The general principle governing estates seems to be that they were
linked with a current head of household. When he died, his estate was divided among his sons, who then created new estates of their own, after
which in most cases the original (father's) estate disappeared. Exceptions
occurred when a father allowed his married sons to establish separate households. This was the case with Jung-hsuan, a man of seventy-five *sui* in 1942,
who had given his eldest and second sons their shares of the estate while
continuing to keep his third son, then a boy of seven, at home. Other exceptions occurred when a son died before his father: This seems to be the reason
why in the second branch the estate was linked with the deceased grandfather of the current eldest male, Jun-shu, who lived in Sian. Jun-shu's
mother managed the household affairs.

A number of exceptions to the principle enunciated above resist easy
explanation. These are estates linked with deceased males whose descendants
had already created separate estates of their own after family division (*fen-
chia*). We have an example of this kind in the senior branch where Shih-tsu's
"I-jen t'ang" estate seems to have survived his death. The most extreme example is found in the fifth branch (see figure 8.3), where estates are linked
with males in every generation.

Were such estates active in the local economy? A search through information on occupations and employment in Yang-chia-kou reveals that four of
the fifteen *t'ang* hiring laborers for farm work were linked with deceased
males, but in these cases a widow survived who was managing the estate.[3]

Our survey of the economic data thus provides no explanation for the
function of estates linked with deceased males whose descendants had
divided the property and established separate estates of their own. We must
conclude that whatever the reasons for such estates, they could not have
been very important in the economy of the Ma because they would not
otherwise have completely escaped the notice of the CCP investigators, who
were particularly intent on uncovering the sources of landlord wealth and
power. Furthermore, there is no evidence that these estates functioned as

---

3. This list included the "Ch'ung-ch'ing t'ang" of Chung-hsuan in the second branch,
Jun-shu's grandfather; the "Hao-i t'ang" of Hung-hsien of the senior branch, who left an
underage son and a widow who managed the household's affairs; the "Chung-yung t'ang" of
Jun-chang in the fourth branch, whose widow managed affairs for the sole heir, a daughter.
Information on stewards employed by landlord estates yielded only one other case, the
"Ming-chih t'ang" of Hung-yung of the senior branch, whose widow managed household
affairs. There was no evidence that the estates linked with deceased males whose descendants
have created estates of their own after *fen-chia* functioned in the village economy.

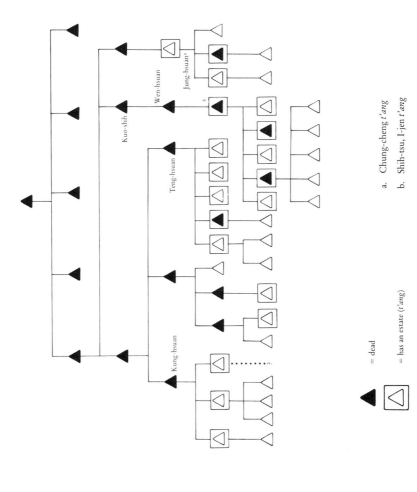

FIGURE 8.2　Adult Male Descendants of the Senior Branch and Their Estates, 1942

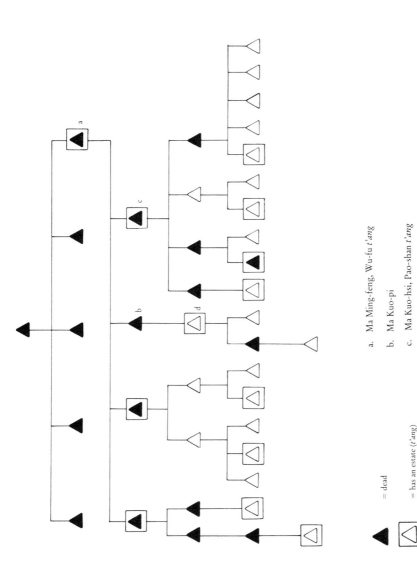

= dead

= has an estate (*t'ang*)

a. Ma Ming-feng, Wu-fu *t'ang*

b. Ma Kuo-pi

c. Ma Kuo-hsi, Pao-shan *t'ang*

d. Ma Wei-hsin, Yen-fu *t'ang*

FIGURE 8.3   Adult Male Descendants of the Fifth Branch and Their Estates, 1942

ancestral estates for branches or subbranches. We must end by noting that the Ma lacked yet another important attribute of lineage organization, possession of corporate property.

Were there any corporate activities to which the Ma subscribed? Here the answer may be yes. Fu-feng chai had a primary school, a highly unusual event in a Shensi village. Its principal was Ma Hsin-min, a landlord; its teaching staff included four other Ma: Jun-lan; Shih-ch'i; and two females, K'o-chien and Jun-hung. We know that Ma children attended this school, but we do not know if the school was supported by a collective effort.

Concerning Ma ritual activities, we are ignorant. The survey does not mention any grave sites or graveside rituals, though evidence from other localities suggests that such rites may well have been carried out.[4]

To summarize: Our scrutiny of the Ma Kuang-yü t'ang leads us to conclude that the Ma had not organized into a lineage. They had no ancestral hall and no corporate property, as far as we can tell, and may or may not have had communal rites for the ancestors. It is clear that they did not replicate features found in dominant lineages in South China by the Watsons (R. Watson 1982; J. Watson 1977), but the Ma still succeeded in establishing rural dominance in their locality.

Ma Local Dominance

The Ma dominance in the locality surrounding Yang-chia-kou is clear when we look at written accounts. Kuan (1934) identified them as landowners whose holdings were so enormous that even they were not sure of precisely how much they owned. Kuan noted that the Ma holdings extended beyond Sui-te and Mi-chih, and he echoes the statistics presented by the KMT rural survey. Since Kuan was a native of Kuan-chia chü, one of the villages whose land was largely owned by the Ma, he had personal knowledge of the situation.

Kuan's report was corroborated by the 1933 KMT sponsored rural investigation (SSNT). When the rural investigators visited Kuan-chia chü in July 1933, they noted that eighty out of ninety households rented land from the Ma, while over 90 percent of the households in nearby Ya-ma-kou village were Ma tenants.

The 1942 survey of the CCP team presents detailed statistics on the regional extent of Ma holdings. Wei-hsin, the "representative landlord," owned over four thousand *mou* of land. This land consisted of 208 plots, rented to over a hundred tenants, and was located in over twenty-three villages. In

---

4. Even though the descendants of Chia-lo counted only six generations, the larger genealogy they held (see note 2 above) identified Chia-lo as a seventh generation descendant of a larger Ma descent group. We know nothing about the ritual expressions of membership in this larger group that may have taken place.

addition, Wei-hsin held rights to lands on which he held mortgages. This mortgage land (*tien-ti*) was turned over to the lender when the loan was made; the lender obtained free use of the land for as long as the loan was unpaid and frequently rented back the land to its original owner. Mortgage land was not owned by the lender; when the loan was repaid, it reverted back to the original owner. A landlord like Wei-hsin collected rent from one to two thousand *mou* of mortgage land each year. About a quarter of such lands were eventually sold to him and added to his permanent holdings (Survey:28–37).

Only 12.5 percent of Wei-hsin's land was actually located within the village boundaries of Yang-chia-kou. Over half of Wei-hsin's permanent landholdings were clustered within a ten *li* radius of his home village; the rest lay within a forty-five *li* radius. Mortgage land was more widely dispersed, scattered over an additional thirty-one villages.

We can also examine the regional distribution of the holdings of another landlord, Ma Jui-t'ang (Survey:33, 37–38). Most of Jui-t'ang's land, totaling over four thousand *mou* (207 parcels) and scattered over thirty-two villages, lay within a forty-five *li* radius of Yang-chia-kou, although some parcels were fifty *li* away.

How did the Ma achieve and maintain local dominance without the institutional advantages offered by the lineage form of organization? In South China, the lineage provided an effective means of combination for households interested in achieving local dominance (R. Watson 1982). Lineage property ensured that the laws of partible inheritance, which tended to dissipate wealth, could be circumvented: Corporate revenues were used to support schools, which gave lineage males a head start in preparation for the civil service examinations and maximized the lineage's chances for placement of its members into the national elite. How do we compare the performance of the Kuang-yü t'ang against the historic performance of the South Chinese lineage?

We have already noted that the Ma moved into Yang-chia-kou in the mid-nineteenth century, having accumulated their first fortune in the regional city, Sui-te. Shortly thereafter they bought up enough land in the villages surrounding their residence to become the major landlords of their locality. They combined landholding with commercial efforts: More *p'u-tzu* were created by various Ma, and these firms also dealt in land purchases, loans, and grain marketing, which were all typical economic activities for households whose major wealth lay in the rural sector. By 1942, villages for a radius of forty-five *li* around Yang-chia-kou were under the economic umbrella of the individual households belonging to the Kuang-yü t'ang. It seems fair to say that the Ma were able to maintain local dominance from the mid-nineteenth century to 1940, when the CCP took control of northern Shensi.

Partible inheritance did act as a factor for downward mobility for the Ma. We can see this most precisely in the case of the fifth branch (see figure 8.3). Ming-feng, the fifth son of Chia-lo, received as his inheritance 3,500 *mou* of land, eighty ingots (*yuan-pao*) of silver, and two pieces (*ken*) of gold, as well as shares in shops (*tzu-hao*). He received shares in the Ch'ung-sheng-hsi shop, begun in 1833 by Chia-lo, and perhaps shares in other shops as well. Ming-feng had four sons. When they divided up his estate in 1885, each received 2,240.75 *mou*. This was the inheritance received by Kuo-pi, the third son. In addition to land, Kuo-pi inherited Chia-lo's shares in the Ch'ung-sheng-hsi firm. Kuo-pi went on to start two new firms: in 1885, he used his own capital to open up the Ch'ung-i chang in Yang-chia-kou village. With his brothers, he established the Ch'ung-yuan hao in nearby Chi-chen market in 1899. During the bad harvests of 1892–93, 1900–1901, 1901–2, Kuo-pi bought up a lot of land. Wei-hsin, the only one of his three sons to survive to maturity, received 2,887.5 *mou* as his inheritance from Kuo-pi.

The ability to pass on an inheritance equal to or greater than the one received from one's father was severely impaired when more than one son survived to maturity. Ming-feng provided substantially less to each of his four sons than he received from Chia-lo as one of five heirs. Kuo-pi was able to pass on more to Wei-hsin than he had himself inherited simply because his other two sons did not live to adulthood. And Wei-hsin's inheritance still did not match the inheritance received by his grandfather, Ming-feng.

By 1942 the economic status of households within the Kuang-yü t'ang had become very diverse. As the report (Survey:1) noted, "In recent decades, the large households (*ta hu*) of the Kuang-yü t'ang have begun to splinter into landlords, middle landlords, and small landlords. Some small landlords have already finally lost their holdings and begun a proletarian way of life." Table 8.3, which presents information on the landholdings of households in the five branches of the Ma group, substantiates this observation. Not only were some Ma households landless; the holdings of other Ma ranged from fairly small to very large properties. There were also significant differences in the average holdings per household by branch.

The fortunes of various Ma households reflected the vagaries of demography and quirks of individual personality and talent. When the head of household was indolent or, even worse, addicted to opium, his inheritance could be easily dissipated, frequently ending up in the hands of more enterprising agnates like Ma Wei-hsin. This member of the fifth branch was, in the words of the 1942 Survey (Survey:21), "the landlord clique's real representative personage," the most entrepreneurial landlord of the descent group. Born in 1886, the sole heir of his father Kuo-pi, Wei-hsin was educated in village schools until the age of seventeen. Because he was the sole surviving son, he did "not seek to make a name for himself in the outside world." Instead, he took over management of the estate from his father in

1904. From that year until the survey period Wei-hsin was in charge of the financial affairs of his household. Wei-hsin's main income was derived from rents; in these decades rents generally contributed more than 60 percent of his income (Survey:133–34). In addition Wei-hsin usually owned shares in several *p'u-tzu*. Between 1909 and 1917, Wei-hsin also tried to make money on the differences in the silver-copper exchange rates at the markets of Mi-chih and Chi-chen. He was quick to lend grain or money to kinsmen with land. When they proved unable to pay their debts, he foreclosed and took their land. The properties of Ma Wei-ch'eng, a member of the fifth branch, passed to Wei-hsin in the period 1921–41. Seventy-one percent of the land acquired by Wei-hsin during that period consisted of parcels previously owned by Wei-ch'eng, who was penniless in 1942.

The richest line in the Kuang-yü t'ang in the late nineteenth and early twentieth century was the result of having single heirs in two successive generations; this was the line of Kuo-shih, second son of Ming-k'o in the senior branch, whose only heir, Wen-hsuan, also had an only son, Shih-tsu (see figure 8.2).[5] At its peak, this household owned 12,250 *mou* of land and six firms (Survey:8).

Despite the negative effect of partible inheritance on individual lines (a phenomenon that can also be witnessed in lineages), the Ma as a whole expanded their interests and wealth in the course of the late nineteenth and twentieth centuries. We can compare the landholdings of the Ma at the end of Chia-lo's life with their total holdings in 1942 (Survey:2–14). During that period, Ma properties increased from approximately 17,500 *mou* to 50,594.25 *mou*, an increase of 290 percent. The Ma did not just maintain, they actually increased their economic power in the locality.

Other data presented in figure 8.1 and table 8.3 show that the Ma were also able to perpetuate their elite status. During the Ch'ing, Ma sons had held degrees; with the twentieth century, they went outside the province for Western education. Ma sons were appointed to posts under the Ch'ing and during the Republic. In 1912, Ma Jung-hsuan was appointed to serve as magistrate of Ching-pien, a county in northern Shensi, under the warlord Ching Yueh-hsiu, who controlled the area from 1911 until his death in 1935 (Selden 1971:16–17). There were Ma serving the KMT: Chung-pi, who in 1942 held a post under the KMT in Yü-lin, and Chung-hsiang, who was working for the county magistrate appointed by the KMT for Mi-chih. Other Ma accepted positions under the CCP Border Region Government, as noted earlier. In the twentieth century Ma had also begun entering military careers. Ma Jun-p'u served under the KMT general Hu Tsung-nan; Ma

5. According to the "Shan-hsi Sui-te Fu-feng Ma-shih shih-shih hsi t'ung piao," Chart 2, Wen-hsuan was the natural son of Kuo-chün, a brother of Kuo-shih, who was adopted as heir to Kuo-shih.

TABLE 8.3

Mobility Indicators for the Ma Branches

	Branches				
	One	*Two*	*Three*	*Four*	*Five*
Number of generations	7	7	5	7	6
Number of males	42	21	7	27	37
Degree-holders?	x	x		x	
Highest degree won	*fu-kung*	*chü-jen*		*chin-shih*	
Higher education after 1911	x	x	x		x
Office-holding	x	x		x	x
Land-holdings, ca. 1942					
Total holdings[a] (*mou*)	12,600.00	14,057.75	8,116.5	7,019.25	6,931.75
Average/household	630.00	2,008.25	2,029.3	638.11	630.00
Number of households holding					
0–175 *mou*	7	0	0	0	4
175–350 *mou*	4	0	0	4	0
350–700 *mou*	1	1	0	3	6
700–1,400 *mou*	5	2	3	3	0
1,400–2,800 *mou*	3	2	0	1	0
Over 2,800 *mou*	0	2	1	0	1

SOURCE: Survey:2–14.
a. The original data was in terms of the local unit, the *hsiang*, which was converted into *mou* at the rate of 1 *hsiang* = 3.5 *shih mou* (Survey:2).

Ling-yun was with KMT forces in Yunnan; Ma Lo, Ma K'o-ch'ien, and Ma K'o-ting were enrolled in the Eighth Route Army. Other Ma entered business and the professions. Ma Shih-i, with an M. S. degree in chemistry from the University of Michigan, was working at the 23rd Arsenal in Lü county, Szechwan.[6] As we noted earlier, the agnates of the third branch, Shih-ju, Shih-liang, and Shih-shang, were all professionals (Survey:6–14). The Ma were thus successful in making the transition from the status occupations of the late Ch'ing to those of the Republican era.

The conclusion of this brief survey is that within the period for which we have detailed information, admittedly a short span covering a little less than a century, the Ma Kuang-yü t'ang was in fact able to expand its economic base, dominate the surrounding villages, and enter the national elite. This achievement was all the more impressive for having taken place during a period when Northwest China and northern Shensi in particular experienced marked economic decline. From the mid-nineteenth century, when the Muslim rebellions of the 1860s devastated the countryside, Shensi had suffered hard times. There were poor harvests and famine in the 1876–79 period, again the 1890s, 1900–1901, and again in 1928–29. Several of these famines were among the worst ever experienced (Ho 1959:chap. 10).

Did kinship ties help the Ma attain wealth and power? What kind of group were they? The concept of a "group" implies collective identity, shared goals, and corporate functions. We have confirmed that the Ma had a collective identity, both in a self-conscious sense and in the eyes of their neighbors. We imagine they shared the desire to achieve or maintain a high economic and social position in their community. But we have failed to find much evidence of corporate functions and collective activities among the members of this descent group. When we compare the Ma with the Lang-yeh Wang studied by Naquin, we find interesting parallels and contrasts. On the one hand, the Ma, like the Wang, had produced degree-holders and could thus be assumed to share many of the aspirations of the Wang. Naquin notes that the desire to underline descent group identity was strongest among the most successful branches of the Wang descent group; we find no such suggestion in the case of the Ma. The difference may be one of time and not place, since conditions in the high Ch'ing, when the Wang genealogy was produced, were far more conducive to presentation of a lineage structure than were the 1940s under a Communist government. Moreover, it is possible that emphasis on economic aggrandizement in the Republican era overrode earlier themes emphasizing literati status: The Ma survey certainly portrays a group whose primary strength lay in the economic rather than the political arena. At the same time, it is difficult to see how household manage-

6. Information on Ma Shih-i's education was provided to me by his son, Professor Lawrence Ma.

ment of wealth could not have conflicted to some extent with collective activities, even in the late imperial era.

The economic activities of the Ma were carried on at the household level. The typical or modal pattern is that of Wei-hsin, who held land, lent grain or cash at high rates of interest, invested in firms, and speculated in the money and grain markets in nearby towns. Occasionally brothers pooled funds to set up the *tzu-hao*: We have cited an example of such cooperation in the founding of the Ch'ung-yuan hao by Ma Kuo-pi. We know that firms of this kind also solicited funds from women: The manager of Kuo-pi's firm, the Ch'ung-i chang, was a man named Feng Shih-fu, who was said to have many social connections. Since the Ch'ung-i chang was undercapitalized, it sought funds from outside, and housewives would take their private money (*t'i chi ch'ien*) to invest it with Feng (Survey:27).

Occasionally economic cooperation extended outside segments, or branches. In 1942, for example, the three sons of Chu-ling in the third branch were all absent from the village. They had divided up their father's estate and entrusted management of affairs to Ma Shih-chen, a male of their generation in the second branch (Survey:11). Of course, such cooperation remained ad hoc and basically improvisatory.

The Kuang-yü t'ang may also have had some functions in the realm of marriage. The general prestige of the descent group may have enabled males from its poorer households to contract better marriages than they would have otherwise attained. This was one of the primary functions of the "great families" of T'ang studied by David Johnson (1977). It is hard to know how important this function might have been for the Ma because we lack sufficient information on marriages. The data we do have concern the sisters and daughters of Ma Wei-hsin, whose household was rich enough to command good marriages without collective support or generalized prestige.

Regional Comparisons

To conclude from our survey of the Kuang-yü t'ang Ma that they prospered and persisted through economic activities conducted on a household level does not of course explain why Northwest China had very few lineages. One factor might be the low level of agricultural productivity in northern Shensi, especially on the loess plateau, which, though in the winter wheat–millet zone, grew more of the inferior crops such as maize, millet, proso millet, and buckwheat than did the richer lands in the Wei and Ching river basins to the south. Drought was a constant menace, bad harvests a recurrent phenomenon. Such an environment produced a sparse population, with population densities that were among the lowest in China (Skinner 1977:213). Settlements were more dispersed, and market towns more distant from one another than in the densely populated regions of South China.

The Kuang-yü t'ang Ma first made their fortune in the urban environment and only subsequently expanded into a rural setting. This may indicate that in northern Shensi productivity was too low to follow a rural strategy as in the Canton delta, where rural dominance might well precede movement into commerce (R. Watson 1982). Commercial involvement through *tzu-hao* or *p'u-tzu* ran through the whole Ma history into the 1930s. This pattern could also be found in South China among the dominant lineages. One significant difference between the Canton delta and northern Shensi lies of course in the prevailing economic trends: As Rubie Watson (1982) demonstrates, economic opportunities in the eighteenth century stimulated the emergence of lineages in the delta, whereas northern Shensi was beginning a long-term economic decline in the mid-nineteenth century when the Ma moved to Yang-chia-kou.

Under the boom conditions of the late seventeenth and early eighteenth centuries, Cantonese rural lineages could, if successful, establish new markets that they then controlled. The Ma never felt they could compete successfully with the merchant-landlords from larger urban centers such as Sui-te or T'ai-yuan. Ma Wei-hsin's agnates included many who had tried and failed in business: His cousin, Ma Wei-han, sold tobacco and eventually fell so deeply into debt that his eldest son committed suicide. The finances of Wei-han's household were ruined by this disaster. Another agnate, Ma Wei-kang, suffered from a mental disorder brought on by business anxieties. According to Wei-kang, "Mi-chih men cannot engage in ordinary business; they are relatively fit only for moneylending and land deals." The Sui-te natives were shrewder and showed good business management, like Shansi businessmen. While other families opened money shops in towns and after 1937 established textile factories, the Ma who stayed at home clung to traditional pursuits: money lending, land, and grain speculation (Survey:26).

Temporal conditions were unfavorable through the period of Ma ascendancy and dominance, and this may have been a factor discouraging lineage formation. The overriding fact, however, is that lineages were rare in Northwest China in any historical period. Was this rarity a product of the mixed ethnic history of the Northwest, which experienced much longer periods of rule by people from the steppe? This is a question for future research. Naquin's chapter on two Wang descent groups, included in this volume, shows that in North China too it was rare to find the lineage with large corporate estates of South and Southeast China. Ebrey's hypothesis is that the north-south differences in descent group organization may originate in the Sung-Yuan era, when elite descent groups such as those studied by Robert Hymes in his paper (included in this volume) began to appear in localities south of the Huai. Yet it is possible, given the variation between Lower Yangtze and Lingnan lineages, that the dominant South China lineage did not appear until a later period, the seventeenth-century transition from Ming to Ch'ing.

Without attempting to answer this question, for now we should note that some of the "ultimate" explanations proffered do not suffice: Freedman's suggestion (1966) that the conditions of wet-rice culture stimulated lineage organization fails because Yang-chia-kou was one of the few villages in northern Shensi that had irrigation works, created by the Ma. The "frontier" explanation also seems doubtful when we consider the unsettled nature of life in the Northwest, which should have raised rather than lowered the need for social organizations that could provide collective defense. The suggestion that it was the elite status of the Ma that dampened the desire for reliance on agnates rather than affines also fails when one seeks to explain the larger regional phenomenon, the absence of lineages. Nor does the relative youth of the Kuang-yü t'ang explain anything: A parallel example may be found in the case of the Ma of T'ung-chou.

The T'ung-chou Ma

The most detailed study of a prominent Northwest China descent group in late imperial times is Terada Takanobu's work (1974) on the Ma of T'ung-chou, an administrative department 120 kilometers northeast of Sian, in the Wei River valley of Shensi. These Ma were a prominent descent line who produced various degree-holders and officials during the Ming and Ch'ing dynasties, including a grand secretary in the sixteenth century. Although the T'ung-chou Ma seem to have compiled genealogies, none has been found in library collections.

Terada's primary source was the Generational Record (*Kuan-hsi Ma-shih shih-hang lu*), a late-nineteenth-century compilation of biographical epitaphs of leading Ma ancestors. The work begins with Ma Ho-ch'ing, the great-great-grandfather of the first appointed official in the line, who was named T'ung. It confines itself to Ma T'ung's descendants through his youngest son, and within this descent line treats only the men of prominence. Terada argues that this descent line's success in retaining a position of privilege over two dynasties was remarkable, especially when compared with the more volatile fortunes of great lineages in the Lower Yangtze. We see the similarity between the T'ung-chou Ma and the T'ung-ch'eng lineages studied by Beattie, but the major and significant difference between the two is that in T'ung-chou we see no trace of any sort of lineage organization: no ancestral halls, no corporate properties, no lineage schools. Like the Yang-chia-kou Ma, management of economic affairs, for which the Generational Record provides abundant information, took place on the household level. We must conclude that here too prominence was in no way the product of collective effort on the part of a lineage.

Kinship and Village Organization

Although we have no information of a comprehensive nature for North-west China, we can reconstruct the dominant types of social organizations in North China villages and compare them with their counterparts in South China. As Potter (1970) noted, single surname villages were rare in North and Northwest China. Hirano (1944) observes that the Mantetsu surveys of the late 1930s and early 1940s found only seven villages in Luan-ch'eng, Hopei, where 88 percent or more of the population shared one surname. The same survey uncovered rudiments of lineages (Uchida 1953) but no examples of dominant rural lineages. These multi-surname villages were arenas for competition between surname groups but also encompassed large areas of ritual and economic cooperation that overrode lineage claims to loyalty.

Uchida noted that ancestral halls and lineages were rare in the villages surveyed by the Mantetsu teams. The few ancestral halls (*chia-tz'u, tz'u-t'ang, chia-miao*) found were located not in villages but in county seats. Even when an ancestral hall was found in a village, it did not necessarily signify the presence of a lineage: This was the case with the Li ancestral hall in Ling-shui kou, a village in Li-ch'eng county, Shantung, which has also been studied by Ramon Myers (1970). The Li constituted half of the village population but were actually dispersed into five lines of descent; only one saw itself as a "lineage," but even though it had a genealogy and owned an ancestral hall, it did not seem to be functioning as a lineage: The hall had never been used for rites, there was no communal worship of the ancestors, and the Li could not recall any occasions when they all met together for a common purpose. The corporate property, owned by one of the three branches into which the Li "lineage" was divided, consisted of one *mou* of "grave protection land" (*hu-ying ti*), whose tiller was obliged to provide materials for the Ch'ing-ming rites.

Scattered cases of communal worship and collective identity are cited for other North China villages by Uchida, who suggests that observance of ancestral grave rites had declined with the economic decline of the region in the late nineteenth and early twentieth centuries. Historical records indicate, however, that these parts of Shantung and Hopei were never dominated by strong lineages, and that corporate property (with the exception of temple land) had never been important in the local economy. Uchida cites over a dozen examples of descent groups that carried out Ch'ing-ming rites at ancestral graves and owned some corporate land, but these estates (usually two or three *mou* in size) were too small to provoke intra-lineage conflict over their use. The land was usually rented to a poor agnate who in turn contributed to the expenses of the grave rites or the communal meal that followed. Even in the rare instances when we find, as with the Li of Ling-shui kou, some of the conventional markers of lineage organization, these are not correlated with local dominance. The lineages are not powerful enough to advance the interests of members (Uchida 1953:83–84).

Indeed, Hirano's examination (1944) of religious organizations in the same villages covered by Uchida shows that solidarity on a village basis, crossing surname lines, was a more important facet of North China villages. Ling-shui kou, the home of the Li cited earlier, had four temples, one dedicated to the Jade Emperor (Yü-huang miao) and the *San-kuan* (Taoist Ruler of Heaven, Ruler of Earth, Ruler of Water); one to Kuan Yü; one to the *San-sheng* (Confucius, Lao Tzu, and Buddha) and earth god; and a small one to Kuan-yin. Villagers organized into temple societies (*miao hui*) that put on festivals and rotated duties of worship. Many villages in the area had temple lands to help provide funds for temple maintenance.

In multi-surname villages, dominant surnames shared the leadership posts, usually in a manner reflecting their proportional numbers and strength. T'ien Te-i's (1934) description of the social and political structure of his native village, Ta pei yin, located in An-tz'u county, Hopei, south of Peking, shows how lineages functioned in a multi-surname village in North China. Ta pei yin had a population of 868 (136 households), residing in four hamlets and belonging to about nineteen surnames. At least four of the surnames were organized into lineages, possessing genealogical knowledge, displaying internal segmentation, owning corporate property, and practicing collective worship at the ancestors' graves during Ch'ing-ming. Since these major lineages resided in distinct parts of the village, Ta pei yin was divisible first into four and eventually into two competing coalitions of hamlets, each dominated by a surname group. Village posts were divided up between the two coalitions. The lineage of the author, the T'ien, dominated the post of village head from the late nineteenth century on, while the Wang dominated the post of assistant during the same period. According to older villagers, before 1911 strife between the leading lineages had tended to promote intra-lineage unity. More recently, the rising need for collective defense against bandits had stimulated the village to organize a "defense group" (*pao-wei t'uan*) manned by representatives from each household in rotation. These new concerns may have dampened lineage solidarity and put new stress on village unity. T'ien noted that inter-lineage relations were currently very amicable.

Because strong descent groups were rare in North China, analysis of village social structure focuses on organizational bonds lying outside the framework of kinship, like those analyzed by Steven Sangren (1984). In fact, North China multi-surname villages tended to resemble some Taiwan villages in their social organization. Harrell's (1981) study of three Hokkien villages in Hai-shan, an area southwest of Taipei, stressed the importance of the environment in determining the social organizational variation. Ch'i-nan, a group of four nucleated settlements, resembles Ta pei yin village in its division into four competing patrilineages, although unlike Ta pei yin, each Ch'i-nan lineage had an ancestral hall. In Ch'i-nan, lineage solidarity over-rode village unity, a fact reflected in Ch'i-nan's lack of a village leader and the absence of village-wide temple associations. We can contrast the temple associations in North China, to which every villager belonged, with Ahern's description (1973:5–9) of rotation of responsibility for the Earth God, Co-su-kong, and Ang-kong festivals among the four single-lineage settlements that constitute Ch'i-nan. Perhaps the stress placed on lineage in Ch'i-nan was a product of internal security during the late Ch'ing and the Japanese regimes; we have already noted that the breakdown of law and order stimu-lated cooperative efforts by villagers in Ta pei yin. Finally, many North and Northwest China villages probably resembled Ploughshare Village, which Harrell notes had no recognizable neighborhoods or lineage organization. Certainly the absence of ancestral halls and continuance of domestic cults in Ploughshare (Harrell 1976) echo findings reported by Uchida for North China (1953).

As several writers have recently pointed out (Twitchett 1982; Ebrey 1983), the dominant South China lineage is an anomaly, whose special char-acter is underlined when we look at contrasting types of descent groups in Northwest and North China. We should stress, like Rubie Watson (1982), that lineage formation was neither a "natural" nor an "inevitable" process in Chinese society. Like the Lang-yeh Wang studied by Naquin, the Ma of Yang-chia-kou and of T'ung-chou were descent groups, producing degree-holders and officials who shared some but not all of the characteristics of a South China lineage. Like them, the Wang and Ma were conscious of a col-lective identity based on descent that was expressed through genealogies, through adoption of common elements in generational names, and occa-sionally through common gravesites. Unlike the South China lineages, these northern groups rarely erected ancestral halls, and, most significantly, they lacked corporate holdings of any size. Not only were they different from the "Kwangtung" or South China lineage, they were also unlike the T'ung-ch'eng lineages studied by Beattie (Beattie 1979; Ebrey 1983) or the more general "Lower Yangtze" type examined by Dennerline and Hazelton in this volume.

Secondary literature on the functions of lineage property (Twitchett 1959:130–33; Potter 1970; Dennerline 1981) tells us that descent groups without such property should be very different from lineages. Without lineage estates, descent groups would have less stake in collective activities. Without estates to soften the divisiveness latent in the economic and social differentiation of households within the group, descent groups should find it more difficult to maintain collective unity over time; they should exercise less power over members and should be relatively impotent to halt the nega-tive effects of partible inheritance and genetic chance on the perpetuation of elite status. Descent group dominance of a rural locality might also be difficult to achieve since effective power resided in households subject to the domestic cycle.

My study of the Shensi Ma and Naquin's of the Lang-yeh Wang contradict the implications in the literature on the importance of corporate properties. The T'ung-chou Ma, like the Lang-yeh Wang, were very successful at perpetuating their degree-winning success over centuries, indeed over two dynasties, even though they do not seem to have possessed lineage estates. The Yang-chia-kou Ma were successful at dominating the countryside around them through a combination of economic and coercive force, even without lineage estates. These case studies remind us that there is frequently "more than one way to skin a cat." Corporate estates were clearly an asset for a collective strategy, but they were apparently not the only organizational tool that could be brought to bear on the problem of how to remain rich and honored over generations. We need to look further at creative regional variations of descent group strategies to tease out the full implications of the Northwest and North China cases presented in this volume.

REFERENCES

Ahern, Emily M. 1973. *The Cult of the Dead in a Chinese Village.* Stanford: Stanford University Press.

Beattie, Hilary J. 1979. *Land and Lineage in China: A Study of T'ung-ch'eng County, Anhwei, in the Ming and Ch'ing Dynasties.* Cambridge: Cambridge University Press.

Brunnert, H. S., and V. V. Hagelstrom. 1912. *Present Day Political Organization of China*, rev. N. T. Kolessoff, trans. A. Beltchenko and E. E. Moran. Shanghai: Kelly and Walsh.

CC.   *Sui-te chou chih* 綏德州志. 1905. Reprint ed. Taipei: Ch'eng-wen, 1970.

Cole, James. N.d. *Survival in Shaohsing: Competition and Cooperation in Late Ch'ing China.* Forthcoming.

Dennerline, Jerry. 1981. "The New Hua Charitable Estate and Local Level Leadership in Wuxi County at the End of the Qing." In *Select Papers from the Center for Far Eastern Studies* (University of Chicago), no. 4 (1979–80): 19–70.

Ebrey, Patricia Buckley. 1983. "Types of Lineages in Ch'ing China: A Reexamination of the Chang Lineage of T'ung-ch'eng." *Ch'ing-shih wen-t'i* 4.9:1–20.

Freedman, Maurice. 1958. *Lineage Organization in Southeastern China.* New York: Humanities Press.

———. 1966. *Chinese Lineage and Society: Fukien and Kwangtung.* New York: Humanities Press.

———. 1979. "The Politics of an Old State: A View from the Chinese Lineage." In his *The Study of Chinese Society: Essays by Maurice Freedman*, selected and introduced by G. W. Skinner, pp. 334–50. Stanford: Stanford University Press.

Harrell, Stevan. 1976. "The Ancestors at Home: Domestic Worship in a Land-Poor

Taiwanese Village." In *Ancestors*, ed. William H. Newell, pp. 373–86. The Hague: Mouton.

———. 1981. "Social Organization in Hai-shan." In *The Anthropology of Taiwanese Society*, ed. Emily M. Ahern and Hill Gates, pp. 125–47. Stanford: Stanford University Press.

HC. *Mi-chih hsien chih* 米脂縣志. 1907 ed.

Hirano Yoshitarō 平野義太郎. 1944. "Hoku Shi sonraku no kiso yōso to shite no sōzoku oyobi sonbyō" 北支村落の基礎要素としての宗族及び村廟 [Lineages and village temples as basic elements in North China villages]. In *Shina nōson kankō chōsa hōkokusho* 支那農村慣行調査報告書 [Report on a survey of village customs in China], ed. Tōa kenkyūjo 東亞研究所, vol. 1, pp. 1–145. Tokyo: Tōa kenkyūjo.

Ho, Ping-ti. 1959. *Studies on the Population of China, 1368–1953*. Cambridge, Mass.:Harvard University Press.

———. 1964. *The Ladder of Success in Imperial China*. New York: John Wiley.

Hsu, Yung-ying. 1945. *A Survey of Shensi-Kansu-Ninghsia Border Region*. New York: Institute of Pacific Relations.

Johnson, David. 1977. *The Medieval Chinese Oligarchy*. Boulder: Westview Press.

Kawachi Juzō 河地重造. 1963a. "Chūgoku no jinushi keizai—nijisseiki, Senhoku Ba shi no bunseki" 中國の地主經濟—二十世紀, 陝北馬氏の分析 [The Chinese landlord economy—analysis of the Ma of northern Shensi in the twentieth century]. *Keizaigaku nenpō* 經濟學年報 (Ōsaka shiritsu daigaku 大阪市立大學) 18:48–125.

———. 1963b. "Nijisseiki Chūgoku no jinushi ichizoku—Sensei-shō Beishi-ken Yōkakō no Ba-shi" 二〇世紀中國の地主一族—陝西省米脂縣楊家溝の馬氏 [A case history of a twentieth-century Chinese landlord clan—the Ma of Shensi province, Mi-chih county, Yang-chia-kou]. *Tōyōshi kenkyū* 東洋史研究 21.4: 507–39.

Kuan Shan 觀山. 1934. "Shan-pei wei-i ti 'Yang-chia-kou Ma chia' ta ti-chu" 陝北唯一的「楊家溝馬家」大地主 [The unique large landlord Ma of Yang-chia-kou, northern Shensi]. *Hsin Chung-hua* 新中華 2.16:84–86.

Meskill, Johanna. 1970. "The Chinese Genealogy as a Research Source." In *Family and Kinship in Chinese Society*, ed. Maurice Freedman, pp. 139–61. Stanford: Stanford University Press.

———. 1979. *A Chinese Pioneer Family: The Lins of Wu-feng, Taiwan, 1729–1895*. Princeton: Princeton University Press.

Myers, Ramon. 1970. *Agricultural Development in Hopei and Shantung, 1890–1949*. Cambridge Mass.: Harvard University Press.

Pai Mei-ch'u 白眉初. 1926. "Shan-hsi sheng chih" 陝西省誌 [Gazetteer of Shensi]. In *Chung-hua min-kuo sheng ch'ü ch'üan chih (4) Ch'in Lung Ch'iang Shu ssu sheng ch'ü chih* 中華民國省區全誌 (4) 秦隴羌蜀四省區誌 [Gazetteer of the Republic of China (4) Shensi, Kansu, Szechwan, and the northwest frontier region]. Peking: Pei-ching shih-fan ta-hsueh.

Potter, Jack. 1970. "Land and Lineage in Traditional China." In *Family and Kinship in Chinese Society*, ed. Maurice Freedman, pp. 121–38. Stanford: Stanford University Press.

Sangren, P. Steven. 1984. "Traditional Chinese Corporations: Beyond Kinship."

Journal of Asian Studies 43.3:391–415.

Selden, Mark. 1971. *The Yenan Way in Revolutionary China*. Cambridge, Mass.: Harvard University Press.

Skinner, G. William. 1977. "Regional Urbanization in Nineteenth-Century China." In *The City in Late Imperial China*, ed. G. William Skinner, pp. 211–49. Stanford: Stanford University Press.

SSNT. *Shan-hsi sheng nung-ts'un tiao-ch'a* 陝西省農村調查 [Village survey of Shensi province], comp. Hsing-cheng yuan, Nung-ts'un fu-hsing wei-yuan hui 行政院, 農村復興委員會. Shanghai: Commercial Press, 1934.

SSZ 1918. *Shina shōbetsu zenshi* 支那省別全誌 [Comprehensive gazetteer of China by provinces], comp. Tōa dōbunkai 東亞同文會. Shanghai: Tōa dōbun gakuin 東亞同文學院.

Survey. Yenan nung-ts'un tiao-ch'a t'uan 延安農村調查團, *Mi-chih hsien Yang-chia-kou tiao-ch'a* 米脂縣楊家溝調查 [Investigation of Yang-chia-kou village, Mi-chih county]. Peking: San-lien.

Taga Akigorō 多賀秋五郎. 1960. *Sōfu no kenkyū* 宗譜の研究 [Investigation of genealogies]. Tokyo: Tōyō Bunko.

Terada Takanobu 寺田隆信. 1974. "Sensei Dōshū no Ba-shi—Min-Shin jidai ni okeru ichi kyōshin no keifu" 陝西同州の馬氏—明清時代における一鄉紳の糸譜 [The Ma of T'ung-chou, Shensi: a rural gentry descent line in Ming and Ch'ing]. *Tōyōshi kenkyū* 東洋史研究 33.3:478–504.

T'ien Te-i 田德一. 1934. "I-ko nung-ts'un tsu-chih chih yen-chiu—chia-tsu chi ts'un-chih" 一個農村組織之研究—家族及村治 [Research on the organization of a village—family and village governance]. *She-hui hsueh chieh* 社會學界 8:107–15.

Ts'ai Shu-fan 柴樹藩. 1979. With Yü Kuang-yuan 于光元 and P'eng P'ing 彭平. *Sui-te, Mi-chih t'u-ti wen-t'i ch'u-pu yen-chiu* 綏德, 米脂土地問題初步研究 [Preliminary research on land questions in Sui-te and Mi-chih]. Peking: People's Press.

Twitchett, Denis. 1959. "The Fan Clan's Charitable Estate, 1050–1760." In *Confucianism in Action*, ed. David S. Nivison and Arthur F. Wright, pp. 97–133. Stanford: Stanford University Press.

———. 1982. "Comment on J. L. Watson's article." *China Quarterly* 92:623–27.

Uchida Tomoo 內田智雄. 1953. "Kahoku nōson ni okeru dōzoku no saishi gyōji ni tsuite" 華北農村に於ける同族の祭祀行事について [Ritual festivals of lineages in rural north China]. *Tōhōgakuhō* 東方學報 22:59–94.

Watson, James L. 1977. "Hereditary Tenancy and Corporate Landlordism in Traditional China: A Case Study." *Modern Asian Studies* 11:161–82.

———. 1982. "Chinese Kinship Reconsidered: Anthropological Perspectives on Historical Research." *China Quarterly* 92:589–622.

Watson, Rubie S. 1982. "The Creation of a Chinese Lineage: The Teng of Ha Tsuen, 1669–1751." *Modern Asian Studies* 16.1:69–100.

Wu, Ching-chao. 1927. "The Chinese Family: Organization, Names, and Kinship Terms." *American Anthropologist* n.s. 19.3:316–25.

NINE

Anthropological Overview:
The Development of Chinese
Descent Groups

James L. Watson

The essays in this volume address a set of issues normally thought to be within the disciplinary purview of social anthropology. Taken together, these seven essays constitute a serious challenge to many of the underlying assumptions that have guided ethnographic researchers for the past twenty-five years. As discussed in chapter 1, anthropological models of Chinese (agnatic) kinship are based primarily on field investigations of the powerful, landowning lineages that are characteristic of the Lingnan region of South China. Studies of this type have been so pervasive that they constitute what might be called a "lineage paradigm." Briefly summarized, this approach derives from the work of Maurice Freedman (1958, 1966), who, in turn, borrowed a set of ideas regarding segmentary lineage societies from his Africanist colleagues (e.g., Evans-Pritchard 1940; Fortes 1945, 1953). Freedman's synthesis of the Chinese ethnographic evidence can be called a paradigm in the sense that it assumes a fundamental model of Chinese society in which the ideology of patrilineal descent takes precedence over all other principles of social organization.[1]

During the past twenty years fieldworking anthropologists have published an impressive collection of studies dealing with various aspects of lineage organization. Some claim to have "proved" the applicability of Freedman's model whereas others have criticized and refined the models—but most have worked within the framework of the lineage paradigm (see e.g., Ahern 1973, 1976; Anderson 1970; Baker 1968, 1979; Cohen 1969;

---

1. Freedman himself was acutely aware of the limitations of his approach, but many who have followed his lead have placed too much emphasis on descent and have underplayed other, equally salient aspects of social organization in Chinese society (such as class, affinity, and ethnic variation).

E. Johnson 1973; Mark 1972; Mathias 1977; Pasternak 1968, 1972; Potter 1968, 1970; Strauch 1983; J. Watson 1975a, 1975b; Woon 1979). This is not to say that all anthropologists have accepted the lineage paradigm (for direct attacks on the approach see Sangren 1984 and R. Watson 1985). But it is generally true that even those fieldworkers who have attempted to work outside the framework of Freedman's models have structured their studies as a critique of the lineage paradigm (see e.g., Harrell 1982; Huang 1980; Pasternak 1969; R. Watson 1981, 1982; Wolf and Huang 1980; M. Wolf 1972).

Out of this research a number of assumptions have emerged regarding the nature of Chinese kinship. These assumptions constitute the "received wisdom" of sinological anthropology as a specialized subdiscipline. It is generally held, for instance, that corporately owned land or some other form of material property is essential to hold people together during the formative stages of Chinese descent groups. Another commonly held view is that uxorilocal residence and nonagnatic adoption are strategies or adaptations that are confined to people near the bottom of the social hierarchy. A cornerstone of the fieldworking anthropologists' received wisdom regarding Chinese social organization is the assumption that women have little to do with the formal structure of agnatic groups and that women rarely have anything to say about the disposition of property (other than their own dowries, and even this is often subject to male controls, see R. Watson 1984). Most anthropologists also operate with the implicit assumption that ritual is a reflection of economic and/or political forces. Ancestral rites, in particular, are thought to be derivative of preexisting corporate activities and are discussed as secondary epiphenomena, rather than as primary motivating forces, in the formation of kinship groups.

These and other received notions regarding the nature of partilineal descent and agnatic organization are critically examined in the preceding essays.[2] Although the authors deal with a variety of historical issues, and often define their problems in ways that differ from the standard anthropological approach, they are all well versed in the ethnographic literature. Furthermore, they have made a conscious effort to speak directly to anthro-

2. It is obvious, however, that the contributors do not speak with one voice on the issues covered in this book. For example, they disagree on the reasons for evoking patrilineal ties and for compiling genealogies. Dennerline emphasizes the notion of "patrilineal authenticity," Hymes stresses the political value of defining a set of potential allies, while Ebrey considers the role of patrilineal descent in Neo-Confucian thought. In explaining the appearance of "modern" descent groups during the late Sung and Yuan, Hymes stresses the political strategies of the elite and Ebrey dwells on the ritual life of commoners. On the issue of historical continuity, Davis and Dennerline point to the dangers of producing too many heirs (thus dispersing property and resources), while Naquin finds a correlation between fecundity and prosperity. Other differences in emphasis and interpretation are apparent in the case studies.

pologists. It seems appropriate, therefore, to conclude this volume with a response from the perspective of social anthropology.

Anthropologists' models of Chinese kinship organization, including the recent counter-models deriving from critiques of the lineage paradigm, are dependent upon interviews with living people. Even those fieldworkers fortunate enough to work with Taiwanese household registers (Pasternak 1983; Wolf and Huang 1980) cannot generalize with any certainty about social organization prior to 1850. Furthermore, the most telling limitation of the anthropologists' approach to Chinese kinship is that we find it difficult, if not impossible, to investigate patterns of social organization that are characteristic of the national and macro-regional elites—what some might call the ruling classes or the scholar-bureaucratic strata. As anthropologists we must face the fact that our models of organization may be relevant only to the lower ranges of China's social hierarchy, namely the general peasantry and the local elites who were not dependent on the imperial bureaucracy for employment or commercial opportunities.

A great strength of the essays in this volume is that they examine people of national visibility who moved easily in the upper reaches of society. Richard Davis, in particular, focuses on a category of people that anthropologists might be tempted to label the "super-elite" of late imperial society. Viewed from the mud flats of rural Kwangtung, the political maneuvers and machinations of the Shih are nothing short of awe inspiring. And yet, Davis, as a political historian, proceeds with the analysis of his case study as if there were nothing particularly unusual about the Shih. To many historians the Shih were *not* unique; life and politics at the pinnacle of power *was* Chinese society to those who concentrate on the super-elite.

The question that all anthropologists and historians must ask is whether the models deriving from fieldwork among living peoples (mostly peasants in the Lingnan and Taiwan regions) have any relevance when analyzing social organization among China's ruling elites. Having read the papers in this volume, along with the earlier publications of these and other social historians,[3] I am not at all convinced that fieldworking anthropologists have the last word on Chinese kinship organization. What follows is an appreciation and a critique of the main issues raised in this book. I wish to stress at the outset that these comments are those of an anthropologist whose notion of "Chinese society" derives largely from long periods of residence in Cantonese peasant villages. It is a long way—in many senses —from the villages of Kwangtung to the corridors of the imperial palace, but it is my firm conviction that research in one sphere can inform studies in the other.

---

3. Publications dealing with the history of Chinese descent groups are discussed at length in J. Watson 1982a; see also chapter 1 of this volume for a partial list of sources covered.

Land, Property, and Corporate Strategies

Many anthropologists have argued that material property, particularly land, is the foundation of Chinese lineage organization (see e.g., Anderson 1970; Freedman 1966; Potter 1970). This may in fact be true for Kwangtung lineages, but evidence from this book suggests that it is most certainly not the case for many descent groups in other parts of China.

Jerry Dennerline's examination of Wu-hsi lineages is the only case study of the six that focuses on corporate land as a major theme, and even here the data do not conform to anthropological models. Dennerline concentrates on the formation of "charitable estates" (*i-chuang*), which appear, on first reading, to be the functional equivalents of "sacrificial estates" (*chi t'ien*), which are characteristic of Kwangtung lineages. But the analogy is deceptive. Rather than serving as the foundation blocks upon which elaborate lineages were constructed, the Wu-hsi charitable estates were not primary but secondary phenomena—one might be tempted to call them epiphenomena were it not for the fact that they play such a central role in the written records of the people concerned. The Wu-hsi estates, as Dennerline describes them, were not designed to hold agnates together through the bonds of corporate landownership—the hallmark of Kwangtung lineage organization. According to Dennerline, these charitable estates were designed and managed with quite another purpose in mind: to attract high-status affines by offering security for in-marrying women (i.e., the daughters of important men). Estates of this nature necessarily emerged long after the lineages in question had been formed. We do not know from the documents whether other types of corporate estates served as the organizational focus of these Wu-hsi lineages. Given the richness of Dennerline's sources, one would expect ancestral estates (sacrificial lands) to emerge as a major theme if they were significant.

The case studies by Davis, Hazelton, Hymes, Naquin, and Rawski do not stress land or material property as a focus for descent group unity. Keith Hazelton (chapter 5) argues that the rent-producing property of the Wu lineage was "too weak a force to hold the group together by itself." Evelyn Rawski (chapter 8), in her study of kinship organization in North China, finds no visible land base for the Ma as a corporate group. Among the Ma, land seems to have been controlled by agnatic lines rather than lineage estates, and was transferred from one generation to the next through the mechanism of personal inheritance and family partition. Land was not concentrated into inalienable estates named in honor of key ancestors, as in Kwangtung. These findings lead Rawski to challenge the anthropologists by turning the tables on them: It is, she suggests, the Kwangtung pattern of lineage organization that is peculiar. By implication it is unreasonable to expect historians to explain why powerful, land-based lineages did not appear in other parts of China, particularly in the North (see also Ebrey 1983).

Robert Hymes, in his study of Sung descent groups (chapter 4), challenges the anthropologists on yet another issue: the nature of corporate unity. Like his colleagues in this volume, Hymes could find no clear evidence that Sung descent groups (not "lineages" in the modern sense) had a foundation in corporately owned property of any kind. Rather, the groups in question were—in his view—defined by corporate marriage strategies. The collections of agnates studied by Hymes constituted "groups" only in the sense that they cooperated to construct genealogies, an activity designed to draw boundaries and distinguish one set of people from other, similarly defined sets. In my reading of Hymes's evidence, the ultimate aim of these corporate activities was to enhance the group's chances in the marriage market. The raison d'être of kinship organization in this case was the nurturing of the group's image as it was projected to potential affines and *not* the construction of a tight-knit body of agnates who confronted outsiders as potential enemies (the latter representation emerges from the anthropological literature on modern lineages). Hymes, in his provocative introduction, summarizes these two perspectives. Historians like Hymes, Dennerline (1981 and chapter 6 this volume), and David Johnson (1977) stress the role of corporate activities in the formation of alliances *between* descent groups whereas most anthropologists have concentrated on the ideology of descent *within* groups. This difference in perspective—internal versus external, or alliance versus descent—is fundamental to all research on unilineal descent groups. It is not surprising that historians should stress the links between competing groups, given the public records (e.g., genealogies) with which they work. Genealogies, in particular, are designed to represent a descent group as a collection of men worthy of marriage, partnership, and political alliance. Anthropologists, on the other hand, normally work with one community of living informants who stress the internal cohesion of their group and, hence, are not concerned exclusively with their image in the outside world.

Richard Davis (chapter 3) explores the corporate activities of a descent group, the Shih, that not only had no foundation in land but also had no effective "roots" in the Chinese countryside. The Shih were held together by shared privileges, a common naming system, and a mutually advantageous adoption strategy. There were no estates of any kind, no halls, no genealogies, no rituals of solidarity, and no evident ties to a "native place" (*hsiang-hsia*, village or town of origin) in the countryside. In Davis's view, it was the sharing of imperial "protection" (*yin*) that transformed the Shih from a loose collection of agnates into a self-conscious group during the Sung. Successful bureaucrats were granted the privilege of nominating a specified number of people for imperial service through the mechanism of *yin*. Not surprisingly, the Shih came to treat imperial privilege as a resource and used it to good effect in promoting the careers of agnates.[4] However, as Davis is careful to point out, this strategy of building descent group solidarity could also backfire—especially during periods of bureaucratic strife and imperial disfavor. Ironically, it was the very success of the Shih in monopolizing high office that eventually brought down the entire group. They became an easy target of criticism once their leading members had fallen from grace. In Davis's view, therefore, the high-risk strategy followed by the Shih was not conducive to the formation of historically viable kinship groups that were capable of surviving the deaths (or the demotions) of leading members.

There are many other documented cases in which the corporate bases of Chinese descent groups are not dependent upon the ownership or management of material property (Mann 1974; J. Watson 1975b). Intangible resources such as information, reputation, and job introductions can serve as the basis of corporate unity. An excellent, if somewhat unusual, example is provided by Susan Naquin in her study of sectarian leadership in Chihli (chapter 7). The "unorthodox" Wang constituted a lineage in the sense that members shared an interest in, and derived income from, the management of a sect. The lineage provided what was, in effect, a pool of reliable proselytizers. The fact that the leadership of a heterodox sect was "imbedded" in an orthodox kinship organization makes this a case of considerable theoretical interest. Given the absence of corporate land or other material resources, it would appear that the Wang lineage survived primarily as an information network. Naquin's study, along with the findings of others in this volume, highlights in a dramatic way the inherent flexibility of Chinese kinship organizations.

Burial Rites and the Formation of Descent Groups

As noted above, it is generally taken as an article of faith among anthropologists that ritual (e.g., ancestral and burial rites) is a reflection of political and economic forces (Ahern 1973, 1981; Baker 1979; Freedman 1966; Potter 1970; J. Watson 1982b; A. Wolf 1970). Anthropologists differ, of course, in their approach to this subject, but few who have worked on Chinese society are prepared to "detach" ancestor worship or burial rites from the economic/political system and treat ritual as anything other than a dependent variable. In this sense, Patricia Ebrey's essay (chapter 2) represents a serious challenge to the sinological anthropologists' approach to

---

4. Davis notes that it was not only agnates who were nominated for *yin* privileges; affines were also honored on occasion. But *yin* privileges appear, from my reading of Davis's account, to have been concentrated in the agnatic line, usually within the category known to anthropologists as descendants of common grandfather.

ritual. Drawing on a wide range of historical sources, Ebrey has come to the conclusion that ritual—in this case burial rites and ancestral observances—was an independent, *determining* factor in the formation of Chinese descent groups. Rather than representing ancestral rites as an outgrowth of preexisting economic and political activities, Ebrey argues that it was the group celebration of ancestral rites that triggered the larger historical change associated with the appearance of corporate descent groups. Here we have the historian standing an anthropological argument on its head. Yet, as Ebrey points out, historical explanations are not the same as sociological ones. Ebrey's stance is so far outside the anthropologists' paradigmatic view of Chinese descent groups that many fieldworkers may suspect that her interpretation is an artifact of historical sources that tend to dwell on burial rites and neglect other aspects of social organization (proper burial is a theme that has preoccupied Chinese commentators since the beginning of written records). Whether or not Ebrey's approach can be proved to the satisfaction of anthropologists, her essay certainly provides fresh insights into a problem of central significance to Chinese studies.

It is particularly interesting, from the anthropological point of view, that the movement to worship ancestors at their graves developed first among commoners and only later was adopted by the bureaucratic elite. Before the T'ang, Ebrey notes, agnates living in separate households did not maintain graves as a "group responsibility." Graves were centrally important but only to individuals and domestic units. By mid-T'ang, however, a major change in popular culture had occurred and the Ch'ing-ming festival had been transformed into a rite of celebration during which groups of agnates gathered at the graves of their common ancestors (see Hazelton's chapter for a description of Ch'ing-ming). The Confucian elite did not promote this ritual transformation, but they were soon forced to accept it.

As a footnote to Ebrey's essay there appears to have been a similar transformation in public rituals associated with the ancestral cult during the late Ming and early Ch'ing. This particular transformation may have occurred only in those areas of Kwangtung and Fukien where powerful lineages predominated. Ch'ing-ming continued to be a rite of grave worship but primarily for "recent" ancestors (up to twelve generations after death); smaller groups of descendants consisting of fewer than 100 people gathered during these spring rites. By mid-Ch'ing, lineages in their full membership of hundreds and even thousands began visiting the graves of their remote founders (up to thirty generations back) during the Chung-yang festival, the so-called "double-nine" celebration—the ninth day of the ninth lunar month. Ch'ing-ming came to be defined as the festival of lineage branch and domestic group observances while Chung-yang took on the trappings of a lineage-wide ritual of solidarity. The redefinition of festivals in the Chinese ritual calendar is a process that continues today in Hong Kong, Taiwan, and even in parts of the People's Republic. Ebrey's work demonstrates how conceptions of kinship and group consciousness are intimately related to this transformation process.

Another important issue to arise from the essays in this volume is the relationship between descent group formation and the location of burials. As Keith Hazelton notes (chapter 5), there has always been a conflict in Chinese society between group burial (in corporate cemeteries) and individualistic burial (seeking advantage by geomantic placement). In chapter 2 Ebrey outlines several attempts by Sung leaders to institute group burial practices among their agnates. Han Ch'i's effort is particularly interesting given that he belonged to a shallow descent group. In laying the plans for a common cemetery, Han Ch'i clearly hoped to create a larger, more impressive descent group by focusing on the dead rather than the living. This is a fascinating insight into the conscious manipulation of burial rites by the educated elite. It also demonstrates that it is entirely possible that some Chinese descent "groups" *existed as corporations only in death*. Burial in a common site may have been the only thing that held certain groups together, and collective worship at the graves may have been the only corporate activity that living members shared.

It is significant in this respect that Han Ch'i railed against the practice of individualistic burial and warned his agnates not to consult geomancers. "Placing the dead" to maximize the luck and good fortune of descendants (see Freedman 1966; J. Watson 1982b) is fundamentally opposed to "collecting in the dead" for common burial (for examples of the latter pattern see Hazelton's chapter). During the Sung, when the notion of kinship groups as economic corporations was not yet highly developed, individualistic burial was a threat to the very existence of nascent groups. In later centuries dispersed burials were less problematic, given that lineages and clans had many other corporate activities to serve as organizational foci. Ebrey's exploration of Sung burial practices has opened up a new field of anthropological research, namely the *mentalités*, or mental structures, associated with descent groups as they are reflected in notions of the afterlife. This is a topic that warrants further research.

In Chapter 7 Susan Naquin discusses an interesting variation of group burial in Yung-p'ing. Rather than collecting in all of their deceased agnates, one of the Wang groups studied by Naquin maintained what might be called a "lineal cemetery." Sons of eldest sons, in a direct line from the designated founder, had rights of burial in this common plot. Although the sources are too fragmentary for us to know for certain, it seems likely that it was a mechanism to ensure the maintenance of the ancestors' graves in the absence of a landed, corporate estate set aside for this purpose. The immediate descendants of every eldest son in line would have the obligation to maintain the common plot until a new generation took over. Lineal cemeteries are thus fundamentally different from the corporate plots proposed by Han Ch'i; one maintains a single line of descent while the other collects in an expanding group of collateral agnates.

It is entirely possible that anthropologists have "placed the cart before the horse" in discussing burial rites and ancestor worship as secondary phenomena, derivative of political and economic activities. Fieldworkers necessarily observe the end product of a centuries-long process of historical transformation. Ebrey contends that a "key element" in the emergence of modern Chinese descent groups was a change in ideas regarding the relationship of individuals to distant ancestors. This change, in turn, fostered a "group consciousness" among local agnates—leading them to create the economic and political trappings that we now associate with modern lineages, clans, and surname groups (see J. Watson 1982a:595–606). Ebrey has challenged one of the fundamental tenets of social anthropology. Sinological anthropologists must either refute her argument or modify their own notions of the role of ritual in historical processes.

The Role of Women: Transactors or Reactors?

In recent years anthropologists have had rather a lot to say about the status of women in late imperial Chinese society (see e.g., Ahern 1975; Cohen 1976; E. Johnson 1975; Sangren 1983; Topley 1975; R. Watson 1981, 1984; J. Watson 1982b; A. Wolf 1975; M. Wolf 1972, 1975). The general conclusion is that Chinese women stood outside the formal structure of Chinese (extra-domestic) descent groups and that they did not exercise jural control over property or human resources. No one would deny that women might influence decisions by informal means, but this could only be accomplished—according to the received interpretation—if the women were able to rise above their formal position in the male-dominated descent group or domestic unit.

Jerry Dennerline challenges this view of Chinese women in chapter 6. Drawing on the written records and oral traditions of two successful lineages in Wu-hsi, Dennerline claims to have found evidence that women (specifically widows) were the primary movers in decisions to establish charitable estates. His whole essay can be read as a critique of the anthropologists' representation of Chinese women as passive reactors who lived in the shadows of an androcentric world. Contrary to everything anthropologists assume they know about the disposition of property in Chinese society, Dennerline asserts that widows in Wu-hsi controlled the personal estates of their deceased husbands.

Given that this is such a radical departure from the standard interpretation of widows' roles, many anthropologists will find the argument difficult to accept without more supporting evidence. One problem is the hagió-graphic nature of Chinese sources relevant to these issues. Even among the most androcentric of lineages in Kwangtung one often finds an oral tradition extolling the virtues of self-sacrificing women who are credited with holding the founder's family, or his agnatic group, together during times of crisis (see e.g., Sung 1973). Richard Davis (chapter 3) describes a virtuous ancestress of this type who is cited for having saved the Shih during their formative period (see also Elvin 1984 on virtuous widows). How much, one wonders, did the lineages studied by Dennerline romanticize the role of widows? As we are dependent on written sources it may never be possible to tell for certain, but Dennerline is by no means the only scholar to have postulated an independent, decision-making role for Chinese women. Ebrey has shown that upper class women in the Sung managed to control their own property (1981, see also chapter 2 in this volume). Furthermore, Rubie Watson's field investigation of Cantonese villagers (1981) shows that women were active participants in the conduct of affinal relations and not the silent bridges for alliances between men. The stereotype of the Chinese woman as a withdrawn, socially incompetent appendage is no longer viable. We know from the recent work of both historians and anthropologists that women were transactors as well as reactors: They were not all puppets in the hands of males.

Many anthropologists operate with the implicit assumption that there is a correlation between "strong" patrilineal descent groups and "weak" social roles for women.[5] This may in fact be true in parts of rural Kwangtung, but the findings of Dennerline and others make it obvious that the correlation does not hold for China as a whole. The lineages studied by Dennerline were "strong" by any measure of corporate unity, wealth, or political cohesion—and yet the women appear to have played an active role in the affairs of both lineage and family. Class differences may also be at issue here. Did upper class women enjoy more freedom of action than peasant women (cf. Ebrey 1981)? It is possible that the growth of lineages and associated phenomena during the Ming and Ch'ing led to a gradual devaluation of women in a symbolic, ritual, and political/economic sense. The androcentric vision of Chinese society may therefore be an artifact of Ming-Ch'ing social engineering associated with lineage building. Much more research needs to be done on notions of gender and the roles of women before any of these questions can be answered.

5. To quote from a prime offender: "Women do not inherit and, hence, are not involved with the landed ancestral estates that form the material foci of Chinese lineages. Furthermore, women are not a matter of concern for any unit larger than the household, which means that they can be bought and sold at will" (J. Watson 1980:224).

Uxorilocal Residence and the Structure of Descent Groups

Anthropologists are, at bottom, dependent on living informants for the clues and insights that help make sense of an alien social system. It should not be surprising, therefore, to learn that fieldworkers often take on the worldview, including the preferences and prejudices, of the people who are the subjects of their investigations. In reading the works of anthropologists who have studied Kwangtung lineages, for instance, it is impossible not to gain the impression that uxorilocal residence, nonagnatic adoption, "little daughter-in-law marriage,"[6] and widow remarriage are slightly disreputable social adaptations associated with those on the margins of society. Conversely, it is assumed that high social status accrues to people who practice patrilocal residence, agnatic adoption, "major marriage,"[7] and discourage widow remarriage. The latter set of traits is generally characteristic of the most powerful lineages in rural Kwangtung. Members who do not conform to the accepted rules of conduct are punished or expelled from the lineage (see e.g., J. Watson 1975a). Tenants and other dependent people who live in the shadows of the powerful lineages are not expected to conform to these social expectations. In rural Kwangtung, therefore, one generally finds a close correlation between low social status and uxorilocal residence; the same is true for nonagnatic adoption, "little daughter-in-law marriage," and widow remarriage. It should be noted that these correlations do not apply in Taiwan (Harrell 1982; Wolf and Huang 1980), but counterevidence of this type has usually been explained away by lineage specialists as a function of Taiwan's "weak" patrilineages and frontier conditions (see e.g., J. Watson 1982a:598–600).

In this respect it may be disconcerting for some anthropologists to learn that social historians who focus on the national elites do not share their notions of what constitutes "proper" behavior, or high social status. Several contributors to this volume treat uxorilocal residence and nonagnatic adoption as routine strategies for perpetuating the patriline or building political alliances. Given that historians spend so much time immersed in the writings, and hence the worldview, of the bureaucratic elite one would surely expect them to have picked up negative clues if these strategies were considered "improper" in any way. No hints of this nature are recorded; what is striking in the sources is the care with which members of the elite recorded cases of uxorilical residence, thereby keeping track of agnates who had married out of the local descent group. In modern Kwangtung lineages, by

6. "Little daughter-in-law marriage" is a union that has its origins in the transfer of a potential bride while she is still an infant. The aim is to marry the girl to the son of her adoptive parents, many years later (see Wolf and Huang 1980).

7. "Major marriage" contrasts to "little daughter-in-law marriage" in that the former involves the full, expensive rites for an adult bride (see Wolf and Huang 1980).

contrast, males who marry uxorilocally are expunged from all genealogical records and their agnates try hard to forget them as quickly as possible.

Based on evidence from this book, there would appear to be at least two types of uxorilocal residence in late imperial China. The first is the version described in the field studies of anthropologists. The strategy in this case is primarily one of biological reproduction: A groom, rather than a bride, is transferred from one household to another—the aim being to reproduce the patriline of the groom's father-in-law. This, of course, is a reversal of the "normal" pattern of patrilocal residence whereby the bride moves and serves as the reproducer of her husband's father's patriline. A male who marries uxorilocally may gain money and security but he loses control over one or more of his sons, who take the surname of their maternal grandfather (see M. Wolf 1972). In this way an heirless man can reproduce himself through the medium of his own daughter.

The contributors report some examples of uxorilocal residence conforming to the reproductive strategy outlined above (see chapter 2). But they also found evidence for another, hitherto undocumented (or at least unanalyzed) form of uxorilocal residence. The strategy in this case is *political* rather than *reproductive*. The groom's aim is to ally himself with a powerful and wealthy father-in-law. He is not expected to reproduce another patriline. Presumably the father of the bride has other, more effective means of perpetuating his own line (by taking secondary wives until a son is born or, if all else fails, by adopting a male heir). In this form of uxorilocal residence the active agent is the groom and not his father-in-law; the groom makes the decision to relocate.

Robert Hymes (chapter 4) and Jerry Dennerline (chapter 6) both report cases of this type (see also Zurndorfer 1984). The men in question did not change their surnames and, in fact, were responsible for starting branches of their own patrilineal descent groups. In effect, uxorilocal residence was the mechanism for lineage segmentation in Wu-hsi (Dennerline's study) and branch formation among agnatic groups in Fu-chou (Hymes). Reading between the lines of these accounts it is clear that moving to the household, or the locality (neighborhood? village? town?), of one's father-in-law was a common strategy of (male) social mobility among the higher elites. But relocation did not always entail severance of the migrants' links to their own patrilines or agnatic groups. Findings of this nature reinforce the view that we are only beginning to understand the structure and variety of social life among the elites of late imperial China.

Future Directions For Collaborative Research

The essays in this volume deal specifically with *agnatic* kinship and the structure of patrilineal descent groups. There are, of course, other means of defining "kinship" in Chinese society, notably through matrilateral ties to one's mother's kin and through affinal links to one's spouse's kin. Anthropologists have explored the nature of these nonagnatic ties among modern peasants (see e.g., Gallin 1960; Harrell 1982; R. Watson 1981), but, to date, little is known about the formal structure of matrilateral and affinal relationships among China's elites. It would appear from the essays in this volume, and from earlier studies (e.g., Dennerline 1981:137–49; Ebrey 1981; D. Johnson 1977:10ff), that affinal links may have been more significant to some scholar-bureaucrats than ties to agnates. More research needs to be done on these problems before any generalizations can be drawn. A joint project on marriage, involving historians and anthropologists, would seem to be the logical sequel to the present set of essays.

There are other problems that have emerged from this book but have not yet been thoroughly investigated. For instance, in considering the historical development of agnatic groups we must not be misled by the self-congratulatory rhetoric so characteristic of Chinese texts. It is obvious that obligations to agnatic kinsmen were sometimes perceived as a *burden* by the wealthy and the famous, irrespective of what they might have said in their memoirs. Robert Hymes (chapter 4) notes that there were two opposing strategies behind the Sung elites' interest in creating estates for the benefit of kinsmen: (1) to build up a local following and (2) to define and limit one's obligations to local agnates. Hymes cites the famous charitable estate established by Fan Chung-yen as an example of the second type (see also Twitchett 1959). Anthropologists have dealt primarily with estates that were created to unite agnates and thereby form a political base for local leaders (see e.g., R. Watson 1982). Accordingly, historians must be careful not to apply anthropological models of lineage or estate formation to their own work without careful consideration of the alternatives. If we have learned anything in the course of this project it is the danger of equating Sung or Ming descent groups with modern, Kwangtung-style lineages.

The formative role of genealogies is another problem that emerges from the essays in this volume. Anthropologists have underestimated the social significance of written genealogies as a means of uniting people. The creation of a written genealogy is a political act that has profound implications for the future direction of the group in question: It freezes the record and makes it more difficult to manipulate the past. The fact that genealogies are *written* also imparts a sense of legitimacy to the enterprise (see especially chapters 2 and 4). Keith Hazelton (chapter 5) gives us a rare glimpse into the motivations that lie behind the creation of genealogies. Among the Wu, Hazelton argues, genealogy-writing was perceived by the office-holding elite as a means of consolidating personal gains made in the wider world of politics and bureaucratic service. He does not, in other words, assume that genealogies were devised with the sole intention of uniting the descent group. This is not to deny that in later generations these written records played an important role in holding the Wu together, but the original "purpose" of the genealogies may have been quite different.

Future research might well focus on the process of genealogy-writing and on the audiences who read, purchased, or consulted the finished product. In modern Kwangtung lineages, for instance, there are both public and private genealogies. The former are produced for political purposes and, hence, are often published in readily available editions whereas the latter are used exclusively for the settlement of internal disputes. Private genealogies are invariably in manuscript form, and they often contain information that is not for public consumption. One wonders whether the elites studied by Davis, Ebrey, Hazelton, and Hymes kept similar records for their private use. The genealogies that have survived are clearly intended for an audience of potential affines and allies. These documents could be treated as if they were projective instruments, revealing something of the thought processes and mental attitudes that went into their construction. Written genealogies of the public variety tell us as much about the political aspirations of the authors as they do about the structure of agnatic groups. This, at least, is a conclusion that derives from the work of Keith Hazelton and Robert Hymes (chapters 4 and 5).

Chapters 2, 3, 7, and 8 all touch on the important subject of generational names—a social pattern easily retrievable from written genealogies. The authors make a number of assumptions regarding the appearance of regularized naming patterns; most conclude that the use of these names can be taken as an indicator of "corporateness" for the groups concerned. On one level there can be no question that this is a correct assumption: A minimum standard of coordination is required to enforce a system of generational naming. Some of these systems are very elaborate indeed (see chapter 3 on the Shih). The question that must be asked, however, is whether or not naming patterns are a reflection of "deeper," more significant forms of corporate activity. In other words are generational names to be taken as the tip of an iceberg, the only surviving vestige of a once thriving corporation? Susan Naquin argues in chapter 7 that the abandonment of naming patterns "mirrors" a decline in the social position and cohesion of the descent group in question. She bases her judgment on the history of two groups in Yungp'ing. Richard Davis (chapter 3) makes a similar claim: Among the Shih, he argues, generational naming patterns constituted the "adhesive" necessary to hold the group together and to define social relationships. Generational names were central to the identity of the Shih as a corporate group.

The modern lineages studied by anthropologists also maintain regularized naming systems, but there is little consistency in their use over the past three hundred years. The Man and Teng lineages of Hong Kong's New Territories, for instance, do not have uniformly applied naming systems for the entire corporate group. Instead, smaller units (lineage branches or sets of agnates defined by descent from a common grandfather) maintain their own naming systems and enforce them with varying intensity. If one were to judge the "corporateness" of the Man or Teng lineages on the basis of names recorded in their genealogies, neither would score very high on a scale of uniformity. And, yet, by any other measure of corporate strength both lineages would far outrank any of the groups investigated in this volume. I am not suggesting that historians abandon generational names as an indicator of corporateness—this would be throwing the baby out with the bathwater. Regularized naming systems are, after all, one of the few aspects of corporateness that can be retrieved from a genealogy. But we need to know more about Chinese naming systems before generalizations are made regarding their social significance. It is perhaps encouraging to note that the study of names and naming systems is a topic of great interest to many social anthropologists (see e.g., Beidelman 1974; Goodenough 1965; Levi-Strauss 1966: 172–216; Ramos 1974; Tonkin 1980). A collective effort to investigate the nature of Chinese naming systems would now seem to be in order.

There are many other important topics discussed in this book that warrant further study: the role of the state in descent group formation (did state intervention help or hinder?), class differences (did different classes form different types of descent groups?), "communal families" as precursors of modern lineages (is there an historical connection as Ebrey suggests in chapter 2?). It is also important to take a long, hard look at the nature of the Chinese surname, to determine how it has changed over time (did it always have the sociological significance that it now carries?). All of these topics would be suitable for joint investigations by historians and anthropologists. And, finally, there is one issue that looms large in the future of Chinese kinship studies: the challenge of historical demography. The conference upon which this volume is based included a workshop on demographic issues;[8] in addition, participants spent many hours discussing the possibilities and limitations of demographic analyses in the field of Chinese studies. Davis, Dennerline, and Naquin (chapter 3, 6, and 7) examine the relationship between fecundity and the historical viability of kin groups. Given that this volume concentrates on specific case studies, the authors cannot be certain how "representative" their data are and how general their conclusions might be. It is hoped that future projects will focus directly on these issues.

It is now apparent to all who have worked on this project that the study of Chinese social institutions must, of necessity, be a multi-disciplinary enterprise. We can no longer afford to view China through the prisms of our

8. The workshop was organized by Richard Barrett, who presented a paper entitled "Historical Demography and the Study of Chinese Kinship: A Preliminary Reconnaisance." The paper was discussed by Eugene A. Hammel and James Lee.

respective disciplines. Furthermore, it is of paramount importance that China specialists develop a more comparative approach to their research. Reading the works of Indianists, Africanists, and Europeanists is the best way to gain an understanding of what is interesting and unique about Chinese society.

Social anthropologists and social historians are ideal partners for the exploration of Chinese society. The historians have already made their intentions clear: They have no qualms whatsoever in raiding the anthropological literature for ideas and insights to inform their own historical research. Anthropologists are only beginning to explore the great ethnographic frontier of Chinese history; in this we fall far behind our anthropologist colleagues who work on European societies. One hopes that, in the future, there will be more collaborative research involving anthropologists and historians, working *together* on the same set of problems.

REFERENCES

Ahern, Emily M. 1973. *The Cult of the Dead in a Chinese Village*. Stanford: Stanford University Press.

———. 1975. "The Power and Pollution of Chinese Women." In *Women in Chinese Society*, ed. Margery Wolf and Roxane Witke. Stanford: Stanford University Press.

———. 1976. "Segmentation in Chinese Lineages: A View from Written Genealogies." *American Ethnologist* 3:1–16.

———. 1981. *Chinese Ritual and Politics*. Cambridge: Cambridge University Press.

Anderson, Eugene N., Jr. 1970. "Lineage Atrophy in Chinese Society." *American Anthropologist* 72:363–65.

Baker, Hugh D. R. 1968. *A Chinese Lineage Village: Sheung Shui*. Stanford: Stanford University Press.

———. 1979. *Chinese Family and Kinship*. London: Macmillan.

Beidelman, T. O. 1974. "Kaguru Names and Naming." *Journal of Anthropological Research* 30:281–93.

Cohen, Myron. 1969. "Agnatic Kinship in South Taiwan." *Ethnology* 15:237–92.

———. 1976. *House United, House Divided: The Chinese Family in Taiwan*. New York: Columbia University Press.

Dennerline, Jerry. 1981. *The Chia-ting Loyalists: Confucian Leadership and Social Change in Seventeenth-Century China*. New Haven: Yale University Press.

Ebrey, Patricia Buckley. 1981. "Women in the Kinship System of the Southern Song Upper Class." *Historical Reflections* 8:113–28.

———. 1983. "Types of Lineages in Ch'ing China: A Re-examination of the Chang Lineage of T'ung-ch'eng." *Ch'ing-shih wen-t'i* 4(9):1–20.

Elvin, Mark. 1984. "Female Virtue and the State in China." *Past and Present* 104:111–52.

Evans-Pritchard, E. E. 1940. *The Nuer*. Oxford: Oxford University Press, Clarendon Press.

Fortes, Meyer. 1945. *The Dynamics of Clanship among the Tallensi*. Oxford: Oxford University Press.

———. 1953. "The Structure of Unilineal Descent Groups." *American Anthropologist* 55:17–41.

Freedman, Maurice. 1958. *Lineage Organization in Southeastern China*. London: Athlone.

———. 1966. *Chinese Lineage and Society: Fukien and Kwangtung*. London: Athlone.

Gallin, Bernard. 1960. "Matrilateral and Affinal Relationships in a Taiwanese Village." *American Anthropologist* 62:632–42.

Goodenough, Ward H. 1965. "Personal Names and Modes of Address in Two Oceanic Societies." In *Context and Meaning in Cultural Anthropology*, ed. Melford E. Spiro. New York: Free Press.

Harrell, Stevan. 1982. *Ploughshare Village: Culture and Context in Taiwan*. Seattle: University of Washington Press.

Huang, Shu-min. 1980. "The Development of Regionalism in Ta-chia, Taiwan: A Non-kinship View of Chinese Rural Social Organization." *Ethnohistory* 27:243–65.

Johnson, David G. 1977. *The Medieval Chinese Oligarchy*. Boulder: Westview Press.

Johnson, Elizabeth L. 1973. "Hakka Lineages in an Industrial City." Paper presented at the 1973 Annual Meeting of the American Anthropological Association, New Orleans.

———. 1975. "Women and Childbearing in Kwan Mun Hau Village: A Study of Social Change." In *Women in Chinese Society*, ed. Margery Wolf and Roxane Witke. Stanford: Stanford University Press.

Levi-Strauss, Claude. 1966. *The Savage Mind*. London: Weidenfeld and Nicolson.

Mann (Jones), Susan. 1974. "The Ningpo Pang and Financial Power in Shanghai." In *The Chinese City between Two Worlds*, ed. Mark Elvin and G. William Skinner. Stanford: Stanford University Press.

Mark, Lindy Li. 1972. "Taiwanese Lineage Enterprises: A Study of Familial Entrepreneurship." Ph.D. dissertation, University of California, Berkeley.

Mathias, John. 1977. "A Study of the *Jiao*, a Taoist Ritual, in Kam Kin, in the Hong Kong New Territories." D.Phil. dissertation, University of Oxford.

Pasternak, Burton. 1968. "Agnatic Atrophy in a Formosan Village." *American Anthropologist* 70:93–96.

———. 1969. "The Role of the Frontier in Chinese Lineage Development." *Journal of Asian Studies* 28:551–61.

———. 1972. *Kinship and Community in Two Chinese Villages*. Stanford: Stanford University Press.

———. 1983. *Guests in the Dragon: Social Demography of a Chinese District, 1895–1946*. New York: Columbia University Press.

Potter, Jack M. 1968. *Capitalism and the Chinese Peasant: Social and Economic Change in a Hong Kong Village*. Berkeley: University of California Press.

———. 1970. "Land and Lineage in Traditional China." In *Family and Kinship in Chinese Society*, ed. Maurice Freedman. Stanford: Stanford University Press.

Ramos, A. 1974. "How the Sanumá Acquire Their Names." *Ethnology* 13:171–85.

Sangren, P. Steven. 1983. "Female Gender in Chinese Religious Symbols: Kuan Yin, Ma Tsu, and the 'Eternal Mother.'" *Signs* 9:4–25.

———. 1984. "Traditional Chinese Corporations: Beyond Kinship." *Journal of Asian Studies* 43:391–415.

Strauch, Judith. 1983. "Community and Kinship in Southeastern China: The View from the Multilineage Villages of Hong Kong." *Journal of Asian Studies* 43:21–50.

Sung, Hok-p'ang. 1973. "Legends and Stories of the New Territories: Kam T'in." *Journal of the Hong Kong Branch of the Royal Asiatic Society* 13:111–32.

Tonkin, Elisabeth. 1980. "Jealousy Names, Civilised Names: Anthroponomy of the Jlao Kru of Liberia." *Man* 15:653–64.

Topley, Marjorie. 1975. "Marriage Resistance in Rural Kwangtung." In *Women in Chinese Society*, ed. Margery Wolf and Roxane Witke. Stanford: Stanford University Press.

Twitchett, Denis. 1959. "The Fan Clan's Charitable Estate, 1050–1760." In *Confucianism in Action*, ed. David S. Nivison and Arthur F. Wright. Stanford: Stanford University Press.

Watson, James L. 1975a. "Agnates and Outsiders: Adoption in a Chinese Lineage," *Man* 10:293–306.

———. 1975b. *Emigration and the Chinese Lineage: The Mans in Hong Kong and London.* Berkeley: University of California Press.

———. 1980. "Transactions in People: The Chinese Market in Slaves, Servants, and Heirs." In *Asian and African Systems of Slavery*, ed. James L. Watson. Berkeley: University of California Press.

———. 1982a. "Chinese Kinship Reconsidered: Anthropological Perspectives on Historical Research." *China Quarterly* 92:589–622.

———. 1982b. "Of Flesh and Bones: The Management of Death Pollution in Cantonese Society." In *Death and the Regeneration of Life*, ed. Maurice Bloch and Jonathan Parry. Cambridge: Cambridge University Press.

Watson, Rubie S. 1981. "Class Differences and Affinal Relations in South China." *Man* 16:593–615.

———. 1982. "The Creation of a Chinese Lineage: The Teng of Ha Tsuen, 1669–1751." *Modern Asian Studies* 16:69–100.

———. 1984. "Women's Property in Republican China: Rights and Practices." *Republican China* 10.1a:1–12.

———. 1985. *Inequality among Brothers: Class and Kinship in South China.* Cambridge: Cambridge University Press.

Wolf, Arthur P. 1970. "Chinese Kinship and Mourning Dress." In *Family and Kinship in Chinese Society*, ed. Maurice Freedman. Stanford: Stanford University Press.

———. 1975. "The Women of Hai-shan: A Demographic Portrait." In *Women in Chinese Society*, ed. Margery Wolf and Roxane Witke. Stanford: Stanford University Press.

Wolf, Arthur P., and Huang Chieh-shan. 1980. *Marriage and Adoption in China, 1845–1945.* Stanford: Stanford University Press.

Wolf, Margery. 1972. *Women and the Family in Rural Taiwan.* Stanford: Stanford University Press.

————. 1975. "Women and Suicide in China." In *Women in Chinese Society*, ed.
    Margery Wolf and Roxane Witke. Stanford: Stanford University Press.
Woon, Yuen-fong. 1979. "The Non-localized Descent Group in Traditional China."
    Ethnology 18:17–29.
Zurndorfer, Harriet T. 1984. "Local Lineages and Local Development: A Case
    Study of the Fan Lineage, Hsiu-ning *Hsien*, Hui-chou, 800–1500." *T'oung Pao*
    70:18–59.

GLOSSARY

A-lu-hui	阿魯灰
An Chih-wen	安志文
An-tz'u	安次
An-yuan	安遠
Ch'a-lin	查林
chai	宅
Chan (surname)	詹
Chan-ch'iao	棧橋
Chang (surname)	張
chang (elder)	長
chang ch'i tsu	長其族
Chang Jung	張榮
Chang Shih-ch'eng	張士誠
Chang Tsai	張載
Ch'ang-feng	長豐
Ch'ang-li	昌黎
chao	昭
Chao Chi-ming	趙季明
chao-mu	昭穆
Chao Ting	趙鼎
Ch'en (surname)	陳
Ch'en Liang	陳亮
Ch'en Lü-tao	陳履道
Ch'en Yü	陳寓
Ch'en Yuan-chin	陳元晉
Cheng Yü	鄭玉
Ch'eng	程
Ch'eng Chü-fu	程鉅夫
Ch'eng I	程頤

Ch'eng Min-cheng	程敏政
Ch'eng-nan	城南
Ch'eng-pei	城北
Ch'eng-shih tsung-p'u	程氏總譜
Ch'eng Shun-tao	程順道
Ch'eng Tseng	程曾
Ch'eng-tu-fu	成都府
chi	祭
Chi-chen	吉鎮
Chi-chou	吉州
Chi-shui	吉水
chi-t'ien	祭田
ch'i	氣
ch'i-ch'in	期親
ch'i-fang	七房
Ch'i-fang-ch'iao	七房橋
Ch'i-men	祁門
chia	家
chia-fa	家法
Chia-hsi	嘉熙
chia-hsiang	家鄉
chia-miao	家廟
chia-tsu	甲族
chia-tz'u	家祠
Chiang-chou	江州
Chiang-hsi	江西
Chiang-t'an	江潭
chieh-fang ch'ü	解放區
chien	間
Chien-ch'ang	建昌
Chien-ch'u ssu	建初寺
chien-sheng	監生
Ch'ien-an	遷安
Ch'ien Cheng-te	錢正德
Ch'ien Ch'eng-p'ei	錢承沛
Ch'ien Chin	錢進
Ch'ien Chung-te	錢種德
Ch'ien Fa	錢發
Ch'ien-hsing yueh-hu	錢姓樂戶
Ch'ien Ju-chang	錢如璋
Ch'ien Ju-lin	錢汝霖
Ch'ien Kuo-yao	錢國耀
Ch'ien Mu	錢穆
Ch'ien Shao-lin	錢邵霖
Ch'ien Shun-te	錢順德
Ch'ien Ting	錢鼎
Ch'ien T'ing-mu	錢廷牧

Ch'ien Tzu	錢梓
Ch'ien Wei-yung	錢維鏞
chih	支
chih-ch'in	至親
chih-p'ai	支派
Chih-ta	至大
Ch'ih-chou	池州
Chin (surname)	金
Chin-ch'i	金溪
Chin-chiang	晉江
Chin-hua	金華
chin-shih	進士
Chin-tan	金丹
ch'in	親
Ching-pien	靖邊
ching tsung shou tsu	敬宗收族
Ching Yueh-hsiu	井岳秀
ch'ing	頃
Ch'ing-ho Ts'ui	清河崔
Ch'ing-ming	清明
Ch'ing-yun	青雲
chiu p'u hsu	舊譜序
Chou (surname)	周
Chou Pi-ta	周必大
Chu (surname)	朱
Chu-ch'i	朱溪
Chu Hsi	朱熹
Chu-tzu fang	朱紫坊
Chu-tzu fang Chin	朱紫坊金
Chu Yuan-chang	朱元璋
chü	聚
chü-jen	舉人
chü shih ming chia	俱適名家
chü-tsu	舉族
ch'ü-chang	區長
Chuan-ch'iao	磚橋
chuan-sheng	轉生
chuang-t'ou	莊頭
Ch'un-hsi	淳熙
Chung-cheng *t'ang*	中正堂
chung shih	中市
Chung-yung *t'ang*	忠勇堂
Ch'ung-ch'ing *t'ang*	重慶堂
Ch'ung-i chang	崇義長
Ch'ung-jen	崇仁
Ch'ung-sheng hsi	崇盛西
Ch'ung-yuan hao	崇元號

Dorgon	多爾袞
E-hu	鵝湖
en-kung	恩貢
Fan (surname)	范
Fan Chung-yen	范仲淹
Fan Sui	范隋
Fan Ying-ling	范應鈴
fang	房
Fang Hsiao-ju	方孝儒
Fang Kang	方綱
fen-chia	分家
Feng-huang	鳳凰
Feng-jun	豐潤
Feng-lin	楓林
Feng Shih-fu	馮世富
feng-shui	風水
feng-shui chia	風水家
Fu (surname)	傅
Fu-chou (Fukien)	福州
Fu-chou (Kiangsi)	撫州
Fu-feng chai	扶風寨
fu-kung	副貢
Fu-ning	撫寧
fu shih	富室
Fu Shou	符綬
Han Ch'i	韓琦
han shih	寒食
hang	行
Hao-i *t'ang*	好義堂
Heng-shan	橫山
Ho (family)	何
ho	合
Ho-ch'a ch'ü	河岔區
Ho Chung	何中
Ho-chung (prefecture)	河中
ho tsang	合葬
ho tsu	合族
Hou-shan Ch'ien	堠山錢
Hou Ting	侯錠
hou yuan	後園
Hsi-men Shao	西門邵
Hsi-ta-ch'eng	西大乘
Hsia Hsiung	夏雄
hsiang	鄉
hsiang-hsia	鄉下
hsiang-huo-miao	香火廟
Hsiang-t'an	湘潭

Hsiao-chia-hang	蕭家巷
Hsieh Fang-te	謝枋得
Hsieh O	謝諤
Hsien-ch'i	鹹溪
Hsien-ch'ien	縣前
Hsien-feng	咸豐
Hsin-an	新安
Hsin-an Ch'eng-shih t'ung-tsung shih-p'u	新安程氏統宗世譜
Hsin-an ta-tsu chih	新安大族志
Hsin-t'ien	新田
hsing	姓
Hsiu-chen	修眞
Hsiu-ning	休寧
hsu (preface)	序
Hsu (family) (chap. 2)	許
Hsu (surname) (chap. 4)	徐
Hsu chia p'u	續家譜
Hsu Ching-jui	徐景瑞
Hsu Shou-hui	徐壽輝
Hsu tzu-chih t'ung-chien ch'ang-pien	續資治通鑑長編
Hsun (surname)	荀
Hu Chu	胡助
Hu Ta-hai	胡大海
Hu-t'ou Ch'ien	胡頭錢
Hu Tsung-nan	胡宗南
Hu Yen-wu	胡炎午
hu-ying-ti	護塋地
Hua	滑
Hua Ch'a	華察
Hua Chin-ssu	華進思
Hua Ch'üan	華詮
Hua Hung-mo	華鴻模
Hua I-lun	華翼綸
Hua-kai	華蓋
Hua San-hsing	華三省
Hua Ts'un-k'uan	華存寬
Hua Tsung-hua	華悰韡
Hua Yun	華雲
Huai-an	淮安
Huai-hai	懷海
Huang (surname)	黃
Huang Ch'ao	黃巢
Huang Chen	黃震
Huang Chin	黃溍
Huang Ch'ung-shih	黃崇實
Huang K'ai	黃開

Huang Kan	黃榦
Huang K'ua	黃栝
Huang San-chieh	黃三傑
Huang Shao-fu	黃紹復
Huang-tun	篁墩
Huang Yun	黃筠
Hui-chou	徽州
Hui-shan	惠山
hui t'ung-tsung	會統宗
hun	魂
Hung-chou	洪州
Hung Mai	洪邁
Hung-sheng-li	鴻聲里
I-ch'eng	儀徵
i-chuang	義莊
I-huang	宜黃
I-jen *t'ang*	依仁堂
i-ping wan-hu	義兵萬戶
i-t'ien	義田
i-ts'ang	義倉
Jao Meng-ch'ih	饒孟持
Jen-tsung	仁宗
jen-tzu	任子
Ju (river)	汝
ju-hu	儒戶
ju-jen	儒人
Kai-chu	蓋竹
Kan-lu	甘露
K'ang Yung-shao	康永韶
ken	根
Ko (surname)	葛
ku-jou	骨肉
Kuan-chia chü	官家咀
Kuan-hsi Ma shih shih-hang lu	關西馬氏世行錄
kuan-tsu	官族
Kuan Yin	觀音
Kuan Yü	關羽
Kuang-yü *t'ang*	光裕堂
Kuei-chi	會稽
Kuei-ch'i	貴溪
Kuei-t'ien	桂田
kung (lord)	公
Kung (surname)	龔
Kung-fang	龔坊
kung-i	公議
kung-p'u	公僕
kung-sheng	貢生

Kuo (surname)	過
kuo	槶
kuo-chia kung-tso jen-yuan	國家工作人員
Lan-tu Ch'en	藍渡陳
Lang-ssu	瑯琊
Lang-yeh	瑯琊
Le-t'ing	樂亭
Li (surname)	李
Li-ch'eng	歷城
li-chia	里甲
Li K'o-lu	李克魯
Li K'o-yung	李克庸
liang-chang	糧長
Lin (surname)	林
Lin Ch'ing	林清
Lin-ch'uan	臨川
Lin-i	臨邑
Ling-shui kou	冷水溝
Liu (surname)	劉
Liu Chieh	劉傑
Liu Ching	劉璟
Liu Hsun	劉洵
Liu K'o-chuang	劉克莊
Liu Tsung-yuan	柳宗元
Liu Yao-fu	劉堯夫
Lo-an	樂安
Lo-shan	羅山
Lo-yang	洛陽
Lou Yueh	樓鑰
Lu (state)	魯
Lu (surname)	陸
Lu Chiu-shao	陸九韶
Lu Chiu-yuan	陸九淵
Lu-ling	廬陵
Lu-lung	盧龍
Lu O	陸諤
Lü Hsi-che	呂希哲
Luan	灤
Luan-ch'eng	欒城
Lung-hsing	隆興
Lung-hua ching	龍華經
Lung-t'ing	隆亭
Lung-wang t'an	龍王壇
Ma (surname)	馬
Ma Chia-lo	馬嘉樂
Ma Chu-k'ang	馬祝康
Ma Chu-ling	馬祝齡

Ma Chung-hsiang	馬鍾祥
Ma Chung-hsuan	馬中選
Ma Chung-pi	馬鍾璧
Ma Ho-ch'ing	馬和卿
Ma Hsin-min	馬新民（醒民）
Ma Hung-hsien	馬鴻獻
Ma Hung-hsun	馬鴻勛
Ma Jui-chang	馬瑞長
Ma Jui-t'ang	馬瑞唐
Ma Jun-chang	馬潤漳
Ma Jun-hung	馬潤宏
Ma Jun-lan	馬潤瀾
Ma Jun-p'u	馬潤普
Ma Jun-shu	馬潤書
Ma Jung-hsuan	馬榮選
Ma K'o-chien	馬克儉
Ma K'o-ch'ien	馬克前
Ma K'o-ting	馬克定
Ma Kuo-hsi	馬國璽
Ma Kuo-hua	馬國華
Ma Kuo-pi	馬國弼
Ma Kuo-pin	馬國賓
Ma Kuo-shih	馬國士
Ma Ling-yun	馬凌云
Ma Ming-feng	馬鳴鳳
Ma Ming-k'o	馬鳴珂
Ma Shih-chen (Chi-an)	馬師貞（繼安）
Ma Shih-ch'i	馬師麒
Ma Shih-i	馬師伊
Ma Shih-liang	馬師亮
Ma Shih-shang	馬師尚
Ma Shih-tsu	馬師祖
Ma Tung	馬東
Ma T'ung	馬通
Ma Wei-ch'eng	馬維城
Ma Wei-han	馬維漢
Ma Wei-hsin	馬維新
Ma Wei-kang	馬維綱
Ma Wen-hsuan	馬文選
men-k'o	門客
Meng Ch'iao-fang	孟喬芳
Meng-ku hsueh-cheng	蒙古學正
Meng Tse	孟澤
Mi-chih	米脂
Mi-ts'un	彌村
miao hui	廟會
mien	宀

ming	名
Ming-chih *t'ang*	明治堂
Ming-chou	明州
mou	畝
mu	穆
mu-t'ien	墓田
mu-tsu	母族
Na-yen-ch'eng	那彥成
Nan-ch'eng	南城
Nan-feng	南豐
Ni (surname)	倪
Ning-ho	寧河
Ou-yang Hsiu	歐陽修
Ou-yang Shou-tao	歐陽守道
pa-kung	拔貢
Pa-ssu-erh-pu-hua	八思爾不花
Pa-ta-yeh	八大爺
Pa-t'ang	巴塘
p'ai	派
p'ai-ming	排名
p'an-kuan	判官
pao-chang	保長
pao-chia	保甲
Pao-shan *t'ang*	寶善堂
Pao-ti	寶坻
pao-wei t'uan	保衞團
Pao-yu	寶祐
pen-tsung	本宗
p'ien-hsiang	偏廂
ping-kung ch'ang	兵工廠
P'ing-ku	平谷
P'ing-yang	平陽
po-hsueh hung-tz'u	博學鴻詞
Po-ling Ts'ui	博陵崔
p'o	魄
P'o-yang	鄱陽
pu-li	補吏
p'u-hsi	譜系
P'u-t'ien	浦田
p'u-tzu	鋪子
San-kuan	三官
San-sheng	三聖
san ta-tsu	三大族
sao-chi	掃祭
Shang-hsi-k'ou	上溪口
Shao-ting	紹定
She	歙

she-ts'ang	社倉
shen	神
shen-chu	神主
shen-pan	神版
shen-shih	紳士
Shen-tsung	神宗
sheng-yuan	生員
shih	氏
Shih An-chih	史安之
Shih Ang-sun	史昂孫
Shih Chai-chih	史宅之
Shih Chang-sun	史暲孫
Shih Ch'ang-ch'ing	史長卿
Shih Ch'ang-ch'ing	史昌卿
Shih Ch'ang-sun	史昌孫
Shih Chao	史詔
Shih Chao-ch'ing	史昭卿
Shih Chen-sun	史震孫
Shih Chen-sun	史眞孫
Shih Ch'en-sun	史辰孫
Shih Chi-ch'ing	史汲卿
Shih Chi-sun	史紀孫
Shih Ch'i-ch'ing	史齊卿
Shih Ch'i-sun	史祺孫
Shih-ch'iao	石橋
Shih Chien	史簡
shih-ch'ien chih tsu	始遷之祖
shih-ch'ien tsu	始遷祖
Shih Ching-sun	史經孫
Shih Chou-ch'ing	史周卿
Shih Chü-ch'ing	史椇卿
Shih Ch'ung-chih	史窓之
shih-feng	食封
shih-fo	石佛
Shih-fo-k'ou	石佛口
Shih Han-ch'ing	史漢卿
Shih Hao	史浩
Shih Ho-sun	史賀孫
shih-hsi	世系
Shih Hsi-ch'ing	史熹卿
Shih Hsia-ch'ing	史夏卿
Shih Hsien-chih	史憲之
Shih Hsien-ch'ing	史顯卿
Shih Hsien-sun	史顯孫
Shih Hsien-sun	史暹孫
Shih Hsuan-chih	史宣之
Shih Hui-sun	史徽孫

Shih I-chih	史宜之
Shih I-sun	史侁孫
Shih K'ang-po	史康伯
Shih K'uan-chih	史寬之
Shih Kung-ching	史公敬
Shih Kung-i	史公頤
Shih-lu	石麓
Shih Man-ch'ing	史曼卿
Shih Mao-ch'ing	史茂卿
Shih Mao-tsu	史茂祖
Shih Mi-cheng	史彌正
Shih Mi-chien	史彌堅
Shih Mi-ta	史彌大
Shih Mi-yuan	史彌遠
Shih Ming-po	史明伯
Shih Pin-chih	史賓之
Shih Sen-ch'ing	史森卿
Shih Shang-ch'ing	史商卿
Shih Sheng-sun	史晟孫
Shih Sheng-sun	史昇孫
Shih Shih-chih	史實之
Shih Shih-chung	史師仲
Shih Shou-chih	史守之
Shih Ssu-ch'ing	史夘卿
shih-su	世俗
Shih Sui	史璲
Shih Sui-chih	史嵩之
Shih Sung-ch'ing	史松卿
shih-ta-fu	士大夫
Shih T'ang-ch'ing	史唐卿
shih-te hsu	世德序
Shih Ti-sun	史悌孫
Shih Ting-chih	史定之
Shih Ting-tsu	史定祖
Shih Ts'ai	史才
shih-tsu (gentlemen descent group)	士族
shih-tsu (multi-generation descent group)	世族
shih tsu (first ancestor)	始祖
Shih Tsung-chih	史宗之
Shih Wei-sun	史暐孫
Shih Wen-ch'ing	史旼卿
Shih Ya-ch'ing	史亞卿
Shih Yen-ch'ing	史儼卿
Shih Yü-chih	史宇之
shou	收
Shou-feng-ssu	壽峯寺

Shu Ti	舒頔
ssu	思
ssu hou	寺後
ssu hou yuan	寺後園
Ssu-kou	寺沟
ssu-ma ch'in	緦麻親
Ssu-ma Kuang	司馬光
Ssu-shih-li p'u	四十里鋪
su	俗
Su Hsun	蘇洵
sui	歲
sui-kung	歲貢
Sui-te	綏德
Sun Yao	孫堯
Sung-chiang	松江
Sung hui-yao	宋會要
Sung Lien	宋濂
ta-chia	大家
Ta-hsi	大溪
ta hsing	大姓
ta-hu	大戶
Ta pei yin	大北隱
ta ssu hou	大寺後
ta ssu hou yuan	大寺後園
ta tsu	大族
Ta-yuan	大原
T'a-ling	塔嶺
Tai Piao-yuan	戴表元
t'ai-shih	太師
tan	石
T'an (surname)	潭
Tang-k'ou	蕩口
tang lai tsu-chang pao-ming yü Wen-ping t'ung tao kuan	當來族長保明與文炳同到官
t'ang	堂
T'ang Hsun	唐勳
T'ang Shun-chih	唐順之
Tao-kuang	道光
T'ao-hua mao chen	桃花坞鎮
Te-sheng ling	得勝嶺
Teng (surname)	鄧
Teng Hsi-yen	鄧希顏
Teng Yuan-kuan	鄧元觀
ti	第
t'i	體
t'i-chi ch'ien	体已錢
tien-ti	典地

t'ing-t'ang	廳堂
Ts'ai (surname)	蔡
Ts'ao (surname)	曹
ts'e	册
Tseng (surname)	曾
Tseng Chiu	曾舊
Tseng Ch'ung-tzu	曾沖子
Tseng Feng	曾丰
Tseng Kung	曾鞏
Tseng Lueh	曾略
Tseng Tzu	曾子
Tsou	鄒
Tsou Fei-hsiung	鄒非熊
tsu (ancestor, grandfather)	祖
tsu (descent group)	族
tsu-chang	族長
tsu-chia tz'u	族家祠
tsu chih yu-li-che	族之有力者
tsu-ch'in	族親
tsu-jen	族人
tsu-p'u	族譜
tsu-ti	族弟
tsu-tse	族澤
tsu-tzu	族子
tsun tsu ching tsung shou tsu	尊祖敬宗收族
tsun tsu mu tsu	尊祖睦族
tsung	宗
tsung-chang	宗長
Tsung-ch'i	宗溪
tsung-fa	宗法
tsung-hui	宗會
tsung-jen	宗人
tsung-miao	宗廟
tsung-p'u	宗譜
tsung-tsu	宗族
tsung-tzu	宗子
tsung-tzu-fa	宗子法
ts'ung-mei	從妹
tu	都
T'u (surname)	涂
T'u Cheng-sheng	涂正勝
T'u Ch'ung	涂沖
T'u Ssu-yu	涂四友
Tung (surname)	董
Tung-ch'i	東溪
Tung Kuan	董觀
T'ung-ch'eng	桐城

T'ung-chih	同治
t'ung-tsung	同宗
t'ung tsung shih-p'u	統宗世譜
tzu	字
tzu-hao	字號
tzu-sun	子孫
tz'u	祠
tz'u-t'ang	祠堂
wang	望
Wang (surname)	汪
Wang An-shih	王安石
Wang Ch'ao-feng	王朝風
Wang Chen	王楨
Wang Cheng	王正
Wang Chi	王機
Wang *chia*	王家
Wang Chien	王監
Wang Chung-mo	王仲默
Wang Hao-hsien	王好賢
Wang Hao-i	王好義
Wang Heng-kung	王亨恭
Wang-hsien	望仙
Wang Hsien	王暹
Wang *hsing*	王姓
Wang-hsing chia-nei	王姓家內
Wang Hsuan-hsi	汪玄錫
Wang Kao	王鎬
Wang K'o-chiu	王可就
Wang Ku	王鹽
Wang K'un	王坤
Wang Lin	王林
Wang Min-ti	王敏廸
Wang Pai-hsi	王伯熹
Wang P'i	王椑
Wang Ping-heng	王秉衡
Wang San-ch'ung	王三重
Wang San-ku	王三顧
Wang San-p'in	王三聘
Wang Tao-sen	王道森
Wang Te-hsiu	王德修
Wang Tien-k'uei	王殿魁
Wang Tsai-hsing	王再興
Wang Tseng	王增
Wang *tsu*	王族
wang-tsu	望族
Wang Yen	王燕
Wang Ying-teng	王應登

Wang Yü	王域
Wang Yun-t'eng	王運滕
Wang Yung	王林
Wei (surname)	危
Wei-feng shan	圍峯山
Wei Liao-weng	魏了翁
Wei Su	危素
Wen-ling	溫陵
Wen T'ien-hsiang	文天祥
Weng T'ung-ho	翁同龢
Wu	吳
Wu Ch'eng (chap. 4)	吳澄
Wu Ch'eng (chap. 5)	吳誠
Wu Ch'eng-tsu	吳承祖
Wu Ch'i	吳琪
Wu Ch'i-tsu	吳齊祖
Wu Ch'ing	吳慶
Wu Chin	吳津
Wu Chin (13th gen.)	吳進
Wu Chin (9th gen.)	吳晉
Wu-chou	婺州
Wu Ch'u-li	吳處禮
Wu En	吳恩
Wu Fang-shu	吳方叔
Wu Fo	吳佛
Wu Fu (name)	吳富
wu-fu	五服
Wu-fu *t'ang*	五福堂
Wu Hai	吳海
Wu Hao	吳號
Wu Hsi	吳錫
Wu Hsuan-nu	吳玹奴
Wu Hsuan-yu	吳玹佑
Wu Jih-ch'i	吳日起
Wu Ju-ling	吳如陵
Wu Ju-shan	吳如山
Wu Jui	吳芮
Wu-kang	五港
Wu K'o	吳可
Wu K'o-sun	吳可孫
Wu Kuei-min	吳貴珉
Wu Le	吳樂
Wu Lei	吳雷
Wu Li	吳禮
Wu Li-i	吳禮翼
Wu Lü	吳驢
Wu Na	吳訥

Wu Shan-ming	吳善銘
Wu Shao-wei	吳少微
Wu She	吳社
Wu shih t'ung t'ang	五世同堂
Wu Shou-t'ung	吳壽童
Wu Ti	鄔廸
Wu-ting	無定
Wu Tsung-chih	吳宗智
Wu Tsung-jen	吳宗仁
Wu Tzu-chih	吳紫芝
Wu Wei-hsin	吳惟新
Wu Wen-ku	吳文古
Wu Wen-tso	吳文佐
Wu Yen	吳琰
Wu Yen-t'ung	吳彥通
Wu-ying shan	無影山
Wu Yung	吳湧
Wu-t'ien	浯田
Wu-yuan	婺源
Ya-pei	衙背
Yang (surname)	楊
Yang-chia-kou	楊家溝
Yang Luan-erh	楊鑾二
Yao (surname)	姚
Yao-yuan	姚源
Yeh shih	葉氏
Yen-fu *t'ang*	衍福堂
Yen-hsiang hsiang	延祥鄉
yin	蔭
yin pu	蔭補
ying	塋
Ying-tsung	英宗
Yung-feng	永豐
Yü (surname)	余
Yü-chang	豫章
Yü Chi	虞集
Yü-huang miao	玉皇廟
Yü-t'ien	玉田
Yü Tou-hsiang	余斗祥
yuan-pao	元寶
Yueh (surname)	樂
Yueh Wen-ping	樂文炳
Yun-kai	雲蓋
Yung-p'ing	永平

INDEX

Wang An-shih, 64, 97, 99
Wang Ch'ao-feng, 227, 228, 231, 232, 239
Wang Chen, 216, 220, 223, 226
Wang Cheng, 212n2, 216, 220, 221
Wang Chung-mo, 216, 218, 219
Wang Hsien, 212, 216, 222
Wang Hsuan-hsi, 145
Wang Kao, 214, 215, 216, 217, 222, 223
Wang K'o-chiu, 230, 231, 232, 233
Wang Pai-hsi, 216, 218, 219, 220; branch of, 221n7, 222, 223, 224, 225, 237
Wang P'i, 215, 216, 217, 218, 222, 223, 240
Wang Tao-sen, 227n11, 228–229, 231, 232, 233; descendants of, 230, 237, 239, 240
Wang Tsai-hsing, 216, 217, 219, 222
Wang Ying-teng, 216, 217, 219, 222
Wang Yung, 33-34
Watson, Rubie S., 186n7, 266, 270, 283
Wei (of Nan-ch'eng), 132
Wei Liao-weng, 97
Wei Su, 111, 117, 119, 127
Wen T'ien-hsiang, 47, 127
Weng T'ung-ho, 201
White Lotus religion, 211-212, 228–229, 230, 232, 233, 234–239, 240–241
Women: activities of, 22, 235, 265; and agnatic groups, 13, 186, 202, 207, 275, 282–283; burial of, 28, 156; and estates, 12, 43, 188, 190–194, 201, 204, 206, 277; in genealogies, 158, 160
Wu (of Hsin-t'ien, Chin-ch'i), 116, 132
Wu (of Hsiu-ning City), 11, 28, 137–167, 277, 286
Wu (of Lin-ch'uan), 104, 105, 106
Wu Ch'eng, 110, 111, 112; prefaces by, 47, 116, 117, 118, 119, 120, 127, 133n16
Wu Ch'i-tsu, 140, 141, 148, 150, 154
Wu Chin (13th generation), 143, 144, 148, 150, 151
Wu En, 116

Wu Fo, 142, 143, 151, 156n16
Wu Hai, 46, 49, 51–52, 53, 55n23
Wu Hao, 120
Wu-hsi county, 12, 54, 170, 182, 184–185, 277, 282, 285; maps of, 174, 175
Wu Hsuan-nu, 141, 142, 143
Wu Jih-ch'i, 147, 148n11, 150
Wu K'o, 112
Wu K'o-sun, 110, 111, 112
Wu Lei, 148, 149, 150
Wu Shao-wei, 138, 139, 140, 143, 146, 152; descendants of, 149, 160, 161, 162, 164
Wu Ti, 111
Wu Tsung-jen, 142, 143, 148, 149, 151, 152
Wu Tzu-chih, 146n9, 147, 148, 151

Yang, widow, 190–191, 192, 194
Yang-chia-kou, 247, 250, 251
Yang Luan-erh, 145
Yao communal family, 31
Yeh, widow, 67, 68, 80, 88
Yeh Hsien-en, 166, 178n5, 187
Yin-pu. See Protection privilege
Yü Chi, 111, 112, 116, 117, 118, 127
Yü Tou-hsiang, 116
Yuan period, 99; communal families in, 30, 32, 34; descent groups in, 53, 55, 114–128, 131–133, 266; disruptions of, 44, 53, 137; genealogies in, 47, 48, 49, 50n20, 129n14; kinship practices in, 27, 28, 51, 152; marriage patterns in, 102–113, 160, 183; Shih descent group in, 74, 77, 80, 81, 84, 90; Wu descent group in, 139, 141, 144, 148, 149, 150, 154; Wu-hsi descent groups in, 176, 179, 181, 185
Yuan Ts'ai, 20n2
Yueh (of I-huang), 130n15
Yung-p'ing (Chihli), 211, 212, 213, 218, 223–227, 229, 235, 237; Manchu invasion of, 214–215, 230

Designer: Lisa Mirski
Compositor: Asco Trade Typesetting Ltd., Hong Kong
Text: 10/12 Stempel Garamond
Display: Stempel Garamond
Printer: Thomson-Shore, Inc.
Binder: John H. Dekker & Sons